Barbarossa to Berlin

*A Chronology of the Campaigns
on the Eastern Front
1941 to 1945*

Volume 2

The Defeat of Germany
19 November 1942 to 15 May 1945

BARBAROSSA TO BERLIN

A CHRONOLOGY OF THE CAMPAIGNS ON THE EASTERN FRONT 1941 TO 1945

Volume 2

The Defeat of Germany

19 November 1942 to 15 May 1945

by

Brian Taylor

SPELLMOUNT
Staplehurst

British Library Cataloguing in Publication Data:
A catalogue record for this book is available
from the British Library

Copyright © Brian Taylor 2004
Maps Copyright © Spellmount Ltd 2004

ISBN 1-86227-228-X

First published in the UK in 2004 by
Spellmount Limited
The Village Centre
Staplehurst
Kent TN12 0BJ

Tel: 01580 893730
Fax: 01580 893731
E-mail: enquiries@spellmount.com
Website:www.spellmount.com

1 3 5 7 9 8 6 4 2

Typeset in Palatino by MATS, Southend-on-Sea, Essex
Printed in Great Britain by
T.J. International Ltd
Padstow, Cornwall

Contents

List of Maps

Preface

In Volume One we followed the advance of the German armies to Moscow, the Soviet counter-offensive around the city and the subsequent campaigns in 1942, which took German arms to the western bank of the Volga at Stalingrad. The colossal advances of the first year and a half of the campaign left the Ostheer massively overextended and had drawn Germany's allies into the battle in significant numbers.

As the winter of 1942 drew in upon Paulus' 6th Army at Stalingrad, the Stavka had planned its most ambitious counter-offensive of the war so far. It is from this point that Volume Two picks up the story of the war on the Eastern Front. Charting the changing fortunes of the combatants as the war raged across Europe from the Volga to the Elbe, this book details the German efforts to halt an ever stronger Soviet enemy, and the growing professionalism of the Red Army and its commanders.

The composition of the book remains the same, the main body of the text covering the combat front while additional information on casualties, production figures and the deployments adds further detail.

As with Volume One, *The Long Drive East*, the book is divided into *sectors*. Readers can if they wish concentrate on the actions of a particular army group or front or follow the campaigns across all sectors simultaneously. There are three main sectors throughout the text: the *Northern Sector*, the *Central Sector* and the *Southern Sector*. Their areas of operation roughly follow the axes of the three main German army groups. The *Northern Sector* concentrates on operations in the Baltic States and, as the campaign developed, the retreat from Leningrad and final surrender of the German forces in Kurland. Similarly, the *Central Sector* covers the theatre of operations of Army Group Centre, detailing the battles on the long road from Moscow, the stunning victory achieved during Operation Bagration, to the defeat of the Germans in Berlin and the end of the Ostheer in Bohemia. The *Southern Sector* largely covers actions in the Ukraine and Balkans, ending with the defeat of the Germans in Hungary and Austria. Each month end aims to give the reader a snapshot of the opposing forces. Under headings such as Ostheer and Red Army, the deployment and commitments of the two combatant armies are detailed.

In addition, numbers of casualties and productive output are detailed throughout in an effort to bring home the human cost of the war.

Importantly, the perspective of the text is neither German nor Soviet but seeks to offer factual detail of the conflict as engaged in by both armies. German orders of battle are given in divisional detail at the beginning of significant operations, but the mainstay of the work concentrates on the actions of the German armies and korps. Similarly, Soviet deployment is given in army and corp detail at the beginning of major phases of operations, but remains largely at army level throughout the text. German divisional or Soviet corp accounts are only included in the detail of military operations when their actions are of significant importance.

CHAPTER I

The Road West

Having secretly mustered its forces against the exposed flanks of the Sixth Army, the Red Army prepared to launch its greatest offensive of the war so far. Methodically planned and prepared, Operation Uranus would herald a new phase of conflict in the East as the German Army began its long retreat towards Berlin.

19 November 1942

SOUTHERN SECTOR

In the dim winter dawn, 3,500 Soviet artillery pieces opened fire, heralding the beginning of the long awaited counter-offensive around Stalingrad. Vatutin's South-West Front and Rokossovsky's Don Front began by attacking the 3rd Rumanian Army. The Soviet artillery strike, though strong, was dispersed and struck indiscriminately rather than at specific targets.

After the barrage, the 5th Tank Army struck the 2nd Rumanian Korp while the 21st Army pounded the Rumanian 4th Korp near Kletskaya. Elements of 65th Army attacked from Melo-Kletski, running into 44th Infantry Division of the 11th Korp. Each of these attacks met ferocious resistance, the 65th Army in particular struggling to make any progress. To add weight to the attack, the 21st and 5th Tank Armies unleashed their armoured forces, in order to blast a path through the Rumanian units. The 21st Army pushed its 4th Tank and 3rd Cavalry Corps into action while 5th Tank Army threw in the 1st and 26th Tank Corps. The two 5th Tank Army corps tore an eight-mile hole between the 2nd and 5th Rumanian Korps and, under this intense pressure, the Rumanians disintegrated. The Soviet armies surged forward and in a short time had isolated units of the 4th and 5th Rumanian Korps around Raspopinskaya. General Lascar, commanding the 4th Rumanian Korp, managed to stabilise the defensive perimeter after bitter fighting with the Soviet forces. During the first day of the Soviet offensive the 3rd Rumanian Army had suffered 55,000 casualties, halving its strength.

1

Reacting quickly to the Soviet threat, Army Group B ordered General Heim's 48th Panzer Korp to drive the Soviets back upon Kletskaya. The Germans marched to meet the 5th Tank Army, sending the 1st Rumanian Armoured Division to attack north of Zhirkovski while the 22nd Panzer Division attacked north-east from Peschany. In confused fighting the two divisions lost touch, fighting widely separated battles that proved ultimately unsuccessful. After suffering heavy casualties the 22nd Panzer broke off its attack and began to withdraw.

Late that night, Army Group B ordered Paulus to take radical measures to break off the fighting at Stalingrad and restore his left wing. Paulus decided to use his three panzer divisions, combined under 14th Panzer Korp command to push the Soviets back.

20 November 1942

CENTRAL SECTOR
Soviet rifle divisions around the Rzhev salient began reconnaissance in force to identify German weaknesses.

SOUTHERN SECTOR
The 48th Panzer Korp continued its effort to restore the 3rd Rumanian Army positions but during heavy fighting its 1st Rumanian Armoured Division was destroyed by the 5th Tank Army. Other elements of 5th attacked the 22nd Panzer Division as it retreated towards the Chir river. Units of 26th Tank Corp advanced towards the Don, taking Perdazovski.

With his left wing exposed, Paulus continued to move the 14th Panzer Korp from the northern suburbs of Stalingrad to the Don bridgeheads, but a shortage of fuel delayed the redeployment. In an effort to co-ordinate his forces more effectively, Paulus moved his headquarters from Golubinskaya to Nizhne Chirskaya.

South of Stalingrad, thick fog over the second attack sector delayed the start of this element of the Soviet offensive. Two hours late, artillery opened fire against the 4th Rumanian Army. After the barrage, spear-heads of 57th Army struck the Rumanian 2nd and 18th Infantry Divisions between lakes Tsa Tsa and Sarpa. The 51st Army then joined the attack, crashing into the Rumanian 1st and 4th Infantry Divisions. After heavy fighting the Rumanians began to crack, prompting the Soviets to commit their armour. The 13th Tank Corp passed through 57th Army to push into the Rumanian rear before swinging north, while Volskii's 4th Mechanised Corp pushed through 51st Army towards Kalach. The 13th Tank Corp ran into stiff opposition from the 29th Motorised Division, which had been ordered to repel the Soviet attack. The 4th Mechanised Corp struck the retreating Rumanian forces hard at Plodovitoye before blundering into a minefield.

During the afternoon the artillery that had supported the 57th Army moved north to support Shumilov's 64th Army. Attacking from Beketovka, Shumilov ran into stiff resistance from the German 4th Korp. The Rumanian 20th Division quickly crumbled but the German 297th Infantry held up the Soviet attack.

By dusk the situation around Stalingrad had changed dramatically. The 3rd Rumanian Army had been comprehensively defeated, a counter-attack to restore its lines had been brushed aside and the 4th Rumanian Army was in a disorderly retreat towards Kotelnikovo, unhingeing the right wing of 6th Army and 4th Panzer Army. Casualties in the 4th Rumanian Army amounted to 35,000 men, half its operational strength.

GERMAN COMMAND

Hitler ordered the creation of Army Group Don in order to stabilise the German southern flank. Built around the headquarters of 11th Army and commanded by Field Marshal von Manstein, the army group was tasked with securing German positions on the Chir and Don rivers prior to restoring the flanks of the 6th Army in its continuing battle for Stalingrad.

21 November 1942

SOUTHERN SECTOR

Elements of 5th Tank Army encountered the 24th Panzer Division near the Don bridges behind the 6th Army. Fighting at Businovka resulted in serious German casualties and a hasty withdrawal. Paulus' plans to shore up his left wing fell apart.

Heavy fighting continued at Raspopinskaya as Group Lascar fought off repeated Soviet attacks. The Soviet 4th Tank Corp took Golubinskaya as its advance into the German rear continued. Paulus and his headquarters staff had only just left the town for Nizhne Chirskaya and evaded capture by a matter of hours. By evening Vasilevsky was able to report to Stalin that the 4th and 26th Tank and 3rd Guards Cavalry Corps were all heading for Kalach.

The drive from the south accelerated as 4th Mechanised Corp reached Zety. Inexplicably, Volskii ordered a halt so he could regroup but was promptly ordered to resume the advance. Elements of Shapkin's 4th Cavalry Corp, supporting Volskii, captured Abganerovo and cut the railway line to Kotelnikovo.

The collapse of his flanks prompted Paulus to request permission to abandon the Volga and pull back to the Don–Chir line. Army Group B agreed with this proposal and issued orders for its implementation, pending approval by Hitler. This early chance to save the 6th Army was lost when Hitler ordered the Volga line be held.

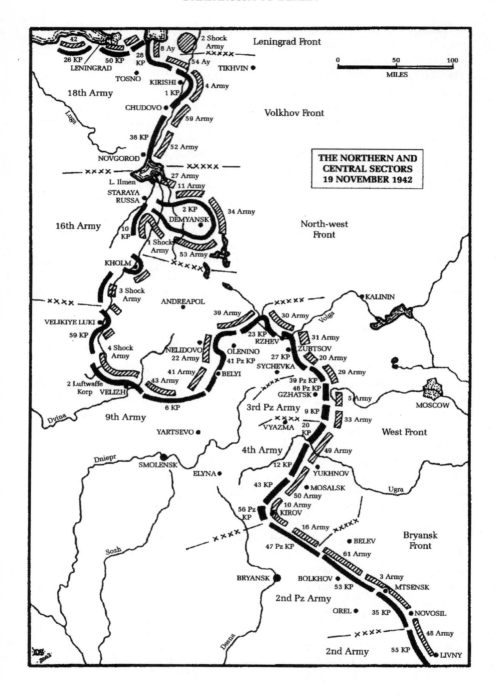

THE NORTHERN AND
CENTRAL SECTORS
19 NOVEMBER 1942

Leningrad Front

2 Shock Army
8 Ay
54 Ay
TIKHVIN
26 KP
50 KP
28 KP
LENINGRAD
TOSNO
KIRISHI
4 Army
1 KP
18th Army
CHUDOVO
59 Army
38 KP
52 Army
NOVGOROD
27 Army
11 Army
L. Ilmen
STARAYA RUSSA
2 KP
34 Army
DEMYANSK
16th Army
10 KP
1 Shock Army
53 Army
KHOLM
3 Shock Army
ANDREAPOL
KALININ
VELIKIYE LUKI
59 KP
39 Army
30 Army
Volga
31 Army
4 Shock Army
23 KP
RZHEV
ZUBTSOV
20 Army
NELIDOVO
22 Army
OLENINO
41 Pz KP
27 KP
SYCHEVKA
29 Army
41 Army
BELYI
39 Pz KP
46 Pz KP
5 Army
MOSCOW
2 Luftwaffe Korp
VELIZH
43 Army
6 KP
GZHATSK
3rd Pz Army
9 KP
33 Army
9th Army
YARTSEVO
VYAZMA
20 KP
West Front
4th Army
49 Army
Dniepr
SMOLENSK
ELYNA
12 KP
YUKHNOV
43 KP
MOSALSK
Ugra
50 Army
56 Pz KP
10 Army
KIROV
16 Army
BELEV
Bryansk Front
Sozh
47 Pz KP
61 Army
BRYANSK
BOLKHOV
3 Army
53 KP
MTSENSK
2nd Pz Army
OREL
35 KP
NOVOSIL
48 Army
Desna
2nd Army
55 KP
LIVNY

Volkhov Front

North-west Front

0   50   100
MILES

Luga
Dvina

4

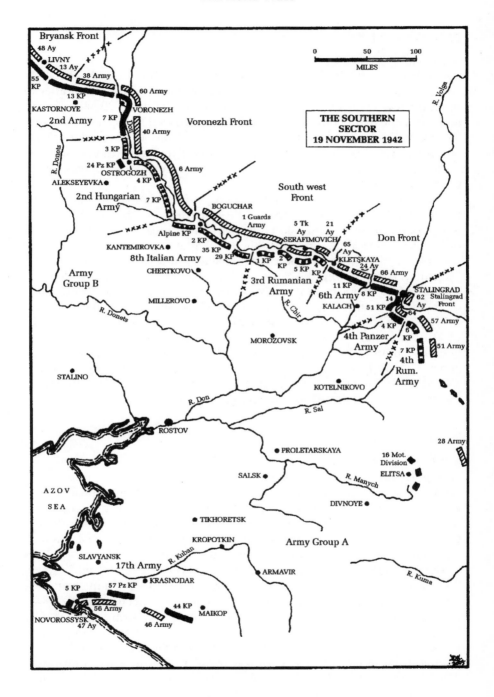

**THE SOUTHERN
SECTOR
19 NOVEMBER 1942**

22 November 1942

SOUTHERN SECTOR

Advancing rapidly, Rodin's 26th Tank Corp closed upon Kalach. The lead tanks audaciously gained control of the bridge over the Don, but an attack upon the town was repulsed by elements of 71st Infantry Division. Later in the day the main body of 26th Tank Corp captured Kalach after the 4th Tank Corp had moved up to provide support. The 24th Army launched new attacks against the 11th Korp, aiming to isolate the Germans between itself and 65th Army. Volskii's 4th Mechanised Corp took Sovetski as it pushed up from the south-east.

The 6th Army was in imminent danger of isolation in Stalingrad. Paulus, having only just moved his headquarters to Nizhne Chirskaya, was ordered back to Gumrak. Hitler was suspicious that Paulus would order a retreat from the Volga on his own initiative. Paulus believed that the only viable course of action was the abandonment of Stalingrad and, informing Army Group B, stressed the urgent need for supplies. Weichs forwarded the request, and an assessment of the situation, to Hitler, who did not respond until after his journey from Berchtesgaden to Rastenburg.

Hoth's 4th Panzer Army was under heavy attack following the collapse of 4th Rumanian Army. Left with the few Rumanian soldiers fleeing before 57th and 51st Armies and 4th Korp, Hoth's army rapidly broke apart. The 4th Korp had become separated, being forced away from the retreating Rumanians. As the pocket was slammed shut on the 6th Army the 4th Korp was handed over to Paulus.

23 November 1942

SOUTHERN SECTOR

Group Lascar made a last attempt to escape from the Raspopinskaya pocket. Some tried to break out towards the Chir but met fierce Soviet resistance. After bitter fighting, a small force punched its way through the Soviet positions, leaving over 27,000 to surrender. With the surrender of Group Lascar the 3rd Rumanian Army practically ceased to exist, having suffered 90,000 casualties since the offensive began.

The 4th Tank Corp linked up with elements of 4th Mechanised Corp at Sovetski where the Germans launched an unsuccessful counter-attack. Other units of 4th Mechanised linked up with 26th Mechanised Corp at Kalach. The encirclement was complete. Paulus' 6th Army, part of 4th Panzer Army (4th Korp) and the remnants of 4th Rumanian Army were isolated around Stalingrad. The Stavka believed they had encircled 90,000 Germans but in fact a force of 267,000 was cut off. This force comprised 256,000 German and 11,000 Rumanian soldiers, 100 panzers, 1,800 artillery pieces, 10,000 motor vehicles and 23,000 horses. Inside the pocket were the headquarters of Jaenecke's 4th, Heitz's 8th, Strecker's 11th, Seydlitz-Kurzbach's 51st and Hube's 14th Panzer Korps, deploying between them fifteen infantry divisions (including the 44th, 71st, 76th, 79th, 94th, 100th, 113th, 295th, 297th, 305th, 371st, 376th, 384th and 389th), three motorised divisions (3rd, 29th and 60th) and three panzer divisions (14th, 16th and 24th) in addition to the 9th Flak Division, 243rd and 245th Assault Gun Battalions and the remnants of two Rumanian divisions. Vasilevsky, reporting the success to Stalin, gained agreement that the most important task was to secure the outer ring and begin the destruction of the trapped forces. The fighting between 19 and 23 November had cost Paulus 34,000 casualties, 450 tanks and 370 artillery pieces lost while 39,000, mainly supply troops and second echelon personnel, escaped the cauldron to fight on along the Don and Chir.

With his army isolated, Paulus called together his subordinate commanders, whose collective decision was to fight their way out of encirclement. Radioing Hitler for permission to break out, Paulus detailed the condition of his army. Weichs had separately contacted Hitler, but the journey from the Obersalzburg prevented communication. Only at midnight did Hitler reach Rastenburg, where Zeitzler went to work to gain his approval for a breakout. Hitler seemed about to agree, but Kietel and Jodl reinforced Hitler's own desire to hold on.

In an effort to force a withdrawal, General Seydlitz-Kurzbach, commanding 51st Korp, ordered his forces to begin to fall back. The 94th Infantry Division began pulling back from the north-eastern face of the pocket. Seydlitz-Kurzbach believed that if he could get the movement started, the withdrawal to the Don would develop of its own accord and neither Paulus nor Hitler would be able to stop it. However, 66th Army struck 94th as it withdrew, and after a running battle the unfortunate division was almost annihilated. Hitler mistakenly took the retreat of the 94th as an attempt by Paulus to force his hand and in a fit of pique removed 51st Korp from his control, making Seydlitz-Kurzbach directly responsible to OKH. Hitler unknowingly rewarded the guilty party.

While Seydlitz-Kurzbach attempted to force the situation, Paulus drew 11th Korp back from its positions in the Don elbow to avoid isolation by 65th and 21st Armies. The withdrawal descended into chaos.

With 6th Army isolated, Army Group B began the task of building up new defences along the Chir and Don rivers. General Hollidt assembled a scratch force to defend the upper Chir while 48th Panzer Korp, badly battered but reinforced by the arrival of 11th Panzer Division, took up positions to his right.

In five days the Red Army fundamentally altered the situation on the southern wing. The well-planned and executed attacks against the Rumanian 3rd and 4th Armies had clearly demonstrated the weakness of

Germany's allies and the new-found confidence of the Stavka and Red Army to carry through a complex offensive operation. Conversely, Paulus' inability to take control without continual reference to Hitler had, even at this early stage of the battle, condemned the Sixth Army to a protracted battle in encirclement.

24 November 1942

CENTRAL SECTOR

Soviet forces around the Rzhev salient prepared to begin Operation Mars. The Stavka had assembled a considerable force around the periphery of the salient in an effort to isolate and destroy the German armies. The 20th Army, 41st, 22nd and 39th Armies were all to play a prominent role in the attack while the 3rd Shock Army of the Kalinin Front faced Velikiye Luki. Zhukov's plan called for the 22nd Army to attack south of Nelidovo along with 41st Army to its right. These armies were to link up with 31st and 20th Armies that would push west between Zubtsov and Sychevka. Once joined, they were to push south and link up with 33rd, 3rd Tank and 5th Armies as they attacked from the west of Vyazma.

The German 9th Army was placed on alert as it was expecting the attack. Model's force comprised 39th Panzer Korp along the Vazuza and Osuga rivers with three infantry and one panzer divisions with a further panzer division in reserve, 27th Korp west of Rzhev with six infantry divisions and 14th Motorised Division, 23rd Korp between Olenino and Rzhev with three infantry divisions and the Grossdeutschland Motorised Division in reserve and 41st Panzer Korp south-west of Belyi with 2nd Luftwaffe Field and two infantry divisions. The 1st Panzer Division was held in army reserve and three more panzer divisions in Army Group reserve.

At Velikiye Luki Group von der Chevallerie comprised the 59th Korp, 2nd Luftwaffe Korp and 6th Korp. The 59th held Velikiye Luki itself while the 2nd Luftwaffe Korp, with two divisions, and 6th Korp with two infantry divisions and a Luftwaffe division, held the long line from the Rzhev salient to Velikiye Luki.[1]

SOUTHERN SECTOR

Paulus struggled to erect a coherent perimeter around Stalingrad, redeploying to cover the exposed western approaches. The 11th Korp deployed to the north, to the north-west was 8th Korp, to the south-west was 14th Panzer Korp, while on the southern face, stretching into the southern suburbs of Stalingrad was 4th Korp. Along the eastern face of the pocket, entrenched inside Stalingrad, was 51st Korp. There was fierce fighting around this perimeter for the next week as Vasilevsky attempted to reduce the pocket.

At Hitler's headquarters an equally fierce battle to free 6th Army continued. Goering stepped into the fray by assuring Hitler that the Luftwaffe could keep 6th Army supplied. Goering maintained that the Luftwaffe, having supplied Demyansk in the winter of '41, would supply the 6th Army. With this assurance, Hitler ordered Paulus to stand fast and await relief. Zeitzler protested vehemently, denouncing Goering's assurance as nothing more than a lie. Even Richthofen, commanding 4th Air Fleet, believed it would be impossible to supply 6th Army fully. With a minimum daily requirement of 750 tons (380 tons of food, 250 tons of ammunition and 120 tons of fuel), the task presented to it was beyond the capability of the entire Luftwaffe transport fleet, let alone those aircraft available locally. A Luftwaffe estimate stated that 6th Army would survive on just 350 tons per day, but with just 298 aircraft 4th Air Fleet was unable to meet even this drastically reduced requirement. Despite all this, at 0830 Hitler sent an order to Paulus, ordering him to hold on to Stalingrad and await relief.

25 November 1942

CENTRAL SECTOR

At 0750 hours the Soviets began Operation Mars. Heavy but inaccurate artillery fire hit the German lines followed by assault units of 20th Army striking the 39th Panzer Korp. Bitter fighting erupted as the Germans prevented major Soviet incursions. Elements managed to gain a small bridgehead across the Vazuza but came under intense German counter-attack. The 31st Army joined the attack. Fierce German fire inflicted crippling losses on the assault units. The Soviets decided to move 6th Tank Corp up during the night to attack in 20th Army's sector.

On the northern face of the salient 39th Army, attacked near Molodi Tud, pushing the Germans back two miles after a day of heavy fighting. Between Nelidovo and Belyi, 22nd Army unleashed its attack. Heavy fighting raged as the rifle units cleared a path for 3rd Mechanised Corp. After severe battles a four-mile salient had been punched in the line. However, the Germans began to move elements of the Grossdeutschland Division up to close the gap.

The 41st Army also attacked near Belyi, hitting the 41st Panzer Korp. After heavy fighting the Soviets smashed a Luftwaffe division and part of an infantry division.

On the far left wing of the 9th Army, the 3rd Shock Army attacked the 59th Korp before Velikiye Luki. Deep penetrations were made into the German positions south of the town.

SOUTHERN SECTOR

The Soviets strengthened their ring around Stalingrad, having erected an inner and outer defensive ring. The outer ring, facing German forces on the Chir and lower Don, consisted of 1st Guards, 5th Tank, 51st and 28th Armies of South-West and Stalingrad Fronts. The 28th Army remained in reserve. Facing 6th Army, forming the inner ring, were 65th, 24th, 66th, 62nd, 64th, 57th and 21st Armies, a force of 490,000 men.

Over the next few days the Germans developed their defences along the Don and Chir. Group Hoth, based around 4th Panzer and 4th Rumanian Armies, was strengthened by the arrival of Kirchner's 57th Panzer Korp from the Caucasus. However, 57th had only the under-strength 23rd Panzer Division at its disposal, while 6th and 17th Panzer Divisions were journeying from France and Orel respectively. The 6th Panzer was fully refitted and near full strength but 17th was badly depleted.

Following Hitler's decision to order 6th Army to stand and fight, the Stalingrad airlift began.

26 November 1942

CENTRAL SECTOR

After heavy fighting the 3rd Shock Army succeeded in isolating elements of the 59th Korp in Velikiye Luki. Other units of the korp were thrown back upon Novosokolniki.

The 20th Army renewed its attack from the Vazuza bridgehead, but was in turn attacked by elements of 5th Panzer Division. The Soviets moved up their armour and repelled the German attack. During the afternoon 6th Tank Corp entered the battle, pushing forward into the German positions but suffering heavy losses. Pushing towards the Rzhev–Sychevka road the Soviets were struck by the Germans during the evening, elements of 9th Panzer Division dealing with the penetration.

The 39th Army continued to push south from Molodi Tud but was meeting strong resistance as the Germans reinforced the line with elements of Grossdeutschland and 14th Motorised Divisions. The 22nd Army renewed its attack, slowly forcing the Germans back but at a high cost. Counter-attacks by other elements of Grossdeutschland brought the advance to a halt.

The 41st Army exploited its previous gains by pushing deeper into the German positions. The Germans erected strong defences against the shoulders of the breakthrough, preventing the broadening of the attack. Lead Soviet units pushed ten miles into the German positions but suffered heavy losses. Behind the line 1st Panzer Division marched west in an effort to contain the break in the line, while elements of the 30th Korp were ordered up to fill the hole.

SOUTHERN SECTOR

Manstein arrived in the Don sector, assuming command of the newly formed Army Group Don. Included in his command were 4th Panzer

Army, 6th Army, 3rd and 4th Rumanian Armies. However, 4th Panzer Army was an army in name only, consisting of 16th Motorised Division at Elitsa and 18th Rumanian Division to its north. The 4th Rumanian Army, reduced to stragglers roaming the steppe around Kotelnikovo, could not be counted on. Despite this Manstein began the formation of screening forces before Kotelnikovo. The 4th Panzer assumed control of the scattered Rumanian units, taking under its command the headquarters of 6th and 7th Rumanian Korps. Paulus' 6th Army, albeit under Army Group Don command, would effectively act only under Hitler's orders. Along the Chir Group Hollidt assumed control of three infantry divisions, all understrength. Hollidt also received two new Luftwaffe field divisions and took control over Knobelsdorf's 48th Panzer Korp fighting in the Nizhne Chirskaya bridgehead. This unit had two panzer divisions, the depleted 22nd and Balck's recently arrived 11th.

27 November 1942

CENTRAL SECTOR
The 6th Tank Corp was unable to advance farther due to difficulties supplying its units. German counter-attacks threatened to sever the corp's communications as the Soviets attempted to push their infantry through to support. Fierce battles raged as 39th and 22nd Armies attempted to force their way forward. Ferocious fighting resulted in heavy casualties to both sides. Heavy fighting around Belyi continued as the 41st Army attacked. There was also very heavy fighting around Velikiye Luki as the 3rd Shock Army attempted to destroy the isolated Germans.

SOVIET COMMAND
While Manstein constructed his defences, the Stavka planned to expand the offensive. While Stalin had decided the main priority was the destruction of 6th Army he also aimed to destroy German and allied forces along the line of the Don from Voronezh to the Azov Sea. Operation Saturn was to follow the success of Uranus. At Stalingrad the 21st Army was transferred to the Don Front.

28 November 1942

NORTHERN SECTOR
Heavy fighting erupted at the base of the Demyansk pocket as the Soviets strove to isolate 2nd Korp.

CENTRAL SECTOR
The 6th Tank Corp drove forward again, smashing its way east but with crippling casualties. The Rzhev–Sychevka road was reached but the corp's

lines were tenuous. Counter-attacks by 5th Panzer Division from the south and 9th Panzer from the north almost cut the 6th Tank Corp off from its supporting units. The Germans began to contain the 39th and 22nd Armies, despite continued strong Soviet attacks. Increasing numbers of German reserves solidified the line.

Heavy fighting continued around Belyi as 41st Army aimed to envelop the town. Elements attempted to force their way east but encountered 1st Panzer Division on its left and 12th Panzer to its front.

SOUTHERN SECTOR

Manstein laid plans for the relief of 6th Army. He intended to begin the operation as soon as possible to break the Soviet outer ring before it was strengthened. Operation Winter-Storm was scheduled to start in early December. Instead of taking the shortest route to 6th Army from the Chir at Nizhne Chirskaya, Group Hoth was to attack from Kotelnikovo where Soviet defences were weaker. From Kotelnikovo the distance to the western tip of the Stalingrad pocket doubled and the relief force had to cross two rivers (the Aksai and Myshkova), each easily fortifiable. To divert Soviet attention towards Nizhne Chirskaya, 48th Panzer Korp was to pin down 5th Tank Army and prevent its reinforcement of the Kotelnikovo axis. Hoth had at his disposal 57th Panzer Korp, the remnants of 6th and 7th Rumanian Korps protecting either flank. The crux of the entire operation though was the ability of the 6th Army to push south-west to meet Hoth when he came within striking distance. Hoth would link up with 6th Army and then pull back to the Don, abandoning the Volga so that 6th Army was extricated.

29 November 1942

CENTRAL SECTOR

Heavy fighting continued around the Rzhev salient as Operation Mars ground on. The 20th Army continued to throw forces into the offensive but suffered massive losses for almost no gain. The 6th Tank Corp, isolated by German counter-attacks, continued to push forward into destruction.

The 41st Army continued to attack Belyi in a vain effort to isolate the German garrison. Despite minor local gains, the Germans again prevented the fall of the town to the Soviets.

SOUTHERN SECTOR

The 4th Cavalry Corp attacked Kotelnikovo, becoming embroiled in heavy fighting with the 57th Panzer Korp as it detrained. The 6th Army was also attacked on its southern perimeter as the Soviets attempted to push it away from the front on the Chir.

30 November 1942

CENTRAL SECTOR
The 6th Tank Corp was all but destroyed in heavy fighting near Osuga. 39th Panzer Korp had successfully contained the 20th Army attack and was regaining the initiative with its 9th and 5th Panzer Divisions. Losses to both sides had been heavy.

The fighting at Belyi wore on, 41st Army's van being forced back towards the town during a strong counter-attack by elements of 20th Panzer and 1st Panzer Divisions.

SOUTHERN SECTOR
The 5th Tank Army launched strong attacks along the Chir, tying down Group Hollidt.

THE RED ARMY
During November the Soviets continued to build up their forces. The Red Air Force activated three more air armies, 7th going to Karelia Front, 13th to Leningrad Front and 18th to South-West Front. [2] Soviet tank strength stood at 4,940 machines, while the air armies had 3,100 planes.

THE OSTHEER
The Ostheer had 3,133 panzers, barely a third of which were operational, together with 2,450 aircraft, again many being out of action.

Of twenty-two Rumanian divisions in the line at the beginning of November, nine had been destroyed, nine more were scattered and could no longer be counted upon, and just four were in the line. Equally disheartening was the struggle through another Soviet winter. Many German divisions lacked proper winter clothing and equipment and suffered the effects of frostbite and hypothermia. Men froze to death as they struggled to survive in their dugouts. At Stalingrad, lacking even the most basic equipment and protection, the frozen ground presented more problems. Once a position was lost the German soldiers found they were exposed on the steppe, the ground being frozen so solid they were unable to dig new defensive positions.

During November the Germans withdrew one infantry division from the line but committed a single new one, their strength remaining at twenty panzer, fourteen motorised and 139 infantry divisions.[3]

1 December 1942

CENTRAL SECTOR
The 20th Army continued its futile attacks for five days, failing entirely to break the now solid German defences between Osuga and Sychevka. To

the west the battle for Belyi was equally unsuccessful, the Germans driving the salient back with heavy losses. At the end of four days' fierce fighting, the 41st Army had been contained, having pushed a ten-mile salient into the German lines. To the north the 22nd Army was similarly beaten, being contained by German counter-attacks.

2 December 1942

NORTHERN SECTOR
Leningrad and Volkhov Fronts received orders to launch Operation Iskra at the beginning of January 1943. This operation was intended to break the siege around the city.

SOUTHERN SECTOR
Fighting along the Chir intensified as 5th Tank Army pinned 48th Panzer Korp down. Battles raged at Oblivskaya, Surovokino and Nizhne Chirskaya. To support the 5th Tank Army the Stavka ordered the 5th Shock Army up to the Chir Front. It would arrive in a week's time. The 51st Army was involved in costly fighting around Kotelnikovo. Around Stalingrad the 21st, 66th and 24th Armies attacked the 6th Army perimeter.

3 December 1942

SOUTHERN SECTOR
The 5th Tank Army had established a bridgehead across the Chir at Nizhne Kalinovka. Romanenko halted to regroup and consolidate. The 51st Army launched strong attacks upon the rail terminals at Kotelnikovo, bringing the sidings under heavy fire. Elements of the 57th Panzer Korp were detraining as the 51st attacked and in fierce fighting it threw the Soviets back. The arrival of 6th Panzer Division surprised the 51st but also alerted the Stavka to the concentration of fresh German forces on this axis.

As the fighting escalated, the Stavka confirmed its intentions for Operation Saturn. The offensive called for the South-West and Voronezh Fronts to isolate the Italian 8th Army and advance south to take the German airbases supplying Stalingrad before Rostov was captured and Army Group Don and A against the Azov Sea and in the Caucasus.

4 December 1942

SOUTHERN SECTOR
Heavy fighting raged along the Chir as 48th Panzer Korp struggled with the 5th Tank Army. Knobelsdorf's 48th Panzer Korp moved to Nizhne Chirskaya to be better able to deal with the attacks by 5th Tank. The 13th

Panzer Division remained on the left wing to bolster the remnants of the Rumanian Third Army. Knobelsdof also took into his command the 11th Panzer and 336th Infantry Divisions plus another Luftwaffe field division. Group Adam, an ad hoc formation, defended the Nizhne Chirskaya bridgehead.[4]

Heavy fighting raged around Kotelnikovo as the 6th Panzer Division threw the 51st Army out of the town.

Vasilevsky reported to Stalin that the armies surrounding Paulus needed substantial reinforcement before they could destroy his army. Stalin had planned to use Malinovsky's 2nd Guards Army, currently in reserve, to bolster the forces of the Don Front. Heavy fighting raged around Stalingrad.

5 December 1942

SOUTHERN SECTOR

Heavy fighting continued along the Chir, around Kotelnikovo and at Stalingrad.

6 December 1942

SOUTHERN SECTOR

Paulus was brought under sustained attack as Don and Stalingrad Fronts probed the German defences.

Lucht's 336th Infantry Division took up defensive positions along the Chir north of Balck's 11th Panzer Division which was at Nizhne Chirskaya. Knobelsdorf intended to operate in tandem with Hoth's relief attack from Kotelnikovo. [5]

7 December 1942

CENTRAL SECTOR

The Germans unleashed a fierce counter-attack against the southern edge of the 41st Army's Belyi salient, 19th Panzer Division slicing through the Soviet lines to isolate 1st Mechanised and 6th Rifle Corps. Bitter fighting raged as the Soviets fought to prevent encirclement.

SOUTHERN SECTOR

Elements of the 5th Tank Army forced their way across the Chir near Surovikino, to the left of 336th Infantry Division. Balck's 11th Panzer Division moved up and lead units checked the Soviet advance. The 5th Shock Army arrived to reinforce the embattled units along the Chir Front.[6]

8 December 1942

CENTRAL SECTOR

The German counter-attack against 41st Army continued, their pincers drawing closer to Belyi as the escape corridor of 6th Rifle and 1st Mechanised Corps became narrower. By the end of the day the German forces were just a mile apart.

SOUTHERN SECTOR

The 6th Army was heavily attacked but managed to repel the Soviet probes. Kirchner's 57th Panzer Korp had still not completed its concentration, only 6th and 23rd Panzer Divisions being in situ. The 17th Panzer had been waylaid by Hitler en route from Orel. It was unlikely that Operation Winter-Storm would begin before 12 December.

After regrouping during the night, the 11th Panzer Division attacked the Soviets to the rear of 336th Infantry Division. The assault struck the Soviets just as they were about to attack and after a bloody battle they were virtually wiped out.

SOVIET COMMAND

As the Soviets prepared to launch Operation Saturn a new 1st Guards Army was raised, the original 1st Guards being redesignated 3rd Guards Army. Lelyushenko commanded 3rd while the new 1st was given to V I Kuznetsov.

9 December 1942

CENTRAL SECTOR

The German pincers at Belyi met, trapping the 1st Mechanised and 6th Rifle Corps.

SOUTHERN SECTOR

Fighting on the Chir intensified as 11th Panzer Division counter-attacked at Oblivskoye, crushing another Soviet bridgehead. The 5th Tank Army suffered heavy casualties as it attempted to break through the Chir line.

The pressure against the 6th Army relaxed as the Soviets assessed the results of the last few days' fighting. It was becoming apparent to the Stavka that the 90,000 men they thought they had encircled were in fact closer to a quarter of a million. This impacted upon Operation Saturn as the encirclement battle demanded a greater number of forces. Therefore, the Stavka modified the objectives to the destruction of the Italian 8th Army and isolation of Group Hollidt. The new plan was codenamed Little Saturn.

10 December 1942

CENTRAL SECTOR
The 6th Rifle and 1st Mechanised Corps launched repeated attacks to try to break out of the pocket south of Belyi. Bitter battles raged until the 15th, when the Soviet force was destroyed.

SOUTHERN SECTOR
With 48th Panzer Korp tied down, the Soviets began a new attack aimed at pinning Group Hollidt. Attacks by 5th Shock Army threatened Hollidt's flank and prevented his transfer of forces to Nizhne Chirskaya for the planned diversionary operation to Winter-Storm.

11 December 1942

SOUTHERN SECTOR
The 11th Panzer Division was forced to fight off additional Soviet attacks across the Chir at Lissinski and Nizhne Kalinovski.

Manstein aimed to launch Winter-Storm on the 12th. Hoth had at his disposal 23rd Panzer Division with thirty tanks and 6th Panzer with 160 panzers and forty self-propelled guns. The 6th Rumanian Korp covered the left flank while 7th Rumanian Korp protected the right.[7] Behind the armoured wedge was the lifeline of 6th Army, a fleet of eight hundred lorries loaded with three thousand tons of supplies. Hoth's force amounted to 30,000 men, with which he was to punch through 51st Army, cross eighty miles of steppe and link up with 6th Army.

Army Group A began its withdrawal from the Caucasus. Heavy fighting erupted along the Terek as the Germans fell back to the Mozdok–Elitsa line.

12 December 1942

SOUTHERN SECTOR
Balck's 11th Panzer Division counter-attacked at Lissinski and wiped out the Soviet bridgehead. Moving north-west the division then attacked the force at Nizhne Kalinovski but failed to destroy this bridgehead.

At 0515 hours Group Hoth began Operation Winter-Storm. With limited air support and a brief artillery barrage, 57th Panzer Korp punched through the 51st Army near Kotelnikovo and pushed north-east. Despite stubborn resistance the 51st was forced to retreat. Due to terrible weather conditions Group Hoth only managed an advance of twelve miles. The heavily laden supply vehicles struggled across the steppe. Eremenko placed Zakharov in command of the forces facing the German attack group and ordered 13th Tank Corp to reinforce 51st Army and halt

23rd Panzer Division. Volskii's 4th Mechanised moved to stop 6th Panzer, deploying at Verkhne Kumski.

13 December 1942

SOUTHERN SECTOR
CENTRAL SECTOR
The 3rd Shock Army launched new attacks against the garrison at Velikiye Luki.

SOUTHERN SECTOR
The 57th Panzer Korp pressed home its attack, 23rd Panzer Division reaching the Aksai river. Hitler agreed to release 17th Panzer Division from behind 8th Italian Army and send it south to aid Hoth's attack. The division had only forty battle-worthy panzers and would arrive too late to support the relief attack, arriving just as the Soviets bolstered their defences. With the German plan apparent and 51st Army retreating to the north-east, Vasilevsky proposed that 2nd Guards Army be used to halt the counter-attack. Stalin angrily refused to sanction this, having intended to use 2nd Guards to help reduce 6th Army. After reasoned argument he gave way though, and 2nd Guards began the move to the Myshkova river.

Along the Chir the 11th Panzer Division was struck on its right flank by strong Soviet forces. Balck redeployed and counter-attacked, defeating the Soviets. However, the fighting had prevented the 11th from finishing off the Nizhne Kalinovski bridgehead.

14 December 1942

CENTRAL SECTOR
The 3rd Shock made significant penetrations into the German defences around Velikiye Luki amid bitter resistance.

SOUTHERN SECTOR
Along the Chir, 5th Shock and 5th Tank Armies continued to attack, pinning down 48th Panzer Korp so it could take no part in the Stalingrad relief attack. The relief force pushed on, but 4th Mechanised and 13th Tank Corps entered the battle against it. Furious fighting developed at Verkhne Kumski as 4th Mechanised tried to halt 6th Panzer Division and gain time for the arrival of 2nd Guards Army.

The Luftwaffe struggled to provide 6th Army with its quota of supplies. German aircraft delivered only one hundred and fifty tons of supplies, far short of the Luftwaffe declared minimum of 350 tons. Sixth Army had to drastically reduce its defensive operations and cut rations to the barest minimum.

With Hoth's relief attack the Soviet High Command postponed Operation Koltso, the reduction of 6th Army.

15 December 1942

SOUTHERN SECTOR
The 48th Panzer Korp evacuated the Nizhne Chirskaya bridgehead. Fighting at Verkhne Kumski intensified.

SOVIET COMMAND
The Stavka completed the planning of Operation Little Saturn. The attack had been revised so that the aim of the campaign was the capture of the Tatsinskaya and Morozovsk airfields and the disruption of communications between Army Groups Don and A Golikov's Voronezh Front employed Kharitonov's 6th Army. Kuznetsov's 1st Guards Army, Lelyushenko's 3rd Guards, Romanenko's 5th Tank and Popov's 5th Shock Armies of the South-West Front would also join the offensive in varying forms. The 5th Tank and 5th Shock Armies were already committed to the Chir sector against 48th Panzer Korp and Group Hollidt, but increased their attacks to prevent the transfer of German units from the Chir to the Don. Total Soviet forces committed to the offensive numbered 425,000 men supported by 5,000 artillery pieces. Garibaldi's 8th Army fielded 216,000 men and just fifty tanks while Army Detachment Hollidt, the remnants of the 3rd Rumanian Army and 48th Panzer Korp had between them 110,000 men and seventy tanks.[8]

16 December 1942

SOUTHERN SECTOR
Voronezh and South-West Fronts opened attacks against the Italian 8th Army at 0800 hours. Artillery fire in the 1st Guards, 6th and 3rd Guards Army sectors hit the Italian lines but thick mist prevented accurate plotting of the barrage. Leading elements of the 1st Guards and 6th Armies began to attack but encountered strong resistance, only managing limited gains. German infantry had been rapidly moved into the Italian positions at the first signs of the attack and opened a withering fire upon the attacking Soviet units. Elements of 27th Panzer Division moved from the reserve to counter-attack, also slowing the offensive. With the attack stalled, Vatutin ordered the commitment of the armour. Units of 18th and 25th Tank Corps of 1st Guards Army surged forward while Sixth Army committed its 17th Tank Corp. Still without effective artillery support and attacking over badly reconnoitred ground, the 18th and 25th Tank Corps ran into minefields, suffering heavy losses.

The 3rd Guards Army hit two German divisions at Krasnokutskaya and

Bokovskaya but after penetrating the line was thrown back by the 22nd Panzer Division.

At Verkhne Kumski the bitter battle between 57th Panzer Korp and 51st Army ended with a slow Soviet withdrawal. Hoth's advance had been seriously delayed and his small force had suffered heavy casualties.

17 December 1942

SOUTHERN SECTOR

Heavy artillery fire renewed the Soviet attack upon the Italian 8th Army. The 6th, 1st Guards and 3rd Guards Armies surged forward once again. Elements of 18th and 25th Tank Corps led the 1st Guards strike, 24th Tank Corp moving up behind the two spearhead corps. Right flank divisions of 6th Army struck from Samodurovka supported by 17th Tank Corp. After heavy fighting the Soviets began to cut open the Italian flank, Soviet forces pressing forward towards the Boguchar river. Slowly but surely the Axis positions began to unravel.

A new Soviet attack struck 336th Infantry Division along the Chir, six miles north of Nizhne Chirskaya. The 11th Panzer Division counter-attacked and drove the Soviets back to the river.[9]

The arrival of 17th Panzer Division to reinforce the 57th Panzer Korp added weight to the German attacks. Leading elements of the 23rd Panzer Division reached the Myshkova.

With the Italian 8th Army on the verge of collapse, Manstein had to remove 6th Panzer Division and send it north. Hoth lost his freshest and strongest unit. Due to the weakness of his remaining panzer forces Hoth grouped all his remaining tanks within 17th Panzer Division.

18 December 1942

SOUTHERN SECTOR

The attack on the Don rolled on. The Germans counter-attacked in an effort to seal a gap in the line at Novaya Kalitva. Fierce battles raged around Boguchar as Soviet attacks gained speed. Elements of 6th Army swung towards Ivanovka while 17th Tank Corp surged forward along the road to Kantemirovka. The 24th and 25th Tank Corps pushed south.

The 11th Panzer Division continued to counter-attack along the Chir but had to meet a new attack from Nizhne Kalinovski. Balck marched his men through the night to deal with this new threat.

The 57th Panzer Korp struggled to maintain its offensive. Elements of 23rd Panzer Division attacked from the right flank of the Myshkova bridgehead while 17th Panzer attacked on the left. Soviet resistance was increasing and later in the day the 23rd Panzer came under heavy attack. The Soviets continued to feed fresh units into the battle, 2nd Guards taking up blocking positions on the Myshkova river. Volskii's 4th Mechanised Corp was renamed 3rd Guards Mechanised Corp.

19 December 1942

SOUTHERN SECTOR
Kantemirovka fell to 17th Tank Corp as Garibaldi's forces disintegrated. The Soviet 6th Army marched hard to catch up with the tanks. More than 15,000 Italians were encircled at Vertyakhovski and suffered heavy losses under concentrated Soviet fire. As the attack gained momentum the Stavka transferred command of 6th Army to South-West Front and ordered 1st Guards to capture Millerovo. The collapse of the 1st Rumanian Korp, on Hollidt's left wing, threatened the rear of the Chir line and of Army Group Don. Units of the 3rd Guards penetrated towards Morozovsk. On the Chir, 11th Panzer Division attacked the Soviet motorised corp at Nizhne Kalinovski. In heavy fighting the Germans destroyed large numbers of tanks, inflicting severe casualties.

The 6th Panzer Division reached the Myshkova river, only thirty miles from Paulus' 6th Army. With the relief force so close, Manstein issued the code word 'Thunderclap', ordering Paulus to break out and link up. General Schmidt, Paulus' chief of staff, informed Hitler of the order and Paulus was told to hold. Despite the fact that the relief force could see the lights from the fighting at Stalingrad on the horizon, 6th Army remained where it was.

20 December 1942

SOUTHERN SECTOR
The 25th Tank Corp was involved in heavy fighting at Kashary, elements of Italian 8th Army retreating under withering Soviet fire. The 3rd Guards advanced upon Morozovsk. Elements of 1st Guards pressed towards Chertkovo and Millerovo, the railway line between Kantemirovka and Millerovo being cut.

Manstein held Group Hoth on the Myshkova as he tried to get Hitler's agreement to allow 6th Army to break out. Manstein asked Zeitzler to intervene but he was equally unsuccessful. The stand fast order remained and 6th Army did not move. On the Myshkova the Germans struggled to hold back furious counter-attacks by 2nd Guards Army. The 17th Panzer Division was down to just eight operational tanks while 23rd Panzer Divisions was similarly depleted.

On the Chir, 11th Panzer Division resumed its attack aimed at throwing the Soviets back over the river. After a promising start the Soviets launched a fierce counter-attack against Balck's right flank. Fighting broke out in the German rear but the situation was quickly restored.

21 December 1942

SOUTHERN SECTOR

As units of 6th Army dug in around Kantemirovka the 17th Tank Corp thrust south.

22 December 1942

SOUTHERN SECTOR

Leading units of 17th Tank Corp closed upon Millerovo while elements of 1st Guards Army encircled Chertkovo, isolating 10,000 Axis troops. The Germans tried to break out over the next few days while 19th Panzer Division launched an unsuccessful relief attempt.

The 48th Panzer Korp was forced to pull back from the Chir in order to cover the rear of Group Hollidt, the Tatsinskaya airbase and the northern approaches to Rostov. As the Germans fell back 24th Tank Corp closed upon Tatsinskaya.

Hoth launched a final attack towards 6th Army. Bitter fighting raged as 2nd Guards threw in its armour to halt the German thrust. Following this last effort Hoth had shot his bolt, his force being exhausted and at the mercy of the stronger Soviet forces opposing it.

23 December 1942

SOUTHERN SECTOR

The 5th Guards Army reached Millerovo, attacking the 3rd Mountain Division. Elements of 19th Panzer were also moving up to support the garrison, the Germans spreading their meagre forces thin. Forces of Soviet 6th Army attempted to reach Novaya Kalitva but were slowed by strong German resistance. As 24th and 25th Tank Corps pressed south the Luftwaffe inflicted heavy losses. After heavy fighting the 306th Infantry Division pulled back upon Morozovsk, enabling 24th Tank to head for Tatsinskaya.

The 57th Panzer Korp again attacked from the Myshkova bridgehead but ran into strong Soviet tank forces. Four hours of fierce fighting followed, bringing the German attack to a halt.

24 December 1942

SOUTHERN SECTOR

The 24th Tank Corp reached Tatsinskaya and, after a brisk battle, took the town and airfield. Luftwaffe losses were heavy as the base was hastily evacuated, seventy-two of 180 transport aircraft being lost.[10] Elements of 25th Tank Corp and 1st Guards Mechanised Corp closed around

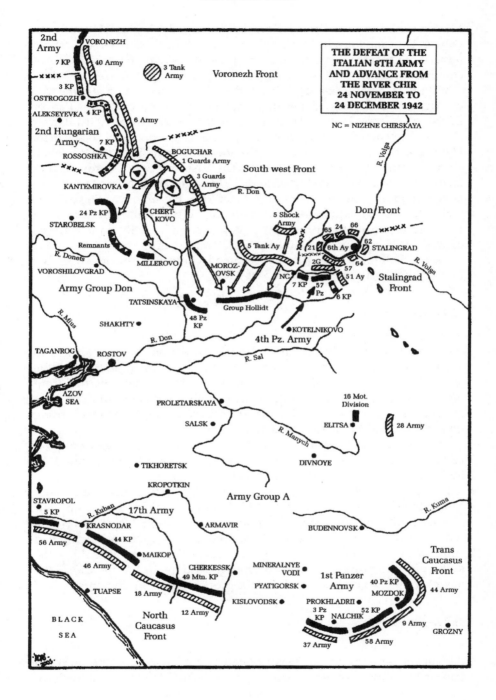

Morozovsk. The 48th Panzer Korp began to redeploy its 11th and 6th Panzer Divisions around Tatsinskaya, intending to destroy the Soviet force. Late in the day a German counter-attack cut the corp's line of communications.

With the Chir line disintegrating and Soviet forces pushing into the rear of Army Group Don, Manstein completed the transfer of 6th Panzer Division to Group Hollidt. Hoth had only the weak 17th and 23rd Panzer Divisions left, a total of only twenty-eight panzers and barely 20,000 men. Having suffered 8,000 casualties and 160 tanks lost since 12 December, Group Hoth was bleeding to death. The 51st and 2nd Guards Armies facing Hoth totalled 149,000 men and 635 tanks and now began to counter-attack, rolling Hoth back towards Kotelnikovo. Fighting was fierce as the Soviets defeated the Rumanian forces on the German flanks, undermining the German positions in the centre. Both 6th and 7th Rumanian Korps disintegrated, opening the flanks of 57th Panzer Korp.

Inside Stalingrad, 62nd Army regained control of the Red October factory after costly fighting with 51st Korp.

25 December 1942

SOUTHERN SECTOR

As Soviet 6th Army dug in on strong positions from Novaya Kalitva to Kantemirovka the Germans moved the 24th Panzer Korp up to cover the area west of Kantemirovka. Detachment Fretter-Pico held the line from Novaya Kalitva to south of Millerovo. Remnants of Italian 2nd Korp were at Voroshilovgrad while the German 17th Korp attempted to erect strong defences around Morozovsk and Tatsinskaya.[11]

The Soviets launched a vicious attack against 57th Panzer Korp as it retreated, forcing the Germans back to the Aksai. Army Group Don informed Paulus that Hoth's attack had failed.

Inside Stalingrad the Soviets pounded the 16th Panzer and 60th Motorised Divisions. Beginning at 0500 hours, the Soviets kept up their attacks until mid afternoon. Despite heavy fighting the German line remained steady. Since the encirclement on 23 November, 6th Army had suffered 28,000 casualties. More serious was the deteriorating health of the survivors, struggling to subsist on meagre rations in the middle of the Soviet winter, with no warm shelter or proper winter equipment.

26 December 1942

SOUTHERN SECTOR

Badanov's 24th Tank Corp was isolated at Tatsinskaya as 11th and 6th Panzer Divisions took up strong positions around the town and airfield. As a sign of the corp's achievement, Stalin redesignated it 2nd Guards

Tank Corp. South-West Front was instructed to make every effort to prevent Badanov's destruction.

Paulus radioed Hitler following the latest delivery of supplies from the Luftwaffe. Only seventy tons of supplies were flown into the pocket of the 350-ton minimum the Luftwaffe promised. Hitler merely replied that 6th Army was to fight to the last man.

The 57th Panzer Korp fell back to Kotelnikovo, closely pursued by 2nd Guards and 51st Armies. Hoth had lost another 8,000 men during the retreat, leaving him with 15,000 effectives, half his original strength.

27 December 1942

SOUTHERN SECTOR
The 3rd Guards Army deployed along the Bystraya river in preparation of a thrust into the rear of Army Group Don. After heavy fighting 11th Panzer Division recaptured Tatsinskaya airfield, forcing 2nd Guards Tank Corp back into Tatsinskaya itself.

The 2nd Guards Army entered Kotelnikovo amid heavy fighting with rearguards of Group Hoth.

28 December 1942

SOUTHERN SECTOR
Badanov's 2nd Guards Tank Corp was under sustained attack at Tatsinskaya, suffering heavy casualties. Vatutin gave permission to launch a break-out attempt.

Kotelnikovo fell to 2nd Guards Army. Other units of the army advanced upon Zimovniki, having taken Sovetnoye. On the flanks of 57th Panzer Korp, 6th and 7th Rumanian Korps ceased to exist after bitter fighting.

With the situation in the Don bend desperate, Hitler agreed to the withdrawal of Army Group A from the Caucasus but insisted upon the retention of the Kuban bridgehead.

29 December 1942

SOUTHERN SECTOR
The 2nd Guards Tank Corp attempted to break out from Tatsinskaya. Heavy fighting raged as Soviet and German armoured forces clashed. Other Soviet forces penetrated to within seven miles of Morozovsk but 17th Korp moved up and halted the Soviet attack. The 11th and 6th Panzer Divisions followed the Soviet break out, hitting their forces on the Bystraya.

30 December 1942

SOUTHERN SECTOR

Badanov's 2nd Guards Tank Corp fought its way into Kostino and along the Bystraya river towards 25th Tank and 1st Guards Mechanised Corps, linking up late in the day. The 11th and 6th Panzer Divisions continued their counter-attack against 3rd Guards Army, inflicting heavy losses.

Far out on the Kalmyuk Steppe 16th Motorised Division began to fall back, enabling the 28th Army to retake Remotnoye.

31 December 1942

SOUTHERN SECTOR

Tomorsin fell to 5th Shock Army as Group Hollidt began to collapse. The Germans reconstituted their 29th Korp around Morozovsk from German, Italian and Rumanian remnants.

Since 19 November South-West Front had lost 64,600 killed and missing and 148,000 wounded in the fighting around Stalingrad while Stalingrad Front lost 43,000 killed and missing and 58,000 wounded. In the Caucasus, since 1 September Northern and Black Sea Groups lost 132,000 killed and missing and 163,000 wounded, 990 tanks, 5,000 artillery pieces and 644 aircraft.[12]

With their Don front in tatters the Germans began the evacuation of the Caucasus, 40th Panzer Korp beginning the withdrawal from the Terek. The 40th Panzer deployed two panzer divisions (3rd and 13th), elements of 5th SS Panzer-Grenadier Division Wiking and three infantry divisions (111th, 370th and 50th). The 1st Panzer Army also included 3rd Panzer Korp at Ordzhonikidze and 52nd Korp at Mozdok while 17th Army comprised 44th Korp near Maikop, 49th Mountain Korp near Elbruz and 5th Korp near Novorossiysk. South Front deployed 393,000 men and Trans Caucasus Front 685,000 against Army Group A.

PRODUCTION

During 1942 the Soviet Union produced 24,446 tanks, 127,000 artillery pieces, 30,400 motor vehicles and 25,436 aircraft.[13]

German production during 1942 included 6,180 panzers and assault guns, 23,200 artillery pieces, 58,049 motor vehicles and 15,556 aircraft. These weapons had to be distributed between the African Front, defence of the occupied territories and the Eastern Front.[14] German oil production stood at 6,600,000 tons of natural oil and 4,600,000 tons of synthetic oil while 7,305,000 tons were consumed.

SOVIET CASUALTIES
The Red Army and Navy lost 515,508 killed and missing in action and 941,896 wounded during the final quarter of 1942.[15]

THE OSTHEER
German deployment on the Eastern Front at the end of December '42 stood at 177 divisions (twenty-one panzer, fourteen panzer grenadier and 142 infantry). The 22nd Panzer Division was disbanded following heavy casualties while 269th Infantry Division was withdrawn. In return 6th and 7th Panzer Divisions and 304th, 306th and 321st Infantry and 5th Luftwaffe Field Divisions entered the line.[16]

Across the entire line the Germans had only 495 operational panzers and assault guns against 8,500 Soviet tanks and Su's. The Ostheer was short of over half a million men while the allied armies had largely been swept away. Only 2nd Hungarian Army remained intact.

1 January 1943

CENTRAL SECTOR
The 3rd Shock Army demanded the surrender of the much-reduced garrison of Velikiye Luki but was refused. Only the citadel still remained in German hands, the remainder of the town having been overwhelmed.

THE RED ARMY
With the reduction of Paulus' 6th Army imminent, the Stavka reorganised its southern commands. Eremenko's Stalingrad Front was renamed South Front and deployed along the outer ring. Rokossovsky's Don Front now took complete responsibility for the pocket, taking 62nd, 64th and 57th Armies under its command. In Stavka reserve a new 1st Tank Army was raised while 2nd Tank Army was created around the core of the 3rd Reserve Army.

2 January 1943

SOUTHERN SECTOR
The 3rd Guards Army captured Morozovsk airfield. Luftwaffe air supply missions now had to fly from Salsk and Novocherkessk.

Kleist's 1st Panzer Army gave up its last outposts on the Terek. Maslennikov's Northern Group operated along the Terek with its 44th, 58th, 9th and 37th Armies, 4th Kuban and 5th Don Cavalry Corps.

3 January 1943

SOUTHERN SECTOR

Fighting on the Chir Front saw the Soviets recapture Chernyakovsky after a bloody battle.

Malgobek and Mozdok were given up by 1st Panzer Army as it fell back to the Kuma river. The 58th and 9th Armies occupied the abandoned towns. Nalchik fell to 37th Army.

SOVIET COMMAND

The Soviet Command scheduled Operation Koltso, the reduction of 6th Army, to begin on 10 January.

4 January 1943

CENTRAL SECTOR

The 59th Korp launched a relief attack with Group Wohler aimed at relieving the survivors of Velikiye Luki. Soviet resistance was intense. The bitter fighting at Velikiye Luki continued as the 3rd Shock attempted to snuff out the last pockets of German resistance.

5 January 1943

CENTRAL SECTOR

Heavy fighting continued at Velikiye Luki with gradual Soviet gains. Wohler continued his relief attack but met considerable Soviet resistance.

SOUTHERN SECTOR

Prokhladrii fell to 58th Army

6 January 1943

CENTRAL SECTOR

Wohler's relief force was being bled white by the Soviets as losses continued to mount. Inside Velikiye Luki the garrison struggled to hold against overwhelming odds. The fighting raged incessantly for the next nine days but the relief attack had already failed.

SOUTHERN SECTOR

As its withdrawal continued, 40th Panzer Korp reached the Kuma. A brief stand was made while the main forces moved north.

7 January 1943

SOUTHERN SECTOR
General Kovacs, chief of staff of the Hungarian 2nd Army, reported to Budapest that a Soviet offensive against 2nd Hungarian was very unlikely, an opinion reinforced by 2nd Army.

8 January 1943

SOUTHERN SECTOR
Having been encircled for more than a month, with Stavka approval Rokossovsky offered 6th Army the opportunity to surrender. The proposal promised proper treatment of the wounded and prisoners. If the offer was rejected the Soviets warned, they would destroy 6th Army and the responsibility for further bloodshed would rest with Paulus. Paulus immediately informed Hitler but was ordered to reject it.

9 January 1943

SOUTHERN SECTOR
Don Front prepared to begin Operation Koltso. The Don Front had 281,000 men, 257 tanks and nearly 10,000 artillery pieces against the 6th Army's 191,000 effectives, 7,700 artillery pieces and mortars and 60 panzers.[17] At the time of the attack the temperature was −35 degrees.

In the period since 23 November Paulus had lost 40,000 killed or missing, suffered 29,000 wounded while 7,000 specialist troops had been flown out of the pocket. No longer able to feed his own men adequately, Paulus ordered all captives to be returned to the Soviet lines. Many, fearing NKVD and OGPU retribution, remained behind the German lines, shunned by both armies.

10 January 1943

SOUTHERN SECTOR
Operation Koltso opened at 0650 hours with a colossal artillery bombardment. The barrage was followed by infantry and armoured attacks. Elements of 24th Army crashed into 113th and 76th Infantry Divisions, while 65th Army struck 384th, 44th and 376th Divisions as it advanced towards Karpovka. The 21st and 57th Armies cut through the Marinovka nose, battering 3rd and 29th Motorised Divisions mercilessly. Under continual attack by Don Front and harassed by 16th Air Army, 6th Army began to disintegrate. Only the 297th and 113th Infantry Divisions survived the attacks, the remainder being wiped out almost to a man. Scattered bands of hunted men retreated across the steppe to the

Rossoshka river and Stalingrad, many falling as the Soviets began a close pursuit.

In the Caucasus, the Soviet began to attack across the Kuma. The 40th Panzer Korp had pulled most of its forces back, only rearguards holding a skeletal line. To the west the 49th Mountain Korp pulled back towards Maikop.

11 January 1943

NORTHERN SECTOR
The Soviet forces in the Leningrad sector began to bombard German positions along the Neva.

SOUTHERN SECTOR
The Marinovka sector of the Stalingrad pocket was crushed, the Soviets herding the Germans back to the Rossoshka. The last remnants of the 29th Motorised and 376th Infantry Divisions were wiped out in bitter fighting. With his army falling apart, Paulus received an order from OKH which stated that 6th Army must not under any circumstances surrender without prior approval.

The advance towards Rostov continued as 51st Army and 2nd Guards Army reached the Manych river, threatening the rear of Army Group A.

In the Caucasus Georgievsk, Pyatigorsk and Mineralnye Vody fell as Army Group A withdrew to the north to avoid isolation. Both 46th and 18th Armies were preparing to attack 44th Korp of the 17th Army and force it back towards the Maikop oilfields, this attack being intended to act as a diversion to draw off German forces from the main attack to the east.

12 January 1943

NORTHERN SECTOR
The Soviets began Operation Iskra around Leningrad. At 0930 hours the 67th Army, fielding 130,000 men, attacked from the southern perimeter of Leningrad. The Soviet aim was to cross the Neva and link up with Volkhov Front. Heavy fighting erupted with 18th Army, the Germans inflicting heavy casualties upon the Soviet units. Aided by artillery and aerial support, the 67th managed to force a crossing of the Neva.

The revitalised 2nd Shock Army, now under Romanovsky and with 114,000 men, began attacking from the Volkhov in order to link up with 67th. Fighting here was also intense against well-entrenched German units.

Fighting at Demyansk died down, having cost the Soviets 10,000 killed and more than 420 tanks lost. The German 16th Army lost 17,000 killed and wounded.

SOUTHERN SECTOR
A new disaster was about to overtake Army Group B. After careful preparation the Soviets launched their offensive against German 2nd and Hungarian 2nd Armies. Golikov's Voronezh and Reiter's Bryansk Fronts, supported by South-West Front, planned to break open the German line on a 300-mile sector between Livny and Kantemirovka. The main attack was undertaken by Moskalenko's 40th Army against the right flank of 2nd Hungarian Army while Rybalko's 3rd Tank Army (including 12th and 15th Tank Corps) was to break through on the left flank. The intention was for the two armies to meet at Alexievka, encircling the bulk of 2nd Hungarian Army. From here they would turn both north and south, rolling up German 2nd Army and remnants of Italian 8th Army. The second phase of the Soviet offensive would draw in 38th and 60th Armies of the Voronezh Front, 13th Army of Bryansk Front and 6th Army of South-West Front. Voronezh Front committed 347,000 men to the attack. Against these forces German 2nd Army had 125,000 men in twelve divisions while 2nd Hungarian had 100,000 men.

Soviet reconnaissance attacks began with 40th Army testing the Hungarian lines. These probes unexpectedly forced the 3rd Hungarian Korp back three miles, prompting Golikov to immediately order the main offensive to begin the next day.

At Stalingrad there was bitter fighting as Don Front tried to crack open the German positions. The fighting between 10 and 12 January had cost Rokossovsky 26,000 casualties and 135 tanks[18], but Paulus had lost 60,000 men and vast amounts of weapons and ammunition.

Kleist pulled back in the Caucasus as the simultaneous diversionary attacks by 46th and 18th Armies at Maikop made slow progress in the face of stiff German resistance.

13 January 1943

NORTHERN SECTOR
At Leningrad the 67th and 2nd Shock Armies continued to attack across the Neva and along the Volkhov, lead units being no more than two or three miles apart by the end of the day. The 26th and 28th Korps had suffered heavy losses during the fighting. Soviet 8th Army joined the attacks, committing its 52,000 men to the battle.[19]

SOUTHERN SECTOR
The Soviet 40th Army launched its offensive against 2nd Hungarian Army. The 7th Hungarian Division took the full weight of the Soviet thrust and after heavy fighting was overwhelmed.

In the Stalingrad pocket the 65th and 21st Armies reached the Rossoshka. Attacks by 64th and 66th Armies from the north and south also forced the Germans back while 62nd Army counter-attacked inside the city.

14 January 1943

NORTHERN SECTOR
The Germans counter-attacked north of Sinyavino, having pulled two infantry divisions up from Kirishi. Fierce fighting ensued as Soviet forces continued their attacks.

SOUTHERN SECTOR
On the upper Don the Voronezh Front smashed the 2nd Hungarian Army. Under cover of thick fog 3rd Tank Army entered the battle, crashing its way through the junction of the Hungarian 4th and 7th Korps and advancing twelve miles.

15 January 1943

NORTHERN SECTOR
Heavy fighting raged around Sinyavino as 67th and 2nd Shock Armies made slow but steady progress.

CENTRAL SECTOR
After a ferocious battle and a desperate break-out attempt, Velikiye Luki fell to the 3rd Shock Army. Just over 180 men from the garrison made it back to the German lines. Some 5,000 men had been lost during the battle while the 59th Korp lost an additional 12,000 fighting around the pocket.[20] The Soviet forces engaged in the battle had lost 31,600 killed and missing and 72,300 wounded.[21]

> The fall of Velikiye Luki brought the largely unsuccessful Soviet offensive in the central sector to an end. Zhukov's plan to isolate Army Group Centre while the 6th Army was destroyed at Stalingrad had failed in the face of overwhelming German resistance. This crucial battle clearly underscored that when faced by German troops in well established defensive positions, the Red Army still had some difficult lessons to learn.

SOUTHERN SECTOR
The isolated garrison of Chertkovo began break-out attempts while 19th Panzer Division launched repeated attacks in an effort to link up.

In Stalingrad the panic gripping 6th Army spread as Pitomnik airfield came under heavy artillery fire.

16 January 1943

SOUTHERN SECTOR

The expected collapse of 2nd Hungarian Army happened as Soviet armies poured west.

Inside the Stalingrad pocket the Germans lost Pitomnik airbase as Soviets advanced towards the city and the only remaining airbase at Gumrak. By this stage of the battle the Soviet spearheads were only six miles west of the Volga.

German forces in the Caucasus withdrew but came under attack by the 44th Army. Luckily for Army Group A the Soviet attacks were badly co-ordinated and unable to disrupt the withdrawal.

17 January 1943

SOUTHERN SECTOR

Chertkovo fell to the Soviets after a bitter struggle.

In the Stalingrad pocket 6th Army struggled to survive. Over half the pocket and ten thousand prisoners had fallen to the Red Army, leaving 6th in possession of only one of the six airfields. Supplies now had to be air dropped and many containers fell into deep snow. Of those dropped in the correct areas, many could not be recovered because of the physical exhaustion of the German soldiers. The battle so far had cost the Don Front dear. Pausing to regroup, Rokossovsky again offered 6th the opportunity to surrender but yet again Paulus refused, as instructed by Hitler.

In the Caucasus 47th Army joined the Soviet offensive.

18 January 1943

NORTHERN SECTOR

Elements of 2nd Shock Army and 67th Army linked up near Schlusselburg, which fell after heavy fighting. A five-mile corridor had been punched through the German positions south of Lake Ladoga, easing the supply situation into Leningrad.

SOUTHERN SECTOR

The 40th Army and 3rd Tank Army linked up at Alexievka, isolating the 4th Hungarian Korp together with large parts of the 3rd and 7th Hungarian Korps and remnants of Italian Alpine Korp.

Inside the Stalingrad pocket the 21st Army brought Gumrak under heavy fire as the Germans tried to bring the primitive airbase back into use. Army Group A pulled out of Cherkessk and Divnoye.

SOVIET COMMAND

General Zhukov was promoted to Marshal of the Soviet Union and made Deputy Supreme Commander of the Soviet Armed Forces.

Vasilevsky presented plans to Stalin for the next phase of the offensive aimed at destroying the German 2nd Army. 13th Army was to attack north of Kastornoye while 40th, 38th and 60th Armies also attacked.

19 January 1943

SOUTHERN SECTOR

The encircled units of the 2nd Hungarian Army surrendered at Ostrogozh, 50,000 marching into Soviet captivity. The offensive had in a week cost the Axis 89,000 captured and 140,000 killed or wounded.

Voronezh Front extended its attacks against Army Group B, elements of the 3rd Tank Army taking Vayluki and Urazovo. Advanced units of the 7th Cavalry Corp entered Vayluki, massacring the Italian forces there.

At Stalingrad the 21st Army was just two miles from Gumrak, bringing the airfield under heavy artillery fire.

20 January 1943

SOUTHERN SECTOR

The South Front crossed the Manych river as it pushed towards Rostov. Elements of the 2nd Guards Army took Manychskaya. Army Group A gave up Nevinomysk to the 37th Army and Proletarskaya to the 28th Army.

21 January 1943

SOUTHERN SECTOR

The 28th Army recaptured Salsk, a major supply base for the airlift into Stalingrad.

22 January 1943

SOUTHERN SECTOR

Following a rapid redeployment, the Don Front renewed the offensive against Paulus' 6th Army. The attack opened with an overwhelming artillery barrage that pulverised the German line. Resistance was weaker than earlier in the month. Gumrak came under intense fire as 21st Army approached Stalingrad.

With his army on the verge of collapse, Paulus requested permission to open negotiations but was again ordered to fight to the last man.

Manstein pulled the 11th Panzer Division away from Hollidt to deal with the 2nd Guards Army threat at Manutchskaya.

23 January 1943

SOUTHERN SECTOR

The Voronezh launched new attacks with 38th Army against the German 2nd Army.

Gumrak fell to 21st Army as the battle for Stalingrad drew towards its bloody conclusion. Paulus moved his headquarters into the city to the Univermaag department store.

In the Manych bridgehead, 11th Panzer Division, with an infantry division in support, hit the 2nd Guards Army. The Soviets were down to just thirty tanks and a handful of riflemen after their fierce battles since December. Bitter fighting erupted as the Germans crushed the Soviet positions, rolling up the bridgehead.

In the Caucasus, Armavir fell to the 37th Army as the German withdrawal continued.

24 January 1943

SOUTHERN SECTOR

The 60th Army forced the 7th Korp out of Voronezh. Elements of the 40th Army began their attack against the southern wing of the 2nd Army in the midst of a blizzard and with temperatures at −20 degrees. Despite these difficulties the Soviets broke the German front and introduced their 4th Tank Corp to battle. To the south, Starobelsk, former headquarters of Army Group B, fell to the Soviet 6th Army.

Hitler decided to pull 1st Panzer Army out of the Caucasus and back into the southern Ukraine to support Manstein's weakened forces. However, the southern flank of 1st Panzer was still as far south as Armavir, which had just been given up to the Trans Caucasus Front, and the bulk of 17th Army was falling back into the Kuban.

The Northern Group of the Trans Caucasus Front, in recognition of its staunch defence in the Caucasus, was elevated to front status, becoming the North Caucasus Front under Maslennikov. The Stavka ordered that the German 17th Army be isolated in the Kuban with 2nd Guards, 51st and 28th Armies of Southern Front. The 44th and 58th Armies were to attack Bataisk while 9th and 37th Armies were to co-operate with the Black Sea Group.

Inside Stalingrad the battle for the city entered its final stage. Paulus again requested that he be allowed to surrender but again Hitler refused and ordered 6th Army to fight to the last man and the last bullet. Manstein also asked Hitler to let 6th Army surrender but received the same response.

25 January 1943

SOUTHERN SECTOR

After heavy fighting the 2nd Guards Army bridgehead at Manychskaya was destroyed. This German success alleviated the threat to the Rostov sector, preventing the early isolation of Army Group A and enabling the 1st Panzer Army to continue its withdrawal into the Donbas.

The Soviets sent emissaries forward to 6th Army to demand its surrender. Paulus again refused.

26 January 1943

SOUTHERN SECTOR

At Stalingrad the German 6th Army was under intense pressure, fighting raging throughout the city as the Soviets pressed from west and east. The hard-pressed 297th Infantry Division, reduced to just 1,800 men from its original 10,000, surrendered to 38th Guards Rifle Division.[22] 65th Army linked up with the 62nd Army between the Mamayev Kurgan and Red October factories, splitting the remnants of Paulus' force into two pockets. Later in the day elements of 21st Army and 64th Army linked up with 62nd Army. The Germans were reduced to a small pocket in the Tractor Factory, consisting of 11th Korp with the 60th Motorised, 16th and 24th Panzer and 389th and 100th Infantry Divisions, while to the south were 4th, 8th, 51st and 14th Panzer Korps together with Paulus and his headquarters, grouped in the city centre.

The Stavka widened the Voronezh Front's objectives to include the capture of the Kursk region. The 38th and 60th Armies were to attack along the Kursk axis while 40th, 69th and 3rd Tank Armies were to move along the Kharkov axis. Facing the Soviets on the Kharkov axis the Germans deployed Army Detachment Lanz from the Oskol river to Kupyansk, comprising one infantry and three Hungarian divisions and the SS Panzer Korp. Between Novy Oskol and Volokolonvka was Panzer Grenadier Division Grossdeutschland and opposite Valuyki a single regiment of the 2nd SS Panzer-Grenadier Division Das Reich. At Kupyansk there were two infantry divisions.[23]

27 January 1943

SOUTHERN SECTOR

The 1st Panzer Army began the final phase of its move out of the Caucasus, entering the eastern Ukraine in force to rejoin the main German combat line. However, over 350,000 men of 17th Army were to be incarcerated in the Kuban.

The 1st Panzer was instructed to deploy along the Donets from

Kupyansk to Voroshilovgrad while Detachment Hollidt covered the line from Voroshilovgrad to the Azov Sea. By the time it redeployed the panzer army comprised 30th Korp, recently redeployed from the central sector, and the 3rd and 40th Panzer Korps. Facing these forces the Soviets deployed their 6th Army, 1st Guards, Group Popov, 3rd Guards Army and 5th Tank Army.

28 January 1943

SOUTHERN SECTOR

Elements of 40th Army, moving north from Alexievka, linked up with 13th Army, encircling the bulk of the German 2nd Army. Only the 55th Korp on the northern wing of the German force was free to withdraw. The encircled units, comprising large parts of the 7th and 13th Korps around Kastornoye, came under heavy attack by 38th Army.

At Stalingrad, Soviet attacks split the 8th and 51st Korps in the city centre apart from the 14th Panzer and 4th Korps around the ruins of the Univermaag department store.

In the Caucasus, 37th Army captured Kropotkin after a brief struggle.

29 January 1943

NORTHERN SECTOR

As the fighting around Leningrad died down, the Soviet armies took stock of their losses. Since 12 January the 67th Army had lost 12,000 killed and missing and 28,700 wounded, while 2nd Shock Army lost 19,000 killed and 46,000 wounded. The 8th Army, which had a minor role in the battle, lost 2,500 killed and missing and 5,800 wounded.[24]

SOUTHERN SECTOR

Heavy fighting continued at Stalingrad as the three pockets were mercilessly attacked.

Kastornoye fell to 38th Army after a ferocious battle. The South-West Front began the next phase of its attacks, aiming to outflank Army Group Don and penetrate the Donbas. Lead units of Soviet 6th Army pushed forward north-west of Starobelsk, aiming to march straight for Balakleya. Elements pushed the Germans back to Kupyansk and crossed the Krasnaya river on both sides of the town. The Germans retreated into Kupyansk and towards Izyum. The 1st Guards Army launched heavy attacks upon 19th Panzer Division near Kabanye and Kremennaya.

30 January 1943

SOUTHERN SECTOR

The 1st Guards Army attacked south-west of Krasny Liman, crossing the Krasnaya to close in around the town. Group Popov moved up between 6th and 1st Guards Armies.

For 14th Panzer, 51st and 8th Korps the battle of Stalingrad ended as they were overrun by 21st and 62nd Armies. Among the prisoners was General Seydlitz-Kurzbach. Paulus' army was reduced to 4th Korp around his own headquarters and the 11th Korp in the factory district.

Tikhoretsk fell to the 9th Army while the Maikop oilfields were cleared by the 12th, 18th and 46th Armies. The 17th Army had now lost contact with the main German line.

31 January 1943

SOUTHERN SECTOR

Paulus was promoted to Field Marshal. This move on Hitler's part was intended to force Paulus' hand, Hitler relying on the fact that no German Field Marshal had ever been taken prisoner. It was therefore expected that Paulus would commit suicide rather than be taken by the Soviets. However, soldiers of 38th Motorised Rifle Brigade entered the Univermaag building and at 0715 hours captured Paulus and his staff. Paulus' surrender effectively ended resistance in the southern pocket, the 4th Korp laying down its arms. Only 11th Korp remained to continue the battle. Hitler was furious at Paulus' capitulation.

Kremennaya fell to 1st Guards Army as 19th Panzer Division was forced back to Lisichansk. Krasny Liman fell. To bolster the line the Germans moved 7th Panzer Division (with thirty-five tanks)[25] up to Slavyansk and 3rd Panzer Division to its east to halt the Soviet advance.

In the Caucasus the rearguard of 1st Panzer Army, 40th Panzer Korp, reached Bataisk. The korp continued to fall back, marching across the frozen Azov Sea to Taganrog.

ASSESSMENT: JANUARY 1943

With the German 6th Army all but destroyed the Soviets could reflect upon the fact that they had also wiped out 2nd Hungarian Army and the greater part of German 2nd Army. The total number of casualties in this battle had risen to 90,000 captured, 80,000 killed and 60,000 wounded by the end of January.

The condition of the Panzerwaffe also reached a new low. As the first month of the New Year ended, the Ostheer had fewer than five hundred operational panzers in the field. Army Group A had fewer than forty operational tanks, Army Groups B and Don a combined force of just under

300 operational machines, Army Group Centre nearly 170 and Army Group North only three panzers in action.

Despite their declining strength, the number of divisions actually increased to nineteen panzer, fifteen panzer grenadier and 149 infantry. One motorised, one infantry and seven Luftwaffe field divisions joined the line but many were below establishment, the Luftwaffe divisions particularly being of dubious fighting quality. Three divisions left the line for a comprehensive refit.[26]

1 February 1943

SOUTHERN SECTOR

There was heavy fighting in the Tractor Factory as Strecker's 11th Korp was pounded by Don Front. Over 4,000 men were killed or wounded as the Red Army launched concentrated tank and infantry attacks, supported by massive artillery fire.

The main part of the Don Front was moving to the west to join the line fighting the Germans in the Ukraine. Voronezh Front began its new attacks towards Kursk and Kharkov, 3rd Tank Army taking Svatovo as it crossed the Oskol near Valuyki. The tank army ran into elements of 2nd SS Panzer Korp north of Kupyansk and was involved in heavy fighting.

South-West Front attacked with its 6th Army and 1st Guards Army. Popov crossed the Donets with his 4th Guards Tank Corp and captured Kramatorsk, while 10th Tank Corp moved up to support. Elements of 1st Guards crossed the Northern Donets west of Krasny Liman, forcing the Germans back to Barvenkovo. Other units entered Lisichansk but were halted by 19th Panzer Division.

GERMAN COMMAND

Hitler's headquarters issued the official communiqué on the defeat at Stalingrad:

'The Battle for Stalingrad has ended. True to its oath to its last breath, Sixth Army, under the exemplary leadership of Field Marshal Paulus, has succumbed to the overwhelming strength of the enemy and to unfavourable circumstances. The enemy's two demands for capitulation were proudly rejected. The last battle was fought under a swastika flag from the highest ruin in Stalingrad.'

2 February 1943

SOUTHERN SECTOR

The epic battle of Stalingrad, which had raged so fiercely in and around the city since 23 August 1942, ended as Strecker and the remnants of 11th Korp surrendered in the Tractor Factory. In all, 91,000 German soldiers had surrendered to the Soviets during the battle and 147,000 were killed. Added to this were the 15,000 who died in the encirclement operation between 19 and 23 November, the 150,000 Rumanians of 3rd and 4th Armies, nearly 100,000 men of Italian 8th Army, 100,000 of 2nd Hungarian and 80,000 of German 2nd Army who also perished in the wave of Soviet attacks that followed the encirclement. Hitler's maniacal obsession with Stalingrad cost Germany and her allies over 650,000 men. Only 30,000 men of 6th Army escaped the pocket during November, many being sucked into the savage fighting on the Chir, and 34,000 were evacuated by air after their encirclement. The Luftwaffe lost over 500 aircraft during the airlift, a large part of its transport fleet, and many irreplaceable experienced pilots were killed or captured.

Don Front losses had been heavy, with 46,000 killed and missing and 123,000 wounded, and the loss of 2,915 tanks, 3,600 artillery pieces and 700 aircraft since 12h January.

The Voronezh Front prepared to launch the next phase of its operations. The 60th Army aimed to reach Kursk, 40th Army was to take Belgorod and penetrate into Kharkov, while 69th Army struck directly into Kharkov and 3rd Tank outflanked the city to the south-west. The 69th Army was a relatively new force, having recently been raised around 18th Rifle Corp. It opened its attack upon Volchansk early in the day, breaking out of its bridgeheads on the Oskol and forcing back the Gross-deutschland Division. Heavy fighting also raged at Kupyansk as 3rd Tank Army attacked the SS Panzer Korp. Co-operating with 6th Army, the two forces had almost isolated Kupyansk, embroiling the Germans in a vicious three-day battle as they fought their way west.

South-West Front attacked with its 6th, 1st Guards, 3rd Guards and 5th Tank Armies. The 17th Air Army provided invaluable support with its 300 aircraft. Group Popov acted as a mobile group in the van of the Soviet attack. Popov was hit by a 40th Panzer Korp counter-attack at Kramatorsk but held off the German armour. In an effort to strengthen their lines, the Germans moved the 3rd Panzer Division east of Slavyansk, in turn bringing other elements of Popov's group to a halt. The 1st Guards Army began its attack upon Slavyansk, becoming embroiled in fierce street fighting. Another 40th Panzer Korp counter-attack halted the 1st Guards advance, but other elements of the army attempted to get around the German flank and separate the two attacking elements of the panzer korp.

The 3rd Guards Army crossed the Donets river near Voroshilovgrad, attacking Group Hollidt and breaking through its defences.

THE OSTHEER IN THE SOUTHERN SECTOR

For the Germans January 1943 had been one long string of disasters. At the beginning of the month the 6th Army had lain encircled at Stalingrad and the forces of Army Group Don struggled to hold the Chir and Donets

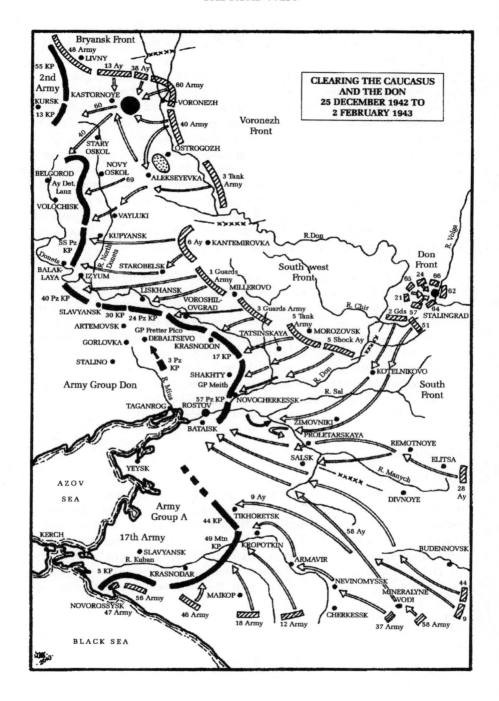

**CLEARING THE CAUCASUS
AND THE DON
25 DECEMBER 1942 TO
2 FEBRUARY 1943**

positions. Army Group A was withdrawing from the Caucasus and Army Group B remained fixed on the Don, albeit without the bulk of 8th Italian Army and 3rd Rumanian Army. Barely a month later, Army Group B had ceased to exist, retaining only the remnants of 2nd Army against the southern and now open wing of Army Group Centre. Army Group Don had been pressed back to the Donets and towards the Mius while attempting to retain Rostov. Army Group A had pulled its 1st Panzer Army back into the southern Ukraine and joined Manstein's Group Don, while 17th Army was isolated in the Kuban, a force of 350,000 men with 2,000 artillery pieces languishing in a backwater when they were badly needed on the main combat line. Such was the scale of the German losses that the Ostheer had no other option than to fight defensive battles all along the line, the cream of the German forces which had been robbed from Army Groups North and Centre in the summer of 1942 now lying wrecked on the steppes of the southern Soviet Union.

The battle for Stalingrad was a costly enterprise for both the Ostheer and the Red Army. Determined, though ultimately misguided, German resistance to the bitter end condemned an army of a quarter of a million men to absolute defeat. Hitler's refusal to accept the principles of a flexible defence, and the lack of resolution among the army generals to act independently in the best interests of their forces, was to be a common theme during the remaining years of the war. Meanwhile, the Red Army had begun the task of understanding the need for methodical preparation and planning. However, the victory at Stalingrad was to be clouded by a German recovery on the southern wing and the failure of the offensive in the centre.

3 February 1943

SOUTHERN SECTOR
The 40th Army joined the Voronezh Front offensive and advanced up to fifteen miles. Kupyansk fell to 3rd Tank Army as the Germans retreated towards the Donets. Elements of the 3rd Tank pushed towards Pechenegi. Farther south, units of the 3rd Guards Army entered Voroshilovgrad but were embroiled in heavy fighting as Group Fretter-Pico fought for every street. Fierce battles also raged at Slavyansk as 40th Panzer Korp attacked 1st Guards Tank Army. Forces of Group Popov closed upon Kramatorsk.

GERMANY: HOME FRONT
The defeat at Stalingrad was announced to the German people over national radio and three days' mourning were declared.

4 February 1943

SOUTHERN SECTOR

After heavy fighting the 69th Army punched a hole between the Grossdeutschland and SS Das Reich Divisions. Due to intense resistance the 69th was unable to fully exploit its gain. The 3rd Tank Army reached the northern Donets at Pechenegi. The newly arrived and up to strength 1st SS Panzer-Grenadier Division Leibstandarte Adolf Hitler began to deploy at Chuguyev and brought the advance of the 3rd Tank Army to an abrupt halt.

Lisichansk was under heavy attack as 1st Guards Army hit the 30th Korp (now part of the 1st Panzer Army). The 40th Panzer Korp was ordered to hold on to Slavyansk. As this battle raged, Group Popov attempted to move north-east of Slavyansk to undermine the German defences.

South Front reached a line from Shakhty to Novocherkessk, having pushed Army Detachment Hollidt away from the lower Donets.

In the Kuban 17th Army was isolated as it attempted to hold a line from Novorossiysk to Krasnodar. In an effort to turn the German flank the North Caucasus Front landed an assault force at Ozereyka Bay, near Novorossiysk and another at Novorossiysk itself. In heavy fighting the force at Novorossiysk was wiped out but those at Ozereyka Bay clawed a foothold, despite fierce German counter-fire.

The fighting in the Caucasus since the New Year had cost the South Front 54,000 killed and missing and 47,000 wounded, while the Trans Caucasus Front lost 12,000 killed and missing and 30,000 wounded. The North Caucasus Front also lost 3,000 killed and missing and 7,000 wounded.[27]

SOVIET COMMAND

The Stavka raised a new Central Front around the core of Rokossovsky's Don Front, planning to move it between the Voronezh and Bryansk Fronts at the end of February. The Central Front included 21st, 65th, 16th Air, 70th and 2nd Tank Armies.

5 February 1943

SOUTHERN SECTOR

Stary Oskol fell to 38th Army as the 40th Army crossed the northern Donets and cut the Belgorod to Kursk road. Units of 40th Army isolated Korocha. Elements of 69th and 3rd Tank Armies attacked the SS Panzer Korp, while other units of 3rd Tank Army attempted to cross the Donets but were held back by Leibstandarte SS Adolf Hitler Division.

Balakleya and Izyum fell to the Soviet 6th Army. The 6th continued between Balakleya and Izyum but the Germans fought a bitter delaying action to evade encirclement. Heavy fighting raged at Lisichansk where the 1st Guards Army continued to attack. At Kramatorsk the Soviets moved 3rd Tank Corp up to support elements of Group Popov.

In the Kuban, Soviet troops captured Yeysk on the Azov coast, severing land communications between 17th Army and Army Group Don. Soviet assault landings at Myoshako and Anapa were successfully beaten off by 17th Army but only after protracted fighting.

6 February 1943

NORTHERN SECTOR

The Soviets began to run trains through to Leningrad along a newly constructed line on the south shore of Lake Ladoga. The trains came under heavy German fire but supplies did reach the city.

SOUTHERN SECTOR

The 40th Army closed upon Belgorod, leading units being just fifteen miles north of the city while others pushed towards Tomarovka. To speed the assault a tank corp was sent up to reinforce the 40th Army's attack. The 3rd Tank Army continued to attack along the Donets, units unsuccessfully trying to cross the river while others advanced south of Chuguyev and secured Andreyevka. At its junction with 69th Army, the 3rd Tank was hit by an SS Panzer Korp counter-attack. Lisichansk fell to 1st Guards Army as 40th Panzer Korp pulled back across the Donets. Other elements of the army crossed at Izyum and pushed on to Barvenkovo. Heavy fighting continued at Slavyansk as 40th Panzer Korp repelled renewed Soviet attacks. South Front closed in around Rostov, Bataisk falling.

GERMAN COMMAND

Hitler, visiting Manstein at his headquarters in Zaporozhe, agreed to the proposed withdrawal of the German right wing to the Mius river, giving up Rostov. However, Manstein's request that the Kuban be evacuated so that 17th Army could be used on the main battlefront was firmly denied. Hitler did agree though to the evacuation of the Rzhev salient, an operation that would release a considerable number of divisions. It was also decided that the defunct Army Group B be disbanded, 2nd Army being handed over to Army Group Centre while Army Group Don took over the entire southern wing of the German line, being redesignated Army Group South. These changes would become effective from 13 February.

7 February 1943

SOUTHERN SECTOR

The Germans pulled out of Korocha after a fierce battle with 40th Army. Other units of the army entered the outskirts of Belgorod, forcing the Grossdeutschland Division back east of the city. The Germans had to punch their way out of the town in a day of bloody action. Elements of the 3rd Tank Army punched their way across the Donets at Andreyevka while Kramatorsk, south of Slavyansk, fell to 1st Guards Army. The 44th Army of South Front took Azov on the Don river.

In the Kuban the 17th Army launched a fierce counter-attack in an effort to destroy the Soviet bridgehead at Novorossiysk. Despite ferocious fighting the 47th Army could not be dislodged.

8 February 1943

SOUTHERN SECTOR

During the night of 7–8 February the 40th Army attacked Belgorod, fighting their way through the city. The Germans drew back to Tomarovka and brought the Grossdeutschland Division back across the Donets to cover the approaches to Kharkov. Kursk fell to 60th Army while the 3rd Tank Army pushed south of Kharkov, threatening the German positions on the Donets. The 6th Army took Andreyevka but then encountered stiff resistance from elements of SS Leibstandarte Adolf Hitler on the road to Zmiyev. Shakhty fell to 5th Shock Army in the Donbas.

9 February 1943

SOUTHERN SECTOR

Units of 40th Army captured Belgorod as 69th Army took Volchansk and Shebekino. The advance of the 3rd Tank Army south of Kharkov was interrupted as the Germans moved elements of the SS Panzer Korp to block its path.

The North Caucasus Front mounted its Krasnodar Offensive Operation with some 390,000 men.[28] Its intention was to break down the 17th Army defences around the town and push the Germans back into the Taman peninsula.

10 February 1943

SOUTHERN SECTOR

The 40th and 69th Armies threw themselves into a direct assault upon Kharkov, becoming embroiled in the German outer defences. Elements of the 40th Army attempted to envelop Kharkov from the west, while other units of the army pushed towards Oboyan, Grayvoron and Bogodukhov. The Germans were forced back upon Borisovka, Zolochev and Olshany.

Units of the Soviet 6th Army reached the river opposite Zmiyev. Heavy fighting ensued as the Germans attempted to prevent their crossing but some succeeded in crossing at Andreyevka. Exploiting the 6th Army success, 3rd Tank Army began an assault crossing of the Donets near Chuguyev. Pechenegi and Chuguyev fell as the SS Leibstandarte Adolf Hitler was forced back. Other units of the 3rd Tank seized Merefa. German defences at Rogan proved too strong for the moment.

The 48th Panzer Korp also came under fierce attack as it withdrew from the Donets to the area north of Stalino.

In the Kuban the Soviet advance along the Black Sea coast succeeded in linking up with those assault forces already at Novorossiysk, threatening the southern flank of the German 17th Army.

SOVIET COMMAND
The Stavka renamed 21st Army the 6th Guards Army. Many of the armies that fought at Stalingrad were renamed in the early part of 1943. Chuikov's 62nd Army became 8th Guards.

11 February 1943

SOUTHERN SECTOR
Fighting at Kharkov intensified as 69th Army pushed deeper into the city. Hausser's 2nd Panzer Korp put up fierce resistance to the attacks but slowly fell back towards the city centre. The SS Panzer Korp counter-attacked and threw the 3rd Tank Army out of Novaya Vodolaga. A renewed 3rd Tank Army attack at Rogan stalled in the face of fierce German resistance. Lozovaya fell to 1st Guards Army. Elements of the army pushed on to take Grishino and Krasnoarmieskoye, Group Popov taking advantage of this to attack the left wing of 40th Panzer Korp. In order to counter this threat the Germans moved units west from Artemovsk to retake Krasnoarmieskoye.

12 February 1943

CENTRAL SECTOR
The Bryansk Front joined the general offensive in the Ukraine as it attacked with its 13th and 48th Armies against 2nd Panzer Army before Orel. These armies attempted to smash through the German line and outflank Orel.

The 40th Army threw its tank corp into the battle, striking the German positions at Zolochev while others pushed towards Dergachi.

The 3rd Tank Army ground its way into the inner defence zone of Kharkov, being involved in bitter fighting with Leibstandarte Adolf Hitler. SS Wiking counter-attacked at Krasnoarmieskoye and Grishino, hitting Group Popov hard. Fierce battles raged all day but eventually the Soviets brought the German attack to a halt. The 7th and 11th Panzer Divisions pushed west from Slavyansk, striking Popov as he tried to move south. Again the German attack stalled.

Vatutin aimed to broaden his offensive in the south. The 6th Army was instructed to take Zaporozhe and Group Popov was to operate in conjunction with the 6th. Popov had just fifty-three operational tanks and 13,000 men left after weeks of hard fighting yet was expected to push towards Stalino and Mariupol. 1st Guards Army was to pin the Germans at Slavyansk while 3rd Guards and 5th Tank Armies were to push west of Stalino.

The Black Sea Group captured Krasnodar from 17th Army after heavy fighting. Slowly but surely the 17th was being squeezed tighter into the Kuban.

13 February 1943

SOUTHERN SECTOR

North of Kharkov the 40th Army pressed the Germans hard, Dergachi being taken in heavy fighting. Borisovka also fell. Other elements of 40th Army closed upon Grayvoron and Bogodukhov and entered the northern suburbs of Kharkov.

Heavy fighting also raged in the eastern suburbs as 3rd Tank Army pushed the Leibstandarte Adolf Hitler back to the city limits. Lanz was personally ordered by Hitler to hold on to Kharkov at all costs in addition to securing a line from Poltava to Dnepropetrovsk with his very limited forces. The fact that the group was already heavily committed to the fighting at Kharkov meant Lanz was unable to fulfil either task.

The 40th Panzer Korp abandoned its counter-attack near Slavyansk and moved towards Kramatorsk. Group Hollidt lost Novocherkessk to the South Front.

Army Group B was officially disbanded and Army Group South came into being once more. Army Group A retained control of 17th Army in the Kuban but was in effect redundant, taking no part in the battles to the north.

14 February 1943

SOUTHERN SECTOR

The 40th Army threatened to cut German communications west and south-west of Kharkov. The Grossdeutschland Division was forced out of Olshany while Soviet units attacked the northern suburbs of Kharkov and pushed towards Lyubotin. Heavy fighting erupted at Grayvoron.

Vvedenka fell to 3rd Tank Army as it pushed south-east of Kharkov, despite fierce resistance from the SS Panzer Korp. However, other elements of the 3rd Tank fell back around Novaya Vodolaga.

With the situation in Kharkov increasingly critical Hausser informed Lanz he must order the evacuation of the city otherwise his force would be encircled and destroyed. Lanz, under direct orders from Hitler, forbade any withdrawal, infuriating Hausser. The heavily embattled German forces were stretched thin around the city. Grossdeutschland attempted to hold to the west while 168th Infantry Division fought in isolation on its left flank. The Das Reich, Leibstandarte and 320th Infantry Divisions tried to hold the eastern and southern approaches to the city. To make matters worse, the civil population began to rise in revolt during the evening.

The 4th Panzer Army disengaged from the Mius line and redeployed to the Dnepropetrovsk area. There it would take command of SS Panzer Korp, Army Detachment Lanz and 48th Panzer Korp. Army Detachment Hollidt held the line from Voroshilovgrad along the Mius river.

After a long and costly battle Voroshilovgrad fell to 3rd Guards Army, while Rostov fell to the 2nd Guards and 28th Armies as the Germans withdrew to the Mius.

15 February 1943

NORTHERN SECTOR

German forces began to withdraw their eleven infantry divisions of the 2nd and 10th Korps from the Demyansk pocket. Hitler had sanctioned the withdrawal earlier in the year but added the clause that it must not be completed until the end of March. During this time 16th Army made extensive preparations to deny the Soviets the use of the captured territory. Mines and booby traps were planted in abundance, making the Soviet advance difficult and costly. As the first units pulled back 11th, 34th and 53rd Armies of the North-West and 1st Shock Army of the Kalinin Front attacked but were unable to break the German line. The North-West Front began the Demyansk Offensive Operation with 327,600 men. [29]

SOUTHERN SECTOR

The battle for Kharkov reached its peak. With Soviet attacks threatening his rear, Hausser again requested permission to evacuate. Having no immediate reply he began to pull his force back at 1300 hours, only to receive a 'hold at all costs' order at 1630 hours. Disobeying Hitler's and General Lanz's direct orders, Hausser continued to withdraw the SS Panzer Korp. With the SS in retreat Lanz had no option but to order the rest of his Army Detachment to evacuate, thus saving his men from certain destruction at the hands of the Soviets.

The 40th Panzer Korp was instructed to abandon Slavyansk and redeploy to Krasnoarmieskoye.

16 February 1943

CENTRAL SECTOR
Army Group Centre informed OKH that it was unable to co-ordinate its actions with those of Army Group South and would therefore only be content with securing the positions of 2nd Army.

SOUTHERN SECTOR
Kharkov fell after a night of fierce fighting with the retreating SS Panzer Korp. The 3rd Tank Army linked up with 40th Army in Dzherzhinsky Square then pushed south to attack the Germans west of Lyubotin. The 40th and 69th Armies began a hurried redeployment north-west of Kharkov.

Hitler unfairly dismissed Lanz, replacing him with Kempf. Group Lanz, renamed Army Detachment Kempf, held under its command SS Panzer Korp and Korp Raus. Zmiyev fell to the Soviet 6th Army.

17 February 1943

SOUTHERN SECTOR
The 40th Army captured Grayvoron and Bogodukhov as the Soviets pushed out from Kharkov. The 69th Army took control of the Bogodukhov sector from 40th Army as it redeployed. As the rifle armies pushed west and north-west, the 3rd Tank Army advanced to the south and south-west, striking the Grossdeutschland and 320th Infantry Divisions of Korp Raus. Slavyansk fell to 1st Guards Army as the offensive from the Donets penetrated deep towards the Dniepr.

With the Soviet position increasingly over extended, Manstein consulted with Hitler. The Führer had arrived in Zaporozhe early in the day, meeting Manstein at the headquarters of Army Group South. Manstein reported that Army Detachment Hollidt had been forced back to the line of the Mius river, closely followed by the South Front but would be able to maintain an effective defence on this position. The 1st Panzer Army had halted the Soviet advance at Grishino but was involved in heavy fighting around Kramatorsk. To the north Army Detachment Kempf continued to fall back to the south-west, nearing Poltava and the Mozh river. During discussions on the 17th and 18th Manstein outlined his plan. Using his meagre forces in concentration, he proposed to bite off the Soviet spearheads and cut their lines of communication. Swiftly regrouping the Germans would then push north, rolling up the Soviet salient that protruded towards the Dniepr. In cooperation with Army Group Centre, Manstein's panzers would finally isolate the forward elements of the Voronezh, Central and South-West Fronts, shortening the combat line and destroying large elements of the Soviets' strike forces. Such a victory would give the Ostheer the chance to restructure and rebuild its armies for the campaign in the summer. After protracted debate Hitler finally agreed to the plan and gave Manstein the freedom of manoeuvre he had been calling for since November '42.

Quickly deploying his forces Manstein aimed to begin the counter-attack almost immediately. Army Detachment Hollidt held firm on the Mius, anchoring the German right wing against the sea, while 1st Panzer Army, with 3rd and 40th Panzer Korps and 30th Korp, deployed behind Hollidt south of Krasnoarmieskoye. This army was ordered to penetrate the rear of 1st Guards Army and Group Popov. To the west, Hoth's 4th Panzer Army would hit 1st Guards Army and 6th Army, now only thirty miles from the Dniepr. Hoth had assembled the three panzer and two infantry divisions of 57th and 48th Panzer Korps before Zaporozhe at Boguslav to cover the river crossing and protect the lines of communication to the German forces in the Donbas. To the north the SS Panzer Korp, having fallen back upon Krasnograd from Kharkov, would strike south-east to trap the advancing Soviet armies between itself and the 48th Panzer Korp. The gap between SS Panzer Korp and 2nd Army, far to the north, was covered by Army Detachment Kempf's Raus Korp. The 40th Panzer Korp was to attack at Krasnoarmieskoye and push north to Barvenkovo to link up with the SS Panzer Korp and 48th Panzer Korp. The 3rd Panzer Korp was to counter-attack south of Slavyansk in order to retake Krasnoarmieskoye and Grishino.

The continuation of the Soviet offensive after Stalingrad had rolled the Germans back from the Don to the Donets, but in the process had over extended the exhausted Soviet armies. Yet again, the Stavka refused to believe its own intelligence information and deluded itself into thinking that German redeployment was a sign of the continuing evacuation of the southern Ukraine. Manstein was about to deliver a sobering lesson in the military art.

NOTES

1   Glantz, *Zhukov's Greatest Defeat*, pp34–5
2   Ellis, *The World War II Databook*, p81
3   Ellis, *The World War II Databook*, p175
4   Mellenthin, *Panzer Battles*, p175
5   Mellenthin, *Panzer Battles*, p175
6   Tarrant, *Stalingrad*, p156
7   Tarrant, *Stalingrad*, p158
8   Glantz, *From the Don to the Dnepr*, p28
9   Mellenthin, *Panzer Battles*, p181
10 Tarrant, *Stalingrad*, p185
11 Glantz, *From the Don to the Dnepr*, pp64–5
12 Kirosheev, *Soviet Casualties and Combat Losses in the Twentieth Century*, Table 67
13 Ellis, *The World War II Databook*, p175
14 Ellis, *The World War II Databook*, p175
15 Kirosheev, *Soviet Casualties and Combat Losses in the Twentieth Century*, Table 67
16 Ellis, *The World War II Databook*, p175
17 Tarrant, *Stalingrad*, p197
18 Tarrant, *Stalingrad*, p199
19 Kirosheev, *Soviet Casualties and Combat Losses in the Twentieth Century*, Table 67
20 Kurowski, *Deadlock Before Moscow*, p366
21 Kirosheev, *Soviet Casualties and Combat Losses in the Twentieth Century*, Table 75
22 Tarrant, *Stalingrad*, p214
23 Glantz, *From the Don to the Dnepr*, p152
24 Kirosheev, *Soviet Casualties and Combat Losses in the Twentieth Century*, Table 75
25 Glantz, *From the Don to the Dnepr*, p99
26 Ellis, *The World War Two Databook*, p176
27 Kirosheev, *Soviet Casualties and Combat Losses in the Twentieth Century*, Table 75
28 Kirosheev, *Soviet Casualties and Combat Losses in the Twentieth Century*, Table 75
29 Kirosheev, *Soviet Casualties and Combat Losses in the Twentieth Century*, Table 75

CHAPTER II
The Ostheer Strikes Back

Kharkov had changed hands for the second time as the Red Army had pushed west after its victory at Stalingrad. It was again to prove the focal point for the massed armies surging across the Ukrainian steppe. Field Marshal von Manstein, Germany's foremost general, was about to deliver a lighting counter-attack with his carefully mustered reserves, an attack that would push the Red Army to the east once more.

18 February 1943

SOUTHERN SECTOR

The 3rd Tank Army, now down to 110 tanks[1] moved forward around Kharkov, attacking the Grossdeutschland Division at Lyubotin and capturing Merefa after a ferocious battle. It then began the push towards Valki.

The 40th Panzer Korp counter-attacked south of Slavyansk and broke into Krasnoarmieskoye. Fierce fighting throughout the day saw the 1st Guards Army halt the Germans in the town centre. Meanwhile, the 1st Guards Army took Pavlograd and Novomosskovsk but at Sinelnikovo was repulsed. The South Front continued its heavy attacks against Group Hollidt but was unable to break through the strengthening German line.

19 February 1943

SOUTHERN SECTOR

Elements of 69th Army redeployed at Bogodukhov and began to push towards Krasnokutsk. Heavy fighting erupted with elements of Korp Raus. After bitter fighting the Germans halted the 3rd Tank Army on the Mzha river, preventing the isolation of units around Lyubotin.

Tanks of the Soviet 6th Army reached the railway station at Sinelnikovo, only thirty miles from Manstein's headquarters at Zaporozhe. However, they could go no farther as they ran out of fuel and were destroyed by German counter-attacks. Hitler, who was still at

Zaporozhe, finished his conference with Manstein and flew back to Germany. Later in the day, the SS Panzer Korp launched a furious attack, smashing into the flank of 6th Army at Zmiyev and pushing to within ten miles of Krasnograd, scattering other elements of the strung-out Soviet 6th Army. The 4th Panzer Army also began its northward thrust towards Pavlograd and Lozovaya, sowing confusion and panic among forward elements of the 6th Army. Grishino was retaken after bloody fighting.

20 February 1943

SOUTHERN SECTOR

West of Kharkov the 40th Army reached a line Krasnopolye–Akhtyka as Korp Raus continued to fall back.

Manstein's carefully prepared counter-attack grew in ferocity as 2nd SS Panzer Korp sliced through the flank of 6th Army, which also came under ferocious Luftwaffe attack at Pavlograd. South of Krasnograd, the SS Panzer Korp linked up with elements of 48th Panzer Korp attacking from Novomosskovsk. This precipitated a Soviet withdrawal across the Samara but some units were isolated west of Novomosskovsk.

The 40th Panzer Korp attacked Group Popov. Popov's understrength tank corps attempted to hold off the German tide but to no avail. Under intense pressure, he requested permission to withdraw but was ordered by Vatutin to continue his attack. Group Hollidt was again heavily attacked along the Mius position.

21 February 1943

SOUTHERN SECTOR

Heavy fighting raged south of Lyubotin as the 3rd Tank Army tried to break into the town. Additional elements of 3rd Tank moved up from the west, placing further pressure upon the Germans.

The Germans mopped up the scattered Soviet units at Novomosskovsk. Despite fierce attacks the Soviet 6th Army continued to push its units ahead, even going so far as to form a mobile group in the Lozovaya and Pavlograd areas to exploit the advance. This group attacked immediately passing east of Sinelnikovo as it drove south.

The 30th Korp began its advance upon Krasnoarmieskoye from the Stalino area while 48th and 57th Panzer Korps moved upon Pavlograd and Lozovaya. Hausser's 2nd SS Panzer Korp and Korp Raus were attacking in conjunction with the 4th Panzer Army towards Pavlograd, aiming to envelop the Soviet forces between them. In addition, 1st Panzer Army attacked with its 40th and 3rd Panzer Korps in the direction of Andreyevka and Izyum.

Detachment Hollidt fought vigorously along the Mius, elements of the

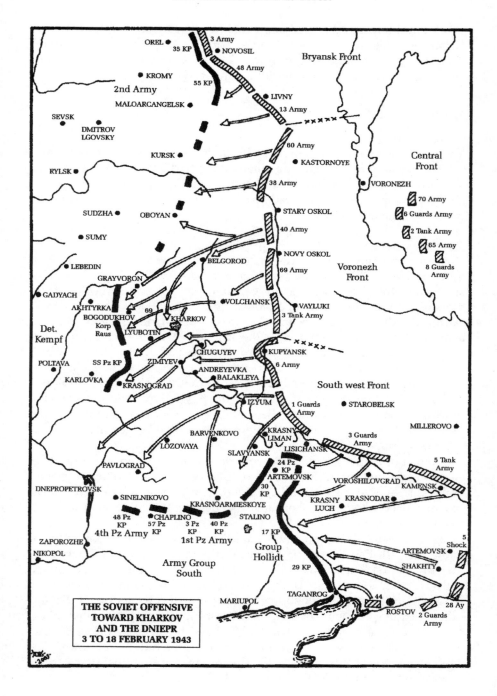

THE SOVIET OFFENSIVE
TOWARD KHARKOV
AND THE DNIEPR
3 TO 18 FEBRUARY 1943

South Front having broken through only to be encircled and destroyed at Debaltsevo station after a fierce battle. With the situation to the south of Kharkov growing increasingly critical Golikov swung his 69th Army and 3rd Tank Army south to aid the ailing 6th Army.

22 February 1943

CENTRAL SECTOR

The Soviets began a new offensive in the Rzhev sector as Army Group Centre prepared to evacuate the salient that jutted forward on the road to Moscow. An attack by the 13th and 48th Armies against the Bryansk and Orel sectors made slow but steady progress in the face of fierce resistance by the German 2nd Army.

SOUTHERN SECTOR

Units of 69th Army forced a crossing of the Vorskla river some twenty-five miles north of Poltava, despite fierce resistance by Korp Raus. To strengthen this sector the Germans began to feed a newly arrived infantry division into the line south of Kotelva. Continued attacks by 40th Army captured Akhtyrka and Lebedin. The Grossdeutschland Division began to abandon Lyubotin, falling back as the 3rd Tank Army took control of the town. Rifle and cavalry units of the 3rd Tank pushed south of Kharkov but were held up by the SS Panzer Korp at Novaya Vodolaga. Other elements of the korp drove the Soviets back upon Pavlograd. This flurry of blows smashed the right wing and centre of the Soviet 6th Army. Despite its obviously dangerous position, the army was ordered to force its mobile group forward. Duly attacking in force, the 6th plunged deeper into Manstein's trap.

Group Popov staggered under the blows of 40th Panzer Korp. The Germans pushed through the broken Soviet group while other elements of the korp swung west to hit them again. Some of Popov's units fell back south of Barvenkovo. The Germans also began to hit the Soviet units at Krasnoarmieskoye.

The 48th Panzer Korp advanced rapidly in the direction of Barvenkovo while the 57th Panzer and SS Panzer Korps moved towards Pavlograd. The 4th and 1st Panzer Armies pushed into the rear of the Soviet armies still advancing towards the Dniepr, the 1st Panzer advancing upon Izyum. As the German attack penetrated deeper into the wings of the Soviet salient, leading elements of the South-West Front were just twelve miles from Zaporozhe only to run short of fuel and be destroyed. The Stavka was slowly becoming aware of the German threat, but its forces were so over extended and weakened by the recent fighting that they were powerless to ward off the German blows.

23 February 1943

NORTHERN SECTOR

Bitter fighting erupted at the base of the Demyansk salient as the Soviet 27th Army tried to isolate the 16th Army. However, the Germans had considerably strengthened this area and were able to hold off the Soviet assaults. The evacuation of the salient was almost complete by this time and had largely proceeded according to plan, the bulk of the 10th and 2nd Korps having escaped the pocket.

CENTRAL SECTOR

There was heavy fighting around Rzhev and Orel as the Soviets pressed home their attacks against Army Group Centre. Here also the Germans were preparing to withdraw from their long held salient.

SOUTHERN SECTOR

In an effort to halt the German advance the Stavka began to pile forces up before them. A rifle, cavalry and tank corp had dug in to try and halt SS Panzer Korp. However, SS forces unleashed a fierce attack, drove to within twelve miles of Lozovaya, and closed upon Pavlograd. In conjunction with this attack the 48th Panzer Korp moved from the southeast, advancing from Chaplino to link up with other forces pushing north towards Boguslav. Elements of 48th Panzer Korp crossed the Samara.

With his 6th Army in tatters, Vatutin ordered a flanking rifle corp from 1st Guards Army to move to the aid of the 6th Army. In addition, 69th and 3rd Tank Armies were ordered to turn south from Bogodukhov to support the 6th.

24 February 1943

CENTRAL SECTOR

The 13th and 48th Armies of the Bryansk Front had pushed the 2nd Army back eighteen miles on the road to Orel in three days of bloody fighting, but German resistance was stiffening all the time.

SOUTHERN SECTOR

The SS Panzer Korp pushed on to Pavlograd, capturing the town after a brisk battle. The Soviet corps committed to stopping the SS began to retreat, abandoning their equipment as they fled. The 48th Panzer Korp continued to develop its attack, pushing east of Boguslav. Strong Soviet forces along the Samara river held up other elements of the korp. Realising the dire straits that the 6th Army was in, Vatutin ordered the already defeated force onto the defensive.

25 February 1943

CENTRAL SECTOR
Central Front joined the attack towards Orel in an effort to smash through the German front line before the onset of the spring thaw. The Stavka intended to turn the southern flank of Army Group Centre and prevent it from giving any support to Army Group South. The 2nd Tank and 65th Armies attacked, with support from 2nd Guards Cavalry Corp.

SOUTHERN SECTOR
Golikov moved an additional tank corp from 40th Army over to assist the 69th Army in the capture of Poltava. The 38th Army lagged well behind the 40th Army's right wing, which was ordered to capture Sumy. Valki and Novaya Vodolaga fell to the 3rd Tank Army.

The SS Panzer Korp attacked in force from Pavlograd. As the Soviet forces fled across the steppe, fierce German fire inflicted heavy losses. The 48th Panzer Korp also moved north, encountering strong resistance at Bogdanovka. However, the Barvenkovo–Lozovaya railway line was severed. On the approaches to Barvenkovo 40th Panzer Korp encounter heavy fighting, elements of Group Popov attempting to hold the German attack.

26 February 1943

NORTHERN SECTOR
There was heavy fighting on the Lovat as the 1st Shock Army tried to close off the much reduced salient.

CENTRAL SECTOR
Central Front, newly committed to this sector, threw its 65th and 2nd Tank Armies into an attack towards Bryansk but was held up by the German 2nd Army.

SOUTHERN SECTOR
Heavy fighting erupted at Lozovaya as SS Totenkopf and SS Das Reich attacked the town. The 6th Panzer advanced east to cut off the Soviet line of retreat. At Barvenkovo the 40th Panzer Korp fought its way into the city despite ferocious resistance.

27 February 1943

SOUTHERN SECTOR
After heavy fighting Lozovaya fell to the SS Panzer Korp. The 48th Panzer Korp was now attacking alongside the SS but had suffered heavy losses during the recent fighting.

SOVIET COMMAND
The Stavka ordered the 1st Guards and 6th Armies back behind the Donets in the face of heavy German attacks. The 3rd Tank Army was ordered south to strike the Germans between Krasnograd and Lozovaya.

28 February 1943

NORTHERN SECTOR
Soviet forces closed up to the Lovat river as the Germans left the Demyansk pocket for good. The North-West Front lost 10,016 killed and missing and 23,647 during the Demyansk Operation.[2]

SOUTHERN SECTOR
Elements of the 40th Army crossed the Psel but were unable to reach Zenkov or capture Sumy, despite heavy fighting.

The 40th Panzer Division recaptured Kramatorsk while 48th Panzer Korp reached the Donets west of Izyum, having forced 1st Guards Cavalry Corp back across the river. The Soviets withdrew from Barvenkovo after a bitter battle and fell back upon Izyum in order to cross the Donets.

ASSESSMENT: FEBRUARY 1943
As February came to a bloody end German commitment in the east stood at sixteen panzer, fifteen panzer grenadier and 140 infantry divisions. The Ostheer had lost three panzer, three motorised and sixteen infantry divisions from its order of battle, the bulk of these at Stalingrad. However, three SS panzer grenadier divisions, six infantry and one Luftwaffe field division had been transferred from other areas to the east and entered the fighting.[3]

The fighting during the winter of 1942–43 had cost Germany's allies thousands of men, Italy losing 185,000, Hungary 140,000 and Rumania 250,000.

1 March 1943

SOUTHERN SECTOR
Soviet casualties so far during the German counter-offensive in the Ukraine had been severe, combat units losing 23,000 killed, 9,000 captured, as well as 615 tanks and 350 artillery pieces destroyed or captured.

The 40th Army went over onto the defensive in positions along the Psel river. The 3rd Tank Army meanwhile attacked from Krasnograd towards Lozovaya with two tank corps, which combined totalled no more than thirty operational tanks.[4] After a short advance the Soviets ran into the SS Panzer Korp and were brought to an abrupt halt.

2 March 1943

SOUTHERN SECTOR

The Germans moved to strike at the 3rd Tank Army. SS Panzer Korp attacked from both the east and west. The remnants of the army's cavalry corp, having already suffered heavy losses, attempted to escape north but the remainder of the army was isolated.

The 3rd and 40th Panzer Korps attacked along a line from the Bakhmutka river to Voroshilovgrad, compelling the 1st and 3rd Guards Armies to pull back over the Donets.

3 March 1943

CENTRAL SECTOR

Rzhev fell to the Kalinin Front. Army Group Centre had begun its withdrawal from the salient where no fewer than thirty divisions were tied down (comprising the 41st Panzer, 23rd, 27th, 39th Panzer, 9th, 20th and 12th Korps). Many of these units would make an appearance later in the year at Kursk, this manoeuvre generating a substantial theatre reserve for the Ostheer. On the southern wing of Army Group Centre the 2nd Army gave up Lgov and Dimitrov Lgovsky.

SOUTHERN SECTOR

The SS Panzer Korp virtually destroyed 3rd Tank Army in a day of ferocious fighting. Minor elements of the army crossed the Donets west of Izyum. Slavyansk fell to 3rd Panzer Korp.

In the fighting since 13 January the Voronezh Front had lost 33,300 killed and missing and 62,000 wounded. The Soviet 6th Army suffered 8,000 killed and 12,000 wounded. Soviet forces also lost 1,000 tanks, 2,100 artillery pieces and 300 aircraft.[5]

4 March 1943

NORTHERN SECTOR

The North-West Front began a new offensive south of Lake Ilmen in an effort to break the 16th Army defences before Staraya Russa.

CENTRAL SECTOR

Olenino and Chertolino fell to Kalinin Front as the 23rd Korp withdrew to the south-west.

SOUTHERN SECTOR

After heavy fighting parts of the 3rd Tank Army were destroyed while others fought their way north-west as they tried to escape. As these battles

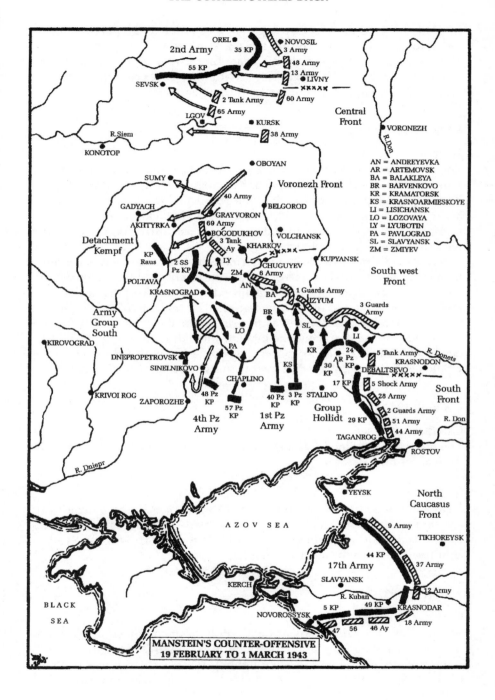

MANSTEIN'S COUNTER-OFFENSIVE
19 FEBRUARY TO 1 MARCH 1943

continued 2nd SS Panzer Korp began to reassemble in preparation for its thrust towards Kharkov. The 4th Panzer Army moved north from Izyum. The 48th Panzer Korp, fighting near Taranovka, aimed to attack in conjunction with the SS Panzer Korp. With their forces reeling, the Stavka ordered its armies in the south onto the defensive.

5 March 1943

SOUTHERN SECTOR

The 4th Panzer Army unleashed a furious attack that destroyed further remnants of the 3rd Tank Army near Krasnograd. Units of the 48th Panzer Korp attacked at Taranovka while the SS pushed the tank army cavalry back. The 3rd Tank Army had lost more than 12,000 killed and over sixty tanks, 200 artillery pieces and 600 motor vehicles during its bloody battle with the German panzer korps.

As the thaw drew ever closer the Germans rushed to redeploy to continue their drive upon Kharkov. General Kempf concentrated his forces west of Krasnograd, deploying the three infantry divisions of Korp Raus along the Psel south of Valki, and placing the refreshed Grossdeutschland Division at Chudovo. Grossdeutschland was to prise apart the remnants of the 3rd Tank and 69th Armies while the infantry hit 40th Army at Akhtyrka. The newly reconstituted 7th Korp, on the southern wing of the 2nd Army, would also push along the Psel river with its three infantry divisions.[6]

6 March 1943

CENTRAL SECTOR

The 5th Army regained Gzhatsk from the 9th Korp as the German withdrawal continued.

SOUTHERN SECTOR

Heavy fighting erupted around Novaya Vodolaga as the SS Panzer Korp enveloped the town. SS units also thrust towards Valki, forcing the Soviets to fall back south of Lyubotin. The 48th Panzer Korp was involved in continued heavy fighting at Taranovka.

7 March 1943

CENTRAL SECTOR

Sevsk fell to 2nd Tank Army as the Central Front continued to push into the southern wing of Army Group Centre. Rokossovsky's 65th and 70th Armies were embroiled in severe fighting with German forces south of Orel, while 60th and 38th Armies tried to turn the left wing of German 2nd Army near Lgov.

SOUTHERN SECTOR
As 48th Panzer Korp unleashed a fierce attack upon Taranovka, SS troops entered Staraya Vodolaga and captured Valki. As these attacks unfolded the Grossdeutschland Division struck 69th Army, forcing it away from the 3rd Tank.

8 March 1943

CENTRAL SECTOR
Sychevka fell to the 20th Army as 39th Panzer Korp withdrew.

SOUTHERN SECTOR
Remnants of 3rd Tank Army abandoned Taranovka and attempted to flee as the 48th Panzer Korp pursued them towards Merefa. The SS Panzer Korp continued its attacks, closing upon Lyubotin while also pushing north of the town. SS units also advanced north from Valki to cut the Bogodukhov–Kharkov railway line.

9 March 1943

SOUTHERN SECTOR
The Grossdeutschland Division attacked towards Bogodukhov, striking elements of the 69th Army. Soviet 40th Army deployed three of its divisions at Bogodukhov in an effort to counter-attack and link up with the hard-pressed 3rd Tank Army. Heavy attacks by the SS Panzer Korp severed the 69th Army from the 40th, enabling its advance east to isolate Kharkov. While the 48th Panzer Korp fought its way along the Mzha river from Merefa to Zmiyev, SS Panzer Korp captured Lyubotin. Amid heavy fighting the Soviets attempted to reinforce the Kharkov defences with new units. Around the city the Leibstandarte SS Adolf Hitler Division pushed west of Dergachi while Totenkopf moved north and captured Olshany, forcing back the remnants of the 3rd Tank Army.

10 March 1943

SOUTHERN SECTOR
German forces north and south of Sumy counter-attacked. The refreshed and redeployed 52nd Korp, with four infantry divisions, and three divisions of the 7th Korp, attacked elements of 40th Army, forcing it out of Lebedin. The Grossdeutschland Division, with an infantry division in support to its left, attacked towards Valki after repulsing a 40th Army counter-attack around Bogodukhov. To the north, two more infantry divisions drove to the north-east towards Kotelva and Akhtyrka in order to establish contact with the 11th Korp on their left.

The 11th had recently been re-formed following its destruction at Stalingrad.

The SS entered the suburbs of Kharkov, Das Reich penetrating from the west while Leibstandarte SS Adolf Hitler pushed north and Totenkopf captured Dergachi. Late in the afternoon elements of the Leibstandarte SS Adolf Hitler entered the north-east suburbs. The 48th Panzer Korp continued its attacks along the line of the Mzha.

11 March 1943

SOUTHERN SECTOR
Bogodukhov fell to Grossdeutschland after a brief struggle. Bitter fighting raged through Kharkov as the SS Panzer Korp plunged deep into the urban sprawl. Leibstandarte SS Adolf Hitler penetrated into the city centre, Das Reich was involved in heavy fighting as it penetrated from the west, while SS Totenkopf captured Krasnokutsk and Murafa, deepening the crisis between 69th and 3rd Tank Armies.

In an effort to prevent the continued deterioration of the situation, the Stavka ordered 1st Tank and 21st Armies to deploy north of Belgorod and began the movement of the 64th Army west from the reserve.

12 March 1943

CENTRAL SECTOR
The 5th Army retook Vyazma as the 20th Korp pulled back.

SOUTHERN SECTOR
SS Das Reich reached the main railway station in the heart of Kharkov while elements of Leibstandarte SS Adolf Hitler cleared the Soviets from the south and south-east quarters. However, the greatest threat to the Soviet forces in the city came from the SS Totenkopf Division as it pushed east and south from its positions north of the city. By nightfall Rogan had fallen and 3rd Tank Army was again in danger of isolation.

13 March 1943

SOUTHERN SECTOR
The Grossdeutschland Division forced a way into the junction of the 69th and 40th Armies and secured Borisovka. The Stavka reinforced the 69th Army with a tank corp.

SS Totenkopf severed the 3rd Tank Army lines of communication, isolating the already shattered army inside Kharkov. The severity of the fighting had considerably reduced the combat strength of the SS korp,

Leibstandarte SS Adolf Hitler Division having only fourteen operational panzers left. In all the battle inside the city cost the Germans 11,500 killed.

14 March 1943

SOUTHERN SECTOR
The SS Das Reich and Leibstandarte Adolf Hitler Divisions cleared the last pockets of Soviet resistance inside Kharkov and began to advance to the east. German forces south-east of the city continued their advance, the 48th Panzer Korp clearing Merefa.

15 March 1943

SOUTHERN SECTOR
The 48th Panzer Korp advanced east from the Mzha river while the SS Das Reich Division pushed along the Kharkov–Chuguyev road.

16 March 1943

NORTHERN SECTOR
The 16th Army's 10th Korp lost Kholm to 3rd Shock Army after a long struggle.

SOUTHERN SECTOR
The 48th Panzer Korp and SS Panzer Korp linked up as they drove east of Kharkov. As the SS advanced out of Kharkov, they forced the Soviets to relinquish control of the factory district, the Tractor Factory falling after a brief struggle. SS Totenkopf cleared Chuguyev and harried the Soviets back to the Donets.

SOVIET COMMAND
The Stavka appointed General Sokolovsky to command of the West Front while Koniev moved to the North-West Front.

17 March 1943

NORTHERN SECTOR
The North-West Front offensive towards Staraya Russa was abandoned after the failure to break through the German lines south of Lake Ilmen.

SOUTHERN SECTOR
The 48th and SS Panzer Korps began their move north towards Belgorod.

18 March 1943

SOUTHERN SECTOR
The Grossdeutschland Division and SS Panzer Korp launched a full-scale attack upon Belgorod, throwing back 69th Army and taking the town. The Stavka immediately moved up the 6th Guards Army (formerly 21st Army) to support the failing 69th while the 1st Tank Army assembled at Oboyan.

> *The loss of Belgorod ended the German counter-offensive in the Ukraine. The onset of the spring thaw brought movement to a halt and prevented Manstein from continuing his drive north to re-establish a strong junction with Army Group Centre. Despite this, Manstein had pulled off an amazing feat, restoring the German southern wing and inflicting a salutary lesson upon Stalin and the Stavka.*

20 March 1943

CENTRAL SECTOR
The 9th Army had almost completed the evacuation of the Rzhev salient. Durovo was evacuated.

23 March 1943

CENTRAL SECTOR
Rokossovksy's Central Front abandoned Sevsk and took up defensive positions east of the town.

24 March 1943

CENTRAL SECTOR
Despite the thaw the Soviets continued to push closer to Smolensk, reaching the German outer defence ring. During their withdrawal from the Rzhev salient Army Group Centre had prepared strong defensive positions around the city.

25 March 1943

SOUTHERN SECTOR
The heavy fighting in the Ukraine had cost 3rd Tank, 40th and 60th Armies of the Voronezh Front 29,800 killed and missing and 28,000 wounded and 6th Army of South-West Front 15,000 killed and 12,800 wounded. The Soviets also lost 300 tanks, 3,000 artillery pieces and 100 aircraft.[7]

31 March 1943

CENTRAL SECTOR
The Kalinin and West Fronts concluded their Rzhev-Vyazma Operation. Of 876,000 men who began the operation, some 38,862 were killed or reported missing and 99,715 wounded.[8]

SOVIET CASUALTIES
The Red Army and Navy lost 726,714 killed and missing in action and 1,425,692 wounded during the first quarter of 1943.[9]

THE OSTHEER
During March the Germans withdrew the 1st Mountain Division and disbanded the 8th Luftwaffe Field Division. The 167th, 327th, 333rd and 335th Infantry Divisions and 12th Luftwaffe Field Division entered the combat line, bringing German strength to sixteen panzer, fifteen panzer-grenadier and 143 infantry divisions.[10] The Panzerwaffe deployed 2,374 tanks but only a fraction of these were operational. Soviet armoured forces totalled more than 7,200 vehicles. The Germans made a number of minor formation adjustments, renaming Army Detachment Hollidt the 6th Army.

Germany's allies still deployed thirty-three divisions in the east (ten Rumanian, five Hungarian, one Slovak, one Spanish and sixteen Finnish).[11] Most, excepting the Finns, were held in the rear echelon on security duties.

11 April 1943

GERMAN COMMAND
Zeitzler outlined a plan calling for the recently formed Kursk salient to be nipped off by two armoured pincers moving from the north and south. The northern pincer would be formed by the newly released 9th Army, substantially reinforced with armoured divisions, while the southern pincer comprised the striking forces of Manstein's Army Group South. However, the proposal split the German command into two distinct factions, those for the attack and those against. Kluge and Keitel were for the attack, proposing that the Ostheer must inflict a crushing blow on the Red Army before it could mount its own offensive. However, Guderian, the recently appointed Inspector General of Armoured Forces, was opposed to the plan, protesting that the weakened Panzerwaffe required time to be strengthened sufficiently. Manstein, the commander of Army Group South, was generally in favour of the attack but only if it began as soon after the thaw as possible, even before the attack forces had been fully assembled. Any delay would give the Red Army the chance to reinforce its armies in the salient and dig extensive defences.

12 April 1943

SOVIET COMMAND
The Soviets began the large-scale mobilisation of civilian labour to dig hundreds of miles of trenches and defence works in the Kursk salient. The Stavka had already identified this area as the most likely location of a renewed German offensive in the summer. By the end of the month more than 150,000 men and women were at work digging trenches and tank traps, while the Voronezh and Central Fronts laid minefields and constructed elaborate anti-tank positions. The Stavka had, after considerable deliberation, decided to fight a defensive battle before unleashing its own counter-offensive.

15 April 1943

GERMAN COMMAND
After protracted debate Hitler issued Operational Order 6, calling for the destruction of the Soviet forces in the Kursk salient. The operation was given the code name Citadel. With speed the crucial element in the plan, the offensive was to begin on 3 May.

17 April 1943

SOUTHERN SECTOR
The German 17th Army came under heavy attack in the Kuban. Fighting continued on and off throughout the summer.

30 April 1943

SOVIET COMMAND
Marshal Novikov was appointed Commander-in-Chief of the VVS (Army Air Force). Novikov was an able commander and under his leadership the Soviets gradually regained control of the skies, greatly influencing the campaigns of the latter stages of the war.

THE OSTHEER
During April the Germans withdrew the 328th Infantry Division from the line but introduced the 39th, 106th, 257th and 282nd Infantry Divisions, leaving the Ostheer with sixteen panzer, fifteen panzer grenadier and 146 infantry divisions. [12]

1 May 1943

CENTRAL SECTOR
At the beginning of May the German forces were still not prepared for Operation Citadel, Hitler continually delaying the start date as he awaited the arrival of the new Panther and Tiger tanks. However, the Soviet began counter-operations against the Germans, May being dominated by fierce air battles over the salient. The Soviets attacked many German airbases in an effort to disrupt the build up of German air forces. Losses to both sides were severe, the Soviets not being strong enough to gain superiority.

SOVIET COMMAND
The Stavka elevated the 3rd Tank Army to Guards status.

2 May 1943

SOUTHERN SECTOR
There was further heavy fighting in the Kuban as 17th Army was forced to give ground in the face of strong Soviet attacks. The Germans were able to prevent any major penetration of their positions, holding a relatively strong front.

4 May 1943

THE AIR WAR
The air war intensified as the Soviets launched a large raid upon the German railway yards at Orsha. A lucky strike by one aircraft hit an ammunition train, the resulting explosions destroying the surrounding area and more than 300 freight wagons.

5 May 1943

SOUTHERN SECTOR
Krymsk and Neberjaisk fell to the North Caucasus Front as the fighting in the Kuban continued.

10 May 1943

GERMAN COMMAND
Hitler postponed Citadel until 13 June. Every day gave the Red Army more time to prepare its defence and lessened the likelihood of a German victory, just as Manstein had stated while the plans were being drawn up.

16 May 1943

SOUTHERN SECTOR
The German 17th Army began a series of counter-attacks in the Kuban.

24 May 1943

SOUTHERN SECTOR
The combat line began to come to life once more as fighting flared up along the Donets. In the Kuban the 5th Korp of 17th Army held strong Soviet attacks. The German ability to repel their attacks prompted the North Caucasus Front to conclude its long running Krasnodar Offensive. Some 66,814 had been killed and 173,902 wounded during the fighting. [13]

26 May 1943

SOUTHERN SECTOR
The 5th Korp was involved in further heavy fighting.

31 May 1943

THE OSTHEER
The opposing forces around Kursk continued to build. The Ostheer was sending the bulk of its replacements to this sector, other sectors having to get by with what they had.

During May the Germans pulled the 4th SS Motorised Division out of the combat line and disbanded the 7th Luftwaffe Division. The 79th Infantry Division entered the line bringing Ostheer deployment to sixteen panzer, fourteen panzer grenadier and 146 infantry divisions. [14]

1 June 1943

THE AIR WAR
As June began the fighting in the air intensified, both air forces struggling to gain supremacy. The Luftwaffe launched heavy raids upon Kursk while the Soviets continued their efforts in the Kuban and along the main line.

3 June 1943

THE AIR WAR
Bombing raids inflicted considerable damage upon the German air bases at Orel.

8 June 1943

Central Sector
The 1st, 2nd and 15th Air Armies began a series of raids against the twenty-eight German airfields in the Kursk region, destroying 220 German aircraft over the next two days.

9 June 1943

Southern Sector
There was renewed fighting at Lisichansk as 3rd Guards Army pressed the junction of 1st Panzer Army and 6th Army.

The Air War
Another heavy air raid, this time at Yaroslavl, inflicted further heavy losses upon the Germans.

14 June 1943

Soviet Command
In an effort to maximise the disruption caused by the partisans in the rear of the German forces, the Stavka ordered the start of the Rail War, an all out attack against the railway network which supplied the combat forces of Army Groups North, Centre and South. These attacks proved extremely troublesome to the Ostheer as greater numbers of men were drawn away from the combat line.

German Command
Despite the passing of yet another D-Day for Citadel, Hitler was still not prepared to begin the offensive.

16 June 1943

German Command
Guderian reported to Hitler that the new Panther tanks were encountering teething problems. Hitler maintained that the Panther was vital to the success of Citadel and pressed them into service regardless, despite Guderian's arguments to the contrary.

21 June 1943

German Command
Hitler set 3 July as the date Operation Citadel was to begin but soon re-scheduled this to 5 July.

24 June 1943

GERMAN COMMAND

As the date of the attack loomed closer, Hitler became increasingly worried at the prospect of failure, confessing to Goebbels that even if the Ostheer vanquished the Red Army in this battle, the opinion of the neutral states in Europe would not be influenced. This was mainly aimed at Turkey, which Hitler had been trying to entice into the Axis camp since the war began.

26 June 1943

GERMAN COMMAND

As another month ebbed away in relative inactivity the offensive had still not begun. Hoth, commanding 4th Panzer Army, observed that the chance of success decreased with every passing day.

30 June 1943

THE OSTHEER

The Ostheer had 3,100,000 men under arms, of whom approximately 1,200,000 were combat troops. The armies in the line also had 2,270 panzers, of which 500 were obsolete models, nearly 1,000 assault guns and 2,500 aircraft. Around Kursk the Germans deployed 10,000 artillery pieces and 2,400 tanks.

The Germans committed the 328th Infantry Division to the combat line, bringing their strength up to sixteen panzer, fourteen motorised and 147 infantry divisions.[15]

THE RED ARMY

The Soviets had 6,422,000 men mobilised, of whom around half were combat soldiers equipped with 103,000 artillery pieces, nearly 10,000 tanks and Su's and over 8,300 aircraft. In the Kursk salient there were 1,300,000 men and 3,500 tanks.

The Red Army and Navy had lost 191,904 killed and missing in action and 490,637 wounded during the second quarter of 1943.[16]

3 July 1943

DEPLOYMENT IN THE NORTHERN SECTOR

On the eve of Operation Citadel, Army Group North had the 16th and 18th Armies in the line. Their forces comprised the following korps.

Facing Leningrad and the Volkhov river was the 18th Army. Around Leningrad the Germans had considerable forces. West of the city, around the Oranienbaum pocket, was the 3rd Luftwaffe Korp (two divisions) and south of Leningrad were 50th and 54th Korps. The 50th Korp had three infantry divisions and 54th Korp four infantry divisions. The 26th Korp, situated east of Leningrad at Mga had seven infantry and one mountain divisions, the 28th Korp near Gruzino, south of Lake Ladoga, had one Luftwaffe and five infantry divisions and the 1st Korp, on the Volkhov, had one Luftwaffe and one infantry division. The 38th Korp around Novgorod had a Luftwaffe division, an infantry division and an SS infantry brigade. A single infantry division constituted the army reserve.

The southern wing of the army group was held by the 16th Army. At Staraya Russa it had the 10th Korp with four infantry divisions while Hoehne's 8th Korp held the link between 10th and 2nd Korps with one Luftwaffe division and two infantry divisions. The 2nd Korp was around Kholm with five infantry divisions. In army reserve were two infantry divisions. Army Group North had a meagre armoured force of just forty-nine operational tanks and assault guns.

Facing the German forces was Govorov's Leningrad Front, with 2nd Shock Army near Lake Ladoga, 42nd Army west of Leningrad and the 55th and 67th Armies south of Leningrad. The 8th Army was also south of Lake Ladoga. Meretskov's Volkhov Front deployed 4th Army and 54th Army along the Volkhov and near Novgorod the 59th Army. South of Lake Ilmen was Korochkin's North-West Front with 1st Shock Army around Demyansk and Kholm, 22nd Army at Kholm and 34th Army at Staraya Russa.

DEPLOYMENT IN THE CENTRAL SECTOR
Army Group Centre fielded the 3rd Panzer, 4th, 9th and 2nd Armies. The northern wing of the army group was secured by the 3rd Panzer Army with its 2nd Luftwaffe Korp (with three Luftwaffe field divisions), the 43rd Korp with one panzer-grenadier and one infantry division and 59th Korp with two infantry divisions grouped around Nevel. The 6th Korp was at Vitebsk with three infantry divisions.

The 4th Army held the Smolensk–Moscow axis with the 12th Korp with three infantry divisions, the 27th Korp north of Yartsevo with four infantry divisions, 39th Panzer Korp before Yartsevo with three infantry divisions, 56th Panzer Korp at Bryansk with three infantry divisions and 9th Korp at Dorogobuzh with three infantry divisions. Two infantry divisions were held in army reserve.

On the northern face of the Orel bulge was the 2nd Panzer Army, comprising 35th Korp near Mtsensk with four infantry divisions, 53rd Korp at Bolkhov with three infantry and one panzer grenadier divisions and 55th Korp at Zhizdra with four infantry divisions. In reserve the army had two infantry divisions.

The southern face of the Orel bulge, comprising the northern arm of the

German pincer at Kursk, held the 380,000 men of Model's 9th Army. The 20th Korp of this force held the line at Ostrovskoye with four infantry divisions and 23rd Korp at Maloarchangelsk with three infantry divisions. The 41st Panzer Korp was near Ponyri with 18th Panzer Division (seventy-five tanks) and two infantry divisions, while 46th Panzer Korp was at Trosna with four infantry divisions. The 47th Panzer Korp had 2nd Panzer Division (136 tanks), 20th Panzer Division (eighty-five tanks), 4th Panzer Division (108 tanks) and 9th Panzer Division (111 tanks) and 6th Infantry Division near Bobrik. In reserve were the 10th Panzer Grenadier Division and 12th Panzer Division (eighty-five tanks). Model had the support of 1st Air Division with 730 aircraft, 21st Panzer Brigade with ninety Elefants, sixty-six Brummbars and sixty-five other tanks. In all the 9th Army had 821 tanks, including thirty Tiger tanks, 250 assault guns and 4,200 artillery pieces[17], while Army Group Centre fielded a total force of 1,900 panzers and assault guns.

The army group had in reserve two infantry divisions, two panzer divisions (5th and 8th), two training and three security divisions, the 7th Hungarian Korp with four infantry divisions and 8th Hungarian Korp with six infantry divisions.

The 2nd Army held the southern wing of the army group. This army comprised 13th Korp before Rylsk with four infantry divisions and 7th Korp around Sumy with five infantry divisions. It had approximately 130,000 men.

Facing Army Group Centre was the Kalinin Front with its 39th Army before Dukhovschina, 3rd Shock Army at Velikiye Luki, 43rd Army facing Yartsevo and 4th Shock Army before Velizh. To the south was the West Front with 10th Army at Kirov, 10th Guards Army and 68th Army in reserve, 11th Guards Army west of Belev, 31st, 33rd, 49th, 5th and 50th Armies on a line running north from Kirov to Dorogobuzh.

The northern face of the Orel bulge was held by Bryansk Front. It held the 11th Army in reserve, 3rd Army south-east of Mtsensk, 4th Tank Army also in reserve, 61st Army north-west of Mtsensk and 63rd Army around Novosil.

The southern wing of the central sector, and the target of the German offensive, comprised the 738,000 men of Rokossovsky's Central Front. This front deployed the 13th Army (five rifle corps and a breakthrough artillery corp) at Ponyri, 2nd Tank Army (two tank and one mechanised corps) in reserve behind 13th Army, 48th Army (seven rifle divisions, two anti-tank brigades) on the right wing, 60th Army (two rifle corps, one artillery division, two tank brigades) on the left wing before Rylsk, 65th Army (four rifle divisions and one rifle brigade) before Sevsk and 70th Army (one rifle division and one rifle corp) between the 65th and 13th Armies. In reserve the Front held two tank corps and had the support of the 16th Air Army with 1,030 aircraft.

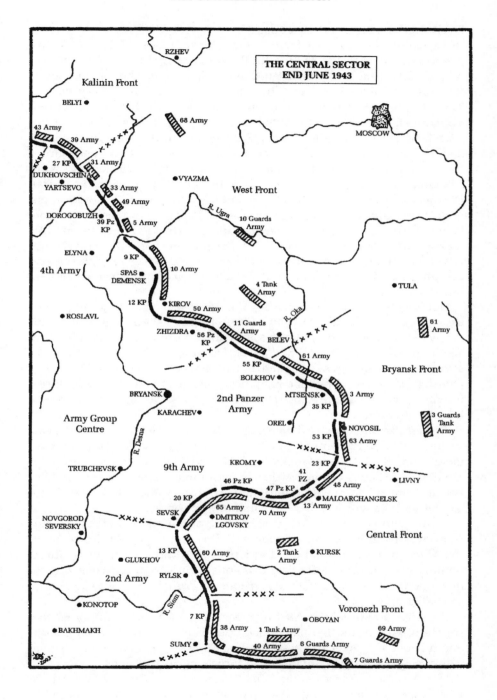

RZHEV

**THE CENTRAL SECTOR
END JUNE 1943**

Kalinin Front

BELYI

68 Army

MOSCOW

43 Army

39 Army

27 KP   31 Army

DUKHOVSCHINA

YARTSEVO

VYAZMA

West Front

33 Army

49 Army

DOROGOBUZH

39 Pz
KP   5 Army

R. Ugra

10 Guards
Army

ELYNA

9 KP

10 Army

4th Army

SPAS
DEMENSK

TULA

4 Tank
Army

12 KP   KIROV   50 Army

ROSLAVL

R. Oka

61
Army

ZHIZDRA   56 Pz
KP

11 Guards
Army

BELEV

Bryansk Front

55 KP

61 Army

BOLKHOV

MTSENSK   3 Army

BRYANSK

2nd Panzer
Army

35 KP

3 Guards
Tank
Army

KARACHEV

OREL

NOVOSIL

Army Group
Centre

R. Desna

53 KP   63 Army

TRUBCHEVSK

9th Army

KROMY

23 KP

LIVNY

46 Pz KP

41
PZ.

20 KP

47 Pz KP

48 Army

NOVGOROD
SEVERSKY

SEVSK

65 Army
DMITROV
LGOVSKY

70 Army   13 Army

MALOARCHANGELSK

Central Front

13 KP   60 Army

2 Tank
Army   KURSK

GLUKHOV

RYLSK

2nd Army

R. Seim

Voronezh Front

KONOTOP

7 KP

38 Army

OBOYAN

69 Army

BAKHMAKH

SUMY

1 Tank Army

40 Army   6 Guards Army

7 Guards Army

75

DEPLOYMENT IN THE SOUTHERN SECTOR

In the south, the German forces were primarily massed for the forth-coming Kursk offensive. Hoth's 4th Panzer Army held the southern face of the Kursk salient with 230,000 men, 902 tanks and assault guns (including fifty-six Tigers and 104 Panthers) and 2,600 artillery pieces. These forces were deployed between Hausser's 2nd SS Panzer Korp from Tomarovka to Belgorod. It fielded its 1st SS Panzer-Grenadier Division Leibstandarte Adolf Hitler with 117 tanks and thirty-five assault guns, 2nd SS Panzer-Grenadier Division Das Reich with 129 tanks and thirty-four assault guns and 3rd SS Panzer-Grenadier Division Totenkopf with 148 tanks and thirty-five assault guns. The 10th Panzer Brigade had 200 Panthers and thirty-one assault guns and would operate in conjunction with these divisions. Knobelsdorf's 48th Panzer Korp held the line between Tomarovka and Kryukovo with its 11th Panzer Division (121 tanks), 167th Infantry Division, 3rd Panzer Division (104 tanks) and Grossdeutschland Panzer Grenadier Division (160 panzers and thirty-five assault guns). On the left flank at Kryukovo was 52nd Korp with three infantry divisions.

Holding the Donets Front were the 160,000 men, 430 panzers and assault guns (including forty-five Tigers) and 1,800 artillery pieces of Army Detachment Kempf. Breith's 3rd Panzer Korp was at Belgorod with 168th Infantry Division, 19th Panzer Division (eighty-two tanks and seventy-five assault guns), 6th Panzer Division (124 tanks) and 7th Panzer Division (103 tanks). The 42nd Korp held the line at Volchansk with three infantry divisions while Raus' 11th Korp was also at Belgorod with two infantry divisions.

The 1st Panzer Army had Nehring's 24th Panzer Korp in reserve near Izyum with 17th Panzer Division and 23rd Panzer Division (seventy-two tanks) and 5th SS Panzer-Grenadier Division Wiking (fifty-two tanks). In the line were 30th Korp at Lisichansk with three infantry divisions, 40th Panzer Korp at Izyum with three infantry divisions and 57th Panzer Korp at Alekseyevka with another three infantry divisions.

To the south, on the extreme right wing of the main German combat front, was Hollidt's Army Detachment. This army had 17th Korp along the Mius river (three infantry divisions), 29th Korp at Taganrog (three infantry and one Luftwaffe field divisions), 4th Korp at Lisichansk with one mountain and two infantry divisions. In army reserve was a panzer-grenadier division.

The 1,100 aircraft of 8th Air Korp, part of 4th Air Fleet, supported the southern wing of the German attack upon Kursk. In total, Army Group South had 2,400 tanks and assault guns. Manstein had a limited reserve comprising a Rumanian infantry and three security divisions.

In the Taman, Army Group A had Ruoff's 17th Army with the 44th Korp (one Rumanian and five German infantry divisions), the 49th

Mountain Korp (two German and one Rumanian infantry divisions) and 5th Korp with two Rumanian infantry and one mountain divisions, one German mountain division and two infantry divisions. In reserve the army group held the 13th Panzer Division and the Kerch Korp (with just a single Luftwaffe field division). In the Crimea, in addition to the Kerch Korp, the Germans had the Crimea Army. This ad hoc force had two training, one infantry and two Rumanian divisions.

The southern sector of the Soviet front was covered by Voronezh, South-West and South Fronts, with the Steppe Front in reserve and North Caucasus Front facing the Kuban peninsula. Vatutin's Voronezh Front, which would feel the weight of the German attack south of Kursk, deployed 1st Tank Army (three tank and one mechanised corps) in operational reserve behind the 6th Guards, 38th Army (one rifle corp, one rifle division, two tank and one anti-tank brigade) on the right wing before Sumy, 40th Army (four rifle corps, five rifle divisions, one artillery, one anti-tank and one tank brigade) to the left of the 38th, 69th Army (five rifle divisions) in reserve behind the left wing, 6th Guards Army (two rifle corps) facing Tomarovka and 7th Guards Army (four rifle corps) on the left wing facing Belgorod to the north and along the Donets river. In reserve the front had two tank corps. Vatutin had at his disposal 534,000 men and the 913 aircraft of 2nd Air Army.

In reserve, behind the Voronezh and Central Fronts, was Koniev's Steppe Front with 27th Army (one rifle and one tank corps), 47th Army (one rifle corp, one mechanised corp and six rifle divisions), 4th Guards Army (one airborne, two rifle and one tank corps), 53rd Army (eight rifle and one break through artillery divisions), 5th Guards Army (formerly the 66th Army with two rifle corps) and 5th Guards Tank Army (three tank and one mechanised corps). In support was 5th Air Army. Koniev could call upon 550,000 men, 7,000 artillery pieces and in excess of 1,500 tanks. In reserve he held 5th Guards Cavalry Corp.

Malinovsky's South-West Front deployed 12th Army in reserve, 1st Guards Army along the Donets between Izyum and Lisichansk, 3rd Guards Army between Lisichansk and Voroshilovgrad, 3rd Tank Army in reserve, 46th Army on the Donets south of Chuguyev, 57th Army on the extreme right wing north of Chuguyev, 6th Army, 8th Guards Army in reserve and 1st Air Army. South Front had 28th Army, 2nd Guards Army and 44th Army along the line of the Mius river, 51st Army on the northern wing near Voroshilovgrad and 5th Shock Army to its south.

Facing the 17th Army was Petrov's North Caucasus Front. This formation had 18th Army in the south at Novorossysk, 56th and 58th Armies in the centre and 9th Army on the northern wing.

DEPLOYMENT IN FINLAND AND NORWAY
In Finland the Germans had limited forces, but from Norway they

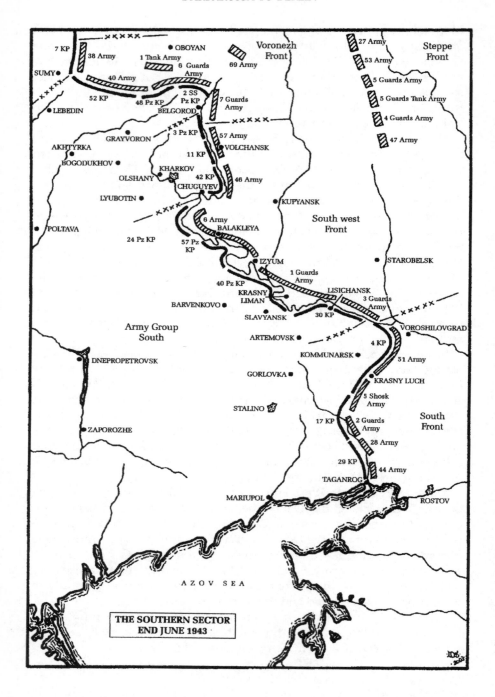

7 KP

38 Army

OBOYAN

1 Tank Army

6 Guards
Army

Voronezh
Front

69 Army

27 Army

53 Army

Steppe
Front

SUMY

40 Army

5 Guards Army

52 KP

48 Pz KP

2 SS
Pz KP

7 Guards
Army

5 Guards Tank Army

LEBEDIN

BELGOROD

4 Guards Army

3 Pz KP

57 Army

47 Army

GRAYVORON

AKHTYRKA

VOLCHANSK

11 KP

BOGODUKHOV

KHARKOV

42 KP

OLSHANY

CHUGUYEV

46 Army

LYUBOTIN

KUPYANSK

South west
Front

POLTAVA

6 Army

BALAKLEYA

24 Pz KP

57 Pz
KP

STAROBELSK

IZYUM

1 Guards
Army

40 Pz KP

LISICHANSK

3 Guards
Army

KRASNY
LIMAN

BARVENKOVO

SLAVYANSK

30 KP

VOROSHILOVGRAD

Army Group
South

ARTEMOVSK

4 KP

51 Army

DNEPROPETROVSK

KOMMUNARSK

GORLOVKA

KRASNY LUCH

5 Shosk
Army

STALINO

17 KP

2 Guards
Army

South
Front

ZAPOROZHE

28 Army

29 KP

44 Army

TAGANROG

MARIUPOL

ROSTOV

A Z O V   S E A

**THE SOUTHERN SECTOR
END JUNE 1943**

deployed 20th Mountain Army. This formation had two korps (18th Mountain with two mountain divisions and 19th Mountain with two mountain and one infantry divisions). In central Finland, near Salla, the Germans had 36th Korp with two infantry divisions.

Against these forces the Soviets had Karelian Front under General Frolov. This force had 14th Army before Murmansk, 23rd and 26th Armies north of Leningrad, 32nd Army in central Karelia and 7th Independent Army along the Svir.

THE RED ARMY

In Stavka reserve the Soviets held three mechanised corps, two Guards cavalry corps, 20th and 21st Armies, 37th, 41st and 52nd Armies.

> *German preparations in the run up to Kursk had been extensive. The Panzerwaffe, now under Guderian's command, had been comprehensively rebuilt while the infantry divisions about to be committed to the battle were all close to full strength. New generations of German tanks had begun to enter the line in greater numbers but some, notably the Panther and Elefant models, had been rushed into service without thorough trials.*
>
> *Meanwhile, the Stavka had decided to gamble and allow the Germans to take the lead this summer. Having so far failed to halt a major German offensive, the battle for Kursk would prove a watershed in Soviet military planning, confirming the Stavka's ability to co-ordinate its forces against the best the German Army could throw at it.*

NOTES

1   Glantz, *From the Don to the Dnepr*, p185
2   Kirosheev, *Soviet Casualties and Combat Losses in the Twentieth Century*, Table 75
3   Ellis, *The World War II Databook*, p176
4   Glantz, *From the Don to the Dnepr*, p189
5   Kirosheev, *Soviet Casualties and Combat Losses in the Twentieth Century*, Table 75
6   Glantz, *From the Don to the Dnepr*, p194
7   Kirosheev, *Soviet Casualties and Combat Losses in the Twentieth Century*, Table 75
8   Kirosheev, *Soviet Casualties and Combat Losses in the Twentieth Century*, Table 75
9   Kirosheev, *Soviet Casualties and Combat Losses in the Twentieth Century*, Table 67
10 Ellis, *The World War II Databook*, p176
11 Ellis, *The World War II Databook*, p178
12 Ellis, *The World War II Databook*, p176
13 Kirosheev, *Soviet Casualties and Combat Losses in the Twentieth Century*, Table 75
14 Ellis, *The World War II Databook*, p176

15 Ellis, *The World War II Databook*, p176
16 Kirosheev, *Soviet Casualties and Combat Losses in the Twentieth Century*, Table 67
17 I have given divisional detail of the deployments at Kursk as the nature of the forthcoming battle depends much upon divisional actions. Kursk deployment details come from the excellent Osprey Campaign Series, *Kursk 1943*.

CHAPTER III
Armoured Fist

Having taken stock after the overwhelming losses of the winter, the Ostheer was poised to launch its next offensive, an effort to regain the initiative and begin the advance east once more. With growing nerve, Stalin and the Stavka had elected to absorb the German offensive before launching their own thrust, a strategy hitherto untried in the east.

4 July 1943

SOUTHERN SECTOR

At 1030 hours, as Hoth's 4th Panzer Army prepared to start its first probing attacks during the afternoon, the artillery of the 6th and 7th Guards Armies opened fire. Their deadly cargo fell upon the German positions, causing considerable casualties and sowing confusion throughout the attack sector. The Stavka had planned to launch pre-emptive artillery strikes in an effort to disorganise the German offensive right from the very start.

Following the barrage the Germans regrouped and at 1445 hours, with aircraft of the 8th Air Korp over the battlefield, the Soviet defences were struck by a ferocious counter-bombardment. Fire rained down on the trenches and artillery sites of the 6th Guards Army. The 48th Panzer Korp moved forward under the cover of the barrage. Grossdeutschland Division advanced between Ssyrew and Luchanino while 3rd and 11th Panzer Divisions attacked on the left and right flanks.[1] By evening the 48th Panzer had secured the important hills around Butovo, but heavy fighting continued through the night as the Soviets launched numerous counter-attacks. Ott's 52nd Korp also attacked and, despite meeting severe Soviet resistance, secured the left flank of 48th Panzer Korp. Meanwhile, Hausser's 2nd SS Panzer Korp began limited reconnaissance attacks to the right of 48th. By 2230 hours General Vatutin had assembled his units for a combined counter-attack, 6th Guards using its ample artillery support to great effect. The ferocity of the fighting alerted the Stavka to the fact that this was the opening move of the German offensive.

During the night the Soviet weather played its part in the battle as a deluge of rain turned the parched summer soil into mud, hindering the movement of the German attack forces to the front line.

5 July 1943

CENTRAL SECTOR

At dawn German forces north of the Kursk salient assembled for their attack. Yet again the Soviets pre-empted the Germans, an artillery barrage by the 13th Army of Central Front causing similar confusion and casualties to 9th Army as suffered by the 4th Panzer Army. Despite this ill wind Model duly launched his attack, aircraft of the 1st Air Division, together with the artillery of the 9th Army, pounding the 13th and 70th Armies as German armour and infantry moved forward on a twenty-five-mile front. Within the first half hour of fighting 13th Army was under intense pressure, but determined defence bogged down the attacks by 258th and 7th Infantry Divisions along the Orel highway. Model halted his forces and regrouped, resuming the attack a couple of hours later on another narrow sector of the line. Throwing the 20th Panzer Division against the 13th Army's 15th Rifle Division, bitter fighting erupted as the Germans tried to overpower 13th Army through sheer weight of numbers. Bobrik fell to 20th Panzer Division after costly fighting, while action on the flanks of the main attack raged as both 48th and 70th Armies resisted furiously. However, numerical superiority did begin to tell as the day lengthened, Butyrki falling to the 6th Infantry Division and Panzer Abteilung 505 at midday. However, the new Elefant self-propelled guns of Panzer Jaeger Battalion 653, attacking alongside 292nd Infantry Division near Aleksandrovka, proved vulnerable to Soviet fire due to their lack of anti-personnel armament. Fighting at Alexandrovka saw the destruction of many Elefants as the Soviets separated the armour from their supporting infantry and then tank busting teams disabled the lumbering giants with mines and anti-tank guns. The 86th Infantry Division attempted to batter its way through to Ponyri, supported by 78th Sturm Division and Panzer Jaeger Battalion 654 to its left. Despite the continued German attacks, the Soviets mounted repeated counter-attacks, wearing down 9th Army from the very beginning of the battle.

SOUTHERN SECTOR

The fighting which had begun on the afternoon of 4 July resumed today. Once again the 6th and 7th Guards Armies began a pre-emptive bombardment of the German lines, but the 48th Panzer Korp launched its own attack shortly after. The attack appeared to develop well, but rain during the night had turned the banks of the small stream in front of the Germans into a morass. The Grossdeutschland Division had difficulty in moving into the attack, being shelled by Soviet artillery as it floundered. Under heavy fire and having run straight into a minefield near Butovo, the Germans lost thirty-six of their new Panther tanks. German infantry then had to fend off ferocious counter-attacks, suffering heavy losses during bloody fighting. The 3rd Panzer Division on the left wing was unable to break into Savidovka despite repeated attacks.[2] The Germans pressed slowly forward though. After hours of ferocious fighting, the 48th Panzer Korp secured Cherkosskoye, its infantry and armour suffering crippling casualties in the minefields and under continual Soviet artillery fire.

Hausser's 2nd SS Panzer Korp resumed its attack but met fierce resistance. The SS divisions managed to break through the Soviet lines and advanced fifteen miles by dusk. The SS Totenkopf Division succeeded in attacking the command post of 69th Army at Yakhontovo, inflicting heavy casualties. Berezov, Gremuchi, Bykovo and Vosnesenski all fell to the German forces. The ferocious German attacks stretched the 6th Guards Army to breaking point, worrying Vatutin that the Germans might break through in this sector.

On the Donets flank, Army Detachment Kempf was unable to advance far due to strong resistance by the 7th Guards Army. Heavy fighting raged throughout the day as Breith's 3rd Panzer Korp launched repeated attacks.

The first day of Operational Citadel had been a failure for the Germans, both the 9th Army and 4th Panzer Army failing to smash the Soviet defences on the wings of the salient. In the north the 9th Army was already becoming bogged down. The fierce fighting on the ground was accompanied by equally vicious battles above, the Luftwaffe and Red Air Force battling for control of the skies. Losses in these battles were equally severe.

6 July 1943

CENTRAL SECTOR

Model threw more divisions into his attack but Rokossovsky in turn placed reinforcements into the line, preventing the Germans from achieving a breakthrough. The 3rd Tank Corp moved forward to Ponyri while 17th Guards Rifle Corp bolstered 13th Army. The 19th and 16th Tank Corps moved west and north-east of Olkhovatka to block any possible German penetration of the first defence belt.

As the fighting developed the 2nd Panzer Division repelled a fierce counter-attack by the 16th Tank Corp. A massive artillery duel also erupted between 13th Army and 9th Army. Having fended off the Soviet counter-attack during the morning, German armour deployed to attack Olkhovatka. The 9th and 2nd Panzer Divisions moved up to attack. Despite the commitment of massive forces, the Germans could not break through the Soviet lines. After heavy fighting the 23rd Korp was held up before Maloarchangelsk. The 9th and 18th Panzer, 86th and 292nd Infantry Divisions pushed south towards Ponyri. So far Model's units had advanced no more than six miles but suffered over 10,000 casualties.

SOUTHERN SECTOR

The 4th Panzer Army, supported by the 8th Air Korp, continued to attack with its 48th and 2nd SS Panzer Korps. The 2nd SS Panzer Korp became embroiled in bitter fighting, but units of the SS Das Reich Division managed to break through at Luchki, opening a gap in the 6th Guards Army defences. The SS then pushed ten miles along the road to Kursk. With 6th Guards clearly in difficulty, Vatutin began to move the 1st Tank Army to its support, a move later criticised as the Soviet armour was drawn into a battle of attrition, rather than being held back to deliver a counter-blow after the Germans were exhausted. The 48th Panzer Korp remained stuck in its positions despite repeated attacks which resulted in fierce fighting.

Beith's 3rd Panzer Korp fought its way slowly north-east of Belgorod. The 19th Panzer Division, supported by 168th Infantry Division, was embroiled in bitter fighting, a battle that raged for the next three days. The 7th Panzer Division also advanced leaving the 106th and 320th Infantry Divisions of 11th Korp to guard its flank. Heavy fighting erupted as the Soviet Volchansk Group attacked 11th Korp. The Soviets were themselves unable to break the German front line.

SOVIET COMMAND

The Stavka ordered the 5th Guards Tank Army of Koniev's Steppe Front to move to the aid of the Voronezh Front. This formation would arrive at the small village of Prokhorovka in the next few days, where it would meet the 2nd SS Panzer Korp.

7 July 1943

CENTRAL SECTOR

Heavy fighting forced Rokossovsky to take units from 65th and 60th Armies to reinforce the hard pressed 13th. Furious battles raged between Olkhovatka and Ponyri. At Olkhovatka 300 panzers and assault guns of the 2nd, 4th, 20th, 18th and 9th Panzer Divisions crashed into 16th and 19th Tank Corps. At Ponyri the Germans advanced into the village, becoming embroiled in bitter hand-to-hand fighting in the School House, Tractor Depot, Railway Station and Water Tower. The fighting continued throughout the day as both armies attacked, counter-attacked and then attacked again. The fighting was so intense that Model reported to Army Group Centre that his forces were beginning to run low on ammunition and would not be able to continue the offensive for much longer.

Manstein pressed forward, 4th Panzer Army slowly gaining ground on the road to Oboyan. After bitter fighting the 48th Panzer Korp took Dubrova. The Grossdeutschland Division broke through the 6th Guards Army positions on either side of Ssyrzew, forcing them back to Gremutshy and Ssyrzewo. The retreating Soviets were hammered by German artillery, suffering heavy losses. Moving forward through the heavily mined ground, the Germans were brought to a halt again during the afternoon at the outskirts of Ssyrzewo. Heavy defensive fire and strong counter-attacks by mechanised and tank forces prevented any further gains. Other elements of the Grossdeutschland Division penetrated to Verchopenje and north of Gremutshy. On the left wing the 3rd Panzer Division closed upon Beresovka.[3]

The 29th Anti-Tank Brigade heavily engaged the 2nd SS Panzer Korp all afternoon as the Germans tried to push forward. After heavy fighting Teterevino fell, the Leibstandarte SS Adolf Hitler and SS Das Reich Divisions pushing on to Greznoye. The Soviet brigade had been virtually wiped out in the bitter fighting.

The 3rd Panzer Korp made rapid progress against the flank of 7th Guards Army, undermining the Soviet positions. Alarmed by this, Vatutin subordinated the artillery of the 38th and 40th Armies to 6th and 7th Guards in an effort to halt the German attack.

8 July 1943

SOUTHERN SECTOR
The fighting at Ponyri and Olkhovatka raged unabated as 9th Army threw in more attacks but with little success. Ferocious fighting developed around Teploye as 4th Panzer Division tried to take the village. Little headway was made against carefully sited Soviet Pak fronts and minefields. Fighting raged at Teploye for three days.

SOUTHERN SECTOR
The Voronezh Front moved its 40th Army up to support the flagging 6th Guards and 1st Tank Armies. A battle group of the 48th Panzer Korp pressed ahead of the main body and reached Height 260.8 from where it wheeled west to push into the rear of the Soviet forces holding up the centre and left flank of the korp. The Grossdeutschland Division began to swing west to ease the pressure on 3rd Panzer Division. Heavy fighting raged around Verchopenje and Height 243.0, before both of which the Germans were held. By noon Syrtsevo had fallen to Grossdeutschland and 3rd Panzer Divisions but a 40th Army counter-attack kept the 48th occupied thereafter.[4]

Vatutin attempted to ambush the 2nd SS Panzer Korp at Gostoschchevo with his 2nd Guards Tank Corp, but a timely Luftwaffe strike destroyed more than fifty tanks, crippling the Soviet force. The 3rd Panzer Korp continued to struggle forward east of Belgorod.

9 July 1943

CENTRAL SECTOR

The 9th Army renewed its efforts at Ponyri as it attempted to take Hills 253.5 and 274 with 6th Infantry Division. Soviet resistance was ferocious, preventing the Germans from achieving either objective. The heavy fighting at Olkhovatka and Teploye also continued as the Germans made minor gains.

SOUTHERN SECTOR

Bitter fighting raged between Verchopenje and Solotino as 4th Panzer Army struck the 1st Tank and 6th Guards Armies. The 48th Panzer Korp was within sixteen miles of Oboyan, but after four days of bloody fighting was almost spent. Its 3rd Panzer Division finally entered Beresovka only for its advance to be checked north of the village as Soviet forces fired from the woods. The 11th Panzer Division struggled to move at all.[5]

Fatigue became a major problem for the Germans as men and machines suffered the effects of five days continuous fighting. The Soviet position was equally bad, Vatutin realising that he had committed his 1st Tank Army too early. The movement of the 5th Guards Tank Army and now also the 5th Guards Army of the Steppe Front to this sector would give the Soviets a crucial advantage in the next few days. Taking advantage of the current Soviet weakness, the 4th Panzer Army redeployed in the Prokhorovka area, from where it planned to resume its attacks. The army was by this stage of the battle down to only 501 operational tanks, having lost nearly half its strength.[6]

The advance of 3rd Panzer Korp had ground to a halt as its flank lengthened. Soviet attacks along this exposed line forced Detachment Kempf to commit greater forces to its protection.

10 July 1943

CENTRAL SECTOR

The 9th Army, almost exhausted after the fighting of the last week, made a last desperate effort to break through the 13th Army. The 4th Panzer Division took Teploye after a brutal battle but the fighting at Ponyri intensified. Model committed his last reserves, 10th Panzer Grenadier and 31st Infantry Divisions attacking alongside 2nd and 4th Panzer Divisions, a force of 300 panzers and assault guns. Fighting was extremely fierce, but by dusk the Germans were no farther forward. Since 5 July the 9th Army had lost 50,000 men and more than 400 panzers. Model therefore ordered his forces onto the defensive. The battle had cost the Central Front 15,300 killed and missing and 18,500 wounded.

SOUTHERN SECTOR

The 48th Panzer Korp struck the 6th Guards and 1st Tank Armies as it tried to push closer to Oboyan. Grossdeutschland wheeled south and mopped up the Soviet forces on the left flank of the korp. Fierce Luftwaffe attacks supported the ground forces, enabling the Germans to trap the Soviets between the guns of the 3rd Panzer and Grossdeutschland Divisions. [7]

The 2nd SS Panzer Korp moved towards Prokhorovka, which 5th Guards Tank Army was also approaching, unknown to the Germans. The SS Totenkopf Division moved onto the korp's left flank to cross the Psel and by dusk had taken Krasny Oktabyr. The 2nd SS Panzer Korp then began to redeploy to attack Prokhorovka the next day. Manstein began to move up 24th Panzer Korp from his reserve at Kharkov to aid the offensive.

WESTERN EUROPE

Events in Western Europe, which would ultimately decide the fate of the German offensive, began to unravel. Allied forces landed in Sicily and began the conquest of Italy. While this invasion did not directly affect the fighting in the east, it gave Hitler a pretext for calling off Citadel. He maintained that the premier SS divisions of the 2nd SS Panzer Korp must be moved west to defend Italy, these forces arriving too late to influence the fighting on Sicily.

GERMAN COMMAND

General Schmidt, commanding 2nd Panzer Army, was relieved of his command. No new commander was appointed in his place as the headquarters of 2nd Panzer Army would leave the east by the end of July for Serbia. Its forces were to be incorporated into the 9th and 4th Armies.

11 July 1943

CENTRAL SECTOR

As the fighting at Ponyri died down the Red Army began Operation Kutuzov, the destruction of the German forces in the Orel bulge. Units of the West and Bryansk Fronts began probing attacks against the 55th, 35th and 53rd Korps of 2nd Panzer Army. The Soviet plan was to force the 11th Guards Army of the West Front through the thin line held by the 55th Korp on the northern face of the bulge, while the 3rd and 63rd Armies of the Bryansk Front attacked from the Novosil area, striking the 35th and

53rd Korps. Once the German line had been breached, the 3rd Tank Army would punch through and roll into the German rear, threatening the positions of the 9th Army on the southern face of the Orel bulge. For the attack the 11th Guards Army deployed 170,000 men and the 50th Army 62,800. The Bryansk Front in total deployed 409,000 men and the Central Front, still heavily committed with the 9th Army, 645,000.[8]

SOUTHERN SECTOR
With 2nd SS Panzer Korp attacking west of Prokhorovka, the 3rd Panzer Korp broke free and pushed up from the south. Leading elements of the 5th Guards Tank Army were arriving near the village and encountered the Germans late in the day. The SS, still attacking all along their line, were unaware of the threat posed by the 5th Guards Tank Army. Hoth's 4th Panzer Army was making great use of its artillery and air support despite the deteriorating visibility brought on by the clouds of dust thrown up by the explosions and movement of armour. The battles in the skies overhead also intensified as the Soviets slowly but surely gained superiority through sheer weight of numbers.

12 July 1943

CENTRAL SECTOR
Following the probing attacks of 11 July, Operation Kutuzov began in force. Infantry of the 3rd and 63rd Armies, supported by artillery fire and the aircraft of Gromov's 1st Air Army, struck the 2nd Panzer Army. Realising that the attack was imminent, the Germans had evacuated their forward positions before the assault. To the north the 11th Guards Army attacked through its own artillery barrage rather than after it, supported in turn by Navmenko's 15th Air Army. A counter-barrage and fierce small arms fire inflicted terrible losses upon the attacking units. General Rendulic called for air support to smash the Soviet forces converging on his 35th Korp but the Luftwaffe was unable to oblige, its 1st Air Division no longer having the strength to provide for both the 9th Army and 2nd Panzer Army. The Soviets renewed their attack during the afternoon but were again repulsed by the 35th and 53rd Korps. These attacks in his rear compelled Model to abandon the battle for Ponyri. Effectively the battle of Kursk was over as far as the 9th Army was concerned; the battle for the Orel bulge had begun.

SOUTHERN SECTOR
During the night the 48th Panzer Korp redeployed in order to resume its offensive toward Oboyan. Unfortunately, Soviet counter-attacks at first light threw the German plan astray, resulting in further bitter battles of attrition.

Early in the day the 2nd SS Panzer Korp attacked at Prokhorovka, the 3rd SS Totenkopf Division leading, followed by 2nd SS Das Reich Division and 1st SS Leibstandarte Adolf Hitler Division. The initial attack was made by 200 tanks north-west of the town but ran into the 5th Guards Tank Army. Rotmistrov was pushing 500 of his 900 vehicles into battle in the first wave. By 0900 hours the battle of Prokhorovka had begun in earnest. A furious Soviet assault threw SS Totenkopf onto the defensive, compelling Hausser to commit his full korp to the fighting. SS Totenkopf clashed with 31st Guards Tank and 33rd Guards Rifle Corps while 2nd Guards Tank Corp mauled SS Das Reich. During the afternoon the SS regrouped and attacked again, hitting 18th Tank Corp west of Prokhorovka. The 10th Mechanised and 24th Guards Rifle Corps were drawn into the fighting as the battle raged on. Overhead the Luftwaffe fought a vicious battle with the Red Air Force, both sides losing many machines. By dusk the SS was forced to give up the field, having suffered heavy losses. The 5th Guards Tank Army had lost nearly 400 tanks and half its men, but crucially, the Red Army was able to replace its losses whereas the Germans could not.

13 July 1943

CENTRAL SECTOR
The slow and costly advance by the 11th Guards Army against the 55th Korp on the northern face of the Orel salient had pushed the 2nd Panzer Army back sixteen miles. However, the skilful defence of the 35th and 53rd Korps to the south-east had exacted a heavy toll upon the attacking divisions of the Bryansk Front's 3rd and 63rd Armies. Model began to move forces from the southern sector of the Orel salient to the north, the 9th Army slowly withdrawing from its hard won territory in order to cover its rear.

SOUTHERN SECTOR
The 2nd SS Panzer Korp continued to attack at Prokhorovka but was unable to push back the 5th Guards Tank Army. It was obvious that the Germans had been unable to achieve the encirclement of the Soviet forces in the Kursk area, let alone break through the formidable Soviet defences that ringed the salient. An indication of the ferocity of the fighting was shown by the strength return of the 2nd SS Panzer Korp, which was down to 180 operational tanks and sixty-four assault guns by the end of the battle for Prokhorovka. The 4th Panzer Army in total had just 505 operational tanks left, half its original strength.[9]

The attacks by the 48th Panzer Korp were suspended as its flanking units were brought under heavy attack. The Germans were forced to relinquished control of Beresovka and Height 247.0. [10]

GERMAN COMMAND

Hitler met with the commanders of Army Groups South and Centre at Rastenburg. Hitler informed both Kluge and Manstein that he was cancelling Operation Citadel, mainly because of the Allied landings in Sicily. In addition, he informed them that they would have to make available armoured units for transfer to the west. Both Kluge and Manstein protested at the withdrawal of units from their already under strength formations. Manstein even went so far as to request that the offensive continue. While he did not support the original decision to attack so late in the season, he maintained that once the attack had begun the only chance of success was to continue until a breakthrough was achieved. He was over-ruled and Army Group South was ordered to abandon its attack.

14 July 1943

CENTRAL SECTOR

The West Front brought up its 4th Tank Army to add weight to the attacks by 11th Guards Army. In addition the 11th Army moved up from reserve to support the 11th Guards. Bryansk Front moved its 3rd Guards Tank Army up behind the 3rd and 63rd Armies to crush the apex of the German salient. Further heavy fighting raged as the Germans slowly withdrew.

SOUTHERN SECTOR

South of Kursk the German attacks were dying down but heavy fighting continued around Prokhorovka. Soviet forces were beginning to launch strong counter-attacks, sapping the strength of the exhausted 48th Panzer and 2nd SS Panzer Korps.

The 48th Panzer Korp counter-attacked in an effort to regain Heights 247.0 and 243.0. As the Germans moved they were brought under intense artillery fire. Soviet attacks from the north and west were beaten off but disrupted the German plan. Despite this the Germans retook Height 243.0.

15 July 1943

CENTRAL SECTOR

Fighting on the northern face of the Kursk salient intensified as the Central Front joined the attack against the 9th Army. Model found it difficult to contain the Soviet attacks, being pressed back from north, east and south.

SOUTHERN SECTOR

The Germans began to pull back to their start lines south of Kursk, the 4th Panzer Army and Army Detachment Kempf going onto the defensive. Manstein believed the Soviet forces facing 4th Panzer were equally exhausted and considered an offensive along the Mius or Donets, which had so far remained quiet, unlikely.

THE COST OF CITADEL

Citadel had bit deeply into both armies. The Germans claimed to have taken 32,000 prisoners and inflicted 85,000 casualties upon the Red Army during the battle while 2,000 tanks and 2,000 artillery pieces were destroyed. Soviet losses had indeed been great, operational tank strength falling to 1,500 machines by the end of the battle. The Red Army in turn claimed that the Ostheer lost 70,000 men, 3,000 panzers, 1,000 artillery pieces and nearly 1,400 aircraft. These figures were exaggerated, but it could not be denied that the struggle had blunted the revitalised Panzerwaffe. Many divisions were reduced to mere remnants, 3rd Panzer having thirty tanks left and 17th Panzer fewer than sixty by the end of the battle. The 19th Panzer Division was in an even worse state with only seventeen operational tanks while 8th Panzer had just eight tanks. The 2nd and 12th Panzer Divisions combined numbered only twenty tanks. Infantry losses had also been high, 106th Division losing 3,224 of nearly 10,000 men, 320th losing 2,839, and 168th losing 2,671 men. The stronger elite divisions also suffered crippling casualties; Grossdeutschland Division had lost 220 of its 300 tanks while the SS Panzer Korp lost 242 of 425 tanks and forty-six of its 100 assault guns.[11]

The failure of Citadel broke the panzers, just as Guderian had feared. His fears were realised as the Soviets demonstrated that their own armoured losses, although severe, were relatively easily replaced.

Defeat at Kursk had cost Germany the initiative in the east for good. Hitler's gamble with his reconstituted panzer force had squandered the German army's last sizeable force. Never again would the Ostheer field such a generously equipped force, and from here on it would fight a battle of attrition against a massively superior foe. Despite this though, the German Army remained fundamentally intact as it waited for the expected Soviet counter-offensive.

16 July 1943

CENTRAL SECTOR

In the Orel salient the 9th Army came under heavy attack by the West, Bryansk and Central Fronts but prevented any penetration of the line.

17 July 1943

CENTRAL SECTOR

The 11th Army supported the attacks of the 11th Guards Army while the

4th Tank Army tried to speed up the advance. The 55th Korp managed to slow the Soviet advance, inflicting heavy losses. To the east the 35th and 53rd Korps continued their dogged resistance against the 3rd and 63rd Armies.

SOUTHERN SECTOR

Tolbukhin's South Front and Malinovsky's South-West Front began probing attacks along the Mius and Donets. Light attacks struck Mackensen's 1st Panzer and Hollidt's 6th Armies, alerting Manstein to what he believed was the next Soviet offensive. He therefore began to move 2nd SS Panzer Korp south to deal with this threat. This move denuded the southern face of the Kursk sector of a significant portion of its armour, 4th Panzer retaining the battered 48th Panzer Korp while 24th Panzer Korp remained in reserve. The latter unit would also soon leave for the Mius line. Manstein was not expecting a major Soviet attack north of Kharkov, believing the Voronezh Front to be spent and being unaware of the existence of large-scale Soviet reserves.

18 July 1943

CENTRAL SECTOR

The 11th Guards and 11th Armies, with the support of the 4th Tank Army, were only twelve miles from Khotinets and Karachev but still faced stubborn resistance from the 55th Korp.

SOUTHERN SECTOR

The South-West and South Fronts continued their attacks on the Donets and Mius, making minor penetrations.

Ruoff's 17th Army came under renewed attack in the Kuban as the North Caucasus unleashed its fourth offensive against the German pocket.

SOVIET COMMAND

The Stavka declared Koniev's Steppe Front operational, 53rd, 47th, 4th Guards, 7th Guards and 69th Armies being brought under its control. The Steppe Front situated itself between the Voronezh and South-West Fronts to strike the German forces around Kharkov.

19 July 1943

CENTRAL SECTOR

The 3rd Guards Tank Army entered the fighting east of Orel. The tank army joined the attacks of the 3rd and 63rd Armies and 3rd Guards Tank, which were pushing the Germans back upon Orel itself. The offensive by the 11th and 11th Guards aimed to capture Bryansk and cut the 9th Army's line of retreat.

20 July 1943

CENTRAL SECTOR
Despite the introduction of their armour, the Soviet advance upon Orel bogged down as the 3rd Guards Tank became enmeshed in the bitter fighting with the 53rd Korp. With its tanks stalled the 3rd Guards Tank turned north-east and joined the thrust of the 3rd Army towards the Oka. Progress picked up but was still very slow.

22 July 1943

NORTHERN SECTOR
The Leningrad Front's 67th Army, situated on the Neva east of the city, and Volkhov Front's 8th Army deployed on the west bank of the Volkhov north of Tosno launched the Mga Offensive Operation, employing a combined total of 253,300 men.[12] The aim of the offensive was to force the Germans away from Leningrad and strengthen the precarious corridor south of Lake Ladoga.

CENTRAL SECTOR
Bolkhov fell to the 61st Army and Mtsensk to the 3rd Army as the slow advance into the Orel salient continued.

23 July 1943

SOUTHERN SECTOR
The 4th Panzer Army was back to its start line of 4 July. Three weeks of heavy fighting had seen the loss of all the territory gained during Operation Citadel and even more importantly, the loss of many valuable men and machines. The 4th Panzer Army had by this time deployed 120,000 men and 150 operational tanks between the 48th Panzer Korp and 52nd Korp. The 7th Korp of the 2nd Army held the junction with the 52nd Korp south of Sumy with its three infantry divisions.

Army Detachment Kempf covered the line from Belgorod to Zmiyev, protecting the right wing of the 4th Panzer. It deployed 80,000 men in the 11th Korp east of Belgorod (four infantry divisions) and 42nd Korp along the Donets (three infantry divisions).

The fighting in and around the Kursk pocket had cost the Voronezh Front 27,500 killed and missing and 46,000 wounded. The Steppe Front lost 27,000 killed and missing and 42,600 wounded. The Voronezh Front continued to deploy 693,000 men, over 1,800 tanks and 110 Su's, 8,728 artillery pieces and 700 Katyusha while the Steppe Front had 287,000 men, 450 tanks, 4,800 artillery pieces and sixty Katyusha.[13]

26 July 1943

CENTRAL SECTOR

The 4th Tank Army attacked in conjuction with the 3rd Army once again but suffered heavy losses to dug-in German anti-tank fire. Model had begun to redeploy some of his armour from the south of the Orel salient to the northern and eastern sectors, strengthening his defences.

30 July 1943

SOUTHERN SECTOR

Hollidt's 6th Army repulsed the South Front probes and restored its positions along the Mius and in the north-east Donbas. The 3rd Panzer Korp, transferred away from Detachment Kempf during these battles, had lost a considerable number of men and tanks, as had the 2nd SS Panzer Korp.

The Voronezh Front began to hand over part of its sector to the Steppe Front. Deploying the 69th, 38th, 40th, 6th Guards, 7th Guards and 1st Tank Armies, the Voronezh Front gave the 69th Army and 7th Guards over to the Steppe Front while the Steppe Front gave its 27th Army up to the Voronezh Front. The 47th Army remained in reserve to support either front as required.

31 July 1943

THE OSTHEER

Over the entire front the Germans had 2,500 combat aircraft against 8,300 Soviet planes, a ratio of 3.3:1 against. During July alone the German armies in the east lost 197,000 men but received only 90,000 replacements, a shortfall of more than 100,000 in a single month.

The Germans added a panzer-grenadier and infantry division to their order of battle while two motorised divisions were re-designated panzer-grenadier divisions. Total German strength in the east stood at sixteen panzer, thirteen panzer grenadier and 150 infantry divisions. [14]

1 August 1943

CENTRAL SECTOR

With the initiative in the east firmly in the hands of the Red Army and Hitler's attention fixed on the west, Army Group Centre was given permission to withdraw from the exposed Orel salient to the Hagen line, an ad hoc defence position east of Bryansk.

THE AIR WAR
The Americans carried out a major daylight raid on the Ploesti oilfields in Rumania, destroying more than forty percent of the refining capability and seriously affecting the supply of fuel to the German units on the eastern front. It was from this period onward that the Germans were to suffer severe damage to their manufacturing and transport infrastructure and in turn their ability to effectively supply the increasingly committed combat armies.

2 August 1943

CENTRAL SECTOR
Fighting in the Orel bulge saw Znamenskaya fall to the Soviets.

SOUTHERN SECTOR
The Red Army was poised to begin its counter-offensive south of Kursk. The Voronezh and Steppe Fronts would unleash Operation Rumyantsev against the unsuspecting 4th Panzer Army and Detachment Kempf.

Vatutin's Voronezh Front deployed the 38th Army opposite Sumy, 40th Army south-east of Sumy, facing the left flank of the 52nd Korp, 27th Army north of Grayvoron, 6th Guards Army north of Tomarovka, 5th Guards Army north-east of Tomarovka, 1st Tank Army in reserve behind the 6th Guards and 5th Guards Tank Army in reserve behind the 5th Guards. Steppe Front deployed the 53rd Army north of Belgorod, 69th Army north and east of Belgorod and 7th Guards Army on the Donets south of Belgorod and north of Volchansk. In addition the South-West Front would commit its 57th Army directly east of Kharkov and 46th Army around Chuguyev. The 4th Guards and 47th Armies were held in operational reserve.

The aim of the operation was to isolate and destroy the 4th Panzer Army and Detachment Kempf and, driving south, liberate Kharkov before unhinging the Germans defences north and south of the city.

The 4th Panzer Army deployed the 52nd Korp on its centre and left, holding a long line from the area south of Sumy to Tomarovka. The 48th Panzer Korp was to its right, holding a narrow front between Tomarovka and Belgorod. Army Detachment Kempf faced east along the Donets, its 11th Korp being deployed east and south of Belgorod, while the 42nd Korp covered the eastern approaches to Kharkov. Manstein's reserves, the 24th Panzer Korp and 3rd Panzer Korp, were still south along the Mius and in the Donbas, following the South-West and South Fronts' diversionary attacks which had drawn them away.

The forthcoming offensive in the Ukraine heralded the Red Army's renewed drive for the Dniepr, an advance which had been so devastatingly cut short in the spring. From this day forward, the Soviets would not cease in their efforts to drive the Germans out of their territory and begin the war to liberate Eastern Europe.

3 August 1943

SOUTHERN SECTOR

The Red Army opened Operation Rumyantsev, its artillery barrage ripping apart Ott's 52nd Korp. After just five minutes the barrage ended, lulling the Germans into a false sense of security. Thirty minutes later the Soviet artillery resumed their fire and the air armies joined the attack. This time they pounded the German lines with unprecedented ferocity for over two hours, inflicting heavy casualties. Tanks and infantry of the 6th and 5th Guards Armies then moved forwards on a thirty-mile front, opening bitter fighting with the right wing of the 52nd Korp and 48th Panzer Korps. The 5th Guards Army developed its attack successfully as the morning progressed, crushing the right flank of the 52nd Korp. Amid heavy fighting lead elements of the 5th Guards closed upon Tomarovka from the north-east. The 5th Guards Tank Army was committed to the fighting and pushed forward in support of the 5th Guards. By evening the two armies were more than fifteen miles into the junction of the two German korps.

The 1st Tank Army had also entered the battle through the 6th Guards Army but was halted in fierce fighting north of Tomarovka. Elements of the 52nd Korp launched a ferocious counter-attack, slowing the 1st Tank Army advance.

The 53rd Army and units of 69th Army attacked the German positions north of Belgorod. The 48th Panzer Korp and 11th Korp struggled to hold back the Soviet tide. Forward German defences quickly fell, but repeated counter-attacks by armoured forces slowed the Soviets down. However, the fighting proved costly as the left flank division of the 11th Korp was all but wiped out by the 53rd Army. The 69th Army struck the centre of the 11th Korp but intense fighting slowed the advance. Other elements of the 69th Army, together with the 7th Guards Army, launched attacks across the Donets but failed in the face of concentrated counter-fire by the right wing of the 11th Korp.

4 August 1943

CENTRAL SECTOR

Elements of the 3rd and 63rd Armies entered Orel amid heavy fighting with the retreating 53rd Korp.

SOUTHERN SECTOR

The Voronezh Front renewed its attack with intense artillery fire and air attacks smashing the German positions around Tomarovka. After thirty minutes of crushing fire, the 6th and 5th Guards Armies again assaulted the 52nd Korp, while the 1st Tank and 5th Guards Tank Armies began their renewed attacks. Bitter fighting raged as the right wing units of the 52nd Korp tried to stop the Soviets from breaking into Tomarovka. Leading elements of 1st Tank and 5th Guards Tank Armies threatened the lines of communication of the three German divisions fighting at Tomarovka. The 5th Guards Tank Army, advancing east of Tomarovka, ran into retreating elements of 48th Panzer Korp and became embroiled in heavy fighting. Luftwaffe strikes hindered the Soviet attack. Reinforcements brought up to strengthen the 5th Guards Tank soon swung the battle around and the Soviets pushed ahead, threatening to isolate two infantry divisions.

Fighting north of Belgorod intensified as the 48th Panzer Korp and remnants of 11th Korp's left wing struggled to hold back the 53rd and 69th Armies. The Soviets fought a slow and costly battle but were unable to break the German defences. Elements of the 11th Korp were forced back into the suburbs and the last remaining German bridgehead on the east bank of the Donets at Mikhailovka came under attack by 7th Guards Army.

Surprised by the ferocity of the Soviet attack and the destruction of the right wing and centre of the 52nd Korp, Manstein lengthened the 48th Panzer Korp sector to cover this unit's now open left flank. During heavy fighting Soviet tanks attacked the headquarters of the 52nd Korp and dispersed it. By evening there was a fifteen-mile gap in the line between the 52nd Korp and the 48th Panzer Korp.

5 August 1943

CENTRAL SECTOR

The Germans relinquished Orel to the 3rd and 63rd Armies.

SOUTHERN SECTOR

The 6th and 5th Guards Armies hammered the tightly packed German divisions around Tomarovka as the 1st and 5th Guards Tank Armies attempted to push into their rear. The 27th Army began its attack west of Tomarovka, being joined later in the day by the 40th Army as it pushed west towards Lebedin.

Heavy fighting raged north of Tomarovka as the 6th Guards Army made an effort to penetrate into the town. However, German armour launched a fierce counter-attack and brought the Soviet advance to a halt in the outskirts. Other elements of the 6th Guards then forced the Germans to give ground. Units of the 5th Guards Army attacked east of Tomarovka with armoured support. Heavy fighting ensued, but again German tanks tried to hold the line together. By dusk the Soviets had penetrated south of Borisovka, while units of the 6th Guards hit the 48th Panzer Korp near Orlovka. By the end of the day the German position at Tomarovka had deteriorated considerably. The three embattled divisions of the 52nd Korp's right wing, now fighting as part of the 48th Panzer Korp, began a fighting withdrawal in an effort to prevent their encirclement.

During a day of heavy fighting, the 1st Tank Army punched its way forward towards Bogodukhov. The new attacks by the 27th Army were lending support to this attack, preventing the 52nd Korp from redeploying to meet the Soviet armoured threat. Leading units of the 27th aimed to reach Grayvoron. In an effort to slow the Soviet attack Manstein moved the 3rd Panzer Korp back up to Zolochev.

Near Belgorod the 53rd Army cut the Belgorod–Kharkov road, while the 69th and 7th Guards Army began the assault on the city itself. By evening the urban area had been cleared, the remnants of the 48th Panzer Korp's right wing and 11th Korp's left wing pulling back along the line of the Donets. The 7th Guards finally established bridgeheads over the Donets south of the city.

6 August 1943

CENTRAL SECTOR
The 9th Army fell back upon the Hagen line, Kromy being given up to the advancing 13th Army.

SOUTHERN SECTOR
During the early hours of the morning the 1st Tank Army launched an attack aimed at isolating the Germans at Borisovka. Lead units of the 27th Army, supporting the attack, smashed the Germans aside and drove upon Grayvoron. Near the town elements of the 52nd Korp launched a counter-attack.

The 5th Guards Tank Army attacked the redeploying 3rd Panzer Korp near Zolochev and became embroiled in heavy fighting. The ferocity of the German defence halted further Soviet progress.

7 August 1943

CENTRAL SECTOR
Sokolovsky's West Front opened an offensive aimed at capturing Smolensk. The 5th, 10th Guards and 33rd Armies attacked the 4th Army between Dorogobush and Kirov. These armies pushed slowly forward east of Spas Demensk while the 10th Army attacked north of Kirov. The

new 68th Army was held in operational reserve for the offensive. Kalinin Front would join the offensive later, attacking the 4th Army and 3rd Panzer Army north of Smolensk. The Soviets committed the 428,000 men of the Kalinin Front and 824,000 men of the West Front.[15]

SOUTHERN SECTOR

The 6th and 5th Guards Armies forced the remnants of the 52nd Korp out of Borisovka. With the 27th Army blocking the line of retreat, the Germans launched a fierce counter-attack and tore a hole in the lines of 1st Tank Army. However, during the fighting the Germans suffered massive losses, the Borisovka pocket costing the Germans 5,000 killed and 2,000 captured.

Bogodukhov fell to 1st Tank Army. Elements of the army encountered the Grossdeutschland Panzer Grenadier Division east of Akhtyrka. Other units of the 1st Tank ran into the 2nd SS Das Reich Division of the 3rd Panzer Korp east of Bogodukhov, sparking a furious tank battle. The heavy fighting at Zolochev between other elements of the 3rd Panzer Korp and 5th Guards Tank Army continued.

8 August 1943

SOUTHERN SECTOR

The remnants of the 52nd Korp retreated to the area east of Akhtyrka where the Grossdeutschland Divisions held off units of the 1st Tank Army. 3rd Panzer Korp continued to attack the 1st Tank Army, forcing the Soviets onto the defensive south and east of Bogodukhov. Zolochev fell to 5th Guards Tank Army as the 3rd Panzer Korp pulled back from the town. Aleksandrovka also fell to the Soviets.

With the Borisovka pocket destroyed the Soviets regrouped their 27th and 6th Guards Armies. These armies were to push south-west towards Akhtyrka and Kotekva while 40th Army pushed towards Trostyanets.

9 August 1943

SOUTHERN SECTOR

Elements of 1st Tank Army, with 6th Guards Army protecting their right wing, took Murafa. The advancing Soviets then ran into more newly arrived elements of the 3rd Panzer Korp and heavy fighting erupted. The 52nd Korp also began to counter-attack near Grayvoron.

The 5th Guards Tank Army began a new attack towards Olshany but encountered fierce resistance from the 3rd Panzer Korp.

10 August 1943

CENTRAL SECTOR
Khotinets fell to the 61st Army as the Bryansk Front closed upon Karachev.

SOUTHERN SECTOR
Heavy fighting raged around Bogodukhov as the 1st Tank Army attempted to bring up additional units to overpower the increasingly strong German forces. Heavy fighting also raged at Aleksandrovka where Soviet mechanised forces were trying to push their way forward to cut the Poltava railway line. The 5th Guards Tank Army continued to attack at Olshany but was held up.

11 August 1943

SOUTHERN SECTOR
Lead elements of the 1st Tank Army reached Vysokoplye and after a hard fight took the town. However, late in the day the 3rd Panzer Korp counter-attacked and retook the town.

As fighting continued at Olshany, the Germans brought up elements of the 24th Panzer Korp. At this point Zhukov ordered the 5th Guards Tank Army to call off its attack. The 6th Guards Army deployed south-west of Bogodukhov in order to stiffen the right wing of 1st Tank Army.

GERMAN COMMAND
Orders were issued for the fortification of the East Wall. Hitler's belated instruction called for a line of fortifications from the Gulf of Finland to the Black Sea.

12 August 1943

SOUTHERN SECTOR
The 1st Tank Army renewed its attack yet again and recaptured Vysokopolye. Once more the Germans launched ferocious counter-attacks. Chuguyev fell to the 57th Army while elements of the Steppe Front entered the outskirts of Kharkov.

13 August 1943

NORTHERN SECTOR
Bitter fighting continued to rage south-east of Leningrad as the Mga offensive laboured on. The 67th and 8th Guards Armies had failed to breach the German lines despite repeated attacks.

CENTRAL SECTOR

The Kalinin Front joined the offensives rippling along the line north of Smolensk. New attacks by the 39th and 43rd Armies of the Kalinin Front towards Dukhovshina made slow but steady progress.

SOUTHERN SECTOR

The Steppe Front fought its way deeper into Kharkov, street fighting raging as the 11th Korp struggled to hold up the tide of Soviet attacks. The towns of Bolshaya and Danilovka fell near Kharkov as the Soviet envelopment drew closer to success.

Malinovsky's South-West Front began its Donbas offensive, attacking the 1st Panzer Army following the removal of the German armoured units to the north. This presented Manstein with a second problem. With the security of the German units around Kharkov undermined, Manstein had drawn the bulk of his forces north to deal with this threat, not realising that the Stavka intended to launch new attacks along the Donets and Mius as soon as this happened. Even if the Germans had realised this was the Soviet plan, Hitler's insistence that not a yard of ground be given up tied the German armies down, preventing the implementation of a mobile defence. For the Donbas operation the South-West Front had 565,000 men and the South Front 446,000 men.[16]

15 August 1943

CENTRAL SECTOR

Karachev fell to the 11th Guards Army.

SOUTHERN SECTOR

The South Front unleashed attacks along the Mius against the German 6th Army, supported by strong artillery fire. Elements of the 5th Shock Army attacked the 17th Korp, aiming to isolate Ropke's 29th Korp against the Azov coast.

At Kharkov bitter fighting continued in the streets as the Soviets resorted to their old method of launching costly wave attacks, thousands of men falling to the German guns and hundreds of tanks being destroyed. Despite the overwhelming numbers of Soviet tanks, the superiority of German gunnery inflicted crippling losses upon the armoured units of the Steppe Front. The six defending German divisions inside or around Kharkov had no more than 160 tanks and assault guns available as the battle for the city raged but accounted for nearly 200 Soviet tanks knocked out. Clearly, while Soviet strategic command had come a long way since 1941, tactical ability remained markedly inferior to that of the Ostheer, the officers in the field regularly resorting to uninspired frontal attacks in order to break through a German position. However, the Soviet offensive rolled on all the same, unstoppable even in the face of crippling casualties.

16 August 1943

Central Sector
Zhizhdra fell to the 50th Army.

18 August 1943

Central Sector
Soviet losses in the Orel bulge had been high since their counter-offensive began on 12 July. The 50th Army had lost 5,400 killed and missing and 17,700 wounded while the 11th Army lost 5,000 killed and missing and 15,000 wounded. The 4th Tank Army suffered 2,400 killed and 5,000 wounded. In all the Bryansk Front lost 39,000 killed and 123,000 wounded and the Central Front 47,700 killed and 117,000 wounded. The two fronts also lost 2,586 tanks, 892 artillery pieces and 1,014 aircraft.[17]

Southern Sector
The South Front attack along the Mius river ripped apart the 17th and 29th Korps of Hollidt's 6th Army. While the 2nd Guards, 28th and 44th Armies pinned the Germans frontally, the 5th Shock Army pushed south towards the Azov coast, threatening to isolate the 29th Korp at Taganrog.

19 August 1943

Southern Sector
Leading units of the 53rd Army cleared the forests west of Kharkov, while Rotmistrov's 5th Guards Tank became bogged down in bitter street fighting with the 11th Korp. Furious battles cost the 5th Guards Tank another 180 tanks disabled. The 6th Panzer Division, fighting the hordes of Soviet vehicles, numbered just fifteen operational panzers. Meanwhile, the 57th Army swung around the German flank south of Kharkov in an effort to take Army Detachment Kempf in the rear. The 69th Army moved to support the 53rd Army.

20 August 1943

Southern Sector
Lebedin fell to the 40th Army as it moved west. At Kharkov, Rotmistrov's 5th Guards Tank Army tried to force the 11th Korp from the city by direct frontal assault. The Germans were lying in wait with concealed panzers and anti-tank guns and exacted terrible punishment on the 5th Guards Tank Army.

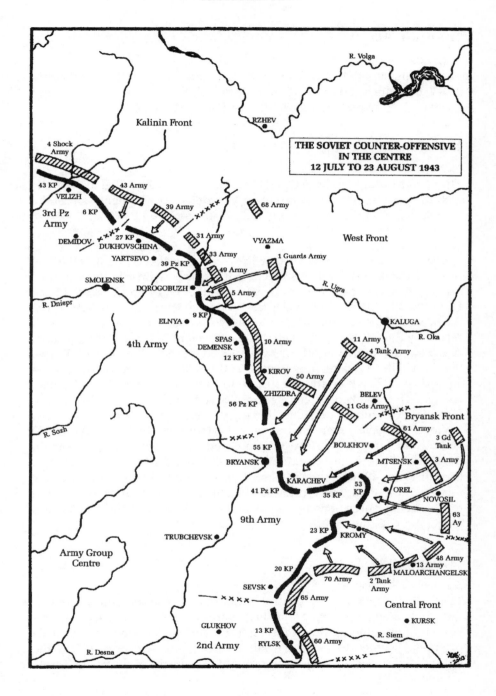

THE SOVIET COUNTER-OFFENSIVE
IN THE CENTRE
12 JULY TO 23 AUGUST 1943

R. Volga

RZHEV

Kalinin Front

4 Shock
Army

43 KP

VELIZH

3rd Pz
Army

6 KP

DEMIDOV.

43 Army

27 KP

DUKHOVSHCHINA

YARTSEVO

39 Army

31 Army

33 Army

39 Pz KP

49 Army

68 Army

VYAZMA

West Front

1 Guards Army

R. Ugra

SMOLENSK

R. Dniepr

DOROGOBUZH

5 Army

9 KP

KALUGA

R. Oka

ELNYA

4th Army

SPAS
DEMENSK

10 Army

11 Army

4 Tank Army

12 KP

KIROV

50 Army

BELEV

ZHIZDRA

56 Pz KP

11 Gds Army

Bryansk Front

61 Army

3 Gd
Tank

R. Sozh

55 KP

BOLKHOV

MTSENSK

3 Army

BRYANSK

OREL

NOVOSIL.

41 Pz KP

KARACHEV

35 KP

53
KP

63
Ay

9th Army

23 KP

KROMY

TRUBCHEVSK

Army Group
Centre

20 KP

48 Army

13 Army

MALOARCHANGELSK

2 Tank
Army

SEVSK

70 Army

65 Army

Central Front

GLUKHOV

13 KP

KURSK

2nd Army

RYLSK

60 Army

R. Siem

R. Desna

21 August 1943

SOUTHERN SECTOR
The fighting along the Mius line since 17 July had cost Hollidt's 6th Army 23,830 casualties and the 1st Panzer Army 27,991. In return the 6th Army received 3,312 replacements and the 1st Panzer Army, 6,174.[18]

22 August 1943

NORTHERN SECTOR
The Stavka brought its Mga Operation to a close, having failed to drive the 26th Korp of the 18th Army out of its Mga defences. The fighting cost the Soviets 20,890 killed and missing and 59,047 wounded.[19]

SOUTHERN SECTOR
Manstein, refusing to risk further losses in a useless battle at Kharkov, ordered the withdrawal of Detachment Kempf, against Hitler's orders. The fighting along the Mius intensified as the South Front pressed back Hollidt's 6th Army. With his forces under attack from Kharkov to the Azov Sea, Manstein was unable to draw upon any reserves. A strength return by the 6th Army showed the sheer weight of Soviet forces against Army Group South. The 6th Army deployed the 29th, 17th and 4th Korps, the 29th with 8,706 men against 69,000 Soviets, 17th Korp with 9,284 against 49,500, while 4th Korp had 13,143 men against 18,000 Soviet troops. The weakened German armoured forces were also facing formidable numbers of Soviet forces; the 4th Panzer Army faced 490 Soviet tanks, Detachment Kempf faced 360 tanks, the 1st Panzer Army 220 and the 6th Army 400.[20] Army Group A, reduced to only the 17th Army in the Kuban, had twenty-one divisions with around 270,000 men between the 5th Korp, 49th Mountain Korp and 44th Korp. Manstein repeatedly requested the withdrawal of these valuable men, the quarter of a million troops being sorely needed against the overwhelming Soviet armies facing Army Group South.

23 August 1943

SOUTHERN SECTOR
The Germans relinquished control of Kharkov for the last time. However, the 3rd Panzer Korp launched strong counter-attacks around Bogodukhov, pinning down the 1st Tank and 6th Guards Armies. This prompted Koniev to move the 5th Guards Tank Army up to aid the struggling armies, which in turn brought movement of the Soviet forces around Kharkov to a standstill.

The battle in the Ukraine had cost the Voronezh Front 48,300 killed and

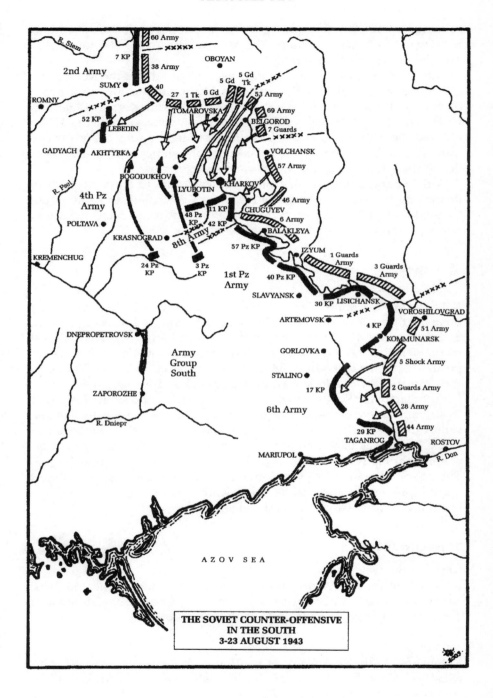

THE SOVIET COUNTER-OFFENSIVE
IN THE SOUTH
3-23 AUGUST 1943

missing and 108,000 wounded and the Steppe Front 23,000 killed and missing and 75,000 wounded. The Soviets also lost 1,864 tanks, 423 artillery pieces and 153 aircraft.[21]

The German 6th Army abandoned its positions along the Mius river, closely pursued by the South Front. The advance of the 5th Shock Army had almost brought about the encirclement of the 29th Korp in Taganrog. Only a timely withdrawal would have prevented its isolation, but Hitler ordered the 29th to stand fast. This policy of fighting for every yard of ground, which had already proved costly in the winter of 1942–43, was to be repeated time and again with disastrous results.

With Kharkov lost, Hitler made a scapegoat of General Kempf, dismissing him from command of his Army Detachment and appointing General Wohler in his place. At the same time the army detachment was renamed 8th Army.

26 August 1943

CENTRAL SECTOR

Rokossovsky's Central Front unleashed a new offensive aimed at breaking through Weiss' relatively intact 2nd Army and reaching Poltava and the Dniepr. For this operation the Central Front employed 579,600 men. Elements of the 65th and 60th Armies pounded the German positions, but the defending 13th Korp put up fierce resistance. The main thrust of the Soviet attack was towards Sevsk and Novgorod-Seversky. Unfortunately for Rokossovsky the 2nd Army had concentrated much of its strength before Sevsk. Yet again though, Soviet strength overcame the skilful German defence and their positions south of the town began to crack. Weiss was unable to prevent Chernyakhovsky's 60th Army from pushing through his front, having no reserves with which to plug the gap. This attack ultimately threatened the entire southern flank of Army Group Centre, pressing it away to the north and creating a gap between the junctions of Army Groups Centre and South.

27 August 1943

CENTRAL SECTOR

Sevsk fell to the 65th Army, but the early commitment of the 2nd Tank Army went disastrously wrong as the armour became bogged down in costly fighting with dug-in German anti-tank units.

SOUTHERN SECTOR

Kotelva fell to the 27th Army as the Voronezh Front pushed west from Kharkov. Near the Mius river the 51st and 5th Shock Armies broke through the positions 4th and 17th Korps.

GERMAN COMMAND
Hitler flew east to his command centre at Vinnitsa where he met with Manstein and his commanders. Manstein called for a policy of flexible defence, leading to the abandonment of territory east of the Dniepr but Hitler would not hear of this, maintaining that where the German soldier stood he remained.

28 August 1943

CENTRAL SECTOR
The Central Front penetrated deeply into the positions of the 2nd Army, rolling north and west and opening up a huge gap in the junction of Army Groups Centre and South.

The West Front rejoined the offensive, beginning a new attack at Elnya in support of the Kalinin Front offensive at Dukhovschina. These attacks pinned down the German 4th Army along its entire length, preventing the transfer of German units to the threatened southern flank of the army group.

29 August 1943

SOUTHERN SECTOR
Heaving fighting saw the fall of Lyubotin to the 5th Guards Tank Army. The 3rd Panzer Korp was making the Soviet force pay dearly for every yard of territory. Behind the Mius line the 2nd Guards and 28th Armies reached the Azov coast and cut off the 29th Korp in Taganrog. The 29th had three infantry, one panzer and one Luftwaffe field divisions.

30 August 1943

CENTRAL SECTOR
The 10th Guards Army and elements of the 5th Army entered Elnya as the 9th Korp of the 4th Army was pushed back.

SOUTHERN SECTOR
Taganrog fell to the 44th Army as the South Front pounded the 29th Korp. The Germans managed to break out of the city and fell back to the west, linking up with the battered remnants of the 6th Army.

31 August 1943

CENTRAL SECTOR
Glukhov fell, the 60th Army having advanced fifty miles into the German lines.

SOUTHERN SECTOR

With the 7th Korp on the southern flank of the 2nd Army now isolated from the rest of the army, it was given over to the 4th Panzer Army. This did not greatly help the 4th Panzer as it took on the extra frontage covered by the 7th Korp. On the southern wing the Germans began a limited withdrawal in the 6th Army sector but this failed to alleviate the situation. Manstein ordered the 1st Panzer and 6th Armies to begin mobile defence operations, this effectively being the prelude to the withdrawal to the Dniepr. Manstein had gained this small victory through long, laboured negotiations with Hitler, who finally relented and allowed a limited withdrawal only as a very last resort.

The Soviet forces operating on the southern wing had reached hitherto unknown strength. The combined strength of the Central, Voronezh, Steppe, South-West and South Fronts stood at 2,630,000 men with 51,200 artillery pieces, 2,400 tanks and Su's and 2,850 aircraft, all of which were attacking weakened German infantry and armoured divisions. Army Group South had around 800,000 men and Army Group Centre approximately 600,000 but as few as a fifth of this number were combat infantry.

THE OSTHEER

As August drew to a bloody close, the Germans counted their losses. More than 218,000 men had been lost during August (133,000 lost by Army Group South alone), of which barely 77,000 were replaced, just 33,000 of which went to Manstein. In addition, more than 570 panzers and 140 assault guns had been destroyed or captured, leaving the Panzerwaffe with 2,555 armoured vehicles in the east, as few as one third of which were operational. Against this skeletal force the Red Army had a fleet of 6,200 tanks.

During August the Germans committed two infantry divisions to the eastern front, but in turn one SS panzer grenadier and one infantry division left, bringing German strength to sixteen panzer, twelve panzer grenadier and 151 infantry divisions.[22]

> Kursk and its aftermath had a lasting affect upon both the Ostheer and the Red Army. For the Ostheer, the loss of its recovered armoured forces was never made good, these divisions slowly being whittled away in one battle after another. Furthermore, the battle signalled the end of the German initiative in the east.
>
> For the Red Army, Kursk was the culmination in a growing state of confidence since the conception of the Stalingrad offensive. The Stavka had successfully held its nerve throughout the German attack and unleashed a series of unprecedented attacks thereafter. It now remained for the Red Army to perfect the use of its immense forces in deep penetrating offensive operations.

NOTES

1   Mellenthin, *Panzer Battles*, p220
2   Mellenthin, *Panzer Battles*, p220
3   Mellenthin, *Panzer Battles*, pp221–3
4   Mellenthin, *Panzer Battles*, p223
5   Mellenthin, *Panzer Battles*, pp223–4
6   Cross, *Citadel*, p230
7   Mellenthin, *Panzer Battles*, p226
8   Soviet army strengths from Kirosheev, *Soviet Casualties and Combat Losses in the Twentieth Century*, Table 67
9   Cross, *Citadel*, p230
10 Mellenthin, *Panzer Battles*, p228
11 Ellis, *Brute Force*, p108
12 Kirosheev, *Soviet Casualties and Combat Losses in the Twentieth Century*, Table 75
13 Glantz, *From the Don to the Dnepr*, p223
14 Ellis, *The World War II Databook*, p176
15 Kirosheev, *Soviet Casualties and Combat Losses in the Twentieth Century*, Table 75
16 Kirosheev, *Soviet Casualties and Combat Losses in the Twentieth Century*, Table 75
17 Kirosheev, *Soviet Casualties and Combat Losses in the Twentieth Century*, Table 75
18 Carell, *Scorched Earth*, p313
19 Kirosheev, *Soviet Casualties and Combat Losses in the Twentieth Century*, Table 75
20 Carell, *Scorched Earth*, p314
21 Kirosheev, *Soviet Casualties and Combat Losses in the Twentieth Century*, Table 75
22 Ellis, *The World War II Databook*, p176

CHAPTER IV
East Wall

The Germans had been thrown irrevocably onto the defensive following Kursk. Retreating towards the Dniepr, the Ostheer expected to find a system of prepared fortifications. However, Hitler had forbidden the construction of defences to the rear and so the retreat to the Dniepr line turned into a race against annihilation. For the Red Army the race to the Dniepr began a pursuit of the enemy that would last until the fall of Berlin in 1945.

2 September 1943

CENTRAL SECTOR
Sumy fell to the 38th Army of Vatutin's Voronezh Front.

SOUTHERN SECTOR
Lisichansk fell to 3rd Guards Army of the South-West Front and Kommunarsk to the 51st Army of the South Front.

3 September 1943

CENTRAL SECTOR
The 60th Army crossed the Desna river at Novgorod Seversky.

SOUTHERN SECTOR
Putivl fell as the Soviets severed the Bryansk–Konotop railway line and communications between Army Group Centre and South.

4 September 1943

SOUTHERN SECTOR
Hitler gave the 17th Army permission to pull out of the Kuban and redeploy to the Crimea.

5 September 1943

SOUTHERN SECTOR
The 3rd Guards Army captured Artemovsk after a hard battle with the 30th Korp of 1st Panzer Army.

6 September 1943

SOUTHERN SECTOR
Konotop fell to the 60th Army of the Central Front, while farther south Kramatorsk and Slavyansk fell to Soviet 6th Army and 1st Guards Army. The 3rd Guards Army succeeded in prising apart the junction of the 6th and 1st Panzer Armies around Konstantinovka, opening a thirty-mile gap. A counter-attack by elements of the 40th Panzer Korp failed to close the gap.

7 September 1943

CENTRAL SECTOR
Boldin's 50th Army launched an assault towards Bryansk but was slowed by fierce resistance from the 55th Korp.

SOUTHERN SECTOR
The 30th Korp of 1st Panzer Army began to withdraw from Stalino, on the extreme right wing of the army.

8 September 1943

SOUTHERN SECTOR
Stalino fell as Fretter Pico's 30th Korp completed its evacuation. The 5th Shock Army moved into the ruined city. Krasnoarmyansk also fell to the 3rd Guards.

GERMAN COMMAND
Manstein and Kleist again met with Hitler at Zaporozhe. Manstein asked permission to pull back to the Dniepr but Hitler refused. However, he did confirm his decision to abandon the Kuban but this was of little help to Army Group South as the men of the 17th Army would go into the Crimea, not the main line.

9 September 1943

SOUTHERN SECTOR
The 60th Army reached Bachmakh, taking the town after a brief struggle.

In the Kuban the 17th Army began its evacuation, pulling out of its forward positions to the Gotenkopf line.

10 September 1943

SOUTHERN SECTOR
Mariupol fell to 28th and 44th Armies as the 29th Korp was forced back. Barvenkovo fell to the 1st Guards Army.

Fighting raged in the Kuban as the North Caucasus Front launched unco-ordinated attacks against the 17th Army, committing nearly 250,000 men to the offensive. The 18th Army entered the outskirts of Novorossiysk and became embroiled in bitter fighting with 49th Mountain Korp. During the remainder of the month the 17th Army evacuated the 250,000 soldiers of its 5th, 49th Mountain and 44th Korps from the Kuban.

11 September 1943

SOUTHERN SECTOR
A German counter-attack succeeded in closing the gap between the 1st Panzer and 6th Armies.

14 September 1943

CENTRAL SECTOR
The German 9th Army began to evacuate Bryansk, heavy fighting raging in and around the city. West Front attacks also drew closer to Smolensk, while the Kalinin Front pushed down from the north. Dukhovschina fell to the 39th Army of the Kalinin Front.

SOUTHERN SECTOR
In the Kuban the German 17th Army withdrew from the Gotenkopf line.

GERMAN COMMAND
Hitler agreed to a withdrawal from Smolensk to reduce the pressure upon Army Group Centre.

15 September 1943

CENTRAL SECTOR
Kalinin, West and Bryansk Fronts began their final offensive aimed at taking Smolensk. Fighting was fierce but progress was again slow.

SOUTHERN SECTOR
Nezhin fell to the 60th Army.

GERMAN COMMAND
After another long discussion with Hitler, Field Marshal Manstein finally got approval for the withdrawal of Army Group South behind the line of the Dniepr. Despite his earlier order of the construction of an Eastern Wall, Hitler had forbidden the construction of fortifications. The 6th Army was ordered back to a line running from Melitopol to Zaporozhe, its 17th and 29th Korps taking up defensive positions along this line while the 4th Korp pulled back via Zaporozhe, where it would then join the 1st Panzer Army. Hollidt's 6th Army was also removed from Army Group South and allocated to Kleist's Army Group A. The 1st Panzer Army was to cross at Dnepropetrovsk and Zaporozhe and then fan out to protect a line from Zaporozhe to Kremenchug. Wohler's 8th Army was to cross at Cherkassy and Dnepropetrovsk and again then had to fan out to cover a sector between the 1st and 4th Panzer Armies. Hoth's 4th Panzer would cross at Kiev and then hand over the 24th Panzer Korp to the 8th Army while redeploying north and south of the city. Manstein moved his head-quarters west to Kirovograd.

SOVIET COMMAND
Stavka ordered Rokossovsky's Central and Vatutin's Voronezh Fronts to converge upon Kiev and destroy the 4th Panzer Army while Koniev's Steppe Front was to move upon Kremenchug. Malinovsky's South-West Front was to march to Dnepropetrovsk, while South Front maintained pressure on the 6th Army, isolating the German forces in the Crimea by reaching Kherson.

16 September 1943

CENTRAL SECTOR
Yartsevo fell to the 31st Army after a bloody battle. The 10th Army crossed the Desna and approached Roslavl while Novgorod Seversky fell to the 60th Army after a long battle.

SOUTHERN SECTOR
Lozovaya fell to Soviet 6th Army while Romny fell to the Voronezh Front. In the Kuban, Novorossiysk fell to the 18th Army after a fierce battle.

17 September 1943

CENTRAL SECTOR
The 11th Guards Army entered Bryansk and, after a brisk battle with

German rearguards, captured the city. Trubchevsk also fell to the 47th Army.

SOUTHERN SECTOR
Berdyansk fell to the 44th Army as Hollidt's 6th Army pulled back to the Melitopol line.

18 September 1943

SOUTHERN SECTOR
The Steppe and Voronezh Fronts captured Priluki, Lubny and Romodan all falling while Pavlograd and Krasnograd fell to the South-West Front. The 6th Army also lost control of Nogaisk as it continued to withdraw.

20 September 1943

CENTRAL SECTOR
Velizh fell to the 4th Shock Army of the Kalinin Front.

21 September 1943

CENTRAL SECTOR
The 43rd Army of the Kalinin Front captured Demidov. The 60th Army of the Central Front entered Chernigov, destroying the defending Germans in a bitter three-day battle.

SOUTHERN SECTOR
Leading elements of the 3rd Guards Tank Army reached the Dniepr opposite Kanev. Farther south, the 1st Panzer Army was pushed back to the Dnepropetrovsk bridgehead. Sinelnikovo fell to the South-West Front.

22 September 1943

SOUTHERN SECTOR
The Central Front reached the Dniepr at the mouth of the Pripyat river.
    Rybalko's 3rd Guards Tank Army crossed the Dniepr at Veliki Bukrin. Elements of the 27th Army provided support, closely followed by the 40th Army. Despite determined efforts to hold the west bank, Wohler's 8th Army was spread too thin. There was heavy fighting at Novomosskovsk as the South-West Front pinned the 1st Panzer Army into the Denpropetrovsk bridgehead.
    Fighting in the Donbas and on the approaches to the Dniepr had cost the South-West Front 40,000 killed and missing and 117,000 wounded, while the South Front lost 26,000 killed and missing and 90,000 wounded.[1]

Meanwhile, the fighting in the Kuban carried on as the German 17th Army continued its orderly evacuation. Anapa fell to the North Caucasus Front but the German lines remained intact.

23 September 1943

CENTRAL SECTOR
Fighting in the Smolensk sector intensified as the Germans were pressed back around the city. Both the Kalinin and West Fronts approached from the north, east and south, hemming in the German 4th Army. Farther south, the 9th Army lost Unecha to the Bryansk Front.

SOUTHERN SECTOR
Poltava fell to the Steppe Front. At Veliki Bukrin there was heavy fighting as the 3rd Guards Tank and 27th Armies extended their bridgehead.

24 September 1943

CENTRAL SECTOR
After a long battle the Germans pulled out of Smolensk, the 31st Army of the Kalinin Front having virtually isolated the city from the north and the 5th and 68th Armies of the West Front from the east and south.

SOUTHERN SECTOR
Borispol fell to the Voronezh Front as it drew closer to Kiev. The 3rd Guards Tank, 27th and 40th Armies consolidated their bridgehead at Bukrin.

25 September 1943

CENTRAL SECTOR
The 31st, 5th and 68th Armies took Smolensk. Roslavl fell to the 10th Army.

SOUTHERN SECTOR
German forces continued to withdraw across the Dniepr, while the 7th Guards Army of the Steppe Front reached it south of Kremenchug, crossing with ease.

26 September 1943

CENTRAL SECTOR
Khotimsk fell to the Bryansk Front

SOUTHERN SECTOR

The Soviet 3rd Airborne Brigade suffered a crushing defeat at Bukrin. Dropped during the night, the 3rd was unfortunate to land in the midst of the 48th Panzer Korp and was virtually destroyed. The 5th Airborne Brigade, also dropped into the bridgehead, suffered heavy casualties.

The 38th Army crossed the Dniepr north of Kiev, establishing a small bridgehead around Lyutezh. Hauffe's 13th Korp (4th Panzer Army) launched a furious counter-attack and almost smashed the 38th, but the Soviets were able to hang on.

Soviet 6th Army crossed the Dniepr near Dnepropetrovsk and established two small bridgeheads. The South Front unleashed a new attack on the Nogaisk Steppe, 5th Shock, 44th and 2nd Guards Armies crashing into Hollidt's 6th Army. South of Melitopol the 28th Army surged forward, heavy fighting erupting along the Molochnaya river.

With the Dniepr line falling apart, the Soviets prepared to begin the Lower Dniepr Operation. Aimed at breaking German resistance in the Dniepr elbow, the Stavka had amassed considerable forces. Steppe Front deployed 463,000 men, South-West Front 461,000 and the South Front 581,000 for this next operation.[2]

27 September 1943

SOUTHERN SECTOR

The 48th Panzer Korp launched a ferocious counter-attack at Bukrin. The Soviet forces in the bridgehead were not expecting an attack of this strength and in the subsequent fighting were almost wiped out. Only through sheer stubbornness did they maintain a small bridgehead on the west bank. Farther south the South-West Front entered Dnepropetrovsk but became embroiled in bitter fighting with Fretter Pico's 30th Korp.

In the Kuban the Germans gave up Temryuk.

29 September 1943

SOUTHERN SECTOR

Kremenchug fell to the Steppe Front after a bloody battle.

30 September 1943

CENTRAL SECTOR

Krichev fell to the southern wing of the West Front.

SOUTHERN SECTOR

The withdrawal of Army Group South behind the line of the Dniepr was essentially complete. Despite being considerably outnumbered, Manstein had evacuated his forces from the east bank, crossed at four widely dispersed locations and then redeployed on the west bank. The 4th Panzer, 8th and 1st Panzer Armies had also evacuated 200,000 wounded during the course of the withdrawal. However, the divisions of Army Group South had been reduced to mere remnants. With thirty-seven infantry and seventeen armoured divisions, Manstein's units had an average combat strength of one thousand men. Soviet losses though had been equally heavy. Since 26 August the Voronezh Front had lost 46,000 killed and missing and 131,000 wounded, the Steppe Front 23,000 killed and missing and 86,000 wounded and the Central Front 33,500 killed and missing and 107,900 wounded.[3]

In the Kuban the 17th Army had given up most of its territory and was back in the Crimea. Jaenecke's 17th had 250,000 men in fourteen German and seven Rumanian divisions, deployed between 5th Korp on the Kerch peninsula and the 49th Mountain Korp farther inland. Against the 17th Army were the 9th, 18th and 56th Armies of the North Caucasus Front.

THE OSTHEER
German strength in the east stood at sixteen panzer, twelve motorised and 151 infantry divisions[4]. Of the 2,300 panzers and assault guns available at the end of September barely 700 were operational, Army Group North having seven operational tanks, Army Group Centre had 199 and Group South 477.[5] Manpower losses were equally severe, 230,000 soldiers being lost in September, of which 112,000 were replaced.

> *Despite the loss of a vast track of territory stretching from Smolensk to the Azov Sea, the Ostheer remained essentially intact. With the Dniepr crossings completed, the Stavka had lost the opportunity to inflict a costly defeat upon Army Group South. Had the Red Army used its armour more aggressively to push ahead of the infantry forces, rather than supporting their attacks, the successful evacuation of Manstein's forces to the west might well have been prevented.*

1 October 1943

SOUTHERN SECTOR
Manstein moved his headquarters from Kirovograd to the former Führer headquarters at Vinnitsa.

2 October 1943

CENTRAL SECTOR
The bitter, two-month long offensive around Smolensk finally died down, having cost the Kalinin Front 28,000 killed and missing and the West Front

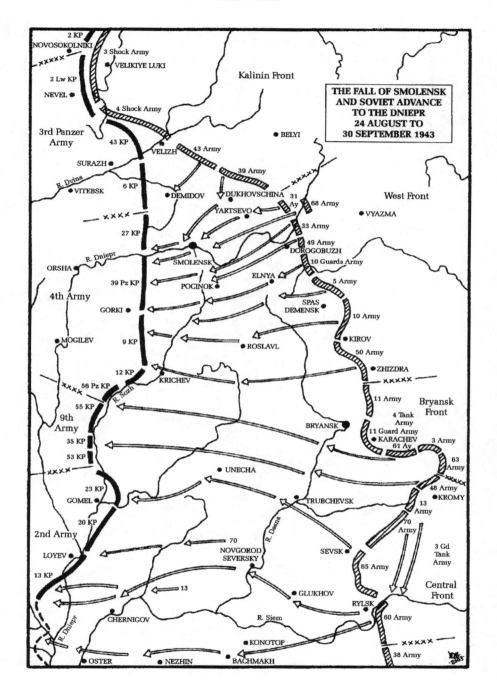

THE FALL OF SMOLENSK
AND SOVIET ADVANCE
TO THE DNIEPR
24 AUGUST TO
30 SEPTEMBER 1943

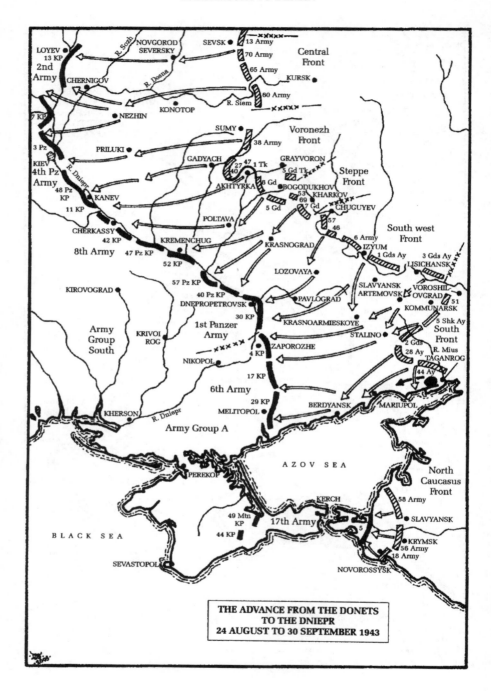

THE ADVANCE FROM THE DONETS
TO THE DNIEPR
24 AUGUST TO 30 SEPTEMBER 1943

79,500 killed and missing and 253,600 wounded. The two fronts also lost 863 tanks, 234 artillery pieces and 303 aircraft.[6]

5 October 1943

SOUTHERN SECTOR
Bitter fighting raged at Dnepropetrovsk as the 8th Guards Army, recently committed to the fighting from the Steppe Front reserve, forced a crossing of the Dniepr south of the town. Farther north, attacks by the 60th and 13th Armies made progress north of Kiev. These two units were also transferred to the Voronezh Front from the Central Front.

6 October 1943

CENTRAL SECTOR
The 3rd and 4th Shock Armies of the Kalinin Front launched new attacks against the junction of Army Groups Centre and North. The main weight of the attack fell upon Luftwaffe field divisions of the 2nd Luftwaffe Korp on the left wing of the 3rd Panzer Army. A rapid Soviet advance led to the early capture of Nevel during the afternoon, severing communications between groups North and Centre.

SOUTHERN SECTOR
Fighting in the Lyutezh bridgehead raged unabated as the Soviets fended off constant counter-attacks by the 13th and 59th Korps. The latter units had been brought down from the Central Sector to reinforce the weak left wing of Army Group South. Only once Soviet armoured units had been brought up was the bridgehead strengthened significantly.

7 October 1943

CENTRAL SECTOR
The 9th Korp, hastily transferred from the 4th Army to the 3rd Panzer Army, launched a fierce counter-attack, bringing both the 3rd and 4th Shock Armies to a standstill. Repeated Soviet counter-attacks failed to push the salient any farther as the Germans stabilised their positions.

SOUTHERN SECTOR
There was heavy fighting at Taman as the last remnants of the German 17th Army evacuated the Kuban peninsula.

8 October 1943

CENTRAL SECTOR
The Bryansk Front was disbanded and its units were handed over to the Central and West Fronts.

9 October 1943

SOUTHERN SECTOR
The long and bitter campaign in the Kuban ended as the 17th Army withdrew to the Crimea. Hitler now detached eight divisions from the 17th Army, distributing them to more needy sectors to the north. The fighting in the peninsula had cost the North Caucasus Front 13,900 killed and missing and 50,000 wounded.[7]

The South Front unleashed a massive artillery barrage upon the 6th Army, followed by an infantry and armoured attack. Hollidt's forces put up fierce resistance, bringing the initial Soviet attack to a halt. However, with numbers on their side, the South Front repeated its attacks. The German positions at Melitopol and the Nogaisk Steppe were the final defence line before the Dniepr river. If they fell, the subsequent retreat would leave the 17th Army isolated in the Crimea. Having just escaped from one pocket the 17th seemed about to become hemmed into another.

10 October 1943

CENTRAL SECTOR
Fighting erupted up on the southern wing of Army Group Centre as Rokossovsky's Central Front attacked the Germans around Gomel.

SOUTHERN SECTOR
The South-West Front attacked the Zaporozhe bridgehead in force, its 8th Guards, 3rd Guards and 12th Armies attacking the 40th Panzer and 17th Korps. The 12th Army attacked from the north, 8th Guards in the centre and 3rd Guards on the left. Fierce fighting erupted as the Germans defended with great vigour.

11 October 1943

CENTRAL SECTOR
The Central Front made slow progress around Gomel, Novobelitsa falling after hard fighting.

SOUTHERN SECTOR
As Soviet troops entered Zaporozhe, bitter street fighting erupted in the town.

13 October 1943

SOUTHERN SECTOR
Most of Zaporozhe had fallen. The German perimeter had been penetrated, 12th Army closing upon the hydroelectric dam. Soviet artillery began to pound the Germans around the dam, inflicting severe damage.

Hollidt's 6th Army was also involved in bitter street fighting in Melitopol as the 28th Army fought its way into the town.

14 October 1943

SOUTHERN SECTOR
After a bloody, four-day battle Zaporozhe fell to the 8th and 3rd Guards and 12th Armies, while the continuing threat to the dam posed by the 12th Army compelled the Germans to abandon their bridgehead. Heavy fighting at Melitopol continued as the 6th Army fought vigorously.

SOVIET COMMAND
The Stavka prepared to launch a major assault aimed at breaking through the German defences on the west bank of the river line and crushing the 8th and 1st Panzer Armies. The South-West Front was to attack between Zaporozhe and Dnepropetrovsk to pin the 1st Panzer frontally while the Steppe Front broke through at the junction of the two armies. For the operation the Steppe Front had the 5th Guards, 7th Guards, 57th and 5th Guards Tank Armies near Dnepropetrovsk and the 53rd, 4th Guards and 52nd Armies nearer Kremenchug. In defence the 1st Panzer Army deployed the 40th and 57th Panzer Korps, 17th, 30th and 52nd Korps.

15 October 1943

SOUTHERN SECTOR
Around Veliki Bukrin the Voronezh Front launched a new assault with the 27th, 40th and 3rd Guards Tank Armies, but met fierce resistance from the 48th Panzer Korp. The German defences were very thin but held the Soviets solidly. Fighting was intense as the Germans tried to wear down the Soviet attack on its start lines.

The 57th Panzer Korp came under sustained attack south-east of Kremenchug and broke apart, the 5th Guards Army smashing the German forward positions. With the forward German defences crushed, the Soviets introduced their armour, the 5th Guards Tank Army pouring into the rear of the 1st Panzer. The Soviet air armies provided crucial support, the 5th Air Army smashing German ground forces as the armies advanced.

16 October 1943

SOUTHERN SECTOR
Bloody fighting continued at Veliki Bukrin as the 48th Panzer Korp fended off repeated Soviet attacks. The German line around Kremenchug also collapsed, enabling the Steppe Front to push south-west towards Krivoi Rog.

17 October 1943

CENTRAL SECTOR
Fighting flared up around Vitebsk as the 43rd Army drove a deep salient into the junction of 9th and 53rd Korps. The 53rd Korp, recently moved to reinforce this sector, fought around the town. On the southern flank of Army Group Centre the Central Front crossed the Dniepr near Loyev and gained a significant bridgehead.

SOUTHERN SECTOR
Inconclusive fighting continued at Veliki Bukrin as the Stavka considered calling off the attack. With the Lyutezh bridgehead now established to the north, the Soviets would be able to turn the northern wing of Army Group South, but it would take time to redeploy forces into this sector. Farther south the 8th Army and 1st Panzer Army were forced back as the Steppe and South-West Fronts exploited the hole blown in the German line. Forward elements of the Steppe Front pushed towards Krivoi Rog.

18 October 1943

SOUTHERN SECTOR
In Melitopol the 28th Army had penetrated to the city centre, the 6th Army beginning to cave in under the repeated Soviet assaults.

19 October 1943

SOUTHERN SECTOR
The Soviets abandoned their attacks at Veliki Bukrin. Vatutin immediately began to move his forces surreptitiously away from this sector to Lyutezh, 100 miles to the north. Unknown to the Germans, the 3rd Guards Tank Army started to pull out of the line and cross to the east bank of the river.

In the Dniepr elbow the South-West Front took Pyatikhati. Vishgorod also fell after a brief battle.

20 October 1943

CENTRAL SECTOR
Army Group Centre reported to OKH that it was in excess of 200,000 men below establishment.

SOVIET COMMAND
The Stavka redesignated its southern fronts, the final major change to the order of battle of the Soviet formations on the southern wing for the remainder of the war. The Voronezh Front was renamed the 1st Ukrainian Front, the Steppe Front became the 2nd Ukrainian, the South-West Front the 3rd Ukrainian and the South Front the 4th Ukrainian Front. Rokossovsky's Central Front became the Belorussian Front, while Eremenko's Kalinin Front was renamed 1st Baltic Front and the old Baltic Front under Popov became the 2nd Baltic.

23 October 1943

SOUTHERN SECTOR
The 6th Army lost control of Melitopol to the 28th Army. With its line broken, 6th Army retreated rapidly to the Dniepr, losing contact with the 17th Army in the Crimea, leaving Jaenecke's force isolated.

24 October 1943

SOUTHERN SECTOR
The 5th Guards Tank Army broke through to Krivoi Rog as the 37th Army moved to support, only to be held back by the 11th Panzer Division. A German counter-attack forced the 5th Guards Tank to pull back its forward units.

On the Nogaisk Steppe the 44th Korp, having been evacuated from the Taman and deployed on the extreme southern wing of the 6th Army, was struck by the 2nd Guards Army and almost overrun. However, the Germans hastily reorganised their units and counter-attacked, halting the Soviet advance.

25 October 1943

SOUTHERN SECTOR
Fighting at Dnepropetrovsk left the 30th Korp shattered, the town falling to the 46th and 8th Guards Armies of the 3rd Ukrainian Front. Dneprozherzinsk also fell. Elements of the 5th Guards Tank Army of the 2nd Ukrainian again reached Krivoi Rog but heavy rain impeded the advance.

26 October 1943

SOUTHERN SECTOR
Kleist ordered the 17th Army to evacuate the Crimea to prevent its isolation in the peninsula. However, Hitler immediately countermanded the order, instructing the 17th to stand fast

27 October 1943

SOUTHERN SECTOR
The 40th Panzer Korp launched a fierce counter-attack near Krivoi Rog. It struck the 5th Guards Tank Army in an effort to prevent the capture of the town. A week of bitter fighting ensued, which succeeded in halting the Soviet drive.

The German 6th Army began to recross the Dniepr at Nikopol. However, the 44th Korp had the farthest to go, having to cross at Kherson to prevent the Soviets from crossing near the mouth of the river. The units of the 44th Korp were severely reduced, its 73rd Infantry Divisions had just 170 combat infantry and the 111th only 200. The 6th Army also only had twenty-five operational tanks and assault guns.[8]

28 October 1943

SOUTHERN SECTOR
The 4th Korp of the 6th Army launched a counter-attack from Nikopol against the flank of 4th Ukrainian Front.

29 October 1943

CENTRAL SECTOR
General Busch was appointed commander of Army Group Centre. Kluge had been injured in a crash and was invalided until the middle of 1944. As if to give Busch his baptism of fire, the West Front renewed its attacks around Orsha and the 1st Baltic Front around Vitebsk.

30 October 1943

SOUTHERN SECTOR
Soviet tanks reached Perekop and cut the main land route out of the Crimea. Genichesk, the last railway route out of the peninsula, was also captured as 17th Army was isolated once again. At this point Hitler relieved Mackensen from command of the 1st Panzer Army, Hube being appointed in his place.

31 October 1943

ASSESSMENT
In the year since November 1942 the Ostheer had suffered 1,886,000 casualties. Some 250,000 had been lost at Stalingrad and of the remainder, 240,000 had been killed, 993,000 wounded and 106,000 captured [9], plus many more missing in action. However, only 1,260,000 men had been replaced. In the four months since Operation Citadel the Germans had lost 911,000 men. Equipment levels had also fallen, German armoured strength standing at 700 operational vehicles. There were in fact 2,300 tanks and assault guns available, but a lack of spare parts prevented many being put back into the line. The Red Army had 5,600 tanks and Su's.

THE OSTHEER
Despite its falling strength, the Ostheer had committed another three panzer, two infantry and one security divisions to the fighting but four infantry divisions left the line. The 1st, 2nd and 3rd SS Panzer-Grenadier divisions had also been redesignated panzer divisions. German strength stood at twenty-two panzer, nine panzer grenadier and 150 infantry divisions.[10]

1 November 1943

SOUTHERN SECTOR
November began with fierce attacks upon the 4th Panzer Army as the 38th Army tried to break into Kiev. In addition the 40th and 27th Armies began new attacks at Veliki Bukrin aimed at diverting German attention from the main offensive which was about to unfold to the north. In the Dniepr elbow, the 40th Panzer Korp counter-attacked around Krivoi Rog in an effort to force back the 2nd Ukrainian Front.

The 4th Ukrainian Front launched strong attacks into the Crimea, heavy fighting erupting around Perekop and Armyansk as 49th Mountain Korp tried to halt 51st Army. The 51st carried out an assault crossing of the Zivash to land behind the Perekop line. A small foothold was gained which the 49th Mountain Korp only managed to contain by swiftly transferring an infantry and flak division from the Perekop isthmus. To the east the 56th Army crossed the Kerch strait and landed around Kerch itself, becoming embroiled in heavy fighting with the 5th Korp.

2 November 1943

SOUTHERN SECTOR
The fighting around Kiev and Veliki Bukrin continued as the 1st Ukrainian Front tried to smash its way through the German defences.

3 November 1943

SOUTHERN SECTOR

At dawn the 1st Ukrainian Front unleashed a storm of artillery fire upon the 13th and 7th Korps opposite the Lyutezh bridgehead, more than 2,000 artillery pieces firing on the 4th Panzer Army. The 38th and 60th Armies led the Soviet attack while the 2nd Air Army provided support and interdiction. In all the 1st Ukrainian Front committed 671,000 men to this next phase of attacks. Not realising that the 1st Ukrainian had switched its strength to Lyutezh, the 4th Panzer was caught by surprise. The 38th Army smashed into three infantry divisions, inflicting crippling casualties. In a vain attempt to quell the Soviet tide, Hoth moved the 20th Panzer Grenadier and 8th Panzer Divisions up to counter-attack. The 7th Panzer Division also moved later and counter-attacked, all to no avail.

On the southern flank the 44th Korp successfully evacuated its forces to the west bank of the Dniepr at Kherson. The 13th Panzer was then detached from the korp and ordered up to Krivoi Rog. On the Kerch peninsula the 56th Army established a secure bridgehead.

4 November 1943

SOUTHERN SECTOR

During a day of heavy fighting and wet weather, the 4th Panzer was unable to hold back the torrent of Soviet attacks and began to crumble. Rybalko's 3rd Guards Tank Army struck the breach in the German line made by the 38th Army. Panic spread, heralding the collapse of resistance around the bridgehead, the 7th and 13th Korps disintegrating under the weight of the Soviet offensive. Soviet forces rapidly enveloped the German positions, compelling the 4th Panzer Army to begin a hurried evacuation from the city. To the south the 2nd Guards Army attacked the 44th Korp at Kherson but was unable to break through the German line.

5 November 1943

SOUTHERN SECTOR

The 38th Army entered Kiev while the 3rd Guards Tank reached Svyatschina. Fighting inside the city was fierce as the 7th Korp attempted to escape from the rapidly advancing Soviet armies. Bitter street battles raged through the night. By the end of the day the main railway station and the greater part of the city were in Soviet hands and the 88th Infantry Division had been all but destroyed.

With the battle of Kiev in progress, the 60th Army swung south-west and drove into the rear of the 4th Panzer, pushing along the edge of the

Pripet Marshes. The attack threw the 59th Korp and 13th Korp back towards Korosten and Zhitomir.

6 November 1943

SOUTHERN SECTOR
The 38th Army completed the capture of Kiev. Only 6,000 Germans had been captured during the battle as the 7th Korp had evacuated the city quickly. The 1st Ukrainian Front now fanned out to the north, west and south, threatening to rip the 4th Panzer Army apart. Manstein began to move the 48th Panzer Korp up from Veliki Bukrin to Belaya Tserkov, from where it would be poised to strike at the base of the rapidly expanding Soviet salient.

7 November 1943

NORTHERN SECTOR
The 2nd Shock Army began to redeploy from its positions along the Volkhov river to the Oranienbaum pocket west of Leningrad. This move was in preparation for the planned attack around Leningrad in January 1944 which aimed to drive the German 18th Army away from the city for the last time.

SOUTHERN SECTOR
Fastov fell to the 1st Tank Army.

8 November 1943

CENTRAL SECTOR
The 3rd and 4th Shock Armies launched new attacks against the 3rd Panzer Army, gaining more ground around Nevel as the junction of the 9th and 53rd Korps was put under intense pressure.

SOUTHERN SECTOR
The 4th Panzer Army was reinforced with the 24th Panzer Korp and 48th Panzer Korp. Limited counter-attacks were launched near Fastov. Vatutin was about to be caught in the same trap Manstein had sprung on him in the spring of 1943 around Kharkov when he neglected to note the build-up of German armour on his exposed flank.

9 November 1943

SOUTHERN SECTOR
The 13th and 7th Korps broke as the 3rd Guards Tank Army pushed towards Zhitomir.

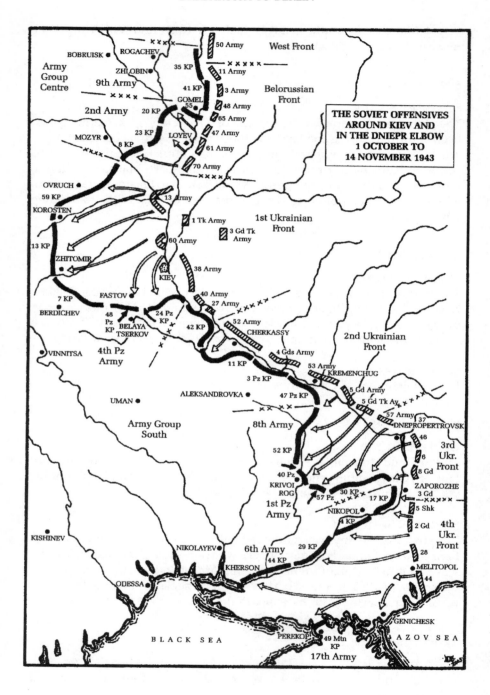

THE SOVIET OFFENSIVES
AROUND KIEV AND
IN THE DNIEPR ELBOW
1 OCTOBER TO
14 NOVEMBER 1943

10 November 1943

CENTRAL SECTOR
The Belorussian Front opened a new attack to the south of Loyev, pushing north-westward into the flank of Army Group Centre.

11 November 1943

SOUTHERN SECTOR
Radomyshl fell as Soviet troops crossed the Teterev river off the march. To the south the 56th Army captured Kerch.

12 November 1943

SOUTHERN SECTOR
Zhitomir and Korostychev fell to the 1st Ukrainian Front. Manstein was poised to launch his counter-attack. As the Soviets pushed west they increased the exposure on their left wing. Manstein planned to retake the territory that had been lost on the west bank and recapture Kiev. To the south-east the 52nd Army forced a crossing of the Dniepr at Cherkassy, pushing back the 11th Korp of the 8th Army.

13 November 1943

SOUTHERN SECTOR
The Kiev offensive had in ten days cost the 1st Ukrainian Front 6,500 killed and 24,000 wounded.[11]

14 November 1943

CENTRAL SECTOR
Rechitsa fell to the Belorussian Front.

SOUTHERN SECTOR
Limited German counter-attacks at Fastov continued as a prelude to the main attack due on the 15th. As the 4th Panzer Army completed its preparations, the 2nd Ukrainian Front prepared to launch a new offensive. The aim of this attack was to drive towards Kirovograd and Krivoi Rog, destroying the German 8th and 1st Panzer Armies.

Soviet attacks in the Crimea continued but were becoming bogged down. The German 17th Army consolidated its positions as its 5th Korp deployed to defend the Kerch peninsula, and the 49th Mountain Korp moved to the Zivash coast and Perekop to defend against attacks from the mainland. The 44th Korp had already been handed over to the 6th Army fighting along the lower Dniepr.

15 November 1943

SOUTHERN SECTOR
With the ground sodden from heavy rain, the 4th Panzer Army counter-attacked west of Kiev. Supported by limited artillery fire, the Germans smashed through the base of the deepening Kiev salient, pushing towards Zhitomir to isolate the vanguard of the armies pressing west. Heavy fighting also raged around Krivoi Rog as the 2nd Ukrainian Front pressed home its attacks against the 52nd Korp of the 1st Panzer Army. The Germans continued to counter-attack locally with the 40th and 57th Panzer Korps.

16 November 1943

SOUTHERN SECTOR
Korosten fell to the 60th Army.

17 November 1943

CENTRAL SECTOR
The Belorussian Front's 48th and 11th Armies had almost encircled Gomel, the defending 9th Army fighting vigorously despite being heavily outnumbered.

SOUTHERN SECTOR
The 48th Panzer Korp recaptured Zhitomir, smashing the Soviet lines of communication west of Kiev and endangering those forces still pushing west. German units also pushed towards Malin and Korosten, threatening the 60th Army. Despite the danger, the 13th Army captured Ovruch as it continued to advance on the northern wing of the 1st Ukrainian Front.

18 November 1943

SOUTHERN SECTOR
The 1st Ukrainian Front began to pull back from the Zhitomir area. Fighting along this line over the next few days continued as the Germans redeployed to strike again and keep Vatutin off balance. So far the fighting had cost the Soviets 3,000 killed, 150 tanks destroyed and more than 320 artillery pieces and anti-tank guns lost.

22 November 1943

CENTRAL SECTOR
The Belorussian Front began another attack aimed at the German 9th Army around Propaisk. Fighting was bitter as the Soviets attempted to break free of the Pripet Marshes and gain a foothold to the north.

23 November 1943

CENTRAL SECTOR
The Belorussian Front forced apart the 2nd and 9th Armies, compelling the Germans to pull back.

25 November 1943

CENTRAL SECTOR
Propaisk fell as the Belorussian Front crossed the Berezina south of Zhlobin. The West Front unleashed a new attack against the 4th Army. Such constant fighting had a severe impact upon the German forces, draining the strength of their thinly stretched divisions.

SOUTHERN SECTOR
The German counter-attack before Kiev ground to a halt. Limited advances were made towards Korosten but Kiev remained in Soviet hands.

26 November 1943

CENTRAL SECTOR
The 48th and 11th Armies forced the 55th Korp of the 9th Army out of Gomel. The attack then continued in the direction of Zhlobin but progress was slow.

29 November 1943

SOVIET COMMAND
The Stavka ordered Vatutin to place the 1st Ukrainian Front on the defensive. To support the hard hit forces in the Berdichev and Korosten areas the 1st Guards Army began to move into the line between the 38th and 60th Armies.

30 November 1943

SOUTHERN SECTOR

Believing the German counter-attack to have ended for the duration of the autumn muddy period, the 1st Ukrainian was taken by surprise when the 48th Panzer Korp unleashed another attack in the Zhitomir area. The 59th Korp also attacked at Korosten and after a bitter battle recaptured the town from the 60th Army.

THE OSTHEER

During November the Germans committed three panzer divisions, two SS panzer grenadier divisions, two infantry divisions and one security division to the front line. One panzer, one mountain and two infantry divisions left or were destroyed, leaving the Ostheer with twenty-four panzer, ten panzer grenadier and 155 infantry divisions.[12]

THE OPPOSING FORCES

From Norway to the Crimea, the Germans had 2,850,000 soldiers. Dietl's 20th Army in Norway had 176,000 men, approximately 40,000 of which were combat infantry, leaving the main line armies with around 2,650,000. Actual combat infantry in the line were becoming a rare breed as losses mounted and replacements became increasingly scarce.

Army Group North, with forty-four infantry divisions, had a battle strength of only 140,000 combat infantry, 100 operational panzers and assault guns and 2,400 artillery pieces. It faced the Leningrad, Volkhov and North-West Fronts with 355,000 combat troops in their rifle divisions, 650 tanks and Su's and 3,700 artillery pieces.

Army Group Centre had forty-six infantry divisions but disposed of only 147,000 combat infantry, 216 panzers and assault guns and 2,600 artillery pieces. Facing it were the Belorussian, West and 1st and 2nd Baltic Fronts with 650,000 combat soldiers, 3,000 tanks and Su's and 6,720 artillery pieces.

Army Group South, the most heavily committed of all the German army groups, deployed forty-four infantry divisions with 140,000 combat infantry, 270 panzers and assault guns and 2,200 artillery pieces while Army Group A had seventeen infantry divisions with 54,000 combat soldiers, 100 tanks and assault guns and 800 artillery pieces. Attacking these armies were the 1st, 2nd, 3rd and 4th Ukrainian Fronts and the North Caucasus Front. Combined, the rifle formations of these fronts totalled 899,000 combat infantry (616,000 facing Army Group South), 4,250 tanks and Su's and 9,300 artillery pieces. It was apparent from these figures that the Ostheer was massively outnumbered.[13] The average German infantry division at the front had a combat strength of just under 3,200 infantry.

2 December 1943

SOUTHERN SECTOR
The 5th Guards Tank Army advanced to within six miles of Znamenka but became embroiled in fierce fighting with the 11th Korp on the right wing of the German 8th Army.

3 December 1943

CENTRAL SECTOR
The Belorussian Front captured Dovsk.

6 December 1943

SOUTHERN SECTOR
The 48th Panzer Korp renewed its attack west of Kiev with the aim of destroying what the 4th Panzer Army believed was a small Soviet grouping at Meleni. Both the 13th and 59th Korps were involved in heavy fighting on either flank, the 13th on the right and 59th on the left.

7 December 1943

SOUTHERN SECTOR
As the 48th Panzer Korp advanced it hit the headquarters of the 60th Army, throwing it into disarray and inflicting heavy casualties.

8 December 1943

SOUTHERN SECTOR
Lead elements of the 48th Panzer reached the Teterev river, having inflicted considerable losses upon the 60th and 13th Armies of the 1st Ukrainian Front. The advance continued in the direction of Malin but Soviet resistance slowed its pace.

Znamenka was isolated by the 5th Guards Tank Army but the 40th Panzer Korp launched a fierce counter-attack in an effort to relieve the town.

9 December 1943

SOUTHERN SECTOR
With the 48th Panzer bogged down south of the Pripet Marshes, the 4th Panzer Army redeployed, the 13th Korp taking over the recently won positions of the 48th.

10 December 1943

SOUTHERN SECTOR
Fierce fighting continued at Znamenka where the 5th Guards Tank Army, now supported by the 5th Guards Army, finally overcame German resistance. Elements of the 4th Guards Army also linked up with the 52nd Army at Cherkassy, the latter having been fighting in isolation since crossing the Dniepr at the end of November.

14 December 1943

NORTHERN SECTOR
The 1st Baltic Front attacked the 3rd Panzer Army around Nevel again. Gains were limited due to considerable German resistance, the 9th Korp fighting hard to prevent any further loss of territory.

SOUTHERN SECTOR
Cherkassy fell to Koroteyev's 52nd Army

16 December 1943

SOUTHERN SECTOR
The 48th Panzer Korp had redeployed and again attacked the 1st Ukrainian Front, aided by the 59th Korp. The main attack hit Meleni, the Germans virtually isolating what they believed was a single Soviet corp but what was later revealed to be a considerably superior concentration. The fighting raged through the next week, the Germans struggling to overcome the numerically superior defending units.

20 December 1943

SOUTHERN SECTOR
The lengthy battles in the Ukraine since the end of September had cost the Soviet armies dear. Koniev's 2nd Ukraine Front had lost 77,400 killed and missing and 226,000 wounded, the 3rd Ukraine 34,000 and 132,000 respectively, and the 4th Ukraine 61,000 killed and 222,000 wounded.[14]

21 December 1943

CENTRAL SECTOR
The Belorussian Front renewed its attacks at Zhlobin, the 48th and 65th Armies inflicting heavy losses upon the hard-pressed 55th Korp and 41st Panzer Korp.

SOUTHERN SECTOR

The 48th Panzer Korp was involved in further heavy fighting at Meleni, it becoming clear to the German commanders that they were facing a major Soviet force. From this it was deduced that the next phase of the Soviet offensive could not be far off.

The German 6th Army lost its hold on the Kherson bridgehead as the 2nd Guards Army of the 4th Ukrainian Front closed up to the mouth of the Dniepr.

23 December 1943

SOUTHERN SECTOR

With the fighting at Meleni increasingly intense, the 48th Panzer called off its attack. The unexpected German assault had succeeded in severely mauling four Soviet corps that had been assembled for the next phase of the offensive in the Ukraine, disrupting the Soviet plans slightly.

Even so, the 1st Ukrainian Front was poised to attack the northern wing of Army Group South once again, the Stavka aiming to turn the left flank of the German southern wing and encircling what was left of it before the Dniestr river. The plan called for the 1st and 2nd Ukrainian Fronts to drive through the 4th Panzer and 8th Armies and reach Mogilev-Podolsky and Pervomaisk while the 3rd and 4th Ukrainian Fronts attacked on the lower Dniepr, between Nikopol and Krivoi Rog.

For the offensive the Stavka had assembled a force of 2,365,000 men. The 1st Ukrainian had 924,000 men, the 2nd 594,000, the 3rd 337,000 and the 4th 550,000. All four fronts combined included more than 2,000 tanks and Su's, 29,000 artillery pieces and 2,360 aircraft in support. Of this number, virtually the entire tank strength was operational and half the infantry were in the combat line. To face this massive force Manstein's Army Group South had forty-three infantry, fifteen panzer and seven panzer grenadier divisions, which when combined with Kleist's Army Group A totalled 1,760,000 men. To support the infantry the army groups had 2,200 panzers and assault guns, barely a third of which were fit for action, and 16,000 artillery pieces. Army Groups South and A had 1,400 aircraft on hand to provide aerial support but again many were out of action due to repairs and lack of fuel. In the Crimea and along the southern bend of the Dniepr were the 17th and 6th Armies of Army Group A. The weak Rumanian 3rd Army was also in the Crimea. Army Group A had eight German infantry divisions, ten Rumanian divisions and one field training division.

The fighting in the autumn of 1943 had proved to be a long string of setbacks for the Ostheer. Forced back across the Dniepr and from Kiev, the German southern wing had been pushed back upon itself. Hitler's insistence that every yard of territory be retained had proved a weight around the German commanders' necks. For the Soviet generals it had been a time to master their art, tank armies and rifle forces learning to operate in conjunction with their resurgent air forces. The renewed Soviet offensive in the Ukraine, and offensives of 1944, would prove the Soviet mastery of the concept of battles of annihilation.

NOTES

1 Kirosheev, *Soviet Casualties and Combat Losses in the Twentieth Century*, Table 75
2 Kirosheev, *Soviet Casualties and Combat Losses in the Twentieth Century*, Table 75
3 Kirosheev, *Soviet Casualties and Combat Losses in the Twentieth Century*, Table 75
4 Ellis, *The World War II Databook*, p176
5 Ellis, *Brute Force*, p114
6 Kirosheev, *Soviet Casualties and Combat Losses in the Twentieth Century*, Table 75
7 Kirosheev, *Soviet Casualties and Combat Losses in the Twentieth Century*, Table 75
8 Carell, *Scorched Earth*, p381
9 Seaton, *The Russo–German War*, p397
10 Ellis, *The World War II Databook*, p176
11 Kirosheev, *Soviet Casualties and Combat Losses in the Twentieth Century*, Table 75
12 Ellis, *The World War II Databook*, p176
13 Ellis, *Brute Force*, Table 29. Strengths are for infantry units only. Added to these must be the armoured forces, which for the Ostheer were in as equally a poor state as the infantry.
14 Kirosheev, *Soviet Casualties and Combat Losses in the Twentieth Century*, Table 75

CHAPTER V
The War of Liberation

The hard fought battles along the line of the Dniepr had established the Red Army in the Western Ukraine, a positioned confirmed by the capture of Kiev. There now began a series of operations on the southern wing that would bend the German front back to the Rumanian border and lay the foundations for the defeat of Army Group Centre in the summer of 1944.

24 December 1943

SOUTHERN SECTOR

The Ukraine erupted into fire once again as the 1st Ukrainian Front began its offensive. Massive artillery bombardment, together with overwhelming aerial support, the likes of which the Germans had not seen before, pulverised the German forward positions. The 1st Guards and 18th Armies attacked the 13th Korp before Zhitomir while the 13th and 60th Armies attacked the 59th Korp to the north and the 38th, 40th and 27th Armies hit the 7th and 24th Panzer Korps to the south. Under massive pressure the German front collapsed, being engulfed in a sea of fire. With resistance broken the 3rd Guards Tank and 1st Tank Armies rushed through the advancing infantry of the 18th and 38th Armies to plunge into the German rear. The 3rd Guards Tank pushed towards Zhitomir while the 1st Tank advanced in the direction of Vinnitsa. With his front line in tatters, Manstein was forced to rush the 48th Panzer Korp into action.

25 December 1943

SOUTHERN SECTOR

The Soviets pounded the German forces with additional artillery fire, grinding down any strong points that continued to resist. To add to the mayhem behind the German lines, the onset of rain prevented the front line units from disengaging to pull back. As the pace of the attack increased, the 40th Army followed in the wake of the 38th Army and 1st Tank Army, pushing along the road to Vinnitsa.

26 December 1943

SOUTHERN SECTOR

Korostychev fell to the 3rd Guards Tank Army while the 60th Army closed upon Korosten. A counter-attack by the 48th Panzer Korp against the 3rd Guards Tank was brushed aside.

27 December 1943

SOUTHERN SECTOR

After heavy fighting elements of the 48th Panzer Korp partially stabilised the Zhitomir sector. Hoth, using the 48th as his fire-fighting unit, directed the korp to the Berdichev sector, but the constant fighting inflicted a terrible price on the combat units, the korp being down to just 150 tanks.

28 December 1943

SOUTHERN SECTOR

The 48th Panzer Korp rushed to counter-attack at Kazatin to halt the 1st Tank Army. Progress was limited as the exhausted unit was halted in its tracks. With his northern wing broken, Manstein began to make an unauthorised movement of his armies. Moving the 1st Panzer Army from the Dniepr bend to the right of the 4th Panzer Army would shorten the sector held by the 4th Panzer Army and also provide stability to the south. However, to move an army headquarters and a number of its units at the height of an enemy offensive was risky venture and it was a credit to the Ostheer and Manstein's exceptional leadership that the manoeuvre was carried out successfully. During the move, the 1st Panzer handed over control of its sectors to the 6th and 8th Armies, the movement beginning on 1 January. Upon its arrival on the northern flank of the army group, the 1st Panzer was to assume control of the 24th Panzer Korp and 7th Korp south-east of Berdichev while the 3rd Panzer Korp, en route, would assemble on the left wing at the junction with the 4th Panzer Army. The 4th Panzer was also to receive the 46th Panzer Korp as reinforcement.

29 December 1943

SOUTHERN SECTOR

The 48th Panzer Korp pulled back from the Berdichev sector to shorten its line. Korosten fell to the 60th Army and Skvira to the 40th Army. Zhitomir was isolated by the 3rd Guards Tank Army. Elements of the 13th Korp, trapped in the town, tried to break out but encountered strong Soviet forces and were held back.

30 December 1943

SOUTHERN SECTOR
The 48th Panzer Korp lost Kazatin to the 1st Tank Army. A drop in the temperature caused the ground to freeze which returned some mobility to the Germans. While this was an advantage it also allowed the Red Army to press ever deeper into the German rear.

31 December 1943

CENTRAL SECTOR
The 9th Korp of the 3rd Panzer Army was again under attack near Nevel while the West Front pressed the 6th Korp back between Orsha and Vitebsk, cutting the road between the towns.

SOUTHERN SECTOR
The 18th Army and 3rd Guards Tank Army recaptured Zhitomir. The 24th Panzer and 7th Korps were reeling back along the road to Vinnitsa, split from the 4th Panzer by a fifty-mile hole in the line. Remnants of the 13th Korp fought in isolation around Zhitomir while fifty miles to the north the 59th Korp was fighting around Korosten and Olevsk. The battered 48th Panzer Korp, having suffered heavy losses as it rushed from one threatened sector to another, was retreating in the Berdichev–Kazatin area.

THE RED ARMY
At the end of 1943 the Red Army had grown to become the most powerful field army in the world. Its strength had risen to 5,570,000 soldiers in the first echelon, with a further 419,000 in reserve. The armies at the front were equipped with 5,600 tanks and Su's and 90,000 artillery pieces, while the air armies had more than 8,800 aircraft at their disposal together with 480,000 personnel. The Soviet Navy remained a minor arm with just 260,000 men, many of who served on land with the marine brigades.[1]

However, there were signs that the supposed bottomless supply of men was nearing its end. Already there were 15- and 16-year-old boys serving with the combat units and many 'liberated' citizens in the Ukraine were pressed into service. Levels of equipment rose significantly though, the Red Army being better equipped than ever before. It was now a truly modern, mobile army. Mechanisation of the infantry was due largely to the Lend Lease trucks supplied by the Western Allies, and the increased mobility of the ordinary rifle divisions would give the offensives of 1944 and '45 a rapidity not seen before in the east.

141

Perhaps the most important development though was the Stavka's ability to co-ordinate its forces effectively. No longer did tanks operate as infantry support weapons, the roles having been reversed. Attacks were now preceded by massed artillery fire and infantry attacks, which broke through the main German lines of resistance. Once this had been achieved the still intact armoured forces were introduced into the battle to thrust into the German rear, cutting communications and sowing confusion behind the enemy lines. It had been a long and hard lesson but the Stavka had learnt it well. Furthermore, the air force was now acting in support of the ground forces, gaining superiority over the battlefield. Against such well co-ordinated all-arms attacks the Germans, with only limited reserves if any at all, could not hope to hold back the tide of the Russian forces.

THE OSTHEER

The Ostheer had suffered crippling losses during 1943 and, despite receiving new equipment, lacked the strength of numbers to compete with the Red Army. The new generation of Tiger and Panther tanks were greatly superior to the Russian models currently in the field but lack of numbers was a real problem. Equipment losses generally had been high and while the Red Army became increasingly mechanised the Germans had to rely more upon horses for their transport needs. Once the Allied Combined Bomber Offensive really began to bite in 1944, the shortage of equipment was made far worse by a shortage of fuel. Manpower though was still the biggest problem faced by the German army, the shortfall of combat infantry growing larger every month as the casualties increased.

During December the German armies lost one SS motorised division and thirteen infantry divisions from their order of battle while receiving one parachute and one infantry divisions in return. Germany's allies had also been hit particularly badly during the course of the year, the Italians and Hungarians having their armies in the east destroyed during the first quarter. The Rumanians, though still present, had far fewer men in the field following the disaster at Stalingrad and could not be relied upon to hold the line when faced by Russian troops. Since June 1941 Germany had lost nearly 3,000,000 men in the east. At the end of 1943 the Ostheer had twenty-four panzer, nine panzer grenadier and 140 infantry divisions in the line,[2] while Rumania had nine divisions, Hungary nine, Slovakia one, Spain one and the Finns sixteen divisions.[3]

PRODUCTION

Both sides continued to produce large amounts of equipment, German production figures rising dramatically during the latter part of 1943 as Armaments Minister Speer's improvements to the industrial might of the Reich began to have an impact. Germany had manufactured 12,063 panzers and assault guns, 46,100 artillery pieces, 74,181 transport vehicles and 25,527 aircraft during 1943, while the Soviets manufactured 24,089 tanks and Su's, 130,000 artillery pieces, 38,845 aircraft and produced or received through Lend Lease 45,000 transport vehicles. The Germans though were supplying increasing numbers of weapons and men to the western regions of the Reich, the fighting in Italy and the build up in France tying down more and more divisions.[4]

1 January 1944

SOVIET COMMAND
The Stavka created a new 6th Tank Army.

3 January 1944

SOUTHERN SECTOR
Olevsk fell to 13th Army and Novgorod Volnysky to 60th as the 59th Korp was forced back. The 3rd Guards Tank Army was only forty miles north of Vinnitsa and the 1st Tank a similar distance north-west of Uman, both of these armies having swung to the south following their initial westward advance. However, the 3rd Panzer Korp was beginning to deploy at Uman in order to block the path of the Russian advance behind the 8th Army.

The 3rd Ukrainian Front launched a strong attack around Kirovograd with its 53rd, 5th Guards and 7th Guards Armies, pinning down the 40th Panzer and 52nd Korps.

4 January 1944

SOUTHERN SECTOR
After a four-day battle the 27th Army took Belaya Tserkov. A rapid advance by the 60th Army pushed the 59th Korp back upon Rovno.

5 January 1944

SOUTHERN SECTOR
Berdichev fell to the 3rd Guards Tank Army and 18th Army as the advance upon Vinnitsa continued.

Koniev's 2nd Ukrainian Front attacked north of the Kirovograd sector, striking the 47th Panzer Korp of 8th Army. The main attack was made by the 53rd Army north of the city, supported by the 4th Guards and 52nd Armies to its right. The attack against the southern wing of the 8th Army was conducted by the 5th and 7th Guards Armies. Koniev held the 5th Guards Tank Army in reserve to exploit any breakthrough.

Wohler's 8th Army comprised Ott's 52nd Korp before Krivoi Rog (one panzer and one parachute and two infantry divisions), Vormann's 47th Panzer Korp north of Kirovograd (three panzer, one panzer grenadier and four infantry divisions) and the 11th Korp on the northern wing near the Dniepr (one panzer and four infantry divisions).

Manstein evacuated his headquarters to Proskurov.

6 January 1944

SOUTHERN SECTOR
The 60th Army crossed the old Russo–Polish border, Rokitno falling.

7 January 1944

SOUTHERN SECTOR
The 5th Guards Tank Army was introduced through the 52nd Army, breaking the 47th Panzer Korp defences around Kirovograd as it fought its way into the town.

8 January 1944

SOUTHERN SECTOR
After heavy fighting Kirovograd fell to the 5th Guards Tank Army.

9 January 1944

SOUTHERN SECTOR
The headquarters of the 47th Panzer Korp was attacked, losing many men in the fighting and throwing the korp into confusion. Aleksandrovka fell to the 4th Guards Army.

10 January 1944

CENTRAL SECTOR
The 61st and 70th Armies of the Belorussian Front launched a limited attack around Mozyr striking the centre of the 2nd Army.

SOUTHERN SECTOR
The 3rd Ukrainian Front began its new offensive, striking the German 6th Army in the Dniepr elbow. The 37th and 46th Armies attacked towards Apostolovo, hitting the 57th Panzer Korp hard.

11 January 1944

SOUTHERN SECTOR
Tolbukhin's 4th Ukrainian Front joined the offensive in the Dniepr elbow, attacking the 4th and 17th Korps with its 3rd Guards and 5th Shock Armies as it tried to link up with the 3rd Ukrainian Front.

12 January 1944

NORTHERN SECTOR
The 1st Baltic Front attacked the 2nd Korp of the 16th Army with the 3rd Shock Army and 10th Guards Army. Heavy fighting erupted around Novosokolinikov.

SOUTHERN SECTOR
Sarny fell to the 13th Army as it reached the Styr and Goryn rivers. The 60th Army closed up to Shepetovka but German resistance was beginning to stiffen, slowing the pace of the attacks.

Bitter fighting raged at Nikopol as the 3rd Guards Army tried to break open the German positions and encircle the left flank of the 6th Army between itself and the 3rd Ukrainian Front. The 6th Army of the 3rd Ukrainian was attacking the 30th Korp behind Nikopol, trying to trap Fretter Pico between itself and the 3rd Guards.

13 January 1944

NORTHERN SECTOR
With the fighting in the Ukraine having raged unabated since the Battle of Kursk in the middle of 1943, the Soviets prepared to turn their attention north. Around Leningrad the Leningrad, Volkhov and 2nd Baltic Fronts had trained hard during 1942 and 1943 to break the 18th Army's grip on Leningrad.

Still in much the same positions as in the winter of 1941, the Stavka aimed to break the siege for good and destroy the German 18th Army before pushing south and west to reconquer the Baltic States. Govorov's Leningrad Front would begin the offensive from the Oranienbaum pocket and the perimeter of Leningrad, encircling the left wing of the German siege positions against the Gulf of Finland. Meretskov's Volkhov Front was to crush the right flank of the 18th Army against the Volkhov while Popov's 2nd Baltic Front pinned down the 16th Army south of Lake Ilmen to prevent the transfer of forces to Leningrad. The Leningrad and Volkhov Fronts had assembled 417,000 and 260,000 men respectively, with 1,200 tanks and Su's, 14,300 artillery pieces and nearly 720 aircraft in support.[5]

Against this formidable array Kuchler's Army Group North deployed forty infantry divisions, one panzer grenadier and two panzer divisions, split between the 18th Army and 16th Army. The 18th Army fielded the 3rd SS Panzer Korp at Oranienbaum, 54th Korp between Oranienbaum and Leningrad, 26th and 28th Korps on the Leningrad perimeter and the 1st Korp along the Volkhov, a total of only 50,000 combat infantry from a complement of over 200,000 men. It was supported by 200 panzers and assault guns, around a third of which were serviceable. South of Lake Ilmen the 16th Army had its 10th, 38th and 2nd Korps strung out on a long and vulnerable line to the junction with the 3rd Panzer Army near Pustoshka.

14 January 1944

NORTHERN SECTOR
The Soviet offensive began, the customary artillery barrage softening the German defences before the main attack was launched. The attack by the 2nd Shock Army from the Oranienbaum bridgehead took the Germans entirely by surprise, ripping Steiner's 3rd SS Panzer Korp apart. The two Luftwaffe divisions allocated the korp took the full force of the blow and collapsed almost immediately.

South of Leningrad the guns of the 42nd and 67th Armies pounded the well dug in German forces in preparation for their attack on the 15th.

To the south, the 2nd Baltic Front's 22nd Army gained ground north of Novosokolnikov.

15 January 1944

NORTHERN SECTOR
Maslennikov's 42nd Army and the 67th Army attacked. Both armies met fierce resistance from the 54th and 26th Korps south of Leningrad, while the 8th Army hit the 28th Korp as it launched diversionary attacks towards Mga. The 54th Army also attacked towards Lyuban, hitting the 1st Korp, while the 59th Army, on the left flank of the Volkhov Front, began to cross the frozen surface of Lake Ilmen to assault the German forces in Novgorod.

16 January 1944

NORTHERN SECTOR
The 42nd and 67th Armies were bogged down in heavy fighting in the German trenches south of Leningrad.

SOUTHERN SECTOR
The 3rd and 4th Ukrainian Fronts called off their attacks against Hollidt's

6th Army. The Soviets had suffered extremely heavy casualties because the 6th Army had constructed a string of strong defences in the Dniepr Elbow. The Stavka decided instead to reinforce and regrouped both fronts prior to the next phase of the attack.

17 January 1944

Northern Sector
The German forces at Leningrad began to crack under the weight of the Russian attacks. The dam at Krasnoye Selo was blown to flood the area and hold up the Russians. So far the 42nd Army had pushed six miles into the positions of the 54th and 26th Korps and was about to turn towards Ropsha to link up with the 2nd Shock Army. However, the German defences held up the advance, enabling Kuchler to extricate his battered divisions despite Hitler's order to fight for every yard. Kuchler expected the Russians to attempt an encirclement operation at Uritsk and Ropsha.

In an effort to slow down the 8th Army at Mga, the 18th Army threw its last reserve of three infantry divisions into a counter-attack.

Southern Sector
The 60th Army took Slavuta.

19 January 1944

Northern Sector
The 2nd Shock and 42nd Armies linked up at Ropsha. A small part of the 54th Korp was encircled at Peterhof and quickly destroyed. However, large amounts of the German siege artillery were captured as Ropsha and Strelna fell, the siege of Leningrad finally being broken for good. The 42nd Army also took Krasnoye Selo and the heights of Voronya Gora. The 1st Korp lost a division in Novgorod as the advancing 59th Army encircled the town.

20 January 1944

Northern Sector
Novgorod fell to the 59th as the Germans broke out. The 2nd Baltic Front launched its diversionary attack against the 16th Army.

21 January 1944

Northern Sector
Mga fell to the 8th Army. Tosno, another major site for the German siege artillery, was threatened but the 18th Army was powerless to halt the

Soviet advance. Kuchler had his hands tied by Hitler's rigid insistence on a static defence.

22 January 1944

NORTHERN SECTOR
Despite a desperate appeal to Hitler, Kuchler was unable to gain authorisation for a withdrawal.

24 January 1944

NORTHERN SECTOR
Pushkin and Pashovsk fell to the 42nd Army while the railway line to Narva was severed by the 2nd Shock Army.

SOUTHERN SECTOR
The Soviets began yet another offensive, this time aimed at encircling the German forces in the Cherkassy salient. The 42nd Korp still held a small section of the west bank of the Dniepr despite the retreat of the 1st and 4th Panzer Armies and was therefore in a very vulnerable position. However, Hitler had insisted that the Dniepr line be held at all costs.

The 42nd Korp was attacked by the 27th Army (1st Ukrainian Front), while the 2nd Ukrainian Front threw its 4th Guards, 52nd and 53rd Armies against the 11th Korp. Despite fierce resistance the German line began to crack near Shpola.

25 January 1944

SOUTHERN SECTOR
The 2nd Ukrainian Front committed its 5th Guards Tank Army to the Cherkassy battle, advancing quickly towards Shpola and into the rear of the 42nd and 11th Korps.

26 January 1944

NORTHERN SECTOR
The 18th Army was pressed back upon Tosno and Lyuban by the 8th and 54th Armies.

SOUTHERN SECTOR
The 27th, 40th and 6th Tank Armies pushed in the direction of Zvenigorodka, striving to link up with the 5th Guards Tank Army as it advanced upon Shpola. The 6th Tank Army had been committed from reserve to strengthen the northern prong of the pincer.

27 January 1944

NORTHERN SECTOR

Govorov announced that the siege of Leningrad was completely lifted, Tosno and Valosovo falling to the 8th Army. The 67th, 8th and 54th Armies threatened to isolate the 28th Korp and elements of the 1st Korp.

SOUTHERN SECTOR

The 60th Army launched strong attacks around Rovno but the going was difficult.

Shpola fell to the 5th Guards Tank Army while the 6th Tank Army captured Lysyanka, the spearheads of the 1st and 2nd Ukrainian Fronts drawing closer together.

28 January 1944

NORTHERN SECTOR

As his army group fell apart, Kuchler issued orders calling for the withdrawal of the 18th Army to the line of the Luga river to prevent its annihilation. Lyuban fell to the 54th Army.

SOUTHERN SECTOR

The 1st and 2nd Ukrainian Fronts linked up near Zvenigorodka, the town falling to the 6th Tank Army after a brief battle. Leib's 42nd and Stemmerman's 11th Korps were isolated. The Stavka immediately called for the destruction of the pocket, the 2nd Ukrainian Front being made responsible for this operation with the 27th, 52nd and 4th Guards Armies. Inside the pocket, centred on Korsun-Shevchenhovsky, some 56,000 men of the 57th, 389th, 72nd and 88th Infantry Divisions, 5th SS Panzer-Grenadier Division Wiking and SS Brigade Wallonie prepared to break out to the west. General Stemmerman, commanding 11th Korp, took control of the combined force. Outside the cauldron, Manstein began preparations for a relief attack, the 3rd Panzer Korp being released from the Uman sector and the 47th Panzer from Kirovograd. The counter-attack would begin as soon as these forces arrived.

29 January 1944

NORTHERN SECTOR

Hitler forced Kuchler to retire from command of Army Group North following his unauthorised withdrawal order of 28 January. General Model, commanding the 9th Army, was appointed to command Army Group North and was allocated two panzer divisions to halt the Soviet offensive. In fact, Model would carry out the withdrawal already ordered by Kuchler. Chudovo fell to the 54th Army and Novosokolniki to elements of the 1st Baltic Front.

SOUTHERN SECTOR

The 13th and 60th Armies crossed the Styr river, forcing back the thinly stretched 59th and 13th Korps.

Manstein tried to pull together his relief force as Group Stemmerman redeployed inside the pocket. Already the Soviets had thrown up strong inner and outer defence rings, ready for any break out or relief attempt. Renewed attacks by the 2nd Ukrainian Front hit Wohler's 8th Army, forcing the 47th Panzer Korp out of Smela.

30 January 1944

NORTHERN SECTOR

Leading elements of the 42nd and 2nd Shock Armies of the Leningrad Front reached the Luga river, behind which the Germans planned to make a stand. The mechanisation of the Soviet forces had enabled them to outpace the 18th Army. The fighting since 14 January had cost the German 18th Army 20,000 casualties.

SOUTHERN SECTOR

The 3rd and 4th Ukrainian Fronts renewed their attacks against Hollidt's 6th Army, this time the main assault being launched by the 46th and 8th Guards Armies of the 3rd Ukrainian Front from the Krivoi Rog area, the 37th and 6th Armies supporting to right and left. To the south the 5th Shock Army, 3rd Guards and 28th Armies of the 4th Ukrainian attacked the Nikopol bridgehead. In all the Soviets committed 257,000 combat infantry to the attack, supported by 1,400 tanks.

Hollidt, with 47,000 combat infantry and 250 tanks between the 4th and 17th Korps in the bridgehead, the 29th Korp around Berislav and the 30th Korp north of Nikopol, with the 57th Panzer Korp in mobile reserve, was unable to hold off these new Soviet attacks. Fretter Pico's 30th Korp was struck hard by the 8th Guards and 46th Armies and came close to collapse.[6]

31 January 1944

NORTHERN SECTOR

The fighting in the Leningrad sector had carried the 2nd Shock Army and 42nd Army to the Luga river north and south of Kingisepp.

SOUTHERN SECTOR

Heavy fighting raged east of Krivoi Rog and around Nikopol as the

1. German infantry attacking during Operation Citadel, July 1943.
(Source: Suddeutscher Verlag)

2. Soviet riflemen push into the ruins of Kiev, November 1943. (Source: Novosti)

3. Panzer IV's and infantry equipped for another winter, late 1943. (Source: Bundesarchiv)

4. A column of Panzer IIIs on the move, summer 1943. (Source: Bundesarchiv)

5. The aftermath of Kursk. Wrecked German equipment litters the battlefield. (Source: Novosti)

6. The battle of Kursk; Soviet forces charge forwards. (Source: Novosti)

7. After a shaky start at Kursk, the Panther proved to be one of the most effective tanks of World War II. (Source: Minin Verlag)

8. Heavily armed German troops dig in, their weapons close at hand. (Source: R Tomasi)

9. Captured German soldiers being led out of Berlin as Soviet tanks drive deeper into the city. (Source: Planeta)

10. The powerful King Tiger tank in Budapest. Note the Zimmerit anti-magnetic mine paste covering the hull and turret to protect against infantry attack. (Source: TRH Pictures)

11. German troops, reduced to using bicycles for mobility, retreat past an armoured column. (Source: TRH Pictures)

12. Soviet assault troops rush past a burning German tank.

13. German civilians flee the advancing Soviets. (Source: Robert Hunt Library)

14. German soldier with panzerfaust. A successful hit has already been scored on an advancing Soviet tank. (Source: Peter Newark Military Pictures)

15. A Panzer V Panther carrying infantry into action, late 1944.
(Source: Robert Hunt Library)

16. German troops preparing to renew their attack in Kharkov, spring 1943. (Source: Orbis Publishing Group)

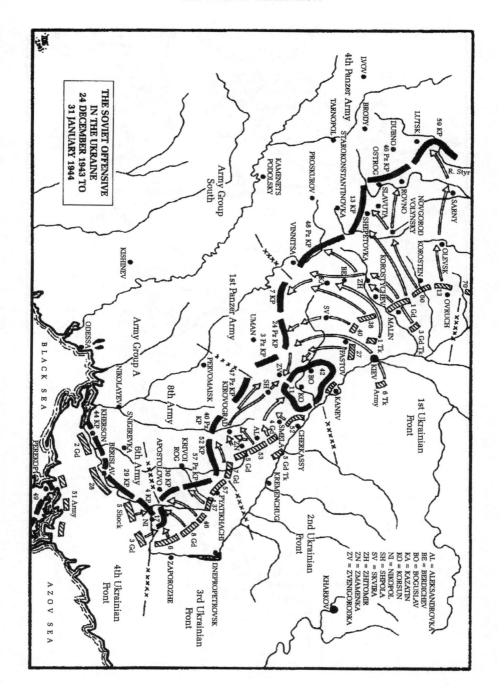

THE SOVIET OFFENSIVE
IN THE UKRAINE
24 DECEMBER 1943 TO
31 JANUARY 1944

4th Panzer Army

LVOV

BRODY

TARNOPOL

DUBNO

LUTSK

59 KP

R. Styr

SARNY

OSTROG

46 Pz KP

STAROKONSTANTINOVKA

PROSKUROV

KAMENETS
PODOLSKY

Army Group
South

KISHNEV

SLAVUTA

ROVNO

NOVGOROD
VOLYNSKY

SHEPETOVKA

13 KP

KOROSTYSCHEV

ZH

48 Pz KP

VINNITSA

BE

SV

KOROSTEN

KOROSTEN

MALIN

60

1 Gd

38

40

27

3 Gd Tk

1 Tk

1 Tk

OLEVSK

OVRUCH

70

13

1st Ukrainian
Front

1st Panzer Army

7 KP

24 Pz KP

UMAN

3 Pz KP

47 Pz KP

ZV

BO

KO

42

FASTOV

KIEV

KANEV

6 Tk
Army

PERVOMAISK

KIROVOGRAD

SH

ZN

Al

4 Gd

ZN

53

SMELA

57

5 Gd Tk

7 Gd

CHERKASSY

KREMENCHUG

2nd Ukrainian
Front

8th Army

ODESSA

NIKOLAYEV

KHERSON

44 KP

2 Gd

BERISLAV

SNIGIREVKA

40 Pz
KP

52 KP

KRIVOI
ROG

APOSTOLOVO

30 KP

37 Pz KP

29 KP

57

4 KP

37

46

8 Gd

6

PYATIKHACHI

DNEPROPETROVSK

6th Army

5 Shock

3 Gd

NI

17

5 Gd

ZAPOROZHE

3rd Ukrainian
Front

KHARKOV

PEREKOP

49

51
Army

28

4th Ukrainian
Front

BLACK SEA

AZOV SEA

Army Group A

AL = ALEKSANDROVKA
BE = BERDICHEV
BO = BOGUSLAV
KA = KAZATIN
KO = KORSUN
NI = NIKOPOL
SH = SHPOLA
SV = SKVIRA
ZH = ZHITOMIR
ZN = ZMAMENKA
ZV = ZVENIGORODKA

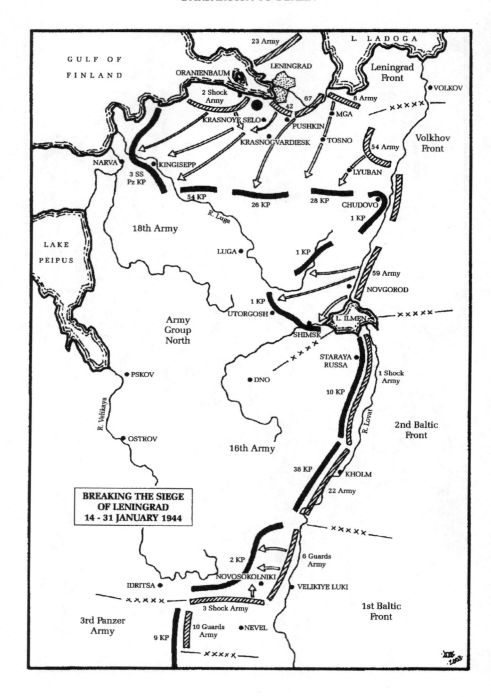

GULF OF FINLAND

23 Army

L. LADOGA

ORANIENBAUM

LENINGRAD

Leningrad Front

VOLKOV

2 Shock Army

67

8 Army

42

MGA

Volkhov Front

KRASNOYE SELO

PUSHKIN

KRASNOGVARDIESK

TOSNO

54 Army

NARVA

KINGISEPP

LYUBAN

3 SS Pz KP

54 KP

26 KP

28 KP

CHUDOVO

R. Luga

1 KP

18th Army

LUGA

1 KP

59 Army

NOVGOROD

1 KP

UTORGOSH

L. ILMEN

Army Group North

SHIMSK

STARAYA RUSSA

1 Shock Army

PSKOV

DNO

10 KP

R. Lovat

2nd Baltic Front

LAKE PEIPUS

R. Velikaya

OSTROV

16th Army

38 KP

KHOLM

22 Army

BREAKING THE SIEGE OF LENINGRAD 14 - 31 JANUARY 1944

2 KP

6 Guards Army

NOVOSOKOLNIKI

IDRITSA

VELIKIYE LUKI

1st Baltic Front

3 Shock Army

3rd Panzer Army

10 Guards Army

NEVEL

9 KP

German 6th Army was crushed by the 3rd and 4th Ukrainian Fronts.

In the Crimea the Germans had erected strong defensive positions. The 49th Mountain Korp deployed one infantry division on the Perekop Isthmus and one infantry and two Rumanian divisions on the Zivash coast facing the 51st Army. The 5th Korp was near Kerch with two infantry and one Rumanian cavalry divisions facing the Independent Coastal Army. In the Jaila Mountains was the 1st Rumanian Mountain Korp, fighting Crimean partisans, while in operational reserve was another infantry division, Mountain Regiment Krym and 9th Flak Division. The 17th Army had a total strength of 235,000 men.

THE OSTHEER

One panzer division, one infantry and two Luftwaffe field divisions were struck off the German order of battle during January but in return one SS motorised division, one infantry and one ski divisions were committed, bringing total German commitment to twenty-three panzer, ten panzer grenadier and 139 infantry divisions.[7] The Luftwaffe had 1,800 aircraft against 8,500 Soviet planes.

1 February 1944

NORTHERN SECTOR

The 2nd Shock Army captured Kingisepp after a fierce battle with the retreating 3rd SS Panzer Korp. Spearheads were just a mile from the Estonian border. The 18th Army launched a counter-attack from Luga city and Utorgosh with elements of the 1st Korp but was unable to halt the 59th Army drive into its right wing.

SOUTHERN SECTOR

The 47th Panzer Korp counter-attacked around Zvenigorodka towards the isolated 42nd and 11th Korps. The attack towards the pocket, centred on the village of Korsun-Schevchenkovsky, became bogged down in mud, the weather in the Ukraine being unseasonably warm for the time of year. Inside the pocket, Stemmerman began to pull his forces back to the south-west, giving up the positions on the Dniepr.

2 February 1944

NORTHERN SECTOR

The 2nd Shock Army forced a crossing into Estonia, capturing Vanakula as the 3rd SS Panzer Korp fell back to the Narva. The 67th Army closed up to the Luga near Luga city.

SOUTHERN SECTOR

Heavy fighting erupted in both Lutsk and Rovno as the 13th and 60th Armies continued to attack. Fighting at Shepetovka also continued.

Around Korsun the 2nd Ukrainian Front held back the weak German attack from Zvenigorodka, while in the Dniepr bend the 3rd and 4th Ukrainian Fronts applied increased pressure to the 6th Army.

3 February 1944

NORTHERN SECTOR

Efforts by the 2nd Shock Army to cross the Narva were repelled by the 3rd SS Panzer Korp after heavy fighting. German counter-attacks near Utorgozh isolated two divisions of the 59th Army but were unable to destroy them. The Russian units resisted for nearly two weeks until they rejoined the main combat line.

SOUTHERN SECTOR

The 3rd Panzer Korp began a relief attack towards the Korsun pocket, deploying the two panzer divisions. This latest attack again met ferocious resistance so to strengthen the attack force Hitler re-routed the 1st SS Panzer Division to this sector. However, the 24th Panzer Division, also earmarked for the counter-attack, was waylaid by Hitler and sent to Nikopol to aid the 6th Army. Heavy fighting continued on the south and south-west perimeters of the Korsun pocket as the 2nd Ukrainian Front tried to prevent German movement towards the relief forces. More territory was voluntarily given up from the north and east as Stemmerman pulled in to a shorter line.

4 February 1944

NORTHERN SECTOR

The 2nd Shock Army reached the mouth of the Narva and the shores of Lake Peipus. Elements crossed and established a small bridgehead while the 42nd Army, having crossed the Luga south of Kingisepp, captured Gdov.

SOUTHERN SECTOR

The 3rd Panzer Korp counter-attacked but was almost brought to a rapid halt in the clinging mud. Strenuous efforts were made to push closer to Stemmerman but the Germans simply lacked the strength and reserves of fuel to break through. The 3rd Panzer Korp attack was led by a strike force of thirty-four Tiger and forty-seven Panther tanks.[8] Inside the pocket the Soviets sent emissaries forward to call upon the Germans to surrender. The offer was rejected.

5 February 1944

SOUTHERN SECTOR
The 2nd Ukrainian Front moved the 2nd Tank Army around from the inner to outer defence ring to counter the threat of a German break-through to Group Stemmerman.

Rovno and Lutsk fell to the 60th and 13th Armies after bitter fighting while in the Dniepr bend the 46th Army captured Apostolovo, encircling a small part of the 30th Korp near the town. The German positions before Krivoi Rog and Nikopol were completely exposed, compelling Hollidt to request the withdrawal of the 6th Army.

6 February 1944

SOUTHERN SECTOR
The 3rd Panzer Korp abandoned its relief attack. The 47th Panzer Korp was finding it equally difficult to move in the face of fierce Russian resistance.

Farther south the 8th Guards Army broke through the 6th Army and stormed across the Ingulets river near Shirokoye.

7 February 1944

SOUTHERN SECTOR
Nikopol fell to the combined attacks of the 6th Army and 3rd Guards Army. Hollidt began to abandon the Dniepr bend but remained in danger of isolation as the 8th Guards and 46th Armies penetrated his rear.

Hitler agreed to a break out by Group Stemmerman from the Korsun pocket. With this authorisation, Stemmerman quickened the pace of the withdrawal, Gorodische and Yanovka being given up to the Russians as the pocket contracted.

8 February 1944

SOUTHERN SECTOR
Heavy fighting raged around the Korsun pocket as the Soviets probed for weaknesses in the line.

9 February 1944

SOUTHERN SECTOR
The 7th Guards Army of the 3rd Ukrainian Front was embroiled in heavy fighting west of Kirovograd.

10 February 1944

SOUTHERN SECTOR
Stemmerman had drawn his forces in tightly by reducing the pocket significantly. The bulk of his force massed to the south as thin rearguards covered the northern and eastern faces. Shepetovka fell to the 60th Army after a protracted battle.

11 February 1944

SOUTHERN SECTOR
The 3rd Panzer Korp renewed its relief attack towards Group Stemmerman, having been reinforced by the arrival of the 1st SS Panzer Division Leibstandarte Adolf Hitler. Bushanka fell after a costly battle while other units of the korp crossed the Gniloy Tikich, a small river running across the line of the German attack. However, the 2nd Tank Army was deploying to counter the German threat.

12 February 1944

NORTHERN SECTOR
The 67th Army entered Luga from the north but became embroiled in bitter fighting with the 28th Korp. The 59th and 54th Armies were also attacking the city from the east, pounding the German defences.

SOUTHERN SECTOR
Elements of the 3rd Panzer Korp took Vinograd. There were fierce tank battles with the 6th Tank Army and 5th Guards Army. Lysyanka fell after bitter fighting, the closest the 3rd Panzer Korp would get to the Korsun pocket. Due to the difficult ground conditions the 3rd Panzer Korp was being air dropped fuel. Inside the pocket the SS Wiking Division launched a determined counter-attack at Shenderovka, aimed at taking the village in preparation for the breakout. However, the Russian forces proved too strong and the SS were beaten back with heavy casualties. Despite this setback, an attack by the 72nd Infantry Division at Novo Buda was successful and the village fell.

13 February 1944

NORTHERN SECTOR
After a bitter battle Luga, Polna and Lyady fell to the advancing Leningrad and Volkhov Fronts.

The Stavka disbanded the Volkhov Front, incorporating its forces into the Leningrad Front. At the same time some minor redeployments were made. The 59th and 8th Armies moved from the Lake Ilmen sector to the Narva line to support the 2nd Shock Army while the 42nd, 67th and 54th Armies faced south to push towards Pskov and the Velikaya river. During the fighting the Volkhov Front had lost 12,000 killed and 38,000 wounded.[9]

SOUTHERN SECTOR
The German relief attack towards Korsun bogged down again as the 3rd Panzer Korp came under fierce attack at Lysyanka. Inside the pocket the SS Wiking Division launched another attack upon Shenderovka as Stemmerman tried to deploy for the breakout. After a costly battle the village fell but the 72nd Infantry Division suffered heavy losses in continued fighting at Nova Buda. Other elements of the 72nd Division were able to take Komarovka. Korsun itself was evacuated.

14 February 1944

SOUTHERN SECTOR
The 2nd Tank Army attacked the 3rd Panzer Korp. Heavy German losses followed but the 2nd Tank was held at bay. As this battled raged 3rd moved additional units up to support those forces already fighting at Lysyanka. Inside the cauldron the 72nd Infantry Division was pressed hard at Novo Buda and Komarovka as the Soviets tried to force Stemmerman away from the relief force. As the rear of the pocket drew in, the SS Wallonien Brigade was heavily attacked.

15 February 1944

NORTHERN SECTOR
Hitler agreed to allow Army Group North to abandon the Luga position and fall back to the borders with the Baltic States.

SOUTHERN SECTOR
In the Korsun pocket the 72nd Infantry Division captured Chilki, but encountered severe Soviet resistance. As casualties mounted the German attacks weakened. Stemmerman knew that if the breakout did not begin soon his korps would succumb to the relentless Russian attacks. However, with the fall of Chilki, he had established a base for the breakout and impatiently awaited Manstein's order. This was duly given, Stemmerman immediately proceeding to move the bulk of his forces to their attack sectors. Only a thin screen was left to cover his rear. Outside the pocket the 3rd Panzer Korp continued its attacks but was simply unable to break the strengthened outer ring.

16 February 1944

SOUTHERN SECTOR

Leading tanks of the 3rd Panzer Korp reached Oktyabr and in heavy fighting took the village. Inside the pocket, the 57th and 88th Infantry Divisions took up their positions to the rear of Group Stemmerman. These two divisions covered the escape of the rest of the group. At 2300 hours Stemmerman began his attack. Bitter fighting erupted as the Germans smashed through the Soviet ring, sheer desperation winning through in the end. Large numbers of men, fighting in independent groups, pushed west through the slush and mud towards the 3rd Panzer Korp. However, Russian resistance pushed the escaping forces away from the 3rd Panzer.

17 February 1944

SOUTHERN SECTOR

Group Stemmerman began to link up with the 3rd Panzer Korp. Hundreds had been killed on the march though, freezing to death as they tried to cross the icy Gniloy Tikich or falling under Russian fire. Among the casualties was Stemmerman, who was killed as his force reached safety. Realizing that the Germans were escaping, the 2nd Ukrainian Front launched an all-out attack upon the pocket, striking the 57th and 88th Infantry Divisions hard.

18 February 1944

NORTHERN SECTOR

South of Lake Ilmen the 10th Korp of the 16th Army relinquished Staraya Russa, the town falling to the 1st Shock Army.

SOUTHERN SECTOR

With the bulk of Group Stemmerman either destroyed as it marched towards the 3rd Panzer Korp, or free, the 57th and 88th Infantry Divisions disengaged and linked up with the main line. After nearly a month of bloody fighting the battle for Korsun had ended. The Germans had managed to save 30,000 of the 56,000 encircled but lost huge amounts of equipment. For the 3rd Panzer Korp the battle was not over though, it having to extricate its panzer divisions from their exposed positions.

SOVIET COMMAND

The Stavka reorganised its front commands in the Central Sector. The Belorussian Front was disbanded and new 1st and 2nd Belorussian Fronts created. Kurochkin's 2nd Belorussian Front (47th, 70th, 61st and 6th Air Armies) deployed between Rokossovsky's 1st Belorussian (3rd, 11th, 48th and 65th Armies plus the 16th Air Army) and Vatutin's 1st Ukrainian Fronts, covering the northern edge of the Pripet marshes.

21 February 1944

SOUTHERN SECTOR
The 8th Guards and 37th Armies fought their way into Krivoi Rog. The Germans had been severely weakened by constant fighting and were close to collapse.

22 February 1944

NORTHERN SECTOR
Dno fell to the combined attacks of the 54th Army from the north and 1st Shock Army from the east.

SOUTHERN SECTOR
Krivoi-Rog fell after heavy fighting.

24 February 1944

NORTHERN SECTOR
The 2nd Shock Army established a bridgehead at Krivasso on the Baltic coast in an effort to break into the rear of the 3rd SS Panzer Korp at Narva. The Germans rushed to counter-attack, making good progress before they were halted by the Soviets.

CENTRAL SECTOR
Rogachev fell to the 11th Army of the 1st Belorussian Front.

26 February 1944

NORTHERN SECTOR
Porkhov fell to the 54th Army.

29 February 1944

SOUTHERN SECTOR
Nationalist partisans in the Ukraine attacked a convoy in the rear of the 60th Army. Marshal Vatutin was in one of the vehicles and was wounded. Zhukov took over command of the 1st Ukrainian Front. Vatutin eventually succumbed to his wounds on 15 April, dying in hospital.

THE OSTHEER

German strength in the east stood at twenty-three panzer, ten panzer grenadier and 134 infantry divisions, eight infantry divisions having left the line and three joined.[10]

ASSESSMENT

Manstein believed that the next Russian offensive would hit the left flank of the army group once again. The 4th Panzer Army was reinforced with units of the 1st Panzer and 8th Armies covering the Vinnitsa and Uman sectors. Raus' 4th Panzer Army (eight infantry, one police and nine panzer or panzer grenadier divisions) deployed the 59th Korp on its left wing around Kovel, 13th Korp around Brody, 48th Panzer Korp in reserve at Proskurov and 3rd Panzer Korp at Tarnopol. Hube's 1st Panzer Army (eight infantry, one artillery and one armoured divisions) was between Starokonstantinovka and Vinnitsa with its 7th Korp, 24th and 46th Panzer Korps, the 1st Hungarian Army being behind the main German front line in this sector while Wohler's 8th Army (five infantry and four panzer or panzer grenadier divisions) was falling back to the Bug between Vinnitsa and Kirovograd. Hollidt's 6th Army (eight infantry and three panzer or panzer grenadier divisions) was on the Ingulets and Dniepr on the southern wing. Behind the 6th Army, a new 3rd Rumanian Army was forming.

Following a number of transfers towards the end of the month, Vatutin's 1st Ukrainian Front deployed the 1st Tank and 3rd Guards Tank Armies in reserve behind its northern wing, the 4th Tank Army in reserve behind its centre, 13th, 60th and 1st Guards Armies on the long northern wing and the 18th Army in the centre and the 38th Army on the left flank. Koniev's 2nd Ukrainian Front deployed the 2nd and 6th Tank and 5th Guards Tank Armies in mobile reserve, 40th and 27th Armies on the right wing, 52nd and 4th Guards in the centre and 53rd, 5th Guards and 7th Guards on the left wing. Malinovsky's 3rd Ukrainian Front completed the main front line to the Black Sea coast. Its 57th and 37th Armies held the left wing, 46th, 8th Guards and 6th Armies were grouped in the centre near Krivoi Rog, 3rd Guards and 5th Shock held between the Ingulets and Dniepr and the 28th Army held the right wing on the east bank of the Dniepr. Group Pliev was in mobile reserve. Tolbukhin's 4th Ukrainian Front had been reduced in frontage to the Crimean periphery. The 2nd Guards and 51st Armies held the Perekop and Zivash sectors and the Independent Coastal Army held the Kerch sector.

Realising the Germans expected the 1st Ukrainian to continue its westward drive, the Stavka planned to unbalance Manstein by throwing the front south-west, against the junction of the 4th and 1st Panzer Armies. This would sever the 1st Panzer, 8th and 6th Armies from the main combat line and force them back into Rumania, leaving the road to Lvov and southern Poland open. Meanwhile, as this attack developed, the 2nd Ukrainian Front would attack the 8th Army and the 3rd Ukrainian the junction of the 8th and 6th Armies and pin the 6th Army frontally.

1 March 1944

NORTHERN SECTOR
The 42nd and 67th Armies closed in upon Pskov. The offensive since 14 January had cost the Leningrad Front 56,500 killed and 170,000 wounded.[11]

4 March 1944

SOUTHERN SECTOR
Supported by overwhelming artillery fire and air interdiction, the 1st Ukrainian Front opened its offensive against the 4th and 1st Panzer Armies. The 1st Guards and 60th Armies smashed into the 59th and 13th Korps, inflicting severe casualties. Within hours a breakthrough was achieved and the 59th Korp began to fall back to the west.

5 March 1944

SOUTHERN SECTOR
Rybalko's 3rd Guards Tank Army and Badanov's 4th Tank Army passed through the advancing 60th and 1st Guards Armies to break into the German rear. Yampol and Ostropol were quickly taken, leaving the 59th Korp scattered. Zbaraz fell to 18th Army.

Koniev's 2nd Ukrainian Front began its attack against the 8th Army and 1st Panzer Army. Before Uman a rain of artillery fire hit the German line. After the bombardment the 5th Guards Army crashed into the right wing of the 8th Army. Once again the weight of the Russian attack proved too great for the Germans, their forces collapsing after a bloody struggle. Koniev then committed the 2nd Tank and 5th Guards Tank Armies to the attack.

6 March 1944

SOUTHERN SECTOR
The 1st Ukrainian Front pushed deeper into the German rear as it developed its attack, a thirty-mile hole having been punched between the 4th and 1st Panzer Armies. Volochisk fell to the 3rd Guards Tank Army. The 2nd Ukrainian Front continued to widen the break between the 8th Army and 1st Panzer Army.

Malinovsky now began his offensive. Following the customary artillery

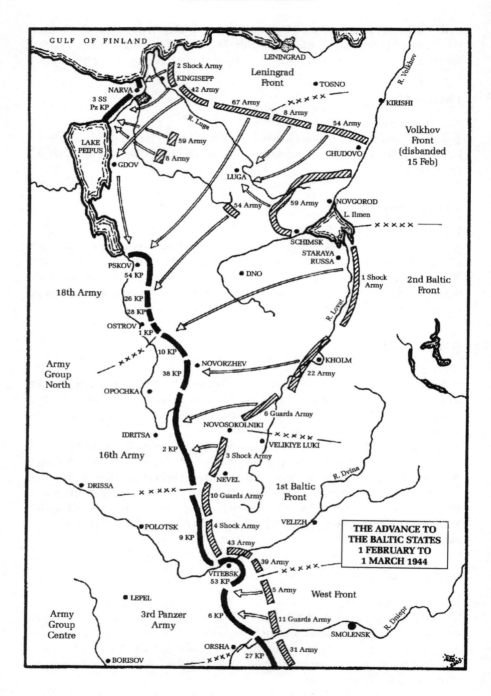

THE ADVANCE TO
THE BALTIC STATES
1 FEBRUARY TO
1 MARCH 1944

barrage, the 8th Guards and 46th Armies attacked the junction of the 8th and 6th Armies, striking the 30th Korp particularly hard. Fierce fighting raged, but by dusk both the 8th Guards and 46th had broken the German line. The Russians immediately pressed into the rear of the 6th Army toward Nikolayev in an effort to isolate it.

7 March 1944

SOUTHERN SECTOR
The 1st Ukrainian Front advanced rapidly. The 60th, 1st Guards and 3rd Guards Tank Armies approached Tarnopol, Chernyi and Ostrov. The 38th Army advanced upon Starokonstantinovka. Hitler ordered Tarnopol held to the last man, even if encircled.

8 March 1944

SOUTHERN SECTOR
The 5th and 7th Guards Armies pushed towards Pervomaisk, throwing the 8th Army back. Novy Bug fell to Group Pliev as the flank of the 6th Army was turned.

With the Ukrainian front in tatters, Hitler declared a number of towns to be fortified places. Local commanders were made responsible for their defence but usually had only meagre resources with which to carry out their assignments. Hitler mistakenly believed that enough of these fortified places could break up the Russian advance and bring it to a grinding halt.

FINNISH SECTOR
Following secret negotiations, the Finns rejected a proposed armistice. The terms dictated by the Soviets were too harsh to accept. However, Finland continued its surreptitious dialogue with the Soviet Union.

9 March 1944

SOUTHERN SECTOR
The 1st Guards Army threw screening forces around Tarnopol. A furious attack was launched into the town but the Germans counter-attacked, forcing the Russians out. Starokonstantinovka also fell to the 38th Army after a brief struggle.

10 March 1944

SOUTHERN SECTOR
The 1st Guards Army was involved in heavy fighting around Tarnopol,

the Germans counter-attacking and forcing the Soviet units out of the town. However, the fortress remained under siege and came under sustained artillery fire. Other units of the 1st Ukrainian Front also pushed towards Proskurov as the 1st Panzer Army fell back.

Uman fell to the 2nd Tank Army, while the 5th Guards Tank and 53rd Armies converged on the town to destroy significant elements of the 8th Army. The fighting on the road to Uman had cost the 8th Army some 200 tanks, 600 artillery pieces and 12,000 motor vehicles. The 3rd Ukrainian Front crossed the Ingul river as it pressed towards the Bug.

11 March 1944

SOUTHERN SECTOR

The 1st Ukrainian came under heavy attack from the 48th Panzer Korp at Cherny Ostrov, temporarily halting the Russian advance. However, Zhukov was about to swing his main thrust south towards the Dniestr to pin the 1st Panzer Army against the river. Heavy fighting raged from Tarnopol, through Volochisk and on to Proskurov.

The 2nd Ukrainian Front pushed its 2nd Tank Army across the Bug river at Dzhulinka while the 6th Tank Army crossed at Gayvoron. Manstein ordered the 8th Army to pull back to prevent its disintegration and isolation on the east bank of the Bug. On the southern flank the 28th Army took Berislav after bitter fighting with the 29th Korp of the 6th Army.

13 March 1944

SOUTHERN SECTOR

After heavy fighting the 48th Panzer began a relief attack towards Tarnopol. The dual role of the attack was also to close the gap between the 4th and 1st Panzer Armies. Fierce, but ultimately unsuccessful fighting would rage for the next week. The 1st Panzer Army fell back across the Bug as its right wing was bent back by the 2nd Ukrainian Front. Kherson fell to the 28th Army on the extreme southern wing after a costly battle with the 44th Korp.

14 March 1944

SOUTHERN SECTOR

As the 8th Guards linked up with the 28th Army, enveloping the right wing of the 6th Army, 14,000 soldiers of the 29th Korp were encircled east of Nikolayev. Under heavy attack the group was forced to surrender later in the day, 4,000 being captured and the bulk of the remainder killed.

15 March 1944

SOUTHERN SECTOR
The 6th Tank Army broke out from its Bug bridgehead and took Vapnyarka. Other elements of the front cut the railway line between Odessa and Zhmerinka near Vinnitsa.

17 March 1944

SOUTHERN SECTOR
The 60th Army of the 1st Ukrainian Front took Dubno, while elements of the 2nd Tank Army reached the Dniestr at Yampol.

18 March 1944

SOUTHERN SECTOR
Zhmerinka fell to Soviet forces. Elements of the 8th Guards Army reached the lower Bug at Novaya Odessa and forced a crossing.

19 March 1944

CENTRAL SECTOR
The 1st Belorussian Front launched a limited attack north of the Pripet Marshes.

SOUTHERN SECTOR
Kovel fell to the 47th Army of the 2nd Belorussian Front after a brisk battle. This army had been deployed on the Front's left wing in order to strengthen the westward thrust. The 2nd Tank Army took Soroki while the 6th Tank Army reached the Dniestr on a broad front around Mogilev-Podolsky. Raus' 1st Panzer Army was virtually isolated by these deep Soviet thrusts, being hemmed in between Mogilev Podolsky and Tarnopol.

DIPLOMACY: HUNGARY
Premier Kallay fled to Turkey as German units crossed the border to bring Hungary under military control. Operation Margaret was successfully carried out as the Ostheer secured its lines of communication for Army Group South.

20 March 1944

SOUTHERN SECTOR
The 1st Tank Army, having redeployed over the last few days from the left wing to the centre of the 1st Ukrainian Front, attacked in conjunction with

the 4th Tank Army between Proskurov and Tarnopol. These new attacks hit the junction of the 4th and 1st Panzer Armies. After a brief struggle the German line was broken again. Vinnitsa fell to Soviet troops.

The 2nd Ukrainian Front's 6th Tank Army captured Mogilev Podolsky. The 5th Guards Tank Army also closed up to the Dniestr to the left of the 2nd Tank Army. Hollidt's 6th Army made a stand on the Bug but was struck all along its line by the 3rd Ukrainian Front.

21 March 1944

SOUTHERN SECTOR

The 48th Panzer Korp, having relieved Tarnopol, was brought under intense attack by the 1st Guards Army and had to fall back. The 1st Tank Army struggled to break through the German positions at Cherny Ostrov, being bogged down by both the mud and severe German resistance.

22 March 1944

SOUTHERN SECTOR

Malinovsky's 3rd Ukrainian Front breached the German line on the Bug. As the fighting raged along the river, the 5th and 7th Guards Armies of the 2nd Ukrainian Front captured Pervomaisk.

SOVIET COMMAND

The Stavka amended the 1st and 2nd Ukrainian Front objectives. The 1st Ukrainian was to complete the encirclement and destruction of the 1st Panzer Army around Kamenets Podolsky, while the 2nd broke free of the Dniestr to threaten the Rumanian borders.

GERMAN ALLIES

As the Red Army drew closer to the border, Marshal Antonescu, the Rumanian dictator, flew to Berlin to meet with Hitler. Antonescu aimed to seek some degree of German support or flexibility against the advancing Communist forces.

With Russian forces also approaching their borders, the 1st Hungarian Army, which had only just begun to form up, entered the combat line near Chernovitsy.

23 March 1944

SOUTHERN SECTOR

The 1st Guards Army renewed its attack around Tarnopol and encircled the town for a second time. The main German combat line was pushed back more than fifteen miles to the west, leaving Group Neinhoff isolated.

General Neinhoff, commandant of the Tarnopol fortress, had just 4,600 men.

To prevent the isolation of the 1st Panzer Army on the Dniestr and its retreat into Rumania, Manstein warned Hube of possible Soviet intentions and ordered him to pull his forces back to the west if threatened with encirclement. However, under intense attack, Hube continued to fall back to the south.

24 March 1944

SOUTHERN SECTOR
After a difficult advance the 1st Tank Army reached the Dniestr river at Zaleschik, severing Hube's westward escape route. After establishing a bridgehead, the 1st pushed on towards Kolomna and Chernovitsy. The 40th Army of the 2nd Ukrainian Front reached the Prut river near Lipkany. Proskurov fell to the 1st Ukrainian Front while the 1st Guards Army repulsed a renewed German relief attack towards Tarnopol and attacked Group Neinhoff inside the town.

25 March 1944

SOUTHERN SECTOR
Heavy fighting raged at Tarnopol. The 1st Guards Army overran the Zagrobela suburb west of the Seret river.

GERMAN COMMAND
Manstein and Kleist flew to Berlin for a meeting with Hitler. Talks were cordial, but privately Hitler was angered by the fact that Army Groups South and A had retreated before the Russian offensive.

26 March 1944

SOUTHERN SECTOR
The 1st Tank Army secured its positions on the Dniestr river, while the 40th Army of the 2nd Ukrainian front crossed the Prut near Lipkany and the 27th Army crossed near Jassy. The 52nd Army approached Jassy from the east. Balta fell.

GERMAN COMMAND
Kleist informed Hitler that if the positions on the Bug were not abandoned and the 6th Army withdrawn to the Rumanian border there was the very real possibility that it would be destroyed. Despite this it took hours of argument before Hitler agreed to even a limited withdrawal. Another result of these conversations was the detachment of 8th Army from Army

Group South to Army Group A. The southerly withdrawal of the 8th had effectively separated it from the remainder of Army Group South.

27 March 1944

SOUTHERN SECTOR
The 4th Tank Army (down to just sixty operational tanks) took Kamenets Podolsky, virtually isolating the 1st Panzer Army between it, the 3rd Guards Army to the north (lately redeployed following the success of the attacks in the Dniepr elbow) and 18th and 38th Armies to the east. The 6th Tank moved along the Dniestr to the south and 40th Army on the Prut. Hube planned to break out to the west rather than to the south as expected.

28 March 1944

SOUTHERN SECTOR
The 6th Tank Army reached Khotin and blocked the 1st Panzer Army's line of retreat to the Prut. The isolated army comprised the 3rd, 24th and 46th Panzer Korps, some six panzer, one panzer grenadier, one artillery and ten infantry divisions.

The 1st Guards Army launched heavy attacks against Group Neinhoff in Tarnopol. The German perimeter broke and bloody fighting erupted inside the town. Farther south the 46th Army of the 3rd Ukrainian Front captured Nikolayev.

29 March 1944

SOUTHERN SECTOR
Kolomna fell to the 1st Tank Army, while at Tarnopol Group Neinhoff was again heavily attacked.

30 March 1944

SOUTHERN SECTOR
The 1st Tank Army captured Chernovtsy.

GERMAN COMMAND
Having returned to the front following their meeting with Hitler, Manstein and Kleist were recalled to the Obersalzburg where both were relieved of their commands. Hitler justified his decision with the statement that the time for great strategic minds had passed, what the armies in the east needed was men of National Socialist will. In their place Hitler appointed Field Marshal Model to command Army Group South and Field Marshal Schorner to Army Group A. At the same time the army

groups were renamed, Army Group South becoming North Ukraine and A becoming Army Group South Ukraine. Just as with Army Group Don, Hitler named his army groups after territory that had already been lost. With Model leaving the northern sector for the Ukraine, General Lindemann took over Army Group North.

31 March 1944

SOUTHERN SECTOR
The 1st Guards Army launched fierce attacks upon Tarnopol, taking the railway station. Neinhoff was confined to the city centre and part of Zagrobela, holding an area less than a mile square. As the 3rd Ukrainian Front pushed towards Odessa, Ochakov was overrun by the 46th Army.

AXIS DEPLOYMENT
As March drew to a close the Rumanian 4th Army began to enter the combat line in northern Rumania, deploying between the 1st Hungarian and 8th Armies.

THE OSTHEER
During March the Ostheer lost three panzer and three infantry divisions from its order of battle but two SS panzer, two SS panzer grenadier, one jaeger, two reserve and four infantry divisions entered the line. However, the newly committed divisions were nowhere near regulation strength, many not even making up a full strength regiment. German paper strength stood at twenty-three panzer, nine panzer grenadier and 140 infantry divisions.[12]

1 April 1944

SOUTHERN SECTOR
Group Neinhoff launched a fierce attack in Tarnopol, inflicting severe casualties upon the 1st Guards Army. However the Germans only repulsed a counter-attack upon the city centre at considerable cost. Around Skala, the 1st Panzer Army was under heavy attack as the 4th Tank Army tried to prevent its movement west.

2 April 1944

SOUTHERN SECTOR
The encircled 1st Panzer Army was presented with an ultimatum, to surrender or be destroyed. The offer was rejected as Hube planned to break out, deploying his army in a mobile hedgehog against the Soviet forces.

The 4th Tank Army crossed the Prut river east of Chernovtsy, while on the extreme southern wing the German 6th Army attempted to fall back across the Dniestr but was hampered by the weather, a fierce storm of sleet hindering the construction of a pontoon bridge.

3 April 1944

SOUTHERN SECTOR
Bitter fighting continued at Tarnopol as the 1st Guards Army tried to crush the last pockets of resistance inside the town.

With sleet falling, the 8th Guards Army of the 3rd Ukrainian Front launched an unexpected attack upon the 6th Army, pushing it back towards Odessa.

4 April 1944

SOUTHERN SECTOR
The 4th Panzer Army launched a limited counter-attack with its 59th Korp that recovered Kovel. Along the Dniestr, as the 1st Panzer Army attacked west, the 1st and 2nd SS Panzer Korps began a relief attack from Buchach, striking the extended flanks of the 1st Guards and 38th Armies. To the south, the 37th Army crossed the Tiligul river, capturing Razdelnaya.

SOVIET COMMAND
The Stavka reorganised its forces in the central sectors. The recently formed 2nd Belorussian Front was disbanded, its forces being allocated to Rokossovsky's 1st Belorussian Front.

As the fighting in the Ukraine bogged down the Stavka planned to unleash two new offensives. The first would hit the German 17th Army in the Crimea while the second, far larger attack was designed to destroy the forces of Army Group Centre in Belorussia. Throughout April and May the Russian forces in this region were comprehensively re-formed and reinforced.

5 April 1944

SOUTHERN SECTOR
The 3rd Ukrainian Front exploited the hole in the German line at Razdelnaya to sever the railway line to Odessa.

6 April 1944

SOUTHERN SECTOR
A small German force was isolated at Razdelnaya and brought under sustained attack.

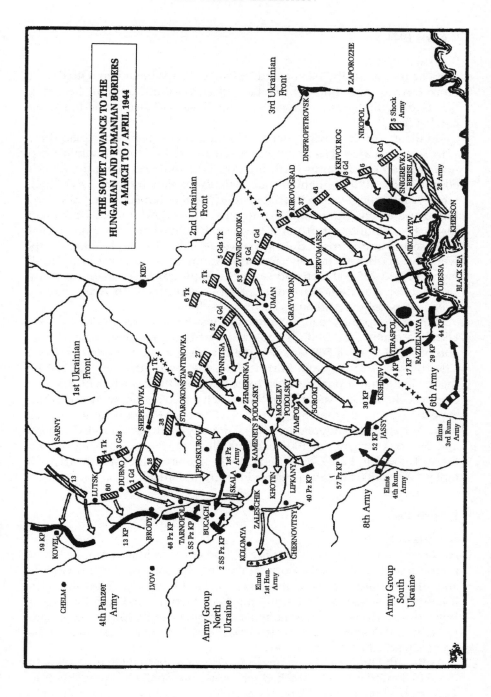

THE SOVIET ADVANCE TO THE
HUNGARIAN AND RUMANIAN BORDERS
4 MARCH TO 7 APRIL 1944

7 April 1944

SOUTHERN SECTOR

After a bitter battle the 1st and 2nd SS Panzer Korps linked up with the 1st Panzer Army near Buchach. Hube had successfully brought his army across difficult terrain, numerous river lines and back into the main combat line.

On the eve of the Soviet offensive in the Crimea, Jaenecke's placed his 17th Army on alert. His force comprised Konrad's 49th Mountain Korp near the Perekop Isthmus (50th Infantry Division) and along the Zivash coast (336th, 10th Rumanian and 19th Rumanian Infantry Divisions), while Allmendinger's 5th Korp defended the Kerch peninsula (98th, 73rd Infantry and 6th Rumanian Cavalry Divisions). Additional Rumanian forces (1st Mountain Korp and two cavalry divisions) were on coastal defence and anti-partisan duties. In reserve, behind 49th Mountain Korp, were the 111th Infantry Division and Mountain Regiment Krym. In all Jaenecke had 235,000 men and seventy assault guns. Yet again the army commander was denied freedom of movement, the 17th Army having been instructed to stand on its current positions.

During the spring the Red Army had considerably strengthened the 4th Ukrainian Front, Tolbukhin's deployed the 51st Army (five rifle divisions and one tank corp of 500 tanks) in the Zivash and 2nd Guards Army (six rifle divisions) at Perekop. Surprisingly, the main attack would not be made via the traditional Perekop route but from the Zivash, which Soviet engineers had made passable for their mechanised and infantry units. Not expecting an attack from this quarter, the Germans had only light defences here. At Kerch, the Independent Coastal Army, with eleven rifle divisions and one tank brigade of 100 tanks, totalling 143,000 men, faced the 5th Korp. Tolbukhin had 278,000 men, 6,000 artillery pieces and nearly 600 tanks. Over 1,200 aircraft supported the ground attack.[13]

8 April 1944

SOUTHERN SECTOR

At dawn concentrated artillery fire by the 4th Ukrainian Front began to pound the 49th Mountain Korp. Following the barrage the 2nd Guards and 51st Armies attacked, the 2nd Guards hitting the 50th and 11th Infantry Divisions and 51st Army the 336th German and 10th Rumanian Infantry Divisions. The German and Rumanian units fought back with ferocity, and despite repeated attacks with artillery and aerial support the Soviets were unable to break through.

As the 4th Ukrainian Front began its offensive, the 1st Guards Army of the 1st Ukrainian Front launched more assaults upon Group Neinhoff in Tarnopol, while Botosani, Dorohoi and Siret fell to 2nd Ukrainian Front in northern Rumania. The 40th and 27th Armies had reached and crossed the Siret river on a sixty-mile front. The German force at Razdelnaya was destroyed by the concentric attacks of the 3rd Ukrainian Front.

9 April 1944

SOUTHERN SECTOR

The 4th Ukrainian Front renewed its attacks against the 49th Mountain Korp. Despite the overwhelming forces against them, the German and Rumanian divisions stood fast. To the east the Independent Coastal Army began its own offensive from Kerch, smashing into the 5th Korp. Once again the Germans resisted with steely determination, preventing a breakthrough.

The 8th Guards, 5th Shock and 6th Armies began to attack Odessa. With only weak German and Rumanian forces opposing their advance, they took most of the city by the end of the day.

10 April 1944

SOUTHERN SECTOR

Odessa fell, cutting one escape route for the German 17th Army. In the Crimea the 49th Mountain Korp began to give on the Perekop Isthmus as 2nd Guards Army bludgeoned its way to the Ishun Narrows. Armyansk fell. On the Zivash sector the 10th Rumanian Division collapsed after hard fighting with the 51st Army. The right flank of the 49th Mountain Korp quickly crumbled, enabling the 51st Army to widen the penetration and threaten the rear of the Perekop defences. Farther east 5th Korp was similarly overwhelmed and began a slow withdrawal. Tolbukhin now launched his armour into the attack, smashing through the thin rearguards left by the 49th and 5th Korps. Against the highly mechanised Soviet divisions the 17th Army was stranded, its infantry divisions having to fight their way back to Sevastopol.

11 April 1944

SOUTHERN SECTOR

The 48th Panzer Korp launched another relief attack towards Tarnopol but became bogged down in heavy fighting at Kozlov.

In the Crimea the 51st Army smashed its way through the rearguards of the 49th Mountain Korp. The Germans immediately fell back in the direction of Sevastopol but suffered heavy casualties. Dzhankoy fell.

12 April 1944

SOUTHERN SECTOR

There was heavy fighting around Tarnopol while to the south Tiraspol fell to the 37th Army as it crossed the Dniestr.

Hitler belatedly gave his authorisation for the withdrawal of German forces to Sevastopol, despite the fact that the 17th Army was in fact already retreating in considerable disorder. Jaenecke urgently requested permission to evacuate the Crimea but this was denied. Despite this he began an unofficial evacuation of non-essential personnel.

Mountain Regiment Krym, part of the 49th Mountain Korp, made a rear-guard stand at Dzhankoy in order to gain time for the main body of the korp to escape to the south. Furious fighting raged as 51st Army hit the German positions. After a bloody struggle the German regiment was virtually annihilated. Fighting on the Kerch peninsula continued as the 5th Korp retreated, the bulk of the korp being at Parpatsch. Under heavy attack the 5th abandoned its line and fell back towards the Jaila Mountains.

13 April 1944

SOUTHERN SECTOR

The 46th Army took Oviodopol at the mouth of the Dniestr. At Tarnopol the 1st Guards Army split Group Neinhoff apart, isolating half on the west bank of the Siret and the other in the Zagrobela suburb.

The 51st Army closed upon Simferopol. Jaenecke planned to make a stand in the Belbek Valley but first had to beat the Soviet forces in the race to Sevastopol. Feodosia fell to the Independent Coastal Army and Evpatoria to the 2nd Guards.

14 April 1944

SOUTHERN SECTOR

The 48th Panzer Korp resumed its counter-attack towards Tarnopol but after a brief advance was brought to a halt.

The 51st Army reached the outskirts of Sevastopol and launched an immediate assault upon the city. Desperate defence by scratch forces held it off while the 49th Mountain assembled.

15 April 1944

SOUTHERN SECTOR

After heavy fighting the 48th Panzer Korp gained a little territory on the approaches to Tarnopol. However, the battle proved costly, many of the German tanks being disabled and much of their available fuel consumed.

Inside Tarnopol the Germans in the Zagrobela suburb prepared to break out. The 1,300 men, forced to leave their 700 wounded behind, would launch their attack the next day. The forces cut off in the second pocket were largely destroyed.

16 April 1944

SOUTHERN SECTOR

At dawn, in two groups of around seven hundred men each, Group Neinhoff began its desperate breakout. Running battles immediately erupted as the 1st Guards Army fought to prevent their escape. The Germans suffered heavy losses under ferocious fire, discipline breaking down as each man fought to save himself. General Neinhoff was killed during the fighting. By dusk the survivors of the first group, just forty-three men in all, reached the 48th Panzer Korp, followed shortly afterwards by five men of the second group. Barely fifty of the original 4,500 strong garrison reached safety.[14]

In the Crimea, the Independent Coastal Army advanced along the southern coast, taking Yalta.

17 April 1944

SOUTHERN SECTOR

The remnants of the 5th and 49th Mountain Korps reached Sevastopol and dug in around the city. The 49th Mountain Korp, with the remnants of two infantry divisions, deployed to cover the northern approaches. However, it came under heavy attack as Soviet forces probed the German defences. The 5th Korp covered the eastern approaches (with three infantry divisions). During the harrowing retreat the 5th and 49th Mountain Korps had suffered terribly, more than 13,000 German and 17,000 Rumanian soldiers being killed or captured in the fighting.

The fighting in the Ukraine had also been costly for the Soviet armies. The 1st Ukrainian Front had, since 24 December 1943, lost 124,000 killed and 332,000 wounded, the 2nd Ukrainian 66,000 killed and 200,000 wounded, the 3rd Ukrainian 55,000 killed and 214,000 wounded and the 4th Ukrainian 22,000 killed and 84,000 wounded.[15]

18 April 1944

SOUTHERN SECTOR

Probing attacks continued against the Sevastopol perimeter as the 51st, 2nd Guards and Independent Coastal Armies searched for weak points in the German defences. Balaklava fell during heavy fighting. At this stage of the battle there were 124,000 Axis soldiers inside Sevastopol.

24 April 1944

GERMAN COMMAND
Hitler sacked General Jaenecke and appointed General Allmendinger as
commander of the 17th Army. Allmendinger had previously commanded
the 5th Korp.

SOVIET COMMAND
Stavka disbanded the West Front in preparation for its reorganisation in
the centre. A 3rd Belorussian Front was created.

27 April 1944

SOUTHERN SECTOR
After a protracted artillery barrage, the Coastal Army launched a fierce
attack upon the 5th Korp holding the southern perimeter of the Sevastopol
defences. Despite bitter fighting the Soviet troops failed to take the Sapun
Heights.

30 April 1944

SOVIET COMMAND
The Stavka implemented a number of command and formation changes.
Meretskov was appointed to command the Karelian Front (7th and 32nd
Armies west and north of Lake Onega). North of Leningrad the 21st Army
had joined the Leningrad Front alongside the 23rd Army. The Leningrad
Front forces south of the city, facing the German 18th Army, were
redesignated Operational Group Narva (2nd Shock and 8th Armies).
South of Lake Peipus was the new 3rd Baltic Front under General
Maslennikov, with Eremenko's 2nd Baltic Front to its left and
Bagramyan's 1st Baltic Front on the southern flank.

New 2nd and 3rd Belorussian Fronts were raised north of the 1st
Belorussian in the place of the now defunct West Front. Sokolovsky
commanded the 3rd Belorussian and General Zakharov the 2nd.
Rokossovsky retained command of the 1st on the long southern flank
from Bobruisk to Kovel.

THE OSTHEER
During April the Germans had committed one SS panzer grenadier and
one infantry divisions to the line but lost one panzer, three infantry and
one Luftwaffe divisions from their order of battle, leaving the Ostheer
with twenty-two panzer, ten panzer grenadier and 137 infantry
divisions.[16]

In the far north, Dietl's 20th Mountain Army, fighting in the Arctic

Circle, had 85,000 men, while in Finland there were 350,000 Finnish soldiers, 180,000 of whom were in the combat line. Despite its heavy defeat before Leningrad in the early months of 1944, Army Group North still deployed 350,000 men while Army Group Centre had around 580,000. In the Ukraine, Army Group North Ukraine deployed 423,000 men while South Ukraine had 360,000. Fighting the partisans in Yugoslavia and Greece the Germans had another 163,000 men.[17]

1 May 1944

SOUTHERN SECTOR
The 4th Ukrainian Front continued its preparations for the final attack against Sevastopol. After the evacuation of many troops to Rumania and its losses in the fighting thus far, the 17th Army was down to an effective strength of only 65,000 men.

2 May 1944

SOUTHERN SECTOR
The 2nd Tank Army and 27th Army launched a spoiling attack at Targul-Frumos, north of Jassy. The 57th Panzer and 4th Korps counter-attacked, inflicting heavy casualties upon the attackers.

3 May 1944

SOUTHERN SECTOR
Heavy fighting continued at Targul-Frumos.

GERMAN COMMAND
The FHO Department (Foreign Armies East) issued a report on the deployment of Soviet forces facing the Ostheer. Gehlen, the head of FHO, believed the Red Army had been considerably reinforced over the last few weeks, despite carrying out major offensives in the Ukraine and Crimea. The next phase of the Soviet attack was expected in the Ukraine, pushing into the Balkans. To counter this perceived threat, Hitler deployed a sizeable portion of his armour in the south. In eastern Hungary the recently formed 1st Hungarian Army was incorporated into Army Group North Ukraine in Galicia while in Rumania the 3rd and 4th Rumanian Armies were being reinforced and re-formed.

4 May 1944

SOUTHERN SECTOR
The Soviet attack at Targul Frumos had been defeated.

5 May 1944

SOUTHERN SECTOR

After a period of redeployment the 4th Ukrainian Front began its final offensive against the 17th Army, some 470,000 Soviet troops, 600 tanks and 6,000 artillery pieces facing 65,000 Germans and Rumanians. Elements of 2nd Guards Army attacked the Mackenzie Heights north of the city, pounding the 49th Mountain Korp. Despite massive attacks and significant losses the 49th maintained its positions.

6 May 1944

SOUTHERN SECTOR

The 2nd Guards Army resumed its attack, but still the 49th Mountain Korp stood fast. However, German strength was rapidly dwindling, the hard-pressed divisions nearing the end of their abilities.

7 May 1944

SOUTHERN SECTOR

With the 49th Mountain Korp on the verge of collapse, the 51st Army unleashed its attack against the 5th Korp. After overwhelming artillery fire the 51st flooded forward, crushing the positions of the 5th Korp on the Sapun Heights. By mid-afternoon the German line had collapsed and Soviet troops broke into the Inkerman Valley. The road to Sevastopol lay wide open.

8 May 1944

SOUTHERN SECTOR

The 2nd Guards and 51st Armies pushed into Sevastopol, cutting off part of the 49th and 5th Korps to the east. As the remnants fell back the 51st Army swept into the city, capturing most of it as the Germans fled to the Khersonnes Peninsula. With the end in sight, Hitler belatedly ordered the evacuation.

9 May 1944

SOUTHERN SECTOR

Some 50,000 German troops packed the Khersonnes Peninsula, pounded by guns and aircraft of the 4th Ukrainian Front. The last rearguards inside Sevastopol were destroyed.

10 May 1944

SOUTHERN SECTOR
Soviets forces launched a ferocious attack upon the Khersonnes Peninsula but were repulsed. As fighting raged on the cliff tops, 15,000 soldiers were evacuated by sea.

11 May 1944

SOUTHERN SECTOR
Continual air attacks and artillery fire inflicted heavy losses upon the Germans on the Khersonnes Peninsula.

12 May 1944

SOUTHERN SECTOR
After a last massive assault, the German line on the Khersonnes Peninsula collapsed, sealing the fate of 25,000 German soldiers. Nearly 15,000 surrendered after a final bloody battle on the cliffs. In all the 17th had evacuated 130,000 of its men from the Crimea but 80,000 were lost during the battle. The army was scratched off the German order of battle.

The fall of the Crimea allowed the Stavka to release the armies of the 4th Ukrainian Front for service on the main combat line. However, most needed reinforcement as the battle for the peninsula had cost the 4th Ukrainian Front 13,000 killed and 50,000 wounded and the Coastal Army 4,000 killed and 16,000 wounded.[18]

THE AIR WAR
The US 8th Air Force had began the concentrated bombing of German oil and fuel production facilities. Germany lost nearly 90% of its fuel production capacity during May alone.

SOVIET COMMAND
The Stavka developed its plans for the next major offensive against the Germans. Deceiving them into believing that the main attack would fall in the Ukraine, the Stavka prepared to launch its offensive in Belorussia against Busch's Army Group Centre.

For this offensive, code-named Bagration, the Soviet armies were considerably strengthened. The 1st Baltic Front received a new tank corp and the 3rd Belorussian Front the 11th Guards Army and 2nd Guards Tank Corp. The 2nd Belorussian received a single rifle corp but Rokossovsky's 1st got the lion's share of the new forces. On his right wing, facing the German 9th Army around Bobruisk, it received the 28th Army and four tank or mechanised corps, while the left wing, projecting out from the Pripet Marshes, received the 8th Guards and 2nd Tank Armies. The 51st Army and 2nd Guards Army, just released from the Crimea, moved into the Stavka reserve.

The Stavka had disbanded the 4th Ukrainian Front and, as Tolbukhin no longer had an active command, the front commanders were moved along the line. Koniev took over at the 1st Ukrainian Front, Malinovsky the 2nd and Tolbukhin the 3rd.

The Stavka also prepared for a major offensive against the Finnish armies north of Leningrad. It planned to knock the Finns out of the war once and for all and regain the territory won during the Winter War of 1939–40. Facing the northern perimeter of Leningrad were the 2nd and 4th Finnish Korps of the South Eastern Army while the Army of Karelia was dug in along the line of the Svir river between Lakes Onega and Ladoga and to the north. The 7th Finnish Korp held the Svir line and the 6th the line north of Lake Onega. By first attacking the South Eastern Army and breaking through its extensive defences, the Leningrad Front hoped to draw in the Finnish reserve and elements of the Karelian Army. Once this had been achieved, the Soviet Karelian Front would unleash its attack. To overcome the 180,000 Finnish soldiers the Leningrad and Karelian Fronts deployed 450,000 men, 10,000 artillery pieces, 800 tanks and Su's and 1,000 Katyusha's. To support the attack there were more than 530 aircraft.[19]

30 May 1944

SOUTHERN SECTOR
The Germans launched a limited counter-attack around Jassy but the fighting was only local and gained little.

31 May 1944

SOVIET COMMAND
The commanders of the Bagration fronts received their orders for the coming offensive.

THE OSTHEER
Having lost the 17th Army in addition to normal wastage, the German armies in the field were reduced by one SS panzer, one motorised and six infantry divisions, while the Ostheer received only two infantry and one of the new Volksgrenadier divisions in return. German strength stood at twenty-one panzer, nine panzer grenadier and 134 infantry divisions.[20] Army Group Centre lost its 56th Panzer Korp from reserve to Army Group North Ukraine.

6 June 1944

The Western Front
The second front was finally opened as the Western Allies invaded Normandy. For the next few weeks Hitler was fixated with the defence of the West and the destruction of the Allied landing force. The Anglo–American invasion of Italy in September 1943 had opened a limited second front against the Germans but failed to tie down sufficient forces to influence the fighting in the east to any great degree. Possibly the most decisive factor in the West was the Allied combined bomber offensive. By attacking the German ability to wage war, the Allied air forces inflicted crippling losses on the German fuel suppliers and production facilities. Furthermore, the raids had drawn the Luftwaffe away to the west, paving the way for the Soviet air armies to gain absolute air superiority. With the loss of thousands of valuable 88mm artillery pieces acting in an anti-aircraft role, the ground forces were deprived of one of their most effective anti-tank guns, a valuable resource considering the Soviet preponderance of armour.

9 June 1944

Finnish Sector
The Leningrad Front began probing attacks against the South Eastern Army. The 7th and 32nd Armies had 202,000 men for the attack, while the 21st and 23rd Armies had 189,000.[21]

10 June 1944

Finnish Sector
The Leningrad Front began its artillery preparation. After a considerable bombardment, Gusev's 21st Army attacked on a nine-mile front, pushing the Finns slowly back across the Sestra. The 23rd Army also began its probing attacks while the 13th Air Army pounded the Finnish defences as the ground troops moved forward.

11 June 1944

Finnish Sector
The 23rd Army joined the offensive. Fighting was bitter as the heavily outnumbered Finns fought to halt the Soviet onslaught. Despite repeated counter-attacks each Finnish position was overwhelmed, Soviet forces drawing close to the second defence line. By evening the first defence line collapsed, forcing the Finns northward.

13 June 1944

FINNISH SECTOR
The second defence line was reached. Elements of the 23rd Army took Terijiko and Yalkena after bloody fighting.

14 June 1944

FINNISH SECTOR
The 23rd and 21st Armies launched a concerted attack upon the second defence line and broke through, pushing the Finns back on an eight-mile front.

GERMAN COMMAND
OKH confirmed that it believed the main Russian attack for the coming summer campaign would be made in the Ukraine, probably against the 4th Panzer Army.

15 June 1944

FINNISH SECTOR
The Finns fell back to their final defence line before Vipurii, closely pursued by the 21st and 23rd Armies.

19 June 1944

THE PARTISAN WAR
With more than 370,000 partisans operating behind Army Group Centre, the Soviets planned to paralyse the German railway network, crippling the German ability to co-ordinate their front line forces and move up reinforcements. Partisans destroyed hundreds of miles of railway lines and brought movement to a halt. In addition, the Soviet air armies launched massive strikes against the Luftwaffe bases in Belorussia.

20 June 1944

FINNISH SECTOR
Soviet forces reached and captured Vipurii, leaving the Finnish South Eastern Army shattered. The scale of the defeat compelled the Finns to draw forces away from the Army of Karelia, exactly as anticipated by the Stavka. The next phase in the destruction of the Finnish army was about to begin.

Central Sector

There had been more than 10,000 partisan attacks on the railways behind Army Group Centre since 19 June.

21 June 1944

Finnish Sector

The Karelian Front began its offensive against the Finnish Karelian Army along the Svir river. The 7th and 32nd Armies, supported by heavy artillery fire, shattered the surprised Finnish forces. The Finns immediately fell back, giving up the Svir line. Elements of the 32nd Army advanced ten-miles while the 7th Army breached the Svir near Lodenoye Pole.

Central Sector

After weeks of preparation the Red Army was poised to strike at Army Group Centre. The Stavka had massed 2,500,000 men for the attack, 1,254,000 in the first echelon, supported by 5,300 aircraft, 5,200 tanks and Su's, 31,000 artillery pieces, 2,300 Katyusha and over 70,000 motor transport vehicles.

Bagramyan's 1st Baltic Front, on the northern wing of the offensive, comprised the 43rd, 6th Guards and 4th Shock Armies with 359,500 men, while the 3rd Belorussian Front to its south had the 11th Guards (formerly 16th Army), 39th, 5th, 31st and 5th Guards Tank Armies with 579,000 men. In the centre of the line was 2nd Belorussian Front with 319,000 men between the 50th, 49th and 33rd Armies, while Rokossovsky's 1st Belorussian, with 1,071,000 men, held the southern flank. For the first phase of the offensive the 1st Belorussian would use only its right wing (61st, 65th, 28th, 3rd and 48th Armies), the left wing not attacking until the beginning of July. Of the 1,200,000 men in the first echelon, more than 595,000 were combat troops, more than Army Group Centre could deploy in total.

The 1st Baltic and 3rd Belorussian Fronts were to crush the flanks of the 3rd Panzer Army and encircle it in Vitebsk before the 1st Baltic exploited the southern wing of Army Groups North. The 3rd Belorussian would press rapidly south-west towards Minsk. To the south the 1st Belorussian Front was to encircle the 9th Army at Bobruisk before pushing north to link up with the 3rd at Minsk. The 1st and 3rd Belorussian Fronts, forming the outer pincers of the encirclement, would then push westward to the Russo–Polish border and force the Germans back into the Baltic states, East Prussia and Poland. While the pincers marched, the 2nd Belorussian would pin the 4th Army frontally. In order to co-ordinate the two prongs of the attack, Marshal Zhukov controlled the 1st Baltic and 3rd Belorussian Fronts while Marshal Vasilevsky co-ordinated the 1st and 2nd Belorussian Fronts.

Busch's Army Group Centre had 580,000 men between the 3rd Panzer, 4th, 9th and 2nd Armies. Reinhardt's 3rd Panzer Army, on the northern flank, deployed 9th Korp (two infantry divisions), 53rd Korp (two infantry and two Luftwaffe field divisions) and 6th Korp (three infantry divisions) with an infantry and security division in reserve. This gave Reinhardt 160,000 men. The 4th Army, under General Heinrici, deployed 27th Korp (one panzer grenadier and two infantry divisions), 39th Korp (three infantry and one panzer grenadier divisions) and 12th Korp (one panzer grenadier and two infantry divisions) with Feldherrnhalle Panzer Grenadier Division in reserve, a force of 165,000 men. On the southern wing was Jordan's 9th Army with the 35th Korp (five infantry divisions), 41st Korp (three infantry divisions) and 55th Korp (two infantry divisions) with 20th Panzer Division in reserve, a force of 170,000 men. On the extreme right wing of Army Group Centre, virtually separated from the rest by the Pripet Marshes, was Weiss' 2nd Army with 23rd, 20th and 8th Korps and 85,000 men. To support the front line forces the German armies had 9,500 artillery pieces and 900 panzers, while the 6th Air Fleet deployed 775 aircraft. Operational availability of panzers and aircraft was around a third of totals. Army Group had a single panzer grenadier division in reserve (the 14th), the bulk of its armour having moved south into the Ukraine.

Busch was expecting a Soviet attack and had placed his armies as close to readiness as he could. Reinhardt's 3rd Panzer Army was badly exposed to attack in the Vitebsk salient. Heinrici's 4th Army remained on the east bank of the Dniepr while Jordan's 9th Army held the southern wing. Hitler had denied Busch operational freedom to manoeuvre.

THE OSTHEER

Since the beginning of May the German armies in the east had been reinforced. Army Group North now had 376,000 men, 138,000 of which were combat infantry, while Army Group Centre had 580,000 (214,000 were combat infantry). To the south Army Groups North and South Ukraine totalled 475,000 and 420,000 men respectively. Only 175,000 and 140,000 were combat infantry.[22]

> *Operation Bagration was one of the most ambitious operations planned by the Red Army so far, an offensive it would not have considered possible even a year earlier. Excellent progress had been made in the use of armoured and air forces during the difficult Ukrainian and Leningrad offensives, so much so that in this new attack the Ostheer would be overwhelmed absolutely. Operation Bagration heralded the final, bloody phase of the Great Patriotic War.*

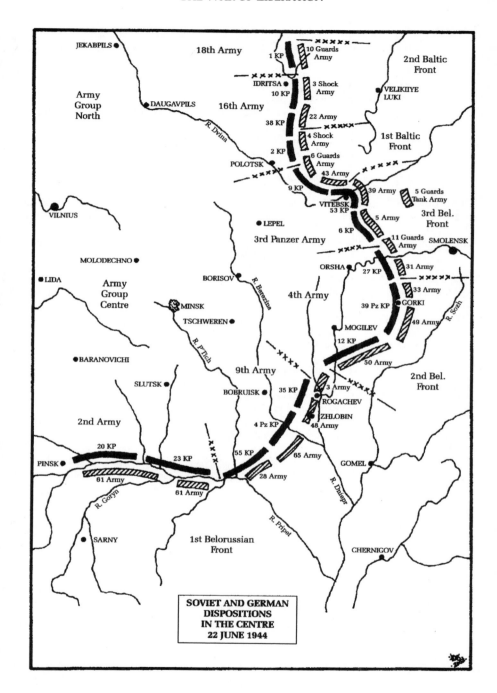

SOVIET AND GERMAN
DISPOSITIONS
IN THE CENTRE
22 JUNE 1944

NOTE

1   Kirosheev, *Soviet Casualties and Combat Losses in the Twentieth Century*, Table 67
2   Ellis, *The World War II Databook*, p176
3   Ellis, *The World War II Databook*, p178
4   Ellis, *The World War II Databook*, pp277–8
5   Kirosheev, *Soviet Casualties and Combat Losses in the Twentieth Century*, Table 67
6   Combat strengths from Ellis, *Brute Force*, Table 34
7   Ellis, *The World War II Databook*, p176
8   Buchner, *Ostfront 1944*, p22
9   Kirosheev, *Soviet Casualties and Combat Losses in the Twentieth Century*, Table 75
10   Ellis, *The World War II Databook*, p176
11   Kirosheev, *Soviet Casualties and Combat Losses in the Twentieth Century*, Table 75
12   Ellis, *The World War II Databook*, p176
13   Kirosheev, *Soviet Casualties and Combat Losses in the Twentieth Century*, Table 67
14   Buchner, *Ostfront 1944*, p93
15   Kirosheev, *Soviet Casualties and Combat Losses in the Twentieth Century*, Table 75
16   Ellis, *The World War II Databook*, p176
17   Lucas, *The Last Year of the German Army*, Table 1, p25
18   Kirosheev, *Soviet Casualties and Combat Losses in the Twentieth Century*, Table 75
19   Kirosheev, *Soviet Casualties and Combat Losses in the Twentieth Century*, Table 67
20   Ellis, *The World War II Databook*, p176
21   Kirosheev, *Soviet Casualties and Combat Losses in the Twentieth Century*, Table 67
22   Lucas, *The Last Year of the German Army*, Table 1, p25

CHAPTER VI

Steamroller

On the third anniversary of Operation Barbarossa, the Red Army was prepared to destroy Army Group Centre. Mirroring the German advance towards Smolensk of 1941, the massive Soviet offensive would eclipse the German victories of the first days of the campaign. Never had the Stavka prepared such an ambitious plan so thoroughly and with such overwhelming force. However, the Soviet armies now not only enjoyed numerical superiority in troops, but in aircraft, tanks and artillery, and perhaps most crucially of all, in motor vehicles. This offensive was to determine for good the fate of the German armies that had once stood just a few miles from Moscow.

22 June 1944

CENTRAL SECTOR

Artillery of the 1st Baltic and 3rd Belorussian Fronts began the bombardment of the 3rd Panzer Army. Massive air attacks accompanied the ground assaults, inflicting severe German casualties even before the main reconnaissance attack had begun. Chistyakov's 6th Guards and Beloborodov's 43rd Armies hit the 9th Korp hard as they began strong probing attacks. Elements of the korp gave ground, being thrown back from Sirotino on an eight-mile front. A five-mile gap was opened near Obol. Massed tank and infantry attacks then simply overwhelmed the Germans. To support the failing defences of the 9th Korp, Army Group North transferred an infantry division but it did no good. The 6th Korp was also under heavy attack by the 39th Army, suffering heavy losses, as another hole opened in the German front, this time south of Vitebsk.

At the end of the day the 1st Baltic Front had forced the 9th Korp back five miles and the 6th Korp had retreated ten miles before the 3rd Belorussian Front. The disintegration of the wings of the 3rd Panzer Army threatened the 53rd Korp positions in Vitebsk.

23 June 1944

CENTRAL SECTOR

After the success of the fighting on 22 June, the 1st Baltic and 3rd Belorussian Fronts began full-scale offensive operations. Bagramyan decided to use his artillery preparation only where the German defences remained strong. Both the 6th Guards and 43rd Armies of the 1st Baltic Front broke through without artillery support, Sirotino falling as the 9th Korp was pushed back to the Dvina. Soviet forces succeeded in cutting the Polotsk–Vitebsk railway line, severing the road west out of the Vitebsk. As these battles raged the 6th Korp suffered a terrible beating. One of the korp's infantry divisions collapsed during bitter fighting and another began to fall back from the north-west. Reinhardt demanded that he be allowed to fall back from Vitebsk but Busch, following Hitler's stand and fight order to the letter, categorically refused. In Vitebsk itself the 53rd Korp was only lightly attacked, the 39th Army pinning the korp down as the pincers of the 1st Baltic and 3rd Belorussian smashed its flanking units. The 27th Korp of the 4th Army was also hit by massive blows on the road to Orsha, delivered by 11th Guards, 5th and 31st Armies on the left flank of the 3rd Belorussian Front. In costly defensive fighting the 25th Panzer Division and 78th Sturm Division inflicted heavy losses upon 11th Guards Army but the German line then began to crumble. To aid the exploitation the Stavka moved up the 5th Guards Tank Army from the reserve to deploy.

Overwhelming artillery fire and air attacks supported the attacks of the 2nd Belorussian Front's 33rd, 49th and 50th Armies towards Orsha and Mogilev. The right wing of the 39th Korp of the 4th Army was heavily attacked around Chausy by elements of the 50th Army. One of the German divisions became separated during the fighting and suffered heavy losses while the division holding the southern flank collapsed, opening the road to the Dniepr and Mogilev. With its combat forces in dire need, the 4th Army had no option but to throw in its small reserve. Feldherrnhalle Panzer Grenadier Division, with only thirty tanks, moved up to aid the ailing 39th Korp. This development endangered the 12th Korp south of the 39th, opening up its northern flank to Soviet attack.

The 1st Belorussian Front began probing attacks against the 9th Army. Busch reported to OKH that he could see no way of restoring his lines.

FINNISH SECTOR

The Finns retreated from the Svir, pursued by the 7th Army. The bulk of the Finnish forces had already left this sector in order to cover the Karelian Isthmus.

24 June 1944

CENTRAL SECTOR

General Zeitzler arrived at the headquarters of Army Group Centre in Minsk to meet with Field Marshal Busch. After the meeting, during which he was informed of the disintegration of the 3rd Panzer Army, Zeitzler telephoned Hitler to request that 3rd Panzer be allowed to evacuate 53rd Korp from Vitebsk. Predictably Hitler ordered it to stand fast and hold at all costs.

As these exchanges took place, the situation at the front deteriorated. Forward units of the 6th Guards Army reached the Dvina river and began to cross, quickly followed by 43rd Army. The 9th Korp attempted to stabilise its lines with a counter-attack but was repelled by the 43rd. By mid-afternoon the 6th Guards Army was across the Dvina at Beshen-kovichi and pushed south to meet the advancing forces of the 3rd Belorussian Front.

General Gollwitzer, commanding the 53rd Korp, asked permission to withdraw from Vitebsk. The 3rd Panzer Army and Army Group Centre headquarters both believed this to be the only logical option but Hitler and the OKH forbade it. The 6th Korp was once again struck by the 5th Army of the 3rd Belorussian Front. Outflanked to the north and south, its remaining units were torn apart by the 39th Army. As the 6th Korp was annihilated, the 53rd Korp was isolated in Vitebsk, both the 43rd Army and 39th Army linking up to open the road to the Dniepr and Mogilev. Hitler belatedly agreed to evacuate the 53rd Korp but ordered the 206th Infantry Division to remain behind and hold on to the last man. The decision came too late though as the entire 53rd Korp was already cut off.

Elements of the 27th Korp of the German 4th Army were severely attacked by 11th Guards Army while the 5th Guards Tank Army moved up to the 5th Army sector. With his 39th Korp falling apart, Tippelskirch requested that he be allowed to pull back behind the Dniepr. Hitler refused, instead allocating two infantry divisions to the 4th Army as reinforcement.

The 1st Belorussian Front began its offensive. Supported by massed artillery fire and waves of ground attack aircraft, the 3rd and 48th Armies crashed into the 35th Korp of Jordan's 9th Army. Fierce fighting erupted as the Germans tried to halt the Soviet tanks and infantry that smashed into their line. However, sheer weight of numbers overwhelmed the 35th, one of its divisions disintegrating. Elements of the 3rd Army began to open the junction of the German 9th and 4th Armies, separating the 35th Korp from the 12th Korp. With his flank in danger of collapse, Jordan committed the 20th Panzer Division from reserve, aiming to halt the Russian attack and plug the hole before it became too large. South of the 35th Korp, in the army's centre, the 41st Korp was also under heavy attack but was held, despite the collapse of its left wing divisions. This prompted the 41st to fall back to the west, away from the 35th Korp.

With Army Group Centre under attack along most of its line, Hitler agreed to the allocation of reinforcements, sending the 5th Panzer Division of 56th Panzer Korp up from the north Ukraine. This single division, with just 130 panzers, was expected to halt the Soviet steamroller which was crushing Army Group Centre.

25 June 1944

CENTRAL SECTOR

The isolated korps of the 3rd Panzer Army fought desperate actions against massive Soviet attacks. Surviving elements of the 9th Korp fell back south-west of the Dvina, pursued by the 6th Guards and 43rd Armies. A counter-attack by the 16th Army's 2nd Korp near Polotsk failed to effect a junction with the 9th, the 4th Shock and 6th Guards Armies blocking Army Group North's efforts.

In Vitebsk the 53rd Korp attempted to disengage from the 39th Army but was involved in fierce street fighting as the Soviets broke into the town. Gollwitzer was trying to assemble his forces for a breakout and by dusk had received the order from army headquarters ordering it to break out but to leave the 206th Infantry Division behind to hold the town. As fighting raged on into the night, the 53rd Korp moved to the southern bank of the Dvina but German sappers blew the Dvina bridges prematurely, stranding most of the 246th Infantry Division on the wrong side of the river. During heavy fighting around the city one of the korp's Luftwaffe field divisions was wiped out.

The 6th Korp launched a weak counter-attack aimed at halting 5th Army. As it assembled it was attacked by the 3rd Air Army, the assault being broken up before it could interfere with the Soviet advance.

The German 4th Army fought its own battles on the east bank of the Dniepr. After a desperate struggle the 27th Korp collapsed, opening up the northern flank of the 4th Army. With the German line in shreds, the 5th Guards Tank Army moved up behind the 11th Guards Army, ready to exploit the gap. The 39th Korp was pounded by the 49th Army and 50th Army as it struggled to pull back west. On the 4th Army's southern flank the 12th Korp was also under furious attack. The counter-attack by the Feldherrnhalle division failed to halt the Russians, the panzers being pushed back away from Suchary. Hitler agreed to a withdrawal but insisted that Mogilev be held at all costs. Having lost the opportunity to fall back intact, the 4th Army struggled under intense Soviet attacks and, like the 53rd Korp in Vitebsk, found it difficult to disengage.

Elements of the 3rd and 48th Armies (1st Belorussian Front) outflanked the 35th Korp near Zhlobin as the 65th and 28th Armies moved up from the south, opening a gap between the 55th and 41st Panzer Korps. The 20th Panzer Division launched a determined counter-attack to support the 35th Korp but was unable to halt the Soviet armour. Destroying more than sixty Soviet tanks in bitter fighting, the 20th had to fall back, being reduced to only forty operational tanks.

GERMAN COMMAND

General Dietl, commanding the 20th Mountain Army, was killed in an air accident. Rendulic took over the vacant command.

26 June 1944

CENTRAL SECTOR

The German situation in Belorussia deteriorated as the Soviet armies deepened their penetration behind Army Group Centre, threatening to encircle the bulk of its forces.

On the northern wing the 53rd Korp began its breakout from Vitebsk. In defiance of Hitler's order that the 206th Infantry Division be left behind, Gollwitzer attacked with all his remaining forces. During the ensuing battle the 206th was wiped out virtually to a man. The Germans aimed to slip away from the town during the night of 26–27 June, but the sound of explosions as engineers destroyed the supply dumps alerted the Russians to the escape attempt. A massive air attack flattened most of the town before a full-scale armoured and infantry assault hit the 53rd. After a brisk battle, during which more than 6,000 German soldiers were killed, Vitebsk fell to the 39th Army. The remnants of the 53rd Korp were isolated a short distance from the southern suburbs of the ruined city.

Tippelskirch's 4th Army was under intense pressure as it fell back to the Dniepr. The 27th Korp, broken after its battle on the left wing, poured back towards the river, hoping to cross before the Soviets could isolate them on the east bank. However, the 5th Guards Tank Army entered the battle and immediately blasted its way through, cutting the road to Orsha and pushing on to Tolochin. This compelled the 27th Korp to fall back south of the town, Orsha falling to the 11th Guards and 31st Armies late in the day. The retreat by the 27th Korp opened up the rear of the 39th Korp and forced it to abandon its crumbling positions. By noon Russian troops reached the Dniepr north of Mogilev, the 49th Army crossing to threaten the rear of the entire 4th Army. With around half of the 4th already across the river, Hitler agreed to its withdrawal to the Berezina. By dusk the 5th Guards Tank Army penetrated to Tolochin, taking the town after a brief battle.

To the south Jordan's 9th Army collapsed. The 35th Korp fell back from Bobruisk but found its line of retreat blocked by 9th Tank Corp. By dusk the korp was encircled by the 3rd and 48th Armies. Elements of the 48th and 65th Armies, pushing up from the south, were only two miles from Bobruisk. Having failed to link up with the 35th Korp, the 20th Panzer Division moved south-west to Bobruisk to prevent the fall of the town. With his army in pieces, Hitler sacked General Jordan, blaming the whole debacle on Jordan's misuse of the 20th Panzer Division. General von Vormann took over the vacant command.

Late in the day, Field Marshal Busch flew to the Obersalzburg to meet with Hitler, pleading with him to be allowed to pull his shattered armies back to try and prevent their total destruction. Hitler was still convinced that the Russian offensive in Belorussia was merely a diversion to the main attack that was expected in the Ukraine and refused Busch freedom of action.

FINNISH SECTOR
Olonets fell to Krutkov's 7th Army.

27 June 1944

CENTRAL SECTOR
Gollwitzer's 53rd Korp broke out from its lodgement south of Vitebsk and moved ten miles to the south-west. As it retreated the 39th Army completed the capture of Vitebsk. Gollwitzer reported to army head-quarters that the breakout was proceeding well but contact was lost shortly afterwards. Under ferocious attack the 53rd broke apart and was destroyed. Gollwitzer and 35,000 of his men were killed or captured during the ensuing fighting.

The 4th Army was also breaking up. Its 27th Korp drew together into a mobile pocket and began to fight west from Orsha. The 39th Korp attempted to rebuild its shattered line as it fell back. On the southern wing the 12th Korp fell back. Behind the northern wing of the 4th Army the 5th Guards Tank Army moved rapidly towards Borisov. However, the 5th Panzer Division had begun to deploy its seventy Panthers and fifty-five Panzer-IV's[1] to block the Soviet advance to the Berezina and gain time for the 4th Army to fall back. Heavy fighting erupted as leading Soviet tanks ran into the panzers.

Farther south the 9th Army was in an increasingly dire situation. The 35th Korp was isolated east of Bobruisk and the 41st to the south of the town. The 55th Korps was falling back to the west along the northern edge of the Pripet Marshes. However, the 41st was ordered to halt its withdrawal and fight its way back towards Bobruisk to support the breakout by the 35th Korp. Inside the pocket the 35th launched its first break-out attempt. With nearly 150 panzers in the lead the Germans tried to smash their way through the 3rd Army, but a combination of ferocious ground fire and attacks by the 16th Air Army managed to break up the German force, inflicting crippling casualties.

Hitler ordered the 3rd Panzer and 4th Armies to establish a line from Polotsk, through Lepel and on to the Berezina, a line that had already been breached by the advancing Soviet forces. In addition, the 12th Panzer Division, released from Army Group North, began to arrive at Marina Gorka to strengthen the 4th Army.

FINNISH SECTOR
The Finns continued their withdrawal east of Lake Ladoga, giving up Petrozavodsk to the advancing 7th Army.

28 June 1944

CENTRAL SECTOR
Soviet forces drew closer to Minsk. The 3rd Panzer Army had been virtually destroyed along the Dvina and its one remaining operational korp, the 9th, was falling back to the west. Attacks by the 43rd Army of the 1st Baltic Front succeeded in securing Lepel.

Heavy fighting raged as the 49th and 50th Armies (2nd Belorussian Front) stormed Mogilev, taking the town after a brisk battle. Soviet losses were high as the 39th Korp defended with great ferocity. The majority of the korp succeed in crossing the Dniepr and fell back to the Berezina. However, the 5th Guards Tank Army was already at Borisov on the Berezina and crossed despite fierce resistance by the 5th Panzer Division.

Farther south the 48th Army crossed the Berezina and entered Bobruisk. With more than 70,000 men of the 35th and 41st Korps isolated in the pocket, the Soviets were hard pressed to prevent a breakout, bitter fighting raging all around the pocket.

At the end of the day the Stavka issued new orders for the liberation of Minsk by the 1st and 3rd Belorussian Fronts and the encirclement of those elements of the 3rd Panzer and 4th Armies still east of the city.

GERMAN COMMAND
Hitler reverted to his policy of sacking generals, Lindemann, commander of Army Group North being dismissed and replaced with Field Marshal Freissner. Field Marshal Busch was also sacked for his failure to halt the Soviet attacks in Belorussia, Model being appointed to command in his place. Model already commanded Army Group North Ukraine and, while retaining this command, gave over operational control to General Harpe.

29 June 1944

CENTRAL SECTOR
Barely a week after the Soviet offensive began, Army Group Centre had

lost 130,000 killed and 60,000 captured and the bulk of its 900 panzers and assault guns destroyed.

On the northern flank the 9th Korp of the 3rd Panzer Army lost Usachi to the 1st Baltic Front while the 4th Army retreated across the Drut. Heavy fighting also raged at Rudnya as the Soviet infantry forces reached the Berezina, and fierce battles raged at Studenka.

To the south the German 9th Army tried to break out from Bobruisk but was repulsed. The 35th Korp practically ceased to exist while the 41st, also encircled following its march east to relieve the 35th, was under heavy fire. In intense fighting the Germans pushed twenty miles north of the town but suffered heavy losses. Rokossovsky continued to drive his forward units towards Minsk, Group Pliev taking Slutsk.

30 June 1944

CENTRAL SECTOR

The 11th Guards and 5th Guards Tank Armies met up at Borisov, effectively isolating a large part of the 4th Army east of the Berezina as its line of retreat was severed. With pressure increasing against the bridgehead, the Germans blew the Borisov bridges and began to fall back.

Having been decisively defeated to the south, Vormann's 9th Army was made responsible for the defence of Minsk. No additional forces were made available.

The 1st Belorussian Front destroyed the Germans north of Bobruisk. A force of 20,000 broke out and reached the 12th Panzer Division at Marina Gorki [2] but the remainder, almost 50,000, were lost.

THE OPPOSING FORCES

Across the Eastern Front the Germans deployed 4,470 tanks and 1,710 aircraft against 11,600 Soviet tanks and 11,800 aircraft. German divisional strength stood at eighteen panzer, nine panzer grenadier and 133 infantry divisions. [3]

1 July 1944

CENTRAL SECTOR

With the Soviet armies fast approaching the Germans began the evacuation of second echelon personnel from Minsk, 8,000 wounded and 12,000 auxiliaries being moved west.[4]

Heavy fighting raged on the Berezina, the 31st and 267th Infantry Divisions attempting to hold open a line of retreat for the 4th Army. Despite the threat posed by the 11th Guards and 5th Guards Tank Armies around Borisov, the 27th Korp got most of its men across near Zhukovets while the 39th and 12th Korps crossed at Berezino. Soviet forces continued to push forwards, trying to get behind the German army and encircle it before it could reach Minsk. Leading tanks entered Tschweren.

2 July 1944

CENTRAL SECTOR
The 5th Panzer Division came under heavy attack east of Minsk as the 1st and 3rd Belorussian Fronts drew closer together. Furious fighting raged at Krasnoye and Molodechno, the latter being retaken by 5th Panzer after ferocious fighting with the 3rd Belorussian Front. However, the 31st Army then sliced through the German defences and, supported by the 5th Guards Tank Army, reached the outskirts of Minsk. Smolovichi fell. The 3rd Army also drew up from the south, outpacing the retreating 9th Army. With the loss of Minsk imminent, Hitler agreed to the evacuation of the city. It was already too late, the bulk of the 4th Army being far to the east.

3 July 1944

CENTRAL SECTOR
Elements of the 5th Guards Tank Army entered Minsk, it and the 31st Army fighting bitter actions with German rearguards. The 3rd Army fought its way in from the south and south-east, linking up with the 3rd Belorussian Front. The German 4th Army, with 100,000 men, was isolated. Heavy fighting raged as the 27th, 39th and 12th Korps retreated, unaware that their escape route had been cut.

4 July 1944

NORTHERN SECTOR
The 4th Shock Army of the 1st Baltic Front took Polotsk, threatening the southern flank of the German 16th Army.

CENTRAL SECTOR
There was heavy fighting around Minsk as the 4th Army tried to escape. Despite repeated attacks, the 27th, 39th and 12th Korps failed to break out. By dusk the Germans had been contained around Pekalin.

5 July 1944

CENTRAL SECTOR
The 27th Korp broke up and attempted to break out in small pockets but many of its men were ambushed and killed. Thousands died in bloody battles in the forests of Belorussia.

6 July 1944

CENTRAL SECTOR

Following the destruction of the 27th Korp, the 12th Korp attacked towards Minsk but it was halted by concentrated Russian fire. Casualties were severe as the Germans rushed the Soviet lines, only to be gunned down in droves. Panic began to spread throughout the remnants of the 4th Army.

The retreating 55th Korp of the 9th Army escaped destruction as it fell back to Luninets. This was the only intact unit left to the 9th Army.

7 July 1944

SOUTHERN SECTOR

The 1st Belorussian Front began limited attacks with its 47th Army, taking Kovel after hard fighting.

8 July 1944

CENTRAL SECTOR

More than 60,000 men of the German 4th Army had fallen during repeated break-out attempts, the majority of its 40,000 survivors being captured by Soviet forces. The 4th Army had effectively ceased to exist.

The 1st and 3rd Belorussian Fronts continued to push west. Elements of the 65th Army, together with Group Pliev and part of the 28th Army, took Baranovichi after a furious battle with remnants of the German 9th Army.

Operation Bagration had succeeded in destroying Army Group Centre. The Stavka and Red Army had successfully broken the individual armies in small-scale encirclement operations before trapping the remnants in a larger cauldron thrown around Minsk. For the Ostheer the defeat eclipsed even Stalingrad, some twenty infantry, one security, three panzer grenadier, one panzer and two Luftwaffe field divisions being destroyed and 350,000 men being lost. The German front in the central sector simply no longer existed.

9 July 1944

CENTRAL SECTOR

The Soviet 5th Army encircled Vilnius, cutting off nearly 15,000 Germans in the city. Other units of the 3rd Belorussian captured Lida as they rushed towards the Niemen.

10 July 1944

NORTHERN SECTOR

The 2nd Baltic Front attacked the southern wing of the 16th Army with its 10th Guards and 3rd Shock Armies. The 2nd Guards and 4th Shock Armies launched new attacks aimed at meeting up with the 6th Guards Army at Daugavpils. With Army Group North now also threatened, Field Marshal Model requested that Freissner be allowed to withdraw behind the line of the Dvina, shortening his line and creating a reserve that could be committed to reinforce the shattered armies of Army Group Centre. Hitler categorically refused.

CENTRAL SECTOR

Utena fell to the 43rd Army and Slonim to the 65th Army of the 1st Belorussian Front.

FINNISH SECTOR

Soviet forces reached the Suvilahti and Lormada rivers, taking Pitkjaranta.

11 July 1944

SOUTHERN SECTOR

The 1st Ukrainian Front was poised to open its offensive against Army Group North Ukraine. For the offensive, Koniev's 1st Ukrainian Front had 840,000 men with 14,000 artillery pieces and 1,600 tanks[5] among the 3rd Guards Army north of Lutsk, 13th Army between Lutsk and Brody, 60th, 38th, 1st Guards Armies massed between Brody and Tarnopol, 5th Guards Army behind the left wing of the 1st Guards Army and 18th Army on the southern wing at Kolomya. The 1st Ukrainian Front's armoured forces, held in the second echelon, consisted of the 1st Guards Tank Army near Lutsk, 3rd Guards Tank Army near Brody and 4th Tank Army near Tarnopol. Two cavalry mechanised groups, held north and south of Dubno, also provided support. The 2nd and 8th Air Armies were also attached and had 2,800 aircraft.

Also facing the northern wing of Army Group North Ukraine was the left wing of the 1st Belorussian Front. This force comprised the 70th, 47th, 8th Guards and 69th Armies concentrated north of Kovel with the 1st Polish Army and 2nd Tank Army in reserve.

Army Group North Ukraine, commanded by General Harpe in the absence of Field Marshal Model, had the 4th Panzer, 1st Panzer and 1st Hungarian Armies. The German forces deployed thirty-four infantry divisions, five panzer divisions and one panzer grenadier division, a total of nearly 500,000 men with 900 panzers, 6,000 artillery pieces and 700 aircraft.

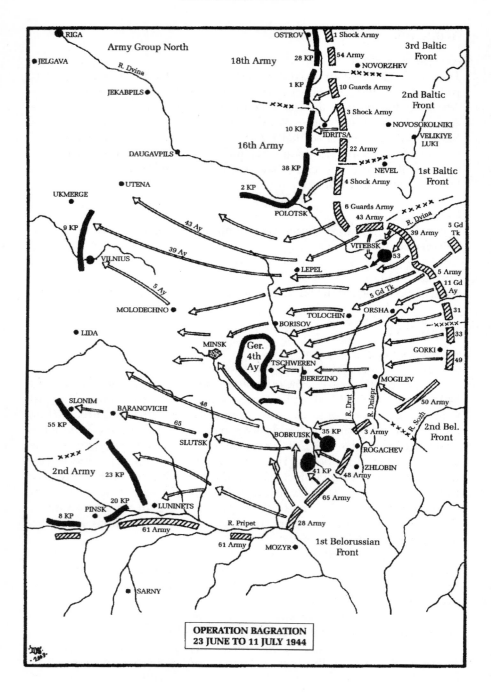

RIGA

Army Group North

JELGAVA

R. Dvina

JEKABPILS

18th Army

OSTROV

28 KP

1 Shock Army

54 Army

NOVORZHEV

3rd Baltic
Front

1 KP

10 Guards Army

2nd Baltic
Front

3 Shock Army

NOVOSOKOLNIKI

VELIKIYE
LUKI

16th Army

10 KP

IDRITSA

22 Army

DAUGAVPILS

38 KP

NEVEL

4 Shock Army

1st Baltic
Front

UTENA

2 KP

POLOTSK

6 Guards Army

43 Army

R. Dvina

5 Gd
Tk

UKMERGE

9 KP

43 Ay

VITEBSK

39 Army

53

5 Army

VILNIUS

39 Ay

LEPEL

5 Gd Tk

11 Gd
Ay

5 Ay

MOLODECHNO

TOLOCHIN

ORSHA

31

33

LIDA

BORISOV

GORKI

49

MINSK

Ger.
4th
Ay

TSCHWEREN

BEREZINO

MOGILEV

SLONIM

48

R. Drut

R. Dniepr

R. Sozh

50 Army

2nd Bel.
Front

55 KP

BARANOVICHI

65

35 KP

3 Army

SLUTSK

BOBRUISK

ROGACHEV

2nd Army

23 KP

41 KP

ZHLOBIN

48 Army

20 KP

LUNINETS

65 Army

8 KP

PINSK

61 Army

R. Pripet

28 Army

1st Belorussian
Front

61 Army

MOZYR

SARNY

**OPERATION BAGRATION
23 JUNE TO 11 JULY 1944**

12 July 1944

NORTHERN SECTOR
The 2nd Baltic Front ripped a fifty-mile hole in the 16th Army, the 10th Guards Army advancing ten miles into the German rear. The 3rd Shock Army had also broken through, reaching the Velikaya river while the 4th captured Drissa. Idritsa fell to the 4th Shock Army of the 1st Baltic Front.

The Stavka strengthened the 1st Baltic Front in its push towards the Gulf of Riga, allocating the 51st and 2nd Guards Armies from the reserve.

CENTRAL SECTOR
Furious battles raged at Vilnius as the 5th Army forced its way into the city.

SOUTHERN SECTOR
Koniev began probing attacks against the junction of 4th and 1st Panzer Armies. The Germans immediately pulled back their forward units to the main defence belt but were observed. Gambling that the Germans would not expect an attack without the usual artillery barrage, Koniev decided to attack on the 13th.

13 July 1944

CENTRAL SECTOR
After a fierce battle the 5th Army took Vilnius, more than 7,000 of the 15,000 strong garrison having fallen during the fighting. The 11th Guards Army crossed the Niemen river at Alytus. German counter-attacks were beaten off with some difficulty

SOUTHERN SECTOR
Koniev launched his offensive without artillery preparation. The 60th and 38th Armies attacked the centre and right of Hauffe's 13th Korp near Brody. Simultaneously the 13th Army began a furious attack against the left wing of the 13th Korp and broke through near Radekhov. Soon after the 38th Army broke through near Zolochev. On either flank of the assault the 46th and 48th Panzer Korps counter-attacked but were hit by the 3rd Guards and 1st Guards Armies.

14 July 1944

CENTRAL SECTOR
The 61st Army and elements of the 28th Army took Pinsk. The 31st Army reached the Niemen at Grodno and crossed to threaten the East Prussian border. Grodno itself was fiercely defended by the SS Totenkopf Division.

SOUTHERN SECTOR

The 1st Ukrainian Front developed its offensive, the 2nd and 8th Air Armies clearing the 4th Air Fleet from the skies. Joining the offensive, the left wing of the 1st Belorussian Front hit the northern wing of the 4th Panzer Army.

The 3rd Guards and 13th Armies resumed their attacks against the junction of the two German panzer armies, the 13th Korp being crushed as the 13th and 38th Armies advanced more than ten miles into its rear. The 60th and 38th Armies developed their attacks towards Lvov but were embroiled in strong German defensive positions. The 48th Panzer Korp tried to launch a counter-attack but suffered heavy casualties to constant Soviet air attacks.

15 July 1944

Opochka fell to the 10th Guards Army.

CENTRAL SECTOR

The Germans counter-attacked at Alytus, hitting the 11th Guards Army. After heavy fighting the Germans were repulsed and the Guards secured their bridgehead.

SOUTHERN SECTOR

The 42nd Korp of the 4th Panzer Army broke, Hauffe's 13th Korp losing contact with its neighbour. As the 60th and 38th Armies struggled to break through the German defences before Lvov, Koniev committed his 3rd Guards Tank Army against the 13th Korp's northern flank and the 4th Tank Army against its southern wing. Counter-attacks by the 46th Panzer Korp hit the 3rd Guards Tank and by the 48th Panzer Korp struck the 4th Tank Army. In intense fighting the 48th suffered heavy losses, being slaughtered by squadrons of Ilyushin ground attack aircraft. However, eventually the German attack halted the 38th Army.

16 July 1944

SOUTHERN SECTOR

The 3rd Guards Tank and 4th Tank Armies smashed aside the German panzer divisions trying to hold them and broke into the rear of the 13th Korp.

17 July 1944

NORTHERN SECTOR

The 3rd Baltic Front joined the offensive now rolling along the line from Lake Peipus to Chernovitsy. Heavy fighting erupted south of the lake as the 1st Shock and 54th Armies hit the dug-in German forces. The 3rd Shock Army captured Sebezh and the 22nd Army Osveya.

CENTRAL SECTOR
Rokossovsky unleashed the full forces of his left wing, hitting the centre and north of the 4th Panzer Army.

SOUTHERN SECTOR
Koniev committed Katukov's 1st Guards Tank Army near Sokal, forcing a crossing of the Bug. The 13th Korp fought its way back to the Prinz Eugen line, meeting fierce resistance as it withdrew. Lelyushenko's 4th Tak Army was embroiled in bitter fighting on the road to Lvov, being bogged down with the 38th Army.

18 July 1944

CENTRAL SECTOR
The 31st Army crossed the East Prussian border and reached Augustow, but ferocious German counter-attacks halted the Soviets. The fighting had reached German soil. As the Russian advance slowed, Model constructed a thin defence line from Kaunas to Bialystok.

SOUTHERN SECTOR
The 8th Guards and 1st Polish Armies attacked north of Kovel and broke through the German line. To the south, leading units of the 1st Guards Army, pushing down from the north, were just twenty miles from Stanislav. The 4th Tank Army took Olshantsa during heavy fighting on the road to Lvov. Meanwhile, elements of the 38th Army linked up with the 13th Army to isolate 65,000 men of the 13th Korp west of Brody.

19 July 1944

SOUTHERN SECTOR
The 13th Korp was hit by a series of concentric attacks, Soviet troops capturing Koltow during the fighting. As the advance upon Lvov developed, the 4th Tank Army launched flanking attacks in an effort to encircle the Germans inside the city. However, the 1st Panzer Army put up strong resistance and deflected the Russian attacks.

20 July 1944

NORTHERN SECTOR
The 1st Shock Army smashed through the German 18th Army to outflank Ostrov. A little to the south the 1st Baltic Front unleashed a new attack

towards Siauliai, using the newly committed 51st and 2nd Guards Armies. The 3rd Panzer Army, already stretched to breaking point, broke under this new attack.

SOUTHERN SECTOR

The 8th Guards Army reached the Bug, having smashed the northern wing of the 4th Panzer Army. With the line breached the 2nd Tank Army was committed to the battle.

Counter-attacks by the 48th Panzer Korp failed to break through to the 13th Korp despite heavy fighting. Rava Russki fell to the 13th Army as the Soviets outflanked Lvov from the north.

GERMAN RESISTANCE

German generals attempted to assassinate Adolf Hitler. While in con-ference at Rastenburg, Colonel von Stauffenberg planted a bomb concealed in his briefcase. The subsequent explosion should have killed Hitler but a German officer, trying to get closer to the operations table, probably saved the Führer's life. Moving Stauffenberg's briefcase behind a thick wooden beam running along the length of the table, the officer shielded Hitler from the full force of the blast. Hearing the sound of the explosion as he left, Stauffenberg telephoned his fellow conspirators in Berlin but their delay gave the Nazis the opportunity to seize the initiative. It was quickly established that Hitler had survived the assassination attempt and the coup quickly collapsed. General Fromm, the head of the Replacement Army who had planned to take control of the Berlin garrison, quickly switched sides and had the conspirators in the War Ministry shot, mainly to cover his own implication in the plot. With total brutality the coup was suppressed across the length and breadth of the Reich. Among those who indirectly lost their lives were Field Marshal Rommel and Field Marshal Kluge.

Reichsführer Himmler, as well as already been head of the SS, head of the State Police, head of the Interior Ministry and many other departments, was appointed commander of the Replacement Army.

21 July 1944

NORTHERN SECTOR

The 1st Shock Army captured Ostrov while the 42nd Army attacked Pskov, the last Russian town still in German hands.

CENTRAL SECTOR

The 2nd Tank Army crossed the Bug near Chelm and pushed on towards the Vistula, separating the 4th Panzer Army from the 2nd Army. The Stavka now ordered the 1st Belorussian Front to liberate Lublin by 26 July.

SOUTHERN SECTOR
The 13th Korp launched a furious attack and after a bloody struggle a small force managed to escape from the pocket. However, the Russians quickly sealed the hole in their line. Only a few men survived the hazardous march to reach the 48th Panzer Korp.

As the Soviets drew closer to Lvov, the Germans moved three divisions up to cover the northern approaches to the city.

FINNISH SECTOR
The steady advance of the Soviet 32nd Army reached the Finnish border, the Finns having fallen back with heavy losses.

GERMAN COMMAND
Almost two years after taking over as Chief of the Army General Staff, General Zeitzler was dismissed. Guderian, once again in Hitler's favour, was appointed in his place. Guderian would hold this post until the final days of the war, being drawn into the unreal atmosphere of the Führer headquarters. Zeitzler's dismissal had largely been as a result of his advice to withdraw from Belorussia earlier in the campaign, advice Hitler did not heed.

22 July 1944

NORTHERN SECTOR
The 42nd Army captured most of Pskov, but German rearguards continued to fight in the town. Panevesus fell to the 51st Army as it pushed west towards Siauliai.

CENTRAL SECTOR
The 2nd Tank Army took Chelm.

SOUTHERN SECTOR
The isolated 13th Korp was destroyed in heavy fighting. More than 35,000 German soldiers were killed during the fighting and another 17,000 captured, 12,000 escaping rejoin the main combat line.[6] Hauffe was captured during the final battle. To the west the 4th Tank Army fought its way into Lvov from the south-east.

23 July 1944

NORTHERN SECTOR
Pskov fell to the 42nd Army.

CENTRAL SECTOR

The 65th Army closed on Brest-Litovsk. The Germans had concentrated the largely intact 2nd Army around the town and prepared to halt the Soviet advance.

Farther south the 8th Guards and 2nd Tank Armies fought their way into Lublin, liberating the Majdanek concentration camp on the outskirts of the town. Inside Lublin itself there was heavy fighting as the 4th Panzer Army put up a strong defence.

SOUTHERN SECTOR

The 1st Guards Tank Army crossed the San river near Yaroslav.

24 July 1944

NORTHERN SECTOR

The 3rd SS Panzer Korp evacuated its Narva bridgehead as Narva Operational Group launched strong attacks. The 20th SS Grenadier Division fell back into Narva itself, destroying the bridges across the river as it withdrew.

CENTRAL SECTOR

Following a bloody battle Lublin fell.

SOUTHERN SECTOR

The 1st Panzer Army began to abandon Lvov as the 3rd Guards Tank Army entered the town from the north and the 4th Tank Army threatened German positions to the south. Yavorov fell to the 3rd Guards Tank Army in heavy fighting. The 4th Tank Army was involved in heavy fighting inside the town, while the 60th and 38th Armies moved up from the east.

GERMAN COMMAND

Freissner moved to command Army Group South Ukraine and Schorner North Ukraine.

25 July 1944

NORTHERN SECTOR

The heavy fighting in the north increased in ferocity as the Narva Operational Group continued to attack the 3rd SS Panzer Korp north of Lake Peipus. The 2nd Shock Army launched a furious attack with heavy artillery support and broke through the German positions. Under fierce attack, the Germans evacuated Narva, falling back to their 'Tannenberg' defence line.

To the south the 10th Guards Army took Kraslava as the 2nd Baltic Front closed upon Daugavpils.

CENTRAL SECTOR

Elements of the 1st Belorussian Front were involved in heavy fighting around Brest Litovsk as the Germans barred the road to the town. Fighting also raged to the west as Group Kryukov of the 70th Army broke into Seidlice. The Germans rushed up reinforcements and launched a strong counter-attack. The Luftwaffe, scarce in these times, even managed a few sorties.

Leading tanks of the 2nd Tank Army reach the Vistula near Deblin while the 1st Polish Army followed in its wake. A surprise attack by the 2nd Tank farther north secured a small bridgehead at Magnuszew.

SOUTHERN SECTOR

Bitter fighting continued in Lvov as the 1st Panzer Army pulled out to escape destruction inside the city.

26 July 1944

NORTHERN SECTOR

The Narva Operational Group began to attack the Tannenberg line north of Lake Peipus but was held up by the 3rd SS Panzer Korp.

After a difficult advance the 51st Army reached Siauliai but failed to take the town, despite bitter fighting.

CENTRAL SECTOR

Group Kryukov resumed its attack at Seidlice, pushing into the town despite fierce German resistance. As the fighting east of Warsaw intensified the Germans activated the newly reformed 9th Army on the southern wing of the 2nd Army and the reconstituted 4th Army in East Prussia.

The 8th Guards Army reached the Vistula west of Lublin, having taken Deblin after a brief battle.

SOUTHERN SECTOR

The 3rd Guards Tank Army launched a strong attack upon Przemysl but became involved in heavy fighting with the 1st Panzer Army. The 1st Panzer had withdrawn the bulk of its forces from Lvov, only rearguards remaining to hold up the Soviets. Stanislav fell to the 1st Guards Army after protracted fighting.

27 July 1944

NORTHERN SECTOR

Daugavpils fell to the 4th Shock Army and elements of the 6th Guards Army. Rezekne also fell to the 10th Guards Army. The 51st resumed its attack at Siauliai, but another strong counter-attack by the 3rd Panzer Army halted the Soviet thrust. Bitter fighting raged throughout the day, but at dusk the 51st Army struck again and threw the Germans back, Siauliai falling by nightfall. The 2nd Guards Army advanced south-west of Siauliai.

CENTRAL SECTOR
The 28th Army from the east and 70th Army from the south launched a surprise attack upon the 2nd Army grouped near Brest-Litovsk, the 70th smashing through to link up with the 65th Army which had fought its way down from the north. Eight German divisions were isolated around the city, which fell in bitter fighting. Intense battles erupted as the Germans launched their efforts to break out from the pocket.

The 2nd Tank Army consolidated its bridgehead at Magnuszew, the 1st Polish Army arriving to reinforce the hard-pressed tankers. Just a few miles south the 69th Army gained another foothold at Pulawy.

SOUTHERN SECTOR
Lvov fell to the 1st Ukrainian Front as the Germans finally abandoned the city.

SOVIET COMMAND
The Stavka set new objectives for the 1st Ukrainian and 1st Belorussian Fronts. Both fronts were to cross the Vistula and establish bridgeheads. To carry out the attacks the 1st Ukrainian Front transferred the 1st Guards and 3rd Guards Tank Armies to support the 13th Army and push out from Sandomierz.

28 July 1944

CENTRAL SECTOR
There was heavy fighting near Brest-Litovsk as Weiss' 2nd Army was pushed back by the 70th and 61st Armies. Elements of 2nd Tank Army pushed north from Magnuszew and hit the 73rd Infantry Division and Herman Goering Para Panzer Division south-east of Warsaw. In southern Poland, Przemysl fell to the 3rd Guards Tank Army after a long struggle.

29 July 1944

NORTHERN SECTOR
The 51st Army turned north from Siauliai to strike towards the Gulf of Riga and isolate the 16th and 18th Armies in Latvia and Estonia. The Germans immediately began to redeploy to secure the narrow corridor that connected the 3rd Panzer Army to Army Group North.

CENTRAL SECTOR

After capturing Vilnius the 5th Army pushed towards Kaunas. The 39th Panzer Korp launched a counter-attack at Wolomin and became embroiled in heavy fighting with the 2nd Tank Army. Lack of fuel hindered the German operation, breaking the momentum of even this limited attack.

SOUTHERN SECTOR

The 3rd Guards Tank Army crossed the Vistula at Sandomierz, gaining a bridgehead on the west bank.

SOVIET COMMAND

With the orientation of the 1st Ukrainian Front north of the Carpathian Mountains, the Stavka re-formed the 4th Ukrainian Front to cover the Slovak border regions. The re-formed front was commanded by General Petrov and had the 1st Guards Army, 18th Army and 8th Air Army. It deployed between the 1st and 2nd Ukrainian Fronts.

30 July 1944

NORTHERN SECTOR

There was heavy fighting at Tukums as the 51st Army attempted to reach the Gulf of Riga. The 2nd Guards Army also attacked at Siauliai to pin down the 3rd Panzer Army and prevent it from transferring forces to the north.

CENTRAL SECTOR

The 5th Army fought its way into Kaunas. The German counter-attack north of Wolomin continued as the 39th Panzer Korp struck the 2nd Tank Army.

To the south, elements of the 1st Guards Tank and 13th Armies crossed the Vistula at Baranow, south-west of Sandomierz. The Germans immediately launched counter-attacks but failed to dislodge the Soviet troops.

31 July 1944

NORTHERN SECTOR

Elements of the 51st Army smashed their way through the exposed German lines west of Riga and reached the Baltic coast, isolating the 16th and 18th Armies in Latvia and Estonia. Army Group North hastily organised for a break-out attempt.

CENTRAL SECTOR

Kaunas fell to the 5th Army, the defending 9th Korp losing more than 40,000 killed and captured in the battle. Seidlice also fell to the 47th Army after fierce fighting.

Leading elements of the 2nd Tank Army broke into Ottwock, entering the Praga suburb of Warsaw but encountered strong German resistance. However, 2nd was under continued heavy attack at Wolomin. The 3rd SS Panzer Division Totenkopf, Hermann Goering Para Panzer and 19th Panzer Divisions were all attacking the depleted 2nd Tank Army.

FINNISH SECTOR

The Karelian and Leningrad Fronts had forced the Finnish armies of Karelia and the South East back to their own borders and inflicted more than 60,000 casualties.

SOVIET CASUALTIES

The Soviet armies in the centre were in urgent need of rest and refit following their month-long offensive against Army Group Centre. The 1st Baltic Front had lost 41,000 killed and 125,000 wounded of its 359,000 men, while the 3rd Belorussian had lost 45,000 killed and 155,000 wounded of its 580,000 men. The smaller 2nd Belorussian Front, with 320,000 men, lost 26,000 killed and 90,000 wounded, while the 1st Belorussian Front (with 1,070,000 men) lost 65,000 killed and 215,000 wounded. [7]

THE OSTHEER

Despite moving up two panzer, one infantry, four Volksgrenadier and one security divisions into the combat line during July the disastrous battles had cost the Ostheer one motorised, twenty-eight infantry, one SS grenadier and two Luftwaffe divisions withdrawn or lost from its order of battle. It now deployed twenty panzer, eight panzer grenadier and 108 infantry divisions.[8]

After its catastrophic defeats, the high command began to scrape together a re-formed 17th Army in the Krakow area.

1 August 1944

CENTRAL SECTOR

With elements of the 2nd Tank Army fighting in the Praga suburb of Warsaw, the Polish Home Army rose in revolt. Led by General Komorowski, the largely civilian army of 38,000 soldiers seized control of large portions of the city, taking the Germans by surprise.

The rear of Vormann's 9th Army, fighting before Warsaw, was threatened by the revolt. The Red Army though was initially unaware that the revolt had begun and could not offer immediate help, its exhausted

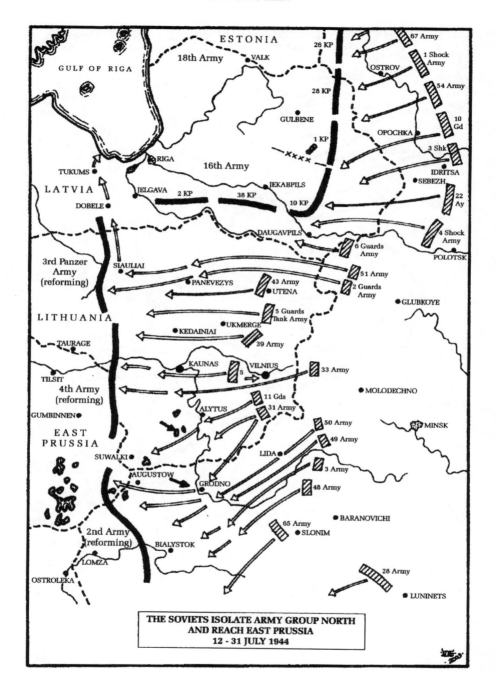

THE SOVIETS ISOLATE ARMY GROUP NORTH
AND REACH EAST PRUSSIA
12 - 31 JULY 1944

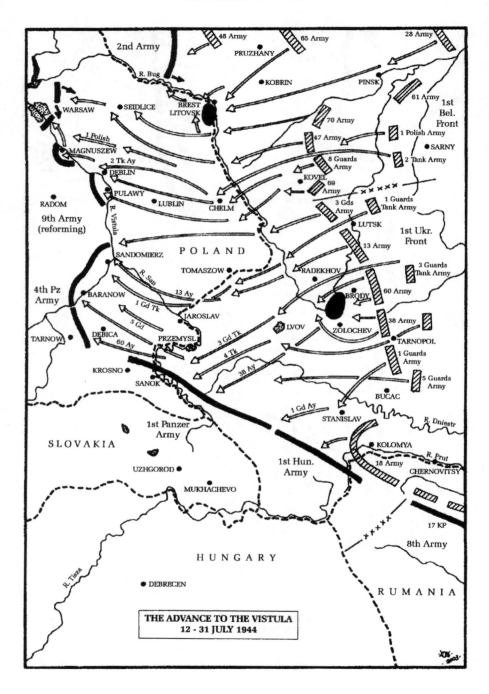

THE ADVANCE TO THE VISTULA
12 - 31 JULY 1944

combat units being at the end of a 400-mile supply line. Indeed as the battle progressed the Russians gave very little aid to the Poles, Stalin pretty much allowing the Germans a free hand to destroy his political enemies in order to install the Communist Lublin-based regime in the capital upon its fall. The Western Allies made repeated requests to air drop supplies to the Poles but only a small amount would be landed, Stalin denying the Allied air forces the use of his airfields.

SOUTHERN SECTOR
The 8th Guards Army attacked at Magnuszew in order to strengthen its bridgehead. The Germans offered stubborn resistance.

FINNISH SECTOR
President Ryti resigned, General Mannerheim taking over as head of state. The Finns were looking for some way out of the war to prevent Soviet invasion and safeguard the territory they had held at the end of the 1939 Winter War.

2 August 1944

CENTRAL SECTOR
The fighting at Wolomin intensified as the Germans threw the 4th Panzer Division in to support the three panzer divisions already in action. The Poles continued their attacks in Warsaw, gaining control of a larger area of the city. Significantly, an assault upon the Okacie airbase failed. The capture of the airfield would have given the Home Army a point of supply for Allied aircraft. The Germans defending the base repelled repeated Polish attacks and inflicted heavy casualties. Hitler appointed SS General Erich von dem Bach-Zelewski to command the forces tasked with the defeat of the Polish revolt.

Along the Vistula, the 69th Army succeeded in crossing at Pulawy to support those armies already across near the town.

3 August 1944

NORTHERN SECTOR
Army Group North had been struggling to concentrate its forces near Riga to re-establish contact with the 3rd Panzer Army. The Soviet High Command began to move the 5th Guards Tank Army up to support the 1st Baltic Front.

CENTRAL SECTOR
At Wolomin the Germans committed yet another division, the 5th SS Panzer Division Wiking hitting 2nd Tank Army. With heavy fighting

inside Warsaw, the Red Army continued to throw forces across the Vistula. Heavy fighting raged around the Sandomierz and Baranow bridgeheads.

4 August 1944

Northern Sector
The 16th Army launched a fierce counter-attack in Latvia, hitting the 51st Army south of Jelgava. Heavy fighting ensued but German progress was slow.

CENTRAL SECTOR
In Warsaw the Poles gained control of the Mokotow, Czerniakow, Powisle, Old Town and Zoliborz districts but came under increasingly heavy German counter-attack. More and more German units, mainly SS, were poured into the city. Some of these units were of the worst type, made up from criminals and murderers, an example being the infamous Dirlewanger Brigade. Elements of the 19th Panzer Division fought their way across the city from the Praga suburb but encountered fierce resistance.

To the south the 1st Ukrainian Front committed the 5th Guards Army to the fighting at Sandomierz.

5 August 1944

NORTHERN SECTOR
The fighting in Latvia intensified as the 4th Shock Army attacked from Krustpils in an effort to drive along the Dvina to Riga. The right wing of the 18th Army absorbed the attack, slowing Soviet progress to a crawl.

CENTRAL SECTOR
The Luftwaffe arrived over Warsaw and bombed the Wola suburb, killing thousands of civilians. The Home Army went onto the defensive, having gained control of three-fifths of the city. German troops launched a fierce attack and, after a bloody battle, captured the Saxon Gardens and Bruehl Palace. This split the Polish pocket in two. An immediate Polish counter-attack forced the Germans onto the defensive but they remained between the two groups.

Hitler made it clear that he wanted Warsaw wiped from the map, the army and SS being given a free hand against the Poles. In just five days' fighting the Poles had lost 15,000 killed. The Germans launched a strong counter-attack against the Magnuszew bridgehead, hitting the 8th Guards Army with the redeployed Hermann Goering Para Panzer Division. Despite heavy fighting the Germans were halted after little progress.

6 August 1944

NORTHERN SECTOR
Laura fell to the 3rd Baltic Front.

7 August 1944

SOUTHERN SECTOR
Sambor fell to the 1st Guards Army of the 4th Ukrainian Front.

8 August 1944

NORTHERN SECTOR
The Stavka had moved the 22nd Army up to aid the 4th Shock Army and after further bitter fighting Krustpils fell.

CENTRAL SECTOR
In Warsaw the Germans established a strong axis from Wola to the Kierbedzia Bridge. Polish counter-attacks continued.

9 August 1944

FINNISH SECTOR
The Russians assessed their losses as the Finnish offensives wound down. The 7th and 32nd Armies had lost 17,000 killed and 46,700 wounded, while the 21st and 23rd Armies lost 6,000 killed and 24,000 wounded.[9]

10 August 1944

NORTHERN SECTOR
The 3rd Baltic Front extended its attack as the 67th and 1st Shock Armies joined the push towards Riga. In heavy fighting on the southern wing of the 1st Baltic Front, the 2nd Guards Army took Rasianiai.

CENTRAL SECTOR
The 3rd and 48th Armies of the 2nd Belorussian Front crossed the Narew near Bialystok.

11 August 1944

NORTHERN SECTOR
After heavy fighting Pechory fell to units of the 3rd Baltic Front.

12 August 1944

CENTRAL SECTOR
The Germans attacked into the Old Town district in Warsaw, hitting the Poles from the south, west and north.

13 August 1944

NORTHERN SECTOR
Verro fell as the 67th Army advanced upon Tartu and the 1st Shock Army upon Valk (now Valga).

CENTRAL SECTOR
Bach-Zelewski realised it was going to take a house-by-house struggle to destroy the Home Army. To blast the Poles into submission, the Germans brought up a 600mm mortar, a pair of 380mm howitzers and two 280mm howitzers.

14 August 1944

NORTHERN SECTOR
The 3rd Panzer Army began a relief attack towards Riga from south of Dobele with a force of 180 panzers and assault guns. After bitter fighting the Germans advanced ten miles along the road to Jelgava. The 51st Army was forced to pull back steadily as it was hit from both the west and east.

CENTRAL SECTOR
The 47th Army attacked north of Warsaw and the 2nd Tank Army to the south, but were both held by powerful German counter-attacks. The 4th SS Panzer Korp, newly committed to this sector, inflicted heavy losses upon the Russian armies.

16 August 1944

NORTHERN SECTOR
The 39th and 40th Panzer Korps attacked north of Siauliai, joining the attack force already in action south of Dobele. Reinhardt had wanted to attack closer to Riga but Hitler had ordered the attack from the Siauliai area.

GERMAN COMMAND
Reinhardt was appointed to command Army Group North and Harpe Army Group North Ukraine. Raus took over the 3rd Panzer Army and Heinrici the 1st Panzer.

17 August 1944

NORTHERN SECTOR
Fighting in Latvia intensified as the 3rd Panzer Army threw more than 300 panzers and assault guns into the attack towards Riga. The 2nd Guards Army was hard pressed by the 3rd Panzer while the 51st was hit by elements of both the 3rd Panzer and 16th Armies. The 16th was continuing to attack south of Jelgava.

CENTRAL SECTOR
The 33rd Army of the 3rd Belorussian Front crossed the East Prussian border and gained a minor bridgehead across the Sesupe river.

18 August 1944

NORTHERN SECTOR
The 5th Guards Tank Army deployed north of the 2nd Guards Army to cover Siauliai. The 39th and 40th Panzer Korps struck the 5th repeatedly but suffered heavy losses in protracted fighting.

SOUTHERN SECTOR
The Stavka planned to unleash its next major offensive, this time against the German and Rumanian forces in Rumania. Prior to the attack the German and Soviet forces had been substantially reinforced. The 2nd and 3rd Ukrainian Fronts were poised to strike the flanks of the German 6th Army, destroying the 3rd and 4th Rumanian Armies in a campaign that mirrored the destruction of the original 6th at Stalingrad.

Malinovsky's 2nd Ukrainian Front comprised the 40th and 27th Armies on the right wing, 52nd and 53rd in the centre and 7th and 4th Guards Armies on the left wing. The 6th Tank Army was in reserve. In all Malinovsky had 771,000 men, 11,000 artillery pieces, 1,300 tanks and Su's and 900 aircraft. Tolbukhin's 3rd Ukrainian had 523,000 men, 8,000 artillery pieces, 600 tanks and Su's and 1,000 aircraft between the 5th Shock Army on the northern wing, 37th and 46th Armies in the centre and 57th Army to the south.

The Stavka plan called for the 2nd Ukrainian Front to crush the Rumanian 4th Army between the Prut and Siret and open up the left wing of the German 6th Army. Other elements of the 2nd Ukrainian Front would simultaneously force the German 8th Army to the west, away from the 6th Army. The 3rd Ukrainian Front was to destroy the 3rd Rumanian Army on the Black Sea coast, unhinging the right flank of the 6th Army. With both its flanks uncovered, the 6th would then be enveloped and destroyed by the inner pincers of the 2nd and 3rd Ukrainian Fronts. The second stage of the offensive would see the 3rd Ukrainian Front seize

Bucharest and the Ploesti oilfields before crossing the Bulgarian border. Bulgaria was in a unique position of being at war with the Western Allies but not with the Soviet Union. A declaration of war by the Russians as the offensive began paved the way for the invasion of Bulgaria. Meanwhile, the 2nd Ukrainian Front was to drive Army Group North Ukraine into Hungary, uncovering the rear of the German forces occupying Greece and Yugoslavia.

Freissner's Army Group South Ukraine deployed the 8th Army, 4th Rumanian Army, 6th Army and 3rd Rumanian Army. Wohler's 8th Army was on the left wing covering the Carpathians with the 17th Korp (one infantry, one mountain divisions), Rumanian 7th Korp (two Rumanian mountain brigades), Rumanian 1st Korp (two Rumanian infantry divisions) and 57th Korp (one German and two Rumanian infantry divisions). This gave 8th Army 43,000 German and 112,000 Rumanian troops. Between the Siret and Prut rivers was General Avramescu's 4th Rumanian Army. This force deployed the 6th Rumanian Korp (two Rumanian infantry divisions, one German infantry division), 4th Rumanian Korp (two Rumanian infantry and one mountain divisions) and Meith's 4th German Korp (two infantry divisions, one Rumanian infantry division) with 43,000 German and 88,000 Rumanian soldiers. Fretter Pico's 6th Army, between the Prut and Dniestr rivers with 212,000 German and 25,000 Rumanian soldiers, had the 7th Korp (two German and one Rumanian infantry divisions), 44th Korp (four infantry divisions), 52nd Korp (three infantry divisions) and 30th Korp (five infantry divisions).

On the Black Sea coast there was the 3rd Rumanian Army under General Dumitrescu with 14,000 German and 75,000 Rumanian troops. This army comprised the 29th German Korp (one Rumanian mountain brigade, one infantry division and the 9th German Infantry Division), the 2nd Rumanian Korp (one infantry division) and 3rd Rumanian Korp (three Rumanian infantry divisions). In reserve the 6th Army and its two Rumanian armies could call upon the 13th Panzer Division. To support the army group the Germans had the 4th Luftwaffe Kommando with 318 aircraft. In all Army Group South Ukraine deployed 340,000 German and 310,000 Rumanian soldiers and 400 panzer or assault guns. When compared to the 929,000 Soviet troops deployed by the 2nd and 3rd Ukrainian Fronts, the Axis forces were facing odds of three to one.

19 August 1944

NORTHERN SECTOR

Elements of the 3rd Shock Army crossed the Oger river but were halted by three divisions of the 18th Army moving south from Estonia. Another Soviet attack at Ergli was also brought to a halt.

CENTRAL SECTOR
The Home Army was under fierce attack in Warsaw as the Germans pounded the city with heavy artillery and air raids. Polish counter-attacks from Zoliborz failed to break the German ring.

SOUTHERN SECTOR
The 2nd and 3rd Ukrainian Fronts began probing attacks in Rumania, the 2nd Ukrainian Front attacking around Jassy and the 3rd at Tiraspol. Both fronts planned to attack on 20 August. Elements of 6th Rumanian Korp pulled back.

20 August 1944

CENTRAL SECTOR
The Poles launched strong attacks from Zoliborz and the Old Town, but suffered heavy casualties.

SOUTHERN SECTOR
Artillery fire smashed into the 4th Rumanian Army and air attacks paralysed its rear. The 2nd Ukrainian Front then attacked, crushing the 4th and 6th Rumanian Korps in the first blow. Elements of the 52nd Army hit the junction of the German 4th and Rumanian 4th Korps near Jassy, while the 27th Army pounded the 6th Rumanian Korp to the left. Despite heavy fighting, the German and Rumanian troops were overwhelmed, Meith's 4th Korp being left high and dry and the Rumanians deserted the field. By midday the 53rd Army had fought its way into Jassy and was across the Bahlui river. Freissner immediately committed his reserves but they were swept aside by the Soviet advance.

The 3rd Ukrainian Front attacked from the Tiraspol bridgehead with its 57th, 37th and 46th Armies, striking the 30th Korp and left flank of the 29th Korp. Initial Soviet attacks were repulsed after bloody fighting but a renewed assault overran the right flank of the 30th Korp. The 29th Korp was also severely damaged in the fighting, its Rumanian divisions abandoning the field en masse. Fretter-Pico began to move his reserve 13th Panzer Division, up but after a hasty counter-attack the division was forced back. There was now a gaping thirty-mile hole in the line between the 6th Army and 3rd Rumanian Army to its right. While this battle raged the 5th Shock Army attacked the 52nd Korp before Kishinev.

21 August 1944

NORTHERN SECTOR
The 3rd Panzer Army recaptured Tukums as it punched a corridor

217

through to Army Group North. Despite the danger around the 16th and 18th Armies, Hitler still refused to allow a withdrawal.

SOUTHERN SECTOR

The fighting in Rumania intensified. As the 52nd Army advanced around Jassy the 10th Panzer-grenadier Division counter-attacked. Heavy fighting followed but the Germans were defeated and forced to retreat. Having shattered the main line of German resistance, Malinovsky committed the 6th Tank Army to the attack. Some 300 tanks ran into and over the remnants of the 10th Panzer-grenadier and its supporting infantry division. In further heavy fighting the 52nd Army completed the capture of Jassy. Meith's 4th Korp attempted to hold along the Bahlui river but was forced back to the south by strong Russian attacks.

The Soviet offensive also struck Wohler's 8th Army. Wohler's Rumanian units abandoned their positions, forcing the remaining German units to begin falling back.

On the southern wing the 6th Army was in the process of disintegration. The 13th Panzer Division had been repulsed before Tiraspol and was in retreat. The 30th Korp was collapsing under the 46th and 37th Army attacks. Two of its divisions had already been practically destroyed and the 13th Panzer had lost all its tanks. German counter-attacks throughout the day failed to halt the Soviet advance, the 46th Army penetrating to within ten miles of the 6th Army headquarters at Tarutino. Freissner now took it upon his own authority to order a general withdrawal to the Prut river. Hitler was furious when he found out.

22 August 1944

SOUTHERN SECTOR

The 6th Tank Army pushed down from the north, behind the main units of the 6th Army to the east, towards Vaslui and Husi. With the complete collapse of the Rumanian armies, Freissner cut the Rumanians out of the command chain, allocating Meith's 4th Korp and the 29th Korp to the 6th Army.

Fierce battles raged south of Jassy as the 4th Korp fell back to the southeast, towards the Prut. Kastuleni and Ungeny fell to 52nd and 4th Guards Armies as they drove along either bank of the river. To the east, elements of the 29th Korp were involved in heavy fighting at Romanovo as the 46th Army plunged deep into the German rear. The 29th was now in full retreat towards the Prut. While the korp retreated, other elements of the 46th Army reached the Black Sea coast and isolated the 9th Infantry Division.

The Rumanians deposed Marshal Antonescu and placed him under arrest. The new government immediately issued orders for all Rumanian units in the field to cease firing upon Russian forces and surrender or go home.

23 August 1944

SOUTHERN SECTOR

Mieth's 4th Korp came under heavy attack from the 6th Tank and 52nd Armies as it pulled back. However, leading units of the 52nd Army severed the German line of retreat by cutting the road to Husi. Heavy fighting raged as the Germans tried unsuccessfully to break through.

On the eastern bank of the Prut the 7th Korp disintegrated as the 4th Guards Army overran its headquarters and attacked all along its lines. Some units did manage to fight their way back to the Prut, crossing at Scoposeni to link up with 4th Korp near Husi.

As more retreating units joined the 4th Korp, Group Meith (as it became known), prepared to launch an attack west to escape isolation and destruction. However, the 6th Tank Army had already outflanked the Germans, pushing deep into their rear as it approached Barlad. Heavy fighting erupted along the Barladul river but the Germans were repulsed, one of Mieth's divisions being wiped out in the fighting.

The 44th Korp and 52nd Korps were falling back from the Dniestr, abandoning Kishinev. However, the imminent collapse of the 52nd Korp endangered the 44th. Under heavy attack the 52nd buckled and was overwhelmed. A little to the south the positions of the 30th Korp had also entirely collapsed.

As the korps in the centre of the 6th Army fell apart, the Soviets pushed deep into their rear. Leovo, on the Prut, fell to the 37th Army as it struck out to meet the 52nd Army pushing down from the north. There now only remained a narrow corridor between Husi and Leovo for the 7th, 44th, 52nd and 30th Korps to escape through.

24 August 1944

NORTHERN SECTOR

Heavy fighting around Lake Peipus forced the 18th Army back into Tartu. The northward thrust by the 67th Army was threatening the rear of the Group Narva, which still held before the 2nd Shock, 59th and 8th Armies.

SOUTHERN SECTOR

The Soviets completed the encirclement of the German 6th Army as the 37th and 52nd Armies linked up between Husi and Leovo. The 4th Guards, 5th Shock, 57th and 37th Armies swung in to destroy the isolated korps, while the 6th Tank, 27th and 52nd Armies of the 2nd Ukrainian Front and 46th Army of the 3rd Ukrainian Front continued to push out on the outer ring. German forces inside the pocket rapidly began to fall apart as the Soviets launched air and artillery strikes, inflicting terrible casualties. Kishinev, abandoned on the 23rd, fell to the 5th Shock Army.

The 30th Korp, on the southern face of the pocket, attempted to assemble its men for a breakout to the west.

Outside the main encirclement, Group Meith fought to prevent its own isolation in bitter fighting with the 52nd Army around Husi. On the Black Sea coast the isolated 9th Infantry Division surrendered, over 13,000 men being captured as the division ceased to exist.

In Bucharest the Rumanians rose in revolt against German authority, firing on German buildings in the city. Hitler ordered punitive action and threw the 5th Flak Division into the fighting in the city. However, the Germans came under heavy fire and had to call upon air support, the Luftwaffe bombing Bucharest. This action spread the revolt and fighting broke out around Ploesti.

25 August 1944

NORTHERN SECTOR
After heavy fighting the 67th Army took Tartu.

CENTRAL SECTOR
The 47th Army attacked near Warsaw, hitting the 4th SS Panzer Korp. Heavy fighting ensued.

SOUTHERN SECTOR
The 6th Army launched repeated attacks in an effort to break out from the Leovo pocket but was beaten back each time. After fierce fighting the 30th Korp was destroyed.

Meith's four-division strong group, with just 20,000 men, continued its own break-out attempts at Husi, but failed to force the Russians back. Only the 29th Korp remained free of encirclement but it was retreating towards the Barladul to the south.

Following the Luftwaffe air-raids the Rumanian government declared war on Germany. All German forces were to be disarmed and interned. The declaration of war threatened the German forces in Greece and Yugoslavia. Lohr's Army Group E took over control of the forces on the Greek mainland and the Aeagean islands, some 315,000 men in all. Weichs' Army Group F assumed command of the German forces in Yugoslavia from its headquarters at Belgrade.

FINNISH SECTOR
The Finns came to terms with the Soviet Union, Moscow agreeing to a Finnish armistice on the condition that all German troops leave Finnish territory by 15 September.

26 August 1944

SOUTHERN SECTOR

The 37th Army reached the Danube at Galati. The remnants of the 6th Army fought their final battle around Leovo while Group Meith continued to attack at Husi. Once more though the Soviet forces were able to repel each German attack and inflict heavy casualties.

The remnants of the 29th Korp, now also in operational encirclement with its 20,000 remaining men, had assembled on the Siret near Focsani in an effort to break out to the west.

With Soviet forces fast approaching its borders, the Bulgarian government ordered the disarming of all German troops and began the evacuation of Thrace.

27 August 1944

SOUTHERN SECTOR

Focsani fell to the 6th Tank Army, trapping the 29th Korp on the east bank. The Ploesti oilfields were threatened with capture.

28 August 1944

SOUTHERN SECTOR

General Meith was killed in heavy fighting as another break-out attempt failed. Through sheer desperate courage the Germans recaptured Vutcani but a Soviet counter-attack retook it. A repeated German assault then captured it for the second time.

Units of the 27th Army seized the Oituz pass and access to eastern Hungary. To the south, Braila fell to the 37th Army.

29 August 1944

SOUTHERN SECTOR

The 6th Army was exhausted and after a last effort to break through Group Meith was destroyed. More than 106,000 men had been captured and 150,000 killed during the fighting, wiping the 6th Army off the German order of battle. Army Group South Ukraine also lost 850 tanks, 3,500 artillery pieces and 35,000 motor vehicles during the battle.[10]

Constanta fell to the 57th Army and Buzau to the 46th Army as Soviet forces closed upon Bucharest and Bulgaria. The Balkan offensive had cost the 2nd Ukrainian Front 7,000 killed and 32,000 wounded and the 3rd Ukrainian 5,800 killed and 21,000 wounded.[11]

DIPLOMACY: HUNGARY
Admiral Horthy removed the pro-German Szotaj government from power and appointed the pro-Soviet Lakatos regime. He did not go so far as to break off relations with Germany though.

30 August 1944

CENTRAL SECTOR
In Warsaw the Germans forced the Poles to pull out of the Old Town. Some 1,500 men with 300 wounded retreated through the sewers to the city centre and 800 went to Zoliborz.

SOUTHERN SECTOR
The vital oilfields at Ploesti fell to the Soviets. Hitler ordered Freissner to establish defensive positions on a line from the Iron Gates to Brasov. This was absolutely unachievable. The newly raised 2nd Hungarian Army was allocated to Army Group South Ukraine but was an army in name only.

31 August 1944

CENTRAL SECTOR
The Germans attacked the Old Town only to find the Poles had withdrawn.

SOUTHERN SECTOR
Bucharest fell to the 53rd Army.

THE OSTHEER
Since Operation Bagration began at the end of June the Ostheer had suffered 916,000 casualties. Despite the commitment of one SS panzer grenadier and ten Volksgrenadier divisions the German armies in the east remained extremely weak, having lost twelve infantry and one Volksgrenadier divisions in the fighting. Paper strength now stood at twenty panzer, nine panzer grenadier and 105 infantry divisions.[12]

1 September 1944

NORTHERN SECTOR
Army Group North was stretched along a 500-mile front in the Baltic States. In the north Boege's 18th Army had the Narva Group (essentially the 3rd SS Panzer Korp) between the Gulf of Finland and Lake Peipus, while south of the lake was the remainder of the 18th Army. Hilpert's 16th Army was grouped in forced around Riga, holding open communications with the 3rd Panzer Army. The army group comprised one panzer, two

panzer grenadier and twenty-nine infantry divisions and three SS brigades.

SOUTHERN SECTOR
Calarasi and Giurgiu fell to Soviet forces in Rumania.

THE OSTHEER
A reformed 17th Army entered the line to the right of the 1st Panzer Army in Slovakia, while a new 6th Army was hastily raised in southern Hungary. The 6th comprised twenty weak battalions grouped around the headquarters of the 29th Korp and the reinforced 13th Panzer and 10th Panzer-grenadier Divisions.

2 September 1944

DIPLOMACY: FINLAND
The Finns broke off diplomatic relations with Germany and demanded that all forces leave their country by 15 September.

3 September 1944

CENTRAL SECTOR
Elements of the 70th Army crossed the Bug river north of Warsaw.

4 September 1944

CENTRAL SECTOR
The Germans launched a furious attack in Warsaw to establish control of the banks of the Vistula. Slightly farther north the 70th and 65th Armies of the 1st Belorussian Front closed up to the Narew river around Pultusk.

SOUTHERN SECTOR
Brasov and Senaia fell to Soviet troops while the 53rd Army reached the Danube at Turnu Severin.

DIPLOMACY: FINLAND
The armistice between Finland and the Soviet Union was ratified, bringing Finland's war to an end.

5 September 1944

CENTRAL SECTOR
Group Panev, operating alongside the 65th and 70th Armies, crossed the Narew near Pultusk.

SOUTHERN SECTOR

The 2nd Hungarian Army counter-attacked with five divisions south of Cluj towards Sibiu, forcing back the newly committed 4th Rumanian Army that was now fighting alongside the Soviet Army. The Rumanians fell back, compelling Malinovsky to move the 6th Tank Army up towards Sibiu to provide support. The main part of the 6th, together with the 27th Army, reached Pitesti.

DIPLOMACY: USSR

The Soviet Union declared war on Bulgaria, the Bulgarian government surrendering the same day.

6 September 1944

CENTRAL SECTOR

Soviet attacks north of Warsaw gained ground slowly as the Germans put up a strong defence. Ostroleka fell to the 48th Army as the Narew was crossed again.

Inside Warsaw, the Germans cleared the Vistula banks of Polish forces, forcing the Poles back into the city centre.

SOUTHERN SECTOR

The 53rd Army crossed the Danube and entered Yugoslavia. With the situation on the southern wing fluid, the Germans committed the 57th Panzer Korp to support the new 6th Army's efforts to halt the Soviet attacks into Hungary.

The 2nd Hungarian Army was brought to a halt south of Cluj. To the east the 40th and 7th Guards Armies hit Wohler's 8th Army on the Hungarian border.

7 September 1944

CENTRAL SECTOR

The Polish Home Army began to negotiate surrender terms with the Germans.

8 September 1944

CENTRAL SECTOR

The Germans launched a series of new attacks against the Poles in Warsaw city centre. Fierce resistance prevented any significant gains. In some sectors of the city, a ceasefire promoted by the Polish Red Cross was honoured, allowing the evacuation of thousands of civilians. However, nearly a quarter of a million remained inside the city. Talks failed to make any headway.

SOUTHERN SECTOR
The 1st and 4th Ukrainian Fronts began new attacks aimed at penetrating the Dukla Pass in southern Poland. The 38th Army, with 99,000 men, supported the 264,000 of the 4th Ukrainian Front.[13] Striking the 1st Panzer Army, fierce battles erupted in the extensive German fortifications.

Army Group E was dangerously exposed by the Russian advance into Yugoslavia. Large-scale partisan attacks pinned the Germans down as they withdrew, slowing their evacuation. Army Group F was already heavily committed to fighting Tito's partisans.

After a brief campaign the 57th and 37th Armies of the 3rd Ukrainian Front overran Bulgaria. A pro-Soviet coup installed a Communist regime, which immediately declared war on Germany.

9 September 1944

SOUTHERN SECTOR
The attacks by the 38th Army in the Dukla Pass made reasonable progress despite determined German resistance. A penetration was made near Krosno but 1st Panzer Army counter-attacks sealed the gap.

10 September 1944

CENTRAL SECTOR
The 47th Army launched a fierce attack into the Warsaw suburb of Praga but was held in the strong German defences.

SOUTHERN SECTOR
The 38th Army fought its way into Krosno but was unable to press any farther due to the arrival of German reinforcements.

11 Septemebr 1944

CENTRAL SECTOR
The Germans launched fierce attacks near the Poniatowski Bridge and in Czerniakow inside Warsaw.

12 September 1944

CENTRAL SECTOR
In Warsaw the 25th Panzer Division attacked in Zoliborz.

SOUTHERN SECTOR

The 6th Tank Army had redeployed at Maros in order to attack the German and Hungarian forces around Cluj. The Stavka elevated the 6th Tank to Guards status.

13 September 1944

NORTHERN SECTOR

The Leningrad, 1st, 2nd and 3rd Baltic Fronts prepared to launch a new offensive aimed at destroying the 18th and 16th Armies between Riga and Narva. While the Leningrad Front drove in from the north, the 2nd and 3rd Baltic Fronts would pin down the German forces south of Lake Peipus. The 1st Baltic Front would sweep around the right wing of the 16th Army to regain the Baltic coast west of Riga and repeat the isolation of the two armies.

The Leningrad Front's 2nd Shock, 59th and 8th Armies along the Narva had 195,000 men, the 1st Baltic Front 621,000 (in the 4th Shock, 6th Guards, 51st, 43rd, 2nd Guards and 39th Armies), the 2nd Baltic 339,000 men (in the 10th Guards, 3rd Shock and 22nd Armies) and the 3rd Baltic Front 345,000 men (in the 42nd, 67th, 1st Shock and 54th Armies). The three Baltic fronts also had 17,000 artillery pieces, 3,000 tanks and 2,600 aircraft.[14] The Army Group North had around 400,000 men with 400 panzers.

CENTRAL SECTOR

The 49th Army crossed the Narew and took Lomza, while the 47th Army cleared the Praga suburb of Warsaw but failed to link up with the Polish Home Army.

14 September 1944

NORTHERN SECTOR

The Soviet offensive against Army Group North began. Supported by heavy artillery fire and air attacks, the 43rd Army at the centre of the thrust by the 1st Baltic Front pushed north around Jelgava. However, the Germans had established strong defences with just such an attack in mind and bogged the Soviet attacks down.

CENTRAL SECTOR

The 25th Panzer Division attacked the Home Army in Zoliborz and Czerniakow.

15 September 1944

NORTHERN SECTOR
Soviet attacks in the Baltic intensified as the 1st Shock Army of the 3rd
Baltic Front launched attacks towards Valk and the 10th Guards, 3rd
Shock and 22nd Armies of the 2nd Baltic Front attacked near Madona.
German resistance was intense, slowing the Soviet armies and inflicting
heavy casualties.

SOUTHERN SECTOR
Freissner had concentrated a significant force around the Cluj salient and
prepared to counter-attack to halt the advance of the 2nd Ukrainian Front.
The 8th Army was deployed on the eastern face of the salient with the 1st
Hungarian Army to its north. At the base of the salient, around Cluj, was
the 2nd Hungarian Army and to its right, around Oradea, the reformed
6th Army.

FINNISH SECTOR
The deadline for German forces to evacuate Finland arrived but
substantial forces were still on the ground. An attack by German units
upon the Finnish port of Suursaari was repulse with heavy casualties, and
as a result of this short-sighted action the 20th Mountain Army was
ordered to withdraw from Finland immediately.

16 September 1944

NORTHERN SECTOR
The fighting in the Baltic intensified as the 3rd Panzer Army launched a
new counter-attack aimed at strengthening the link with Army Group
North. More than four hundred panzers struck the 51st and 5th Guards
Tank Armies. Bitter fighting ensued as the Germans advanced slowly. To
the east, the 22nd Army was hit by a 16th Army counter-attack at Dobele.

CENTRAL SECTOR
Elements of the 1st Polish Army crossed the Vistula at Magnuszew and
began to attack north in an effort to break through to the Home Army.
However, the 9th Army put up a ferocious defence, inflicting heavy
casualties. Inside Warsaw the 25th Panzer Division had pushed the Poles
back about half a mile in Zoliborz after fierce battles. Progress was also
made in Czerniakow as the Poles lost their last grip on the Vistula.

SOUTHERN SECTOR
The 2nd Hungarian Army and 8th Army attacked east of Cluj, hitting the
7th Guards, 4th Rumanian and 40th Armies hard.

17 September 1944

NORTHERN SECTOR
The 3rd Baltic Front attacked around Tartu as they tried to drive into the rear of the German Narva Group. During the last week the 2nd Shock Army had been transferred from its positions north of Lake Peipus to the Tartu sector. The 2nd attacked alongside the 42nd and 67th Armies, and after bitter fighting broke through the 18th Army defences.

18 September 1944

NORTHERN SECTOR
The German defences at Tartu collapsed. As the 2nd Shock, 42nd and 67th Armies advanced the Narva Group began to abandon its increasingly exposed positions. The 8th and 59th Armies pressed along the Estonian coast, harrying the Narva Group.

19 September 1944

NORTHERN SECTOR
The 2nd Shock Army, moving up from Tartu, linked up with the 8th Army at the north-west tip of Lake Peipus. Valk fell to the 1st Shock Army as other attacks threatened to isolate the left wing of the 18th Army in Estonia.

SOUTHERN SECTOR
Fierce battles raged around Cluj as the 8th and 2nd Hungarian Armies pounded the 2nd Ukrainian Front.

20 September 1944

GERMAN COMMAND
With its armies already fighting in the eastern provinces, the Hungarians were presented with a German ultimatum. Unless they accepted integration of their forces in the German chain of command they would be disarmed and Germany would sieze control of the state. Horthy had little option but to comply.

The Germans formed the Volkssturm, a collection of battalion-sized units made up from men and boys between the ages of 16 and 60. The first draft called 1,200,000 up for service. The new units were given the most basic training and sent to fight the experienced Allied and Soviet soldiers.

22 September 1944

NORTHERN SECTOR
Lead elements of the 59th and 8th Armies reached Tallinn and captured the city as the 18th Army rapidly evacuated its units south to avoid encirclement.

The 3rd Panzer Army had to abandon its counter-attack in Latvia, having lost more than 140 panzers during bitter fighting. The 43rd and 4th Shock Armies immediately counter-attacked and forced the 16th Army back upon Riga.

23 September 1944

NORTHERN SECTOR
Parnu fell to the 2nd Shock Army. Minor elements of the 18th Army were isolated to the north but retreated towards the coast at Haapsalu and the Moonzund Islands.

CENTRAL SECTOR
The Germans halted the 1st Polish Army north of Magnuszew and in bitter fighting inflicted crippling losses.

Inside Warsaw the Poles pulled back into Mokotow under ferocious attack. Constant artillery fire, Luftwaffe attacks and street fighting flattened most of the city. Hitler aimed to wipe Warsaw off the map.

SOVIET COMMAND
Having struggled to make any headway, the Stavka suspended the offensive in the Baltic States. It now intended to move the emphasis of the attack south to hit the 3rd Panzer Army rather than the 16th Army, throwing the Germans back to the Baltic near Memel. This would isolate the 16th and 18th Armies in Latvia but open the north-eastern approaches of East Prussia.

24 September 1944

CENTRAL SECTOR
The 19th Panzer Division attacked the Poles in Mokotow, pushing them slowly back. German attacks from the south and west also made progress.

SOUTHERN SECTOR
Army Group South Ukraine's counter-attack near Cluj wore itself out after costly fighting.

GERMAN COMMAND

Hitler redesignated his army groups in the southern sector, renaming Army Group North Ukraine, Army Group A and Army Group South Ukraine, Army Group South.

25 September 1944

NORTHERN SECTOR

Haapsalu fell to the 8th Army. The Germans had taken around 11,500 men across the straits to the Moonzund Islands.

SOUTHERN SECTOR

Tito's partisans captured Banja Luka.

26 September 1944

CENTRAL SECTOR

Following a bitter, three-day battle, 2,000 Polish fighters were forced to surrender in Mokotow. Elements of the Polish Mokotow detachment attempted to escape through the sewers to the city centre but the Germans killed most of them, just 600 managing to escape. Komorowski knew the end was near but continued to resist the German attacks.

27 September 1944

NORTHERN SECTOR

Units of the 8th Army landed on Vormsii Island and quickly overran the island. The 13th Air Army provided support.

CENTRAL SECTOR

The Germans launched renewed attacks against the Polish forces in the Zoliborz district and Kampinos Forest. The Poles attempted to push south of the forest and break out.

28 September 1944

SOUTHERN SECTOR

Gagen's 57th Army attacked from Vidin towards Belgrade but met determined resistance from Army Group F.

29 September 1944

NORTHERN SECTOR

The 8th Army overran Muhu Island.

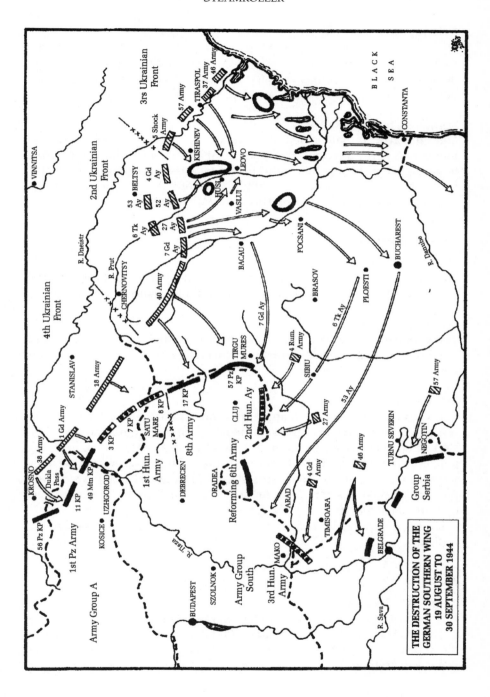

THE DESTRUCTION OF THE
GERMAN SOUTHERN WING
19 AUGUST TO
30 SEPTEMBER 1944

CENTRAL SECTOR

The battle for Warsaw entered its final phase. Polish forces in the Kampinos Forest reached the Skierniewice–Zyrandow railway but were held up by German units. A fierce German attack destroyed the Poles, only 100 of the 2,500 strong force escaping to link up with other units.

SOUTHERN SECTOR

Fighting at Cluj intensified once again as the 6th Army and 2nd Hungarian Army attacked. To the south the 57th Army continued its drive towards Belgrade, together with the 4th Guards Mechanised Corp. This force comprised 200,000 men while the 46th Army, supporting the northern wing of the attack, had another 93,500 men.[15]

30 September 1944

CENTRAL SECTOR

After a final stand the 1,500 remaining defenders of the Zoliborz district surrendered, leaving only the city centre in Polish hands.

SOVIET COMMAND

The conquest of Rumania had cost the Soviet forces 47,000 killed and 171,000 wounded, while 2,000 artillery pieces, 2,200 tanks and 530 aircraft were destroyed.[16]

THE OSTHEER

The Germans lost seven infantry divisions from their order of battle, receiving in return one panzer, one SS panzer grenadier and five Volksgrenadier divisions. Strength now stood at twenty-one panzer, ten panzer grenadier and 103 infantry divisions.[17] The replacement divisions were nowhere near divisional strength. The Ostheer also deployed 4,186 panzers (against 11,200 Russian tanks).[18] Barely a third of the armour was operational at any time and that was short of fuel.

Hungary deployed nineteen divisions and four brigades alongside the Ostheer.

2 October 1944

NORTHERN SECTOR

Elements of the Soviet 8th Army land on Dago Island.

The 3rd Panzer Army, having identified the build up of Soviet forces on the Memel axis, redeployed two panzer and one motorised divisions from Jelgava to Memel.

CENTRAL SECTOR

The last units of the Home Army surrendered in Warsaw, bringing the bloody uprising to an end. In the fighting the Poles had lost 15,000 military and 200,000 civilian dead. The scale of atrocities committed by the SS was considerable. Calls by army generals during the fighting to curb these excesses were largely ignored, Kaminski only being brought to book after the battle was over. The fighting cost the Ostheer 10,000 killed, 7,000 missing and 9,000 wounded.

SOUTHERN SECTOR

The 57th Army isolated part of the German Serbia Group near Negotin.

3 October 1944

NORTHERN SECTOR

The Soviet 8th Army landed on Hiumi. The Germans gave up the islands relatively easily, Dago being cleared.

SOUTHERN SECTOR

Bitter fighting raged on the road to Belgrade. Elements of the 46th Army, approaching Belgrade from the north-east, reached Pancevo but met stubborn resistance from Army Group F. Gagen's 57th Army linked up with Tito's partisans at Negotin as the German Serbia Group was defeated.

> *Between June and September 1944 the Soviet Army had inflicted a series of crushing defeats upon the Ostheer. The loss of Belorussia and Army Group Centre dealt a crushing blow to the German Army, but the destruction of Army Group South Ukraine in Rumania brought it to its knees. Soviet forces had moved from reconquest of their own territory to conquest of the occupied states of Eastern Europe. However, the 'liberation' did not come soon enough for the Poles in Warsaw. Whether Stalin held back the Soviet armies before the city will remain a matter for debate. What is undeniable was the build up of German forces around the city at the time of the rebellion, and the exhausted state of the Soviet forces.*

NOTES

1   Adair, *Hitler's Greatest Defeat*, p121
2   Adair, *Hitler's Greatest Defeat*, p141
3   Ellis, *The World War II Databook*, p176 for German divisional strengths, p230 for armoured strengths and p233 for aircraft strengths.
4   Buchner, *Ostfront 1944*, p163
5   Seaton, *The Russo–German War*, p446
6   Buchner, *Ostfront 1944*, p236

7   Soviet casualties from Adair, *Hitler's Greatest Defeat*, Appendix IV, p177
8   Ellis, *The World War II Databook*, p176
9   Kirosheev, *Soviet Casualties and Combat Losses in the Twentieth Century*, Table 75
10 Buchner, *Ostfront 1944*, p299
11 Kirosheev, *Soviet Casualties and Combat Losses in the Twentieth Century*, Table 75
12 Ellis, *The World War II Databook*, p176
13 Kirosheev, *Soviet Casualties and Combat Losses in the Twentieth Century*, Table 67
14 Kirosheev, *Soviet Casualties and Combat Losses in the Twentieth Century*, Table 67
15 Kirosheev, *Soviet Casualties and Combat Losses in the Twentieth Century*, Table 67
16 Kirosheev, *Soviet Casualties and Combat Losses in the Twentieth Century*, Table 75
17 Ellis, *The World War II Databook*, p176
18 Ellis, *The World War II Databook*, Table 14, p230

CHAPTER VII
Germany Stands Alone

The defection of Rumania and Bulgaria during the Balkan campaign and the negotiated peace made by Finland had stripped Germany of her eastern allies. Only Hungary remained in the field, press-ganged into the defence of her territory.

For the Soviet Union their objective was in sight. Germany's borders had been breached and Soviet troops were poised to attack from the Baltic to the Adriatic. The massive preponderance of Soviet arms no longer brought the conclusion into any doubt. It was now merely the application of this force that remained.

5 October 1944

NORTHERN SECTOR

Elements of the 8th Army landed on Yezel Island but encountered strong German resistance.

Using thick fog as cover, the 1st Baltic Front opened its offensive towards Memel. Over the preceding couple of weeks the front had redeployed the 51st and 5th Guards Tank Armies around Siauliai. Between Dobele and Rasianiai the 1st Baltic Front had the 3rd Shock, 42nd, 4th Shock, 6th Guards, 51st, 5th Guards Tank, 43rd and 2nd Guards Armies. Supporting the southern wing, based just south of Rasianiai, was the 39th Army of the 3rd Belorussian Front. To the north, around Riga, the 1st Baltic had the 43rd and 4th Shock Armies, while the 2nd Baltic had the 22nd and 10th Guards Armies east of Riga and the 3rd Baltic Front, north-east of Riga, had the 54th, 61st, 1st Shock, 67th and 2nd Shock Armies.

Concentrated artillery fire hit the 3rd Panzer Army between Siauliai and Rasianiai, inflicting heavy casualties. The 43rd and 6th Guards Armies quickly crossed the Venta river and advanced ten miles. The 2nd Guards Army forced the Dubissa river despite ferocious German resistance.

Aware of Soviet intentions, Army Group North accelerated the withdrawal of the 18th Army from Latvia, the army abandoning its positions around Sigulda.

6 October 1944

NORTHERN SECTOR

The 5th Guards Tank Army was committed to the attack in the Baltic, advancing in the wake of the 2nd Guards Army and 43rd Army before punching through to the German rear. The 3rd Panzer Army quickly collapsed under the massive Soviet blows and, as the fog lifted, was slaughtered by the 1st Air Army. The 39th Army also began to hit the southern flank of the 3rd Panzer Army, supporting the 2nd Guards as it moved towards the Niemen river. Elements of the 4th Shock and 6th Guards Armies pushed north-west on the right wing, while in the centre the 51st, 43rd and 5th Guards Tank Armies pushed west.

Schorner ordered the withdrawal of the 18th and 16th Armies from their positions east of Riga. Hitler refused to allow the abandonment of the city.

SOUTHERN SECTOR

The 2nd Ukrainian Front launched a new attack into southern Hungary, striking the German line between Oradea and Arad. The 53rd Army and Group Pliev attacked west of Arad supported by the 46th Army to the left. The 7th Guards Army supported the right wing. Units of the 6th Guards Tank Army attacked the 6th Army close to Oradea, while the 40th Army attacked the 8th Army from the east towards Vatra Dornei. The 27th Army held the centre between the 40th and 6th Guards Tank. After bitter fighting the 53rd Army crushed the 3rd Hungarian Army, inflicting heavy casualties.

Against the north-eastern face of the salient in Hungary, held by the 1st Panzer and 1st Hungarian Armies, the 4th Ukrainian Front committed its 1st Guards and 18th Armies. Farther south, other elements of the 46th Army took Pancevo after a fierce battle.

7 October 1944

NORTHERN SECTOR

Army Group North pulled its forces back through Riga as it continued the evacuation of territory east of the city. To the south-west, the 5th Guards Tank Army reached the outer suburbs of Memel. The 43rd Army was advancing behind the 5th to provide support.

FINLAND AND NORWAY

The Soviet 14th Army attacked towards Petsamo, striking the German 19th Mountain Korp.

8 October 1944

SOUTHERN SECTOR
Fierce battles raged in Hungary. Group Pliev had penetrated nearly seventy miles behind the German front and was closing in on Karcag. The 6th Tank Army though was held up by elements of the German 6th Army near Oradea while the 46th Army crossed the Tisza river near Szeged.

The 57th Army of the 3rd Ukrainian Front attacked across the Morava river to seize Velika Plana. This move severed the railway line between Belgrade and Nis. The 1st Bulgarian Army began to attack elements of Army Group E at Nis, as did Tito's 13th Corp.

9 October 1944

SOUTHERN SECTOR
After heavy fighting the 3rd Hungarian Army completely disintegrated, the 53rd Army having advanced more than fifty miles in three days of fierce fighting.

10 October 1944

NORTHERN SECTOR
Palanga fell to the 51st Army, isolating the 16th and 18th Armies in the Kurland Peninsula and around Riga. The 5th Guards Tank Army also reached the Baltic coast near Memel as the 43rd Army struck the 28th Korp inside the town. The 2nd Guards Army pushed towards Tilsit.

The 1st, 2nd and 3rd Baltic Fronts launched concentric attacks upon the German units crammed into the Riga defences. After costly fighting the Soviets were repulsed, enabling the 18th Army to evacuate the bulk of its units to Kurland. Attacks continued throughout the day and finally pierced the outer defences.

> *The isolation of Army Group North in the Kurland Peninsula severed a large group of forces from the German line in the east. Hitler's continued insistence that every yard of ground be held condemned the half million men of this army group to a secondary role for the remainder of the war.*

SOUTHERN SECTOR
The 40th Army pushed the 8th Army and 2nd Hungarian Army back from the Cluj region. West of Cluj, the 6th Tank Army closed upon Debrecen. However, a ferocious counter-attack encircled a large part of the army near the town.

Petrovac fell to units of the 57th Army as it consolidated its hold across the Belgrade–Nis railway.

11 October 1944

NORTHERN SECTOR

Heavy fighting continued in Riga. Schorner was trying to establish a defensive perimeter from Libau, via Dobele and Tukums, to Riga. The 16th Army held the line around Riga and to the west while the 18th Army was redeploying from Libau to the junction with the 16th Army.

SOUTHERN SECTOR

Cluj was encircled as the 40th and 27th Armies linked up, trapping minor elements of the 2nd Hungarian Army. After a brief struggle the town fell. The German 8th Army was now hurriedly pulling its forces back upon Debrecen. Szeged fell to the 46th Army after a protracted struggle.

The 4th Guards Motorised Corp linked up with elements of the 14th Yugoslav Corp which had pushed along the river from Nis.

12 October 1944

NORTHERN SECTOR

The 18th Army attempted to stand on the Riga–Tukums line but came under fierce attack. The 67th Army crossed Lake Kis.

SOUTHERN SECTOR

Oradea fell to the 7th Guards Army as the Soviets destroyed the German division holding the town. There was continued heavy fighting at Debrecen where a counter-attack by elements of the 6th Tank Army freed their isolated corps near the town.

In northern Yugoslavia the 46th Army and Yugoslav partisans took Subotica. Farther south the 57th Army and 4th Guards Motorised Corp moved towards Belgrade from the south, launching a fierce attack upon the city. Elements of the 1st and 14th Yugoslav Corps supported the attack. Army Group F still had considerable forces in the city area, 22,000 troops being inside the city, 20,000 to the south and 15,000 facing the advancing 57th Army to the south-east.

13 October 1944

NORTHERN SECTOR

The 67th Army penetrated the German defences around Riga. Schorner had managed to throw up a defence line at Tukums and halted a drive by the 67th, 1st Shock and 22nd Armies into his left flank. After days of bitter fighting the line would be stabilised and a perimeter from which the 16th and 18th Armies would fight the rest of their war erected.

14 October 1944

SOUTHERN SECTOR
Army Group F struggled to hold off the attacks of Tito's 1st Corp, the 4th Guards Motorised Corp and 57th Army as they all converged on Belgrade. Despite ferocious fighting the Soviet and Yugoslav troops isolated the city, the 12th Yugoslav Corp cutting all of the roads south of the Sava river. The bulk of the German units in the area were cut off, barely 12,000 managing to escape to the north. Heavy fighting erupted inside the city as the Soviet and Yugoslav forces press into the urban area.

15 October 1944

NORTHERN SECTOR
Riga fell after a bloody struggle.

SOVIET COMMAND
The Stavka disbanded the 3rd Baltic Front, allocating the 1st Shock and 14th Air Armies to the 2nd Baltic Front and the 61st Army to the 1st Baltic Front.

NORWAY
The 14th Army secured the Petsamo mining region after a brief struggle with the 19th Mountain Korp. The Germans pulled back into Norway, having lost more than 6,000 killed in the fighting.

16 October 1944

NORTHERN SECTOR
The Soviets began their first offensive against the German forces trapped in Kurland, attacking the 16th and 18th Armies in an effort to reduce the extensive pocket. The 6th Guards Army attacked towards Skrunda and 51st hit Libau. Bitter fighting raged for three days but with little Soviet success.

CENTRAL SECTOR
The 3rd Panzer Army was attacked north of Tilsit by elements of the 2nd Guards Army as the Soviets attempted to push towards the Niemen. The 5th Army and 11th Guards Army attacked along the Gumbinnen–Konigsberg axis, throwing the southern wing of the 3rd Panzer Army back six miles.

SOUTHERN SECTOR
Soviet and Yugoslav forces around Belgrade fought their way towards the

city centre. The Germans resisted fiercely, fighting for every house and street.

DIPLOMACY: HUNGARY

Horthy broadcast on national radio that he believed the Germans were on the verge of total defeat and Hungary had no alternative but to seek an armistice with the Soviet Union. When news of this reached Hitler he flew into a rage and ordered Horthy's arrest. Otto Skorzeny's elite commando unit entered Budapest in the early hours of 16 October and, in a lightning operation, secured the radio station and palace. Horthy was placed under arrest and flown to Germany. The pro-Nazi Arrow Cross regime was established but the damage to German security in Hungary had already been done. Increasing numbers of Hungarian soldiers began to desert from their units.

17 October 1944

CENTRAL SECTOR

The 31st Army attacked the 2nd Army near Suwalki, while the 39th Army attacked near Tilsit to support the 2nd Guards on its right and 5th Army to its left. Elements of 11th Guards crossed the East Prussian border and pushed close to Goldap.

18 October 1944

NORTHERN SECTOR

Kremeny fell to the 1st Shock Army as it drove west from Riga. However, the 16th Army had established strong defences around Tukums and halted the Soviet drive.

CENTRAL SECTOR

The 3rd Belorussian Front continued its attacks into East Prussia but met fierce German resistance.

19 October 1944

CENTRAL SECTOR

The 11th Guards Army finally broke the first defence zone on the Gumbinnen–Konigsberg axis. Elements of the 5th Army, 31st and 39th Armies also penetrated the German defences, the 3rd Panzer Army pulling back to its secondary defence zone.

SOUTHERN SECTOR

A relief attack towards Belgrade by General Weichs' Army Group F was repulsed with heavy losses. Inside the city the Soviet and Yugoslav forces took Ratko Island.

In Hungary the 6th Tank Army broke into Debrecen after nearly three weeks of heavy fighting on the approaches to the town.

NORWAY
The 14th Army resumed its attack from Petsamo, driving the southern wing of 19th Mountain Korp back.

20 October 1944

CENTRAL SECTOR
The 11th Guards Army closed upon Gumbinnen.

SOUTHERN SECTOR
The battle for Belgrade ended as Kalemegdan fortress was captured. Partisan troops linked up with the 4th Guards Mechanised Corp after destroying the German garrison. During the fighting in the city the Germans had been wiped out, 15,000 being killed and 9,000 captured. The 57th Army and 4th Guards Mechanised Corp lost 3,000 killed and 9,500 wounded and the 46th Army, which had a limited role in the operation, lost 1,100 killed and 5,000 wounded.[1]

In Hungary, Debrecen fell to Group Pliev and the 6th Tank Army after a bitter battle. Other partisan forces in Yugoslavia captured Dubrovnik.

21 October 1944

CENTRAL SECTOR
Eydtkuhnen fell as the 3rd Belorussian Front made limited progress on the road to Konigsberg.

SOUTHERN SECTOR
The 4th Guards Army of the 2nd Ukrainian Front captured Baja in southern Hungary.

22 October 1944

CENTRAL SECTOR
In East Prussia the 3rd Panzer Army counter-attacked near Gumbinnen and destroyed leading elements of the 11th Guards Army. The Soviet advance was brought to a halt with heavy casualties.

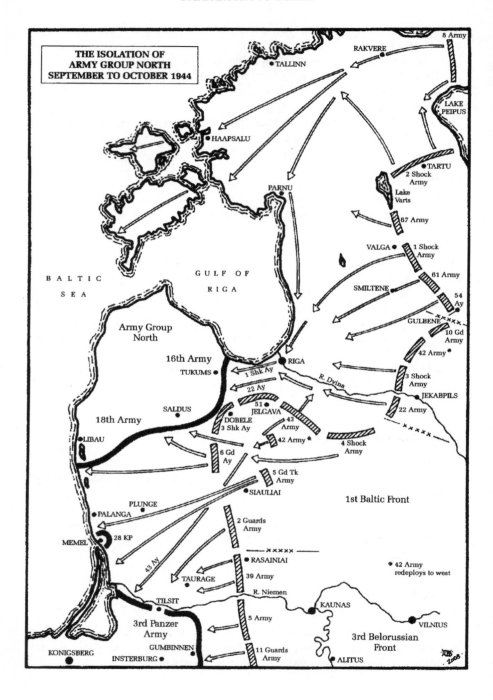

THE ISOLATION OF
ARMY GROUP NORTH
SEPTEMBER TO OCTOBER 1944

8 Army

RAKVERE

TALLINN

LAKE
PEIPUS

HAAPSALU

TARTU
2 Shock
Army
Lake
Varts

PARNU

67 Army

VALGA
1 Shock
Army

61 Army

SMILTENE
54
Ay

GULBENE

BALTIC
SEA

GULF OF
RIGA

10 Gd
Army

42 Army *

Army Group
North

16th Army
TUKUMS

RIGA

1 Shk Ay

R. Dvina

3 Shock
Army

JEKABPILS

22 Ay

22 Army

51
JELGAVA

SALDUS

18th Army

DOBELE
3 Shk Ay

43
Army

42 Army *

4 Shock
Army

LIBAU

6 Gd
Ay

5 Gd Tk
Army

1st Baltic Front

PLUNGE

SIAULIAI

PALANGA

2 Guards
Army

MEMEL

28 KP

* 42 Army
redeploys to west

43 Ay

RASAINIAI

TAURAGE

39 Army

R. Niemen

TILSIT

5 Army

KAUNAS

VILNIUS

3rd Panzer
Army

GUMBINNEN

11 Guards
Army

3rd Belorussian
Front

KONIGSBERG

INSTERBURG

ALITUS

242

SOUTHERN SECTOR
Group Pliev took Nyireghaza, threatening the rear of the 8th Army. In Yugoslavia, Zemun fell as the 57th Army advanced north from Belgrade.

NORWAY
The 14th Army was twelve miles east of Kirkenes and continued to push the 20th Mountain Army back.

23 October 1944

SOUTHERN SECTOR
The 3rd Panzer Korp was redeployed into Hungary and committed to protect the rear of the 8th Army. The 17th and 29th Korps were fighting west to avoid encirclement east of Nyireghaza.

24 October 1944

CENTRAL SECTOR
The 4th Army joined the counter-attack in East Prussia, supporting the 3rd Panzer Army as it recaptured Gumbinnen from the 11th Guards Army.

25 October 1944

SOUTHERN SECTOR
The 3rd Panzer Korp recaptured Nyireghaza, opening an escape route for the 8th Army. Satu Mare and Carei Mare fell to the 40th Army.

NORWAY
Kirkenes fell to 14th Army.

26 October 1944

SOUTHERN SECTOR
Uzhgorod fell to the 18th Army. Elements of the 18th Army linked up with the 40th Army at Mukhachevo but narrowly missed isolating the 8th Army and 1st Hungarian Army.

27 October 1944

CENTRAL SECTOR
The fighting in East Prussia died down as the 3rd Belorussian Front abandoned its attacks.

28 October 1944

SOUTHERN SECTOR

Malinovsky was ordered by Stalin to attack with all the forces at his disposal to take Budapest as soon as possible. Malinovsky replied that he only had the 46th Army immediately available and would prefer to wait until he could muster a more substantial force. Stalin ordered the 2nd Ukrainian Front to begin its attack on 29 October.

29 October 1944

SOUTHERN SECTOR

The 46th Army attacked the 3rd Hungarian Army before Kecskemet. The 7th Guards Army also attacked across the Tizsa and smashed through the 6th Army. Initial progress was encouraging.

The German 8th Army, aided by the 3rd Panzer Korp, fought its way free of the Nyireghaza salient. Heavy fighting with Group Pliev resulted in 25,000 Soviet casualties and 600 tanks lost.[2]

31 October 1944

SOUTHERN SECTOR

The 46th Army reached Kecskemet but became embroiled in bitter fighting with the 24th Panzer Korp.

THE OSTHEER

In the ten months since January the Ostheer had lost in excess of 1,500,000 men, 6,700 panzers and assault guns, 28,000 artillery pieces and 12,000 aircraft. The last three months alone accounted for 672,000 of this total. Of this latter figure, barely 201,000 were replaced. German divisional strength stood at twenty-one panzer, eleven panzer grenadier and 106 infantry divisions, most woefully short of men and equipment.[3]

1 November 1944

SOUTHERN SECTOR

Kecskemet fell to the 46th Army as the 24th Panzer Korp fell back. The Soviet troops then pushed north-west towards Budapest while the 7th Guards Army aimed for Vac. German forces though were building up north of Kecskemet as the 23rd and 24th Panzer Divisions, 13th Panzer, Feldherrnhalle Panzer Grenadier Division and 8th SS Cavalry Division Florian Geyer began to concentrate in order to secure the line of the Tisza river.[4]

2 November 1944

SOUTHERN SECTOR
On the Dalmatian coast Tito's partisans took Zadar.

3 November 1944

SOUTHERN SECTOR
The 46th Army entered the outer defences around Budapest, having broken through the positions of the 22nd SS Cavalry Division near Soroksar. Soviet troops were now just four miles from the city. Elements of the 8th SS Cavalry Division and 12th Hungarian Division counter-attacked but failed to push the Soviets back.

4 November 1944

SOUTHERN SECTOR
The 46th Army penetrated into the suburbs of Budapest but could do no more. Lead elements of the Soviet spearhead were threatened by two counter-attacking panzer divisions (the 1st and 3rd). The Germans had, in the first few days of November, deployed the 3rd Panzer Korp before the city, the 4th Panzer Korp at Jaszbereny and the 57th Panzer Korp around Cegled and Szolnok.[5] The 7th Guards Army took Cegled and Szolnok as it lagged some way behind the 46th. In Dalmatia, Tito captured Sebenico.

6 November 1944

SOUTHERN SECTOR
Monastir fell to Yugoslav partisans. An attempt by the 46th Army to cross the Danube at Csepel Island failed with heavy losses.

7 November 1944

SOUTHERN SECTOR
The 3rd Ukrainian Front renewed its attacks in Hungary, striking the German and Hungarian forces at Mohacs and Apatin. The 57th Army forced the Danube near Batina and Apatin while the 4th Guards Army advanced towards Lakes Velencei and Balaton.

9 November 1944

SOUTHERN SECTOR
Elements of the 3rd Ukrainian Front cross the Danube at Kiskoszeg.

11 November 1944

SOUTHERN SECTOR
Malinovsky began a general assault towards Budapest in order to support the exhausted 46th Army. The new offensive aimed to break the 8th Army defences along the Tizsa. Fierce fighting ensued as the Germans put up a stiff defence.

13 November 1944

SOUTHERN SECTOR
Army Group E was attacked by the 1st Bulgarian Army and forced out of Skopje. This cut the railway line between Salonika and the north, but fortunately for the Germans most of their forces had left this axis and were retreating along the coastal axis through Albania.

14 November 1944

SOUTHERN SECTOR
The 2nd Ukrainian Front was reinforced prior to the resumption of its attack upon Budapest. The 6th Guards Tank Army was ordered to operate in conjunction with the 7th Guards Army to encircle Budapest from the north. The 46th Army made another effort to cross the Danube south of Budapest but was again repulsed.

15 November 1944

SOUTHERN SECTOR
The 2nd and 3rd Ukrainian Fronts penetrated into Army Group South's defences, Jaszbereny falling to the 6th Guards Tank Army. South of Budapest, another attempt to cross the Danube failed.

16 November 1944

SOUTHERN SECTOR
Yet again the 46th Army tried to cross the Danube at Csepel Island but failed to gain a foothold.

18 November 1944

SOUTHERN SECTOR
More attacks by the 46th Army failed to gain a bridgehead on the west bank of the Danube.

21 November 1944

SOUTHERN SECTOR
Tirana and Durazza fell to Albanian rebels. The 46th Army finally gained
a foothold on Csepel Island and immediately pushed strong forces across.
The Germans begin to move elements of the Feldherrnhalle Division
south to counter this threat.

23 November 1944

SOUTHERN SECTOR
The Soviet attacks around and towards Budapest were becoming bogged
down as forward units outran their supplies. North of the city there was
heavy fighting in the Matra hills.

24 November 1944

NORTHERN SECTOR
Yezel Island fell to the Soviet 8th Army, clearing remaining Germans from
the Moonzund Isles. Since the middle of September the Leningrad Front
had lost 6,000 killed and 22,500 wounded, the 1st Baltic 24,000 killed and
79,000 wounded, the 2nd Baltic 15,000 killed and 58,000 wounded and the
3rd Baltic 11,800 killed and 43,000 wounded.[6]

26 November 1944

SOUTHERN SECTOR
The 6th Guards Tank Army captured Hatvan after a brief struggle. The
Stavka had been steadily shifting forces from the 2nd to 3rd Ukrainian
Fronts in order to resume the attack upon Budapest from the south-east.
Malinovsky's attack north of the city would form the northern pincer to
Tolbukhin's southern one south of the city.

28 November 1944

SOUTHERN SECTOR
Mohacs fell to the 57th Army. Pecs was attacked by other elements of the
57th and the 4th Guards Army.

29 November 1944

SOUTHERN SECTOR
Pecs fell to the 3rd Ukrainian Front.

30 November 1944

SOUTHERN SECTOR
The 53rd Army of the 2nd Ukrainian Front broke the 6th Army positions around Eger and captured the town. The Russian forces then pressed on towards Miskolc but German resistance was severe.

THE OSTHEER
Despite a rise in strength to 5,202 panzers (facing 14,000 Soviet tanks), the fuel situation throughout the Reich had reached catastrophic proportions. Significant elements of the Luftwaffe were grounded and the mobile divisions of the army forced to rely on horse drawn transportation. The Allied combined bomber offensive had wreaked havoc among oil production facilities and the capture of the Ploesti oilfields in Rumania severed a major source of oil. Only Hungary's oilfields were left and were already threatened by the Soviet advance.

German divisional strength stood at twenty-one panzer, eleven panzer grenadier and 107 infantry divisions. Hungarian strength was fifteen divisions and three brigades.[7]

1 December 1944

SOUTHERN SECTOR
The 46th Army was held up around Budapest but the 57th Army continued to make progress near Pecs. Elements of the 4th Ukrainian Front attacked the 1st Panzer Army along the Ondava river.

2 December 1944

SOUTHERN SECTOR
With the threat of a Soviet breakthrough in Hungary the Germans brought the 2nd Panzer Army back into the line, deploying it south of Lake Balaton. The main objective for the army was the protection of the Hungarian oilfields at Nagykanitza.

North of the lake Army Group South deployed Fretter Pico's 6th Army between the lake and Hatvan with the 3rd Panzer, 72nd and 57th Panzer Korps, while the 8th Army under Wohler was around Miskolc.

3 December 1944

SOUTHERN SECTOR
Miskolc fell after heavy fighting.

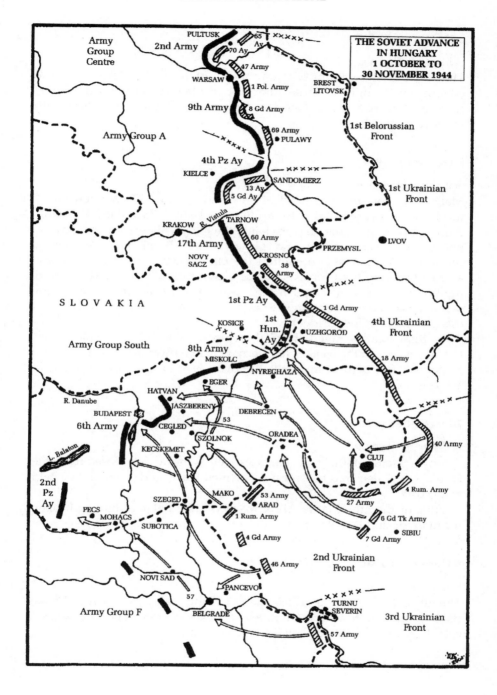

THE SOVIET ADVANCE
IN HUNGARY
1 OCTOBER TO
30 NOVEMBER 1944

4 December 1944

SOUTHERN SECTOR

The 2nd Ukrainian Front began an attack with its 46th Army aimed at crossing the Danube at Ercsi. Attacking just before midnight the Soviet force met overwhelming German counter-fire and was repulsed with massive losses.

5 December 1944

SOUTHERN SECTOR

Malinovsky continued to attack at Ercsi and also unleashed a new attack north of the city. Preceded by artillery and air strikes, the 7th Guards Army launching a ferocious attack into the Ipoly Valley, supported by the 6th Guards Tank Army and Group Pliev. Bitter fighting ensued prompting Malinovsky to commit the 6th Guards Tank to support the attack. The armoured forces suffered heavy losses in the close quarters fighting but managed to push their way forward towards Vac. To the south the 46th Army continued to suffer heavy losses before Ercsi but did establish some minor bridgeheads.

As these battles raged the 57th Army of the 3rd Ukrainian Front advanced against the weaker southern wing of Army Group South, taking Szigetvar. The 37th Army took Vukovar as it crossed the Danube in Yugoslavia.

7 December 1944

SOUTHERN SECTOR

Adony fell to the 46th Army. Barcs also fell as the Soviets closed up to the Drava. Hitler declared Budapest a 'Fortified Place' and ordered it be held at all costs.

Units of the 4th Guards Army reached Lake Balaton, having broken through the 2nd Panzer Army.

8 December 1944

SOUTHERN SECTOR

The 4th Guards Army attacked the 3rd Hungarian Army north of Lake Balaton, moving to within ten miles of Szekesfehervar. The 57th Armies established firm positions between the lake and the Danube.

9 December 1944

SOUTHERN SECTOR
Following a fierce battle Ercsi fell to the 46th Army. Leading elements of the 46th linked up with the 4th Guards near Lake Velencze. Along the Slovak–Hungarian border Balassagyarmat fell to the 7th Guards Army, while elements of the 6th Guards Tank Army reached the Danube at Vac. German counter-attacks by the Feldherrnhalle and 13th Panzer Divisions at Vac were repulsed after heavy fighting.

12 December 1944

SOUTHERN SECTOR
The Stavka ordered the 3rd Ukrainian Front to support the attacks by the 2nd Ukrainian Front upon Budapest. It transferred command of the 46th Army to the 3rd Ukrainian Front. While Malinovsky pinned the Germans north of the city, Tolbukhin was to slice through the weaker defences between Lake Balaton and Budapest, then swing north to envelop the German and Hungarian forces inside the city. The 2nd Ukrainian Front was also to push its 40th and 27th Armies and 4th Rumanian Army from the Hungarian border into Slovakia to threaten the 8th Army.

13 December 1944

SOUTHERN SECTOR
Leading units of the 7th Guards Army were just six miles north and eight miles east of Budapest, having drawn the 6th Army north to protect the approaches to Budapest. Hitler ordered Freissner to throw the Soviet armies back but Freissner refused to counter-attack, arguing that he would not attack before the heavily waterlogged ground north of Lake Balaton had frozen.

14 December 1944

SOUTHERN SECTOR
Ipolysag fell to the 6th Guards Tank Army as it supported the right wing of the 7th Guards.

16 December 1944

THE WESTERN FRONT
The last German offensive in the west began as Hitler launched his Ardennes thrust. Bitter fighting until the end of January 1945 would cost Germany valuable soldiers and vehicles and huge stocks of fuel.

17 December 1944

SOUTHERN SECTOR

The 2nd Ukrainian Front came within five miles of Budapest.

19 December 1944

SOUTHERN SECTOR

The 3rd Panzer Korp was ordered to leave its panzers south of Budapest and march its infantry to Hatvan to reinforce this threatened sector.

20 December 1944

SOUTHERN SECTOR

The 6th Guards Tank Army smashed its way through to the Hron river while the 7th Guards Army reached the Ipel valley and began to push upon Esztergom. German counter-attacks halted the Russian advance. Heavy fighting raged on these positions for nearly a week.

South of Budapest the 3rd Ukrainian Front began its new offensive. Despite being heavily outnumbered, the Germans launched continuous armoured counter-attacks, slowing the Soviet advance to a crawl.

21 December 1944

SOUTHERN SECTOR

The attacks by the 3rd Ukrainian Front between Lake Balaton and Budapest compelled Fretter-Pico to commit the last reserve available to the 6th Army. Hitler once again resorted to sacking generals for defeats at the front. Freissner and Fretter-Pico were both dismissed, Wohler being appointed to command Army Group South and Balck the 6th Army.

22 December 1944

SOUTHERN SECTOR

Under intense pressure the German line between Erd and Lake Velencze began to crack, enabling the 3rd Ukrainian Front to push its units forward. Elements of the 4th Guards Army struck Szekesfehervar and became involved in bitter fighting.

23 December 1944

SOUTHERN SECTOR

The 3rd Ukrainian Front tore a sixty-mile hole in the 6th Army. Szekesfehervar and Bicske fell as the 4th Guards and 46th Armies pushed north towards Esztergom. Fierce counter-attacks by the 8th Panzer Division were pushed aside. By dusk the fighting had spread into Esztergom, leaving only a narrow corridor open to the west. The 4th Guards Army, supporting the attacks by the 46th Army, severed roads and railway lines out of the city. Erd fell after serious fighting.

24 December 1944

SOUTHERN SECTOR
Budapest was on the verge of encirclement. The 6th Guards Tank Army attacked towards Esztergom north of the Danube but met fierce resistance from the 6th Army. The Germans hurriedly redeployed the 8th SS Cavalry Division to Buda to block the roads into the city from the west. German defences in this area were extremely weak.

25 December 1944

SOUTHERN SECTOR
Soviet tanks reached Tatabanya and Csolnok. Forces closed upon Esztergom from the south. The 2nd Ukrainian Front began an offensive against the Pest defences, pushing the Germans and Hungarians steadily back towards urban Budapest. Under intense pressure the 13th Panzer Division and Feldherrnhalle Panzer Grenadier Division had to give ground, losing considerable numbers of men as they fell back.

26 December 1944

SOUTHERN SECTOR
The 6th Guards Tank and 7th Guards Armies reached the Danube north of Esztergom, narrowing the corridor out of Budapest still further. A fierce attack finally brought leading units of the 3rd Ukrainian Front up to join the 2nd Ukrainian to the north, trapping the 11th SS Mountain Korp inside the city together with other Hungarian and German divisions deployed to secure the so-called fortress. A force of five divisions (four German, including the 13th Panzer, Feldherrnhalle, SS Horst Wessel and SS Florian Geyer and the 10th Hungarian Division) was isolated, some 188,000 Hungarian and German soldiers.

Hitler ordered Wohler to leave these forces inside the city, proposing that Gille's 4th SS Panzer Korp relieve them. Gille, with the SS Totenkopf and SS Wiking Divisions, was currently deployed around Bratislava.

The long Soviet drive to capture Budapest had finally resulted in the isolation of the city and encirclement of sizeable German and Hungarian forces. Stalin's insistence that the 46th Army make an early drive on the city had resulted in a protracted battle of attrition as Hitler continued to throw forces into this theatre. The protection of Hungarian oil would prove of major importance to Hitler during the final months of the war, drawing forces away from the defence of Germany itself.

27 December 1944

SOUTHERN SECTOR
Soviet forces began the reduction of the garrison of Budapest, the 2nd Ukrainian Front continuing its attacks into Pest. During heavy fighting Soviet forces entered the suburbs.

28 December 1944

SOUTHERN SECTOR
The battle for Pest raged unabated as the 2nd Ukrainian Front continued to press the German and Hungarian forces back. Hungarian defences in the north-east of the Pest district were destroyed, opening a route into the city for the Soviets. In Buda, Soviet forces were just a mile from the Danube and continued attacking along the Varosmajor Grange toward the Castle District.

29 December 1944

SOUTHERN SECTOR
Desperate Hungarian defence in Pest managed to stabilise the line but was not enough to halt the Soviet advance. Hungarian counter-attacks in southern Buda made progress but soon came under intense Soviet pressure and had to fall back.

After two days of bitter fighting the Soviets offered the Budapest garrison the opportunity to surrender. Two parties of emissaries from the 2nd Ukrainian Front were send into no-man's-land in both Pest and Buda to offer terms to the Germans. The Germans killed the Pest emissary on their way into the city but the Buda party managed to get through the front line to deliver their message. The Buda group then returned to their own lines but, during the journey across the battlefield, Soviet artillery fire hit the German lines. In the ensuing chaos the Buda emissary was killed but others in their party managed to regain their lines.[8]

30 December 1944

SOUTHERN SECTOR
After the German rejection of their surrender demand, the Soviets unleashed an overwhelming barrage upon Pest. Three days of artillery fire

began, striking the defenders and civilians alike. The 2nd Ukrainian Front also resumed its attacks into Pest, striking all along the German and Hungarian perimeter.

31 December 1944

SOUTHERN SECTOR

The Germans launched a fierce counter-attack in Pest and held up the Soviet advance. Heavy artillery fire continued to strike the city.

THE OSTHEER

Possibly the greatest factor hindering the German army was the catastrophic shortage of fuel. The Western Allies pounded German industry day and night, yet German manufacturing continued to increase. However, once the bombing of the oilfields began the Allies saw immediate results. The Luftwaffe, still numerically very strong, was grounded by lack of fuel and the armies in the field had to resort to pressing thousands of horse-drawn vehicles into service.

At the end of 1944 the Germans, despite having some of the most sophisticated equipment of all the combatants (including 4,785 tanks on the eastern front) were basically no more mobile than the armies of the First World War. German divisional strength in the east stood at twenty-one panzer, thirteen panzer grenadier and 107 infantry divisions.[9]

PRODUCTION

German manufactured 39,807 aircraft, 19,002 panzers and assault guns, 67,375 lorries and 70,700 artillery pieces during 1944 against the Soviet production of 40,246 aircraft, 28,963 tanks and Su's, 52,600 lorries and 122,400 artillery pieces. [10]

THE OPPOSING FORCES

As the year ended the opposing forces were deployed on a long line running north from the Dalmatian coast, through Hungary, Slovakia and Poland and on to the Baltic coast in East Prussia. From here there was a gap between the German forces, Army Group North fighting in isolation with its twenty-seven divisions in Kurland.

Schorner's Army Group North had 250,000 men between the 16th and 18th Armies while Reinhardt's Army Group Centre, rebuilt after the defeat in Belorussia, had the 3rd Panzer, 4th and 2nd Armies with thirty-four infantry, four panzer grenadier and three panzer divisions, a force of 580,000 men, 750 panzers and assault guns and 500 aircraft. Deployed around Warsaw and along the Vistula was Harpe's Army Group A with the 9th, 4th Panzer, 17th and 1st Panzer Armies. This army group had twenty-four infantry divisions, four panzer divisions (16th and 17th with

4th Panzer Army, 19th and 25th Panzer Divisions with 9th Army) and two panzer grenadier divisions, a total of 400,000 men, 770 panzers, 4,100 artillery pieces and assault guns and nearly 300 planes.

In Hungary and Slovakia was Wohler's Army Group South with the 8th and 6th Armies, a force of approximately 300,000 men. The 3rd Hungarian Army was also with Army Group South but had lost thousands of men following the collapse of the Horthy regime. Army Group South had more than 180,000 of its men incarcerated in Budapest, leaving the armies in the main combat line stretched extremely thin. South of Lake Balaton, and not within Army Group South's command chain, was the 2nd Panzer Army. Still farther south, withdrawing from the Balkans, were Weich's Army Group F and Lohr's Army Group E, a combined force of nearly 500,000 soldiers. The Ostheer had in full a little over 2,000,000 men, 4,785 panzers and assault guns and 29,000 artillery pieces.

The Soviet Army deployed a host of armies against this drastically reduced German force. From the Baltic Sea to the Danube river the Soviets had 11,500,000 troops, 6,700,000 of them with the first echelon armies. The Soviets were also equipped as never before, deploying 108,000 artillery pieces, 2,700 Katyushas, nearly 15,000 tanks and Su's and 15,000 aircraft. In addition the Poles, Rumanians and Bulgarians deployed a further 350,000 men.

The Leningrad Front had the 40th, 23rd and 32nd Armies against the 16th Army in Kurland. Facing the 18th Army was the 2nd Baltic Front with its 1st Shock, 8th, 22nd and 42nd Armies. To the south the 1st Baltic Front faced the 28th Korp in Memel and the 3rd Panzer Army in northeast East Prussia. This front had the 4th Shock, 6th Guards, 43rd, 51st and 61st Armies, while the 3rd Belorussian Front, situated on the eastern approaches to East Prussia opposite the flank of the 3rd Panzer Army, the 4th Army and the northern wing of the 2nd Army, had the 2nd Guards, 5th, 11th Guards, 20th, 31st and 39th Armies.

North of Warsaw was the 2nd Belorussian Front with the 2nd Shock, 3rd, 5th Guards Tank, 48th, 49th, 50th, 65th and 70th Armies while south of the city, along the line of the Vistula, was the 1st Belorussian Front with the 1st Polish, 1st Guards Tank, 3rd Shock, 5th Shock, 8th Guards, 33rd, 47th and 69th Armies. In southern Poland, from the Vistula–San bridgehead to the Slovakian border was the 1st Ukrainian Front with the 3rd Guards, 4th Guards Tank, 5th Guards, 6th, 13th, 21st, 52nd, 59th and 60th Armies, while in Slovakia there was the 4th Ukrainian Front with its 1st Guards, 18th and 38th Armies.

On the southern wing were the 2nd and 3rd Ukrainian Fronts, fighting Group South. The 2nd Ukrainian had the 6th Guards Tank, 7th Guards, 27th, 40th and 53rd Armies, while the 3rd Ukrainian had the 4th Guards, 46th, 26th, 37th and 57th Armies.

After the spectacular advance in Belorussia and the Balkans, the Stavka prepared a new offensive designed to destroy the German armies on the Vistula. The 2nd and 3rd Belorussian Fronts were to attack into East Prussia and Pomerania, deploying 1,600,000 men (708,000 in the 3rd and 881,000 in the 2nd Belorussian), 28,000 artillery pieces, 3,300 tanks and Su's and 3,000 aircraft, while the 1st Belorussian and 1st Ukrainian Fronts would destroy the main part of Army Group A and advance to the Oder river. These two fronts had 2,200,000 soldiers (1,028,000 in the 1st Belorussian and 1,083,000 in the 1st Ukrainian), 32,000 artillery pieces, 6,500 tanks and Su's and 4,700 aircraft. At Magnuszew the 1st Belorussian Front had packed more than 400,000 men and 1,700 tanks into the small bridgehead. Once the German front had been pierced, the 1st Belorussian and Ukrainian Fronts would advance to the Oder and Neisse before turning to their flanks in Pomerania and Silesia. Stalin placed great importance upon capturing the industrial region of Silesia intact.

The 2nd and 3rd Belorussian Fronts were to strike Army Group Centre in East Prussia. The main blow was to be delivered along the Narew by the 2nd Belorussian Front which was then to push into Pomerania, while Chernyakhov's 3rd Belorussian struck directly into East Prussia.

1 January 1945

SOUTHERN SECTOR
Bitter fighting continued in Pest as the Soviets pounded the 10th and 12th Hungarian Divisions. Soviet forces had finally entered the main metropolitan area of Pest after some hard fighting.

2 January 1945

SOUTHERN SECTOR
The 4th SS Panzer Korp counter-attacked from Komarno, pushing back the surprised 4th Guards Army. In bitter fighting the SS threw the Soviets back twenty miles. At Bicske the 4th Guards tried to halt the German drive before it reached Budapest. Bloody fighting raged through the day. There was also heavy fighting inside Budapest as the German and Hungarian forces counter-attacked.

3 January 1945

SOUTHERN SECTOR
Soviet troops advancing in Pest were just under half a mile from the Racecourse, which the Germans were using as an airfield. Counter-attacks by the 13th Panzer Division failed to halt the Soviet thrust. In Buda there was bitter fighting for Sashegy Hill and Rozsadomb Hill. Sashegy Hill was crucial for the continued defence of Buda by the German and Hungarian forces.[11]

6 January 1945

SOUTHERN SECTOR
The 6th Guards Tank Army and 7th Guards Army launched a major attack along the Hron and gained a bridgehead. A German counter-attack recaptured Esztergom on the south bank of the Danube. In the Pest bridgehead the 22nd SS Cavalry Division abandoned Soroksar. Soviet forces were able to bring the Racecourse airfield under intense artillery fire and put it out of action.

ALLIED DIPLOMACY
Churchill enquired if Stalin could bring forward his forthcoming offensive in Poland to draw some of the pressure off the Allied forces in the Ardennes. Stalin ordered the Vistula–Oder operation be brought forward from 20 to 12 January.

7 January 1945

SOUTHERN SECTOR
The 3rd Panzer Korp began a new counter-attack at Mor in an effort to break through to Budapest. In Pest the 13th Panzer Division was down to just 887 men, the 10th Hungarian to 507 and the Feldherrnhalle to only 865. The 22nd SS Cavalry Division also had around 800 men.[12]

8 January 1945

SOUTHERN SECTOR
Kispest fell to Soviet troops. The 3rd Panzer Korp counter-attack bogged down, while to the north the 6th Guards Tank Army of the 2nd Ukrainian Front pushed along the northern bank of the Danube towards Komarom in an effort to destroy the 57th Panzer Korp.

9 January 1945

SOUTHERN SECTOR
The Soviets began a major attack aimed at splitting the Pest bridgehead in two. The Racecourse fell to Rumanian forces fighting alongside the Soviets.

North of the city the 4th SS Panzer Korp launched a counter-attack from Esztergom, pushing along the Danube towards Budapest.

10 January 1945

SOUTHERN SECTOR

The 4th SS Panzer Korp counter-attack made good progress through the Pilis Hills towards Budapest.

11 January 1945

SOUTHERN SECTOR

The 3rd Panzer Korp attack from Mor fizzled out, the Germans being exhausted after days of bitter fighting. Heavy fighting continued in Pest as the Soviets captured Ujpest, pushing the Feldherrnhalle Division back. Bitter fighting erupted in the Varosliget Park.

SOVIET COMMAND

Following Churchill's appeal, Stalin brought the start date for the offensive in Poland forward to the 12th. The attacks were to be staggered, starting first in the south and then rolling to the north, de-stabilising and ultimately destroying Army Groups Centre and A.

> From the Baltic theatre in the north to the Hungarian plains in the south, the Ostheer was reeling back upon its homeland. The Soviets were poised to unleash their next great offensive, an advance which would take them to the gates of the Reich capital and begin the final, bloody collapse of the German Army.

NOTES

1   Kirosheev, *Soviet Casualties and Combat Losses in the Twentieth Century*, Table 75
2   Seaton, *The Russo–German War*, p494
3   Divisional strengths from Ellis, *The World War II Databook*, p176
4   Ungvary, *The Battle for Budapest*, p6
5   Ungvary, *The Battle for Budapest*, p12
6   Kirosheev, *Soviet Casualties and Combat Losses in the Twentieth Century*, Table 75
7   German divisional deployment from Ellis, *The World War II Databook*, p176, Hungarian from p178
8   Ungvary, *The Battle for Budapest*, pp96–100
9   Ellis, *The World War II Databook*, p 176
10 Details of production figures from Ellis, *The World War II Databook,* Tables 87 (tanks), 88 (Artillery), 91 (trucks) and 92 (aircraft)
11 Ungvary, *The Battle for Budapest*, p130
12 Ungvary, *The Battle for Budapest*, p109

CHAPTER VIII

Germany at Bay

Everywhere along the combat line the Ostheer struggled to hold back the host of Soviet forces pressing into the Reich. As the German armies in the west failed in their attempt to drive a wedge between the Americans and British, Stalin brought his offensive towards the Oder forward. Millions of Soviet troops with thousands of tanks stood ready to crush the Ostheer, a force of increasingly limited military capability as its supplies and replacements failed to materialise. From its Vistula bridgeheads the Red Army would bring the war to the very gates of Berlin.

12 January 1945

CENTRAL SECTOR

1st Ukrainian Front artillery struck the 4th Panzer and 17th Armies, churning their front and rear positions to shreds. Forward battalions attacked the stunned Germans, causing them to mistake these probes for the main attack. A few hours later artillery opened up again, unleashing a two-hour barrage. During the bombardment the headquarters of 4th Panzer Army was hit, two thirds of German artillery disabled and almost a quarter of their personnel killed or wounded. Around midday the 1st Ukrainian Front surged forward. Graeser's 4th Panzer Army was badly hit, the 13th Army slamming into Recknagel's 42nd Korp. After bloody fighting the German line had collapsed, enabling Koniev to commit the 4th Tank Army to the battle. The remnants of the 42nd Korp were pushed aside as Soviet tanks advanced upon Kielce. In an effort to restore his line, Graeser threw in Nehring's 24th Panzer Korp from the reserve. On the right wing the 48th Panzer Korp suffered an equally severe pounding, being forced to give ground under heavy attack.

SOUTHERN SECTOR

Bitter fighting continued in Pest as the Varosliget Park largely fell to the Soviets. The 4th SS Panzer Korp penetrated to within twelve miles of Budapest but was then ordered to pull back.

13 January 1945

CENTRAL SECTOR

Accompanied by a massive artillery barrage the 3rd Belorussian Front opened its offensive against the German forces in East Prussia. Bad weather prevented complete air support and led to some inaccuracy during the barrage. As leading units began to advance, they encountered exceptionally strong German defensive fire. Fierce fighting developed around Kattenau.

The gains made by the 1st Ukrainian Front were consolidated today as its spearheads began to encounter increasingly strong German resistance. Elements of the 59th Army pushed towards Krakow but the 24th Panzer Korp, striking with more than two hundred panzers and assault guns around Chmelnik, engaged the main attack force of the 1st Ukrainian Front. The 4th Tank Army was brought to a halt amid heavy fighting, but after a brutal counter-attack, smashed the Germans aside. Nehring's korp was left in tatters, reeling west as the 4th Tank Army pushed forward. Additional attacks by the 3rd Guards Tank, 52nd and 5th Guards Armies also succeeded in breaking through to the west, the 48th ranzer Korp having been smashed under the weight of these latest attacks.

SOUTHERN SECTOR

Heavy fighting raged in Pest as Soviet troops completed the capture of the Varosliget Park.

14 January 1945

CENTRAL SECTOR

Heavy fighting raged around Kattenau as the 3rd Belorussian fought its way through the town. With its line still intact but under intense pressure, the 3rd Panzer Army committed the 5th Panzer Division from its reserve. After hard fighting Kattenau was retaken, prompting Chernyakhovsky to move the 11th Guards Army from the centre to the right. This move was intended to support the 39th Army, currently attacking the Germans north of Schlossberg.

The 2nd Belorussian Front began its attack into East Prussia from the Narew river, aiming to push into the Danzig region of eastern Pomerania. The main attack was led by the 2nd Shock, 48th and 3rd Armies, while the 5th Guards Tank was held ready to exploit any breakthrough. Secondary attacks on the Pultusk axis pinned down the German reserves. Heavy snowfall prevented the Soviets from utilising their overwhelming air power and after only a short time German resistance stiffened considerably.

Even this early into the offensive, Reinhardt had recognised that the 2nd

Belorussian Front attack presented a major threat to his flank and requested permission to pull back forces to a shorter front line. Hitler naturally refused.

With attention fixed around Baranow, the Germans were taken by surprise as the 1st and 2nd Belorussian Fronts unleashed their offensives to the north. At Magnuszew the Soviets had massed 3rd and 5th Shock Armies, 1st Polish Army and 2nd Tank Army, a force of 400,000 men with 1,700 tanks against the German 8th Korp, while to the south there was 8th Guards, 69th and 1st Guards Tank Armies against the 56th Panzer Korp (19th and 25th Panzer Divisions) of Luttwitz's 9th Army which held the Pulawy sector. In reserve the Germans held the 40th Panzer Korp but this was to cover the entire army group area.

At 0830 hours both the Pulawy and Magnuszew bridgeheads exploded into action as Soviet artillery pulverised the Germans. Pushing rapidly forwards, the attacking forces penetrated twenty miles into the German rear. The 2nd Tank Army entered the battle at Magnuszew almost immediately. By 1030 hours the 56th Panzer Korp had moved to counter-attack with its 19th and 25th Panzer Divisions, but instead of fighting as a single, powerful unit, the 19th moved to tackle the 69th and 8th Guards Armies while 25th attempted to stop the 5th Shock Army. Despite heavy fighting the Soviets drove on, pushing west and north from Magnuszew to envelop Warsaw, while at Pulawy attacks to the west and south-west aimed to encircle the junction of the 9th and 4th Panzer Armies against the Vistula. The 3rd and 5th Shock Armies ripped apart the 8th Korp while the 8th Guards crushed the 56th Panzer. Despite a desperate defence the German forces were simply overwhelmed.

The 1st Ukrainian Front had completely ripped open the German line before Baranow. Nehring's 24th Panzer Korp had been destroyed as a coherent force while the remnants of Recknagel's 42nd Korp fought in isolation as the 13th and 3rd Guards Armies poured around the broken flanks. Recknagel was killed during the fighting. In order to restore the situation Hitler ordered the Grossdeutschland Panzer Korp to move from Army Group Centre to Army Group A.

SOUTHERN SECTOR
The 27th Army of the 2nd Ukrainian Front captured Lunenec in Slovakia as it pushed north from the Hungarian border. The weakness of the Soviet forces in this sector prevented any further exploitation of this gain.

15 January 1945

CENTRAL SECTOR
Fighting in Poland intensified as the Russians continued to attack from East Prussia to the Slovak border. Reinhardt was forced to commit his

slender reserves to the battle. The 2nd Belorussian Front smashed the 2nd Army on the Narew, but at a terrible cost. As the weather cleared the Soviet air armies began to work over the German divisions. The 4th Air Army logged up hundreds of sorties as it pounded anything that moved on the German side of the line.

A little to the south the 5th Shock Army crossed the Pilica river. German counter-attacks were beaten off. The 8th Guards Army struck west towards Radom. With the front fluid the 2nd Guards Tank Army moved up through the 5th Shock Army and the 1st Guards Tank forward through the 8th Guards. The 1st Guards Tank Army pushed towards Lodz and Posen.

Around Warsaw the Soviets began to throw a ring around the 9th Army, elements of the 47th Army attacking from the north and the 1st Polish Army from the south, from Magnuszew.

Still farther to the south the 1st Ukrainian Front advanced unimpeded by the Germans, Kielce falling as the 3rd Guards and 13th Armies wiped out part of the 42nd Korp. The remnants of Nehring's 24th Panzer Korp fought bitterly north of Kielce, in operational isolation.

SOUTHERN SECTOR
Soviet forces in Buda took Sashegy Hill but a German counter-attack regained control.

GERMAN COMMAND
Hitler confirmed the order for the Grossdeutschland Panzer Korp to re-deploy the Herman Goering Panzer and Brandenburg Panzer-grenadier Divisions from East Prussia to Kielce. This move took away Army Group Centre's only effective reserve.

16 January 1945

CENTRAL SECTOR
Warsaw was encircled by the 1st Polish, 61st and 47th Armies, trapping elements of the 46th Panzer Korp. Army Group A ordered the abandonment of the city just before the Soviet forces completed their encirclement. Farther south the 69th Army and 1st Guards Tank Army took Radom. The two armies then continued to push on towards Lodz.

Heavy fighting raged around Kielce as the 24th Panzer Korp struggled against overwhelming odds. Realising the futility of his stand, Nehring broke out to the north during the night of 16–17 January.

Elements of the 3rd Guards Tank, 5th Guards and 52nd Armies of the 1st Ukrainian Front reached Czestochowa, threatening to turn the northern wing of the beleaguered 17th Army.

GERMAN COMMAND

Hitler confirmed his intention to move the 6th SS Panzer Army from the Western Front to Hungary, despite the total collapse of the German forces in Poland. The deployment of the army here was designed to restore the German positions on the Danube and safeguard the oilfields around Nagykanitsa. Guderian argued strongly that the 6th SS should be moved immediately to Poland but Hitler would not be swayed. In a towering rage Hitler sacked Harpe as commander of Army Group A, appointing Schorner in his place. Luttwitz also lost his command of the 9th Army. General Rendulic took over command of Army Group North.

17 January 1945

CENTRAL SECTOR

Warsaw fell to Soviet and Polish troops after more than five years of Nazi occupation. A large part of the civilian population had been murdered during the occupation and uprising of autumn 1944. Of the 1,310,000 strong population in 1939 barely 162,000 remained in the city.[1] To the west the 2nd Guards Tank Army captured Sochaczew, the 47th and 61st Armies pushed north-west in the wake of 2nd Guards.

Elements of the 2nd Shock Army took Ciechanow while the 5th Guards and 3rd Guards Tank Armies closed upon Krakow. The 59th launched attacks directly into the city, smashing the southern wing of the 17th Army. As these bitter battles raged the 60th Army approached Navy Sacz and the 3rd Guards took Radomsko. Elements of the 52nd Army captured Zawiercie.

SOUTHERN SECTOR

The 2nd Ukrainian Front had largely conquered the Pest district of Budapest, only the last remnants of the German and Hungarian force still fighting. The bridges over the Danube were blown, stranding some forces on the Pest side but most of the survivors had managed to fall back to Buda. As this battle neared its conclusion, the 4th SS Panzer Korp redeployed to Szekesfehervar with the aim of crashing through the thinly stretched 4th Guards and 26th Armies between Lake Balaton and Lake Velencei.

18 January 1945

CENTRAL SECTOR

Tilsit came under fierce attack by the 43rd Army of the 1st Baltic Front, pressing the 3rd Panzer Army back upon Konigsberg. Elements of the 70th Army took Modlin while Naselsk and Plonsk fell to the 65th Army.

Saucken's Grossdeutschland Panzer Korp deployed around Lodz, fighting elements of the 1st Guards Tank Army whose advance threatened its rear. The battered 24th Panzer Korp retreated north from Kielce but found strong Soviet forces barring its path. Turning west, Nehring linked up with the survivors of the 42nd Korp.

The 60th Army pinned the 17th Army before Krakow while the 59th and 4th Guards Tank Armies pushed in from the north and west. Very heavy fighting ensued around the city.

SOUTHERN SECTOR
The battle for Pest came to an end after a month of bloody fighting. Between Lakes Balaton and Velencei the 4th SS Panzer Korp unleashed its attack and advanced rapidly towards the Danube. The Germans aimed to reach the river at Dunapentele and turn north to relieve Budapest.

19 January 1945

CENTRAL SECTOR
The 3rd Belorussian Front captured Schlossberg (now Pillkallen) with its 11th Guards Army. Meanwhile the 5th Guards Tank Army (2nd Belorussian Front) took Mlawa and the 70th Army captured Wloclawek. Tilsit also fell to the 43rd Army of the 1st Baltic Front as it broke the line of the Niemen. Farther south the 1st Belorussian and 1st Ukrainian Fronts advanced rapidly, Lodz falling to the 8th Guards Army and Tarnow to the 59th Army. Krakow also fell relatively unscathed as the 17th Army hastily abandoned its positions. The 3rd Guards Tank Army penetrated the German frontier between Breslau and Czestochowa.

SOUTHERN SECTOR
In the fighting in Budapest, Soviet troops landed on Margit Island. A German counter-attack failed to dislodge them.

The 4th SS Panzer Korp brushed aside a counter-attack by the 26th Army and reached the Danube at Dunapentele, effectively severing the Soviet combat units from their second echelon. The main thrust of the German attack immediately swung to the north to drive towards the garrison of Budapest but encountered increasingly stubborn Soviet resistance. In an effort to slow the German drive the 27th Army was transferred from its positions north of Budapest with the 2nd Ukrainian Front, to the southern wing to support the 26th Army.

20 January 1945

CENTRAL SECTOR
The 2nd Shock Army of 2nd Belorussian Front closed upon Tannenberg, scene of the German victory in World War One, while a little to the north

Insterberg fell to the 5th Army of the 3rd Belorussian. The 43rd Army poured out of its bridgehead across the Niemen near Tilsit.

Group Nehring continued its retreat, crossing the Pilica river near Tomaszow. Farther south, in Slovakia, Presov and Kosice fell to the 1st Guards and 18th Armies while the 38th captured Novy Sacz.

With the 2nd Belorussian Front advancing rapidly the Stavka ordered it to turn its four central armies north to drive behind the flank of the 4th Army. However, as the 2nd moved north the 1st Belorussian found its right wing deprived of support.

SOUTHERN SECTOR
In Hungary the 4th SS Panzer Korp pushed north towards Budapest. The German 6th Army began a new attack from Szekesfehervar but was held up by the 4th Guards Army as it fought desperately to halt this new thrust. South of Lake Balaton the 57th Army was fighting 2nd Panzer Army attacks but largely held its ground.

21 January 1945

CENTRAL SECTOR
The Germans evacuated Tannenberg, the monument to Hindenburg being destroyed and the remains of the Field Marshal and his wife taken west. The 2nd Shock Army punched behind the right wing of the 4th Army, aiming to isolate the 2nd, 4th and 3rd Panzer Armies inside East Prussia. Elements of the 5th Guards Tank Army were close to Deutsch Eylau as they advanced in support of the 2nd Shock. Forward units were as far ahead as the Elbing railway station. Gumbinnen fell to the 28th Army as the junction of the 4th and 3rd Panzer Armies was fractured before Konigsberg.

With Soviet forces deep inside the borders of the province, the populace of East Prussia had taken to the roads, seeking safety in the west. More than two million people were migrating, walking and dying under heavy artillery fire and savage air strikes.

Hitler agreed to the evacuation of Memel, Gollnick's 28th Korp and the thousands of civilians in the town beginning the evacuation immediately. He also sanctioned the withdrawal of the 4th Army to cover the open southern flank at Wormditt, the 2nd Army having been driven away to the west into Pomerania as the Soviets advanced. Soviet attacks had exposed the rear of the 4th Army and 3rd Panzer Army, threatening to overwhelm Army Group Centre.

Lead tanks of the 1st Guards Tank Army crossed the Warthe and entered Posen. Group Nehring had fallen back to the Warthe, having skirted south of Lodz.

SOUTHERN SECTOR

The Soviets increase their forces on Margit Island in Budapest and slowly gained more territory. A Hungarian counter-attack in Buda recaptured Varosmajor Grange.

22 January 1945

CENTRAL SECTOR

Allenstein fell to the 48th Army and Deutsch Eylau to the 5th Guards Tank Army. During the night of 21–22 January, General Hossbach began to withdraw sizeable units of the 4th Army away from inland positions to create a strike force closer to the sea. Despite Hitler's withdrawal order of the 21st, this move had not been sanctioned and Hossbach was acting without approval.

On the main Polish front, the 47th Army reached Bromberg while the 2nd Guards Tank Army took Gneizno. The 3rd Shock Army, following in the wake of the 47th, began to invest Bromberg.

The 1st Ukrainian Front also gained significant territory, the 4th Tank Army taking Rawicz while other units took Kronstadt and Gross Strehlitz. Elements of the 5th Guards Army reached the Oder at Brieg. Assault units quickly crossed and established a bridgehead on the west bank. During the night the 4th Tank Army threw units across the river near Goeben. The Germans were unaware that Soviet forces had penetrated this far west.

The Grossdeutschland Panzer Korp, fighting in isolation, was strengthened as Nehring's ragged 24th Panzer Korp joined it. Both forces continued their retreat to the Oder.

SOUTHERN SECTOR

Heavy fighting raged south of Budapest as the 4th SS Panzer Korp hit the 4th Guards Army. The Russians were also under pressure from the 6th Army and began to concede land to the Germans around Szekesfehervar. After heavy fighting Szekesfehervar fell to the Germans.

GERMAN COMMAND

Hitler decided to form a new army group on the Vistula, as suggested by Guderian. Guderian had proposed General von Weichs as commander but Hitler decided upon the Reichsführer SS, Heinrich Himmler, a man without any military experience whatsoever.

23 January 1945

CENTRAL SECTOR

The German 4th Army abandoned the heavily fortified Loetzen defences as it withdrew. Hossbach was continuing to re-deploy his forces in order to strengthen his right flank. He informed Reinhardt of his moves, who, approving of the measures, also neglected to tell Hitler.

The 5th Guards Tank Army continued its drive to the sea, taking Mohrungen as it closed upon Elbing. A single corp thrust its way into Elbing from the east but met fierce resistance from mixed units that the 4th Army pulled together in the town.

Kalisz fell to the 4th Tank Army while to the south the 21st Army reached the Oder near Oppeln. With other elements of the 4th Tank already across at Goeben, the 13th Army moved to support and established a strong bridgehead based upon Steinau. Heavy fighting raged around the town. Oels also fell but the Germans managed to escape before the town was destroyed. As the threat to Breslau increased the 169th Infantry Division was rushed into defensive positions around the city. Army Group A recognised the increasing threat to its forces in Upper Silesia but was hamstrung by Hitler's orders to hold.

SOUTHERN SECTOR

After heavy fighting the 3rd Ukrainian Front began to contain the German thrust around Lake Balaton and along the Danube. The 2nd Ukrainian Front unleashed a new attack with its 40th Army and 4th Rumanian Army along the Slovak–Hungarian border, aiming to undermine the southern wing of the 8th Army.

24 January 1945

CENTRAL SECTOR

Hitler learned of the fall of Loetzen and descended into a mammoth rage. Hossbach's unauthorised withdrawal was no longer a secret, and was to cost both him and Reinhardt their commands.

The 5th Guards Tank Army captured Mulhausen and moved into Elbing. Soviet tanks advanced steadily through the town and reached the Frisches Nehrung at midnight, isolating the 3rd Panzer Army and 4th Army in East Prussia. Some eight divisions of the 2nd Army, all of the 4th Army and the remnants of the 3rd Panzer Army, a force of 400,000 men, had been severed from the main combat line. With Hitler's usual hold-to-the-last-man order in force, the bulk of Army Group Centre was condemned to destruction.

The 2nd Shock Army pushed towards the Vistula delta to the west of the 5th Guards Tank, attacking Weiss' 2nd Army around Marienberg. The 2nd was at this point brought under the control of new Army Group Vistula.

In Poland the 1st Ukrainian Front attacked in force into Silesia from the Oder. Gleiwitz fell to the 60th Army while the 24th and Grossdeutschland Panzer Korps Germans tried to force the 21st Army away from Oppeln.

Heavy fighting erupted but the Germans were not strong enough to dent the Soviet bridgehead. Elements of the 1st Guards Tank Army bypassed Posen, effectively isolating the German garrison.

The Soviet advance to the Baltic in East Prussia severed yet another German army group from the main combat line. Isolated, the German 4th and 2nd Armies would be systematically destroyed by the overwhelming might of the Soviet armies. The horrendous losses suffered by the German military units were mirrored by the horrors inflicted upon the civil populace as it attempted to flee the Soviet advance.

SOUTHERN SECTOR

The 4th SS Panzer Korp penetrated to within twenty miles of Budapest, capturing Baracska, but the Germans were spent. Increasingly fierce resistance by the 4th Guards Army combined with terrible ground conditions, and a catastrophic supply situation all played their part in breaking the momentum of the attack. Budapest remained isolated.

25 January 1945

CENTRAL SECTOR

In East Prussia there was fierce fighting at Elbing as the 5th Guards Tank Army struggled to destroy those elements of the 2nd Army still in the town. In Memel the 28th Korp prepared to abandon its rearguard defences and fall back along the long strip of land between the port and East Prussia. The bulk of the korp had already escaped by sea.

In Poland the 8th Guards Army, following behind the 1st Guards Tank, encircled the Germans in Posen. The 1st Ukrainian Front captured Oels (now Olesnica) and Ostrov on the line of the Oder river. Breslau was directly threatened by the attacks of the 52nd Army from the north. The 4th Tank Army captured Goeben after a fierce battle.

Hitler dismissed Reinhardt and Hossbach and appointed Rendulic commander of Army Group Centre. General Muller took over the 4th Army.

SOUTHERN SECTOR

The Soviets unleashed a major attack on the Varosmajor Grange in Buda. Limited progress was made after ferocious fighting.

26 January 1945

CENTRAL SECTOR

Heavy fighting raged along the Vistula as the 2nd Shock Army wrestled Marienberg away from the 2nd Army. After a bitter struggle the 5th Guards Tank Army finally overcame German resistance in Elbing. The

48th Army attempted to follow the 5th Guards Tank but was held up by probing attacks launched by the German 4th Army. This was the result of Hossbach's redeployment and a first effort to link up with the 2nd Army.

The 2nd Belorussian Front also pushed west, its 70th Army encircling Thorn (now Torun). A little to the south already encircled Bromberg fell to the 3rd Shock Army. In Silesia the 1st Ukrainian Front took Hindenburg as the 60th Army pushed back the 17th Army. Schulz, commanding the 17th, again asked for permission to pull back but was denied. Some 100,000 German troops were in immediate danger of encirclement as the 1st Ukrainian forced its way into the rear. Elements of the 3rd Guards Tank Army were already close to Rybnik but were ordered to turn on Ratibor. The 21st Army was to begin frontal attacks upon the 17th Army from around Oppeln.

Heavy fighting raged at Posen as the 8th Guards Army launched a fierce attack upon the German perimeter defences. Two divisions attacked the southern defences, capturing important fortifications after bloody fighting. Inside the city the Germans had 60,000 troops, mostly stragglers from retreating divisions and Volkssturm. Major Mattern commanded this mixed force.

THE OSTHEER

Despite that fact that their armies in the field were in an advanced state of collapse, the German High Command redesignated its army groups. Army Group North, long isolated in Kurland, was renamed Army Group Kurland. Its twenty-seven divisions were sorely needed but Hitler refused to allow their evacuation. Army Group Centre, some twenty-six divisions of which were incarcerated in East Prussia, were renamed Army Group North. This army group now only comprised the 3rd Panzer and 4th Armies, the 2nd Army having been separated in Pomerania. In Pomerania the Germans had raised Army Group Vistula around the 2nd Army and a new 11th Army. Commanded by Reichsführer SS Heinrich Himmler, Vistula was an army group in name only, numbering barely 50,000 men. To the south were the forces of the new Army Group Centre, old Army Group A. Stretched on a massively over-extended line from Pomerania to Slovakia, it comprised the 9th, 4th Panzer, 17th and 1st Panzer Armies.

27 January 1945

CENTRAL SECTOR

After a long and bloody battle Memel fell to the elements of the 43rd Army. On the main combat line the 3rd Belorussian Front threw a ring of steel around Konigsberg, trapping a panzer, two Volksgrenadier and an infantry division inside the city.

The 4th Army unfolded during the day. Aiming to link up with the 2nd

Army fighting on the west bank of the Vistula at Marienberg, Muller struck the 48th Army around Wormditt with two infantry, one panzer grenadier and two panzer divisions while two infantry divisions attacked at Mehlsack and another two at Braunsberg. Initial progress was promising as the Germans sliced through the surprised Soviet army. However, the 2nd Belorussian Front reacted quickly and moved elements of the 2nd Shock Army from the Vistula to support the hard pressed 48th. Furthermore, the complete superiority of the Soviet air armies considerably hindered the German efforts, inflicting severe casualties.

The 19th Army, recently committed to the battle, supported the attacks of the 70th Army on Thorn. In Silesia the 1st Ukrainian Front had drawn up to the Oder around Breslau and prepared to encircle the German units inside the city. Elements of the 59th and 60th Armies were involved in fierce fighting at Rybnik as they attempted to close the trap upon the 17th Army. Fighting fiercely the 17th began to abandon the Kattowitz pocket. Schorner authorised the withdrawal of the army at the eleventh hour, consigning the Silesian region over to the Russians. Army Group Vistula took the 9th Army under its command.

SOUTHERN SECTOR
The German 6th Army maintained the pressure on the 3rd Ukrainian Front between lakes Balaton and Velencei, retaking Szekesfehervar after a bitter struggle. However, Gille's 4th SS Panzer Korp had become totally bogged down and was under intense pressure from the 3rd Ukrainian as it counter-attacked.

28 January 1945

CENTRAL SECTOR
With the threat to Konigsberg acute the 3rd Panzer Army pushed an infantry division up from the south-west into the city. The division immediately counter-attacked to strengthen the northern perimeter.

The 4th Army continued its attack at Wormditt but suffered heavy casualties under intense Soviet counter-fire. As these battles raged the 3rd Belorussian Front took Bischofsberg and Sensberg, the 4th Army being pushed back towards the sea.

In Pomerania the 1st Belorussian Front pushed back the right flank of the German 2nd Army, capturing Sepolno. Attacks into Brandenburg saw the 1st Guards Tank Army cross the Obra near Meseritz.

The 1st Ukrainian Front captured Katowice and Leszno as the 17th Army hurried along its evacuation of Silesia. A counter-attack by elements of the 24th Panzer Korp near Glogau was stopped after brief but bitter fighting. The Grossduetschland Korp also joined the attack but was similarly unsuccessful.

At Posen, Major Mattern was relieved as commander of the garrison and Major-General Gonell appointed in his place.

SOUTHERN SECTOR
After bloody fighting Margit Island finally fell to the Soviet forces advancing in Budapest.

29 January 1945

CENTRAL SECTOR
Heavy fighting raged around Konigsberg as 39th Army penetrated to the Frisches Haff, west of the city. This latest gain severed communications between the Germans in Samland and those in the city.

The German 4th Army managed to reach to within six miles of Elbing but had shot its bolt. The 2nd Belorussian Front had successfully slowed the German attack by piling more and more forces into the line, gradually wearing down the weaker Germans in a battle of attrition. During heavy fighting Marienwerder fell. In Pomerania Schonlake and Woldenberg fell.

Upper Silesia had largely fallen to the 1st Ukrainian Front. Despite some heavy fighting the Russians had captured the German industrial infrastructure without causing significant damage. However, the German 17th Army had managed to escape annihilation in the Kattowitz pocket by the narrowest of margins as the Soviet forces concentrated on the capture of territory rather than the destruction of the enemy field army.

The capture of the Silesian industrial region dealt a body blow to the German war effort. The loss of crucial coal production areas and armaments factories left a massive hole in the ability of German industry to continue to supply the field armies. With the Ruhr under intense Allied bombardment, the loss of Silesia effectively brought the end of the Third Reich within reach. The German struggle to replace their massive equipment losses became acute, Speer's considerable achievements in productive efficiency during 1944 being destroyed by the loss of this vital industrial region.

SOUTHERN SECTOR
A German and Hungarian counter-attack along the Varosmajor Grange in Buda failed to drive the Soviets back. The attackers suffered very heavy casualties.

30 January 1945

CENTRAL SECTOR
The German forces in East Prussia were confined to three pockets. The most northerly pocket comprised the four divisions of Gollnick's 28th

Korp in Samland, while there were five divisions fighting in isolation at Konigsberg. The largest pocket lay to the south-west and comprised twenty divisions of the 4th Army. Elements had reached to within five miles of Elbing during the recent counter-attack. As they failed to push farther west a frontal attack by the 5th Guards Tank Army pinned down the exhausted troops. The 3rd and 50th Armies then also struck the exposed southern flank.

Russian attacks near Posen captured Stolzenberg. Leading units of the 1st Guards Tank Army captured Calau before pushing upon Schweibus. The 69th and 33rd Armies were moving behind the tanks. Elements of the 2nd Guards Tank and 5th Shock Armies advanced past Zorndorf as they pushed towards the Oder.

The 4th Tank Army took Steinau after a fierce battle while the 3rd Guards Army reached the Oder and secured the armies right flank. The 1st Ukrainian Front undertook new preparations in an effort to destroy the 17th Army along the Oder.

31 January 1945

CENTRAL SECTOR
During heavy fighting in East Prussia the Soviets captured Heilsberg (now Lidzbark Warminski) and Freidland (now Mieroszow).

The 2nd Guards Tank reached the Oder river west of Berlin, capturing Zehden after a brief struggle. Elements of the 8th Guards Army approached Kustrin but encountered difficulties as it ran short of supplies and the exhaustion of the combat troops began to show. Units of the 5th Shock crossed the Oder at Kienitz but met stiff German resistance.

THE OSTHEER
The Germans deployed 4,881 tanks against 14,200 Russian vehicles[2] while the Luftwaffe had 1,430 aircraft against 14,500 Soviet planes[3]. A fraction of the German machines were operational whereas the majority of the Soviet ones were. The Ostheer had a paper strength of twenty-five panzer, thirteen panzer grenadier and 116 infantry divisions.[4]

1 February 1945

CENTRAL SECTOR
The 70th Army began its final attack upon the 30,000-strong garrison of Thorn, fighting its way into the town during the day. German resistance was extremely protracted and it would take more than a week for the town to be captured.

In Pomerania the 1st Belorussian Front launched a new attack against the 11th Army at Schneidmuhl. Ratzebuhr (now Olonek) fell after a bloody battle. Elements of the 1st Guards Tank Army were isolated at Kunersdorf by a 5th SS Mountain Korp counter-attack. After heavy fighting the Germans were repulsed and then struck by the 33rd, 69th and 1st Guards Tank Armies as they counter-attacked. A bloody retreat followed as the Soviets raced to reach the Oder.

The headquarters of the 3rd Panzer Army began its evacuation from East Prussia to re-deploy in Pomerania. In the three weeks since the offensive in Poland began the Germans had lost 400,000 killed, wounded or captured and the equivalent of thirty-five divisions had been destroyed.

SOUTHERN SECTOR
Soviet forces in Buda were fighting along Margit Boulevard, in Szell Kalman Square and Vermezo Meadow. Sashegy Hill continued to hold under intense attack.[5]

2 February 1945

CENTRAL SECTOR
The 8th Guards Army began to attack across the frozen Oder while the 1st Guards Tank Army attacked in Kustrin. Both units met furious resistance from the 9th Army. Despite repeated attacks the 1st Guards Tank was unable to take Kustrin but it was mistakenly reported to the Stavka that the town had fallen.

SOUTHERN SECTOR
The 26th Army and 4th Guards Army linked up at Adony, rejoining the Soviet defences in Hungary.

3 February 1945

NORTHERN SECTOR
There was heavy fighting in Kurland as the 2nd Baltic Front tried to break through the German positions around Libau.

CENTRAL SECTOR
The Germans launched a fierce counter-attack from Samland aimed at reaching Konigsberg. Bitter fighting raged near Thierenberg. Elsewhere, the 2nd and 3rd Belorussian Fronts pressed the 4th Army hard, the 31st and 2nd Guards Armies capturing Landsberg and Bartenstein.

In Pomerania Army Group Vistula fought to halt the Russian thrusts which pushed north towards the Baltic coast. Fierce battles raged from Elbing to Pyritz, the German 2nd and 11th Armies launching desperate counter-attacks to no avail.

There were severe battles at Kustrin as the Luftwaffe made a brief sortie to hit the 1st Guards Tank Army. In Silesia the 6th Guards Army took Brieg and Ohlau on the Oder. Steinau also fell after ten days of fierce fighting. Overnight a thaw along the Oder brought the Russian offensive to a standstill. As the river thawed many Soviet units were isolated on the west bank. German reinforcements also began to flood into the area.

The fighting from the Vistula to the Oder had so far cost the 1st Belorussian Front 17,000 killed and 60,000 wounded and the 1st Ukrainian Front 26,000 killed and 89,000 wounded.[6]

4 February 1945

CENTRAL SECTOR

Zhukov ordered the 5th Shock Army to expand its Oder bridgehead north of Kustrin but German resistance was intense. The Soviet force also struggled in difficult terrain.

5 February 1945

CENTRAL SECTOR

At Posen the 8th Guards Army launched a strong attack upon the German garrison.

SOUTHERN SECTOR

The Soviets began a major attack against the German and Hungarian forces still resisting in Buda. Heavy fighting raged around Sashegy Hill and Nemetvolgy Cemetery. The Hill was isolated after bitter fighting, freeing the Soviets to push deeper into the German defences.

6 February 1944

SOUTHERN SECTOR

A counter-attack by the 8th SS Cavalry Division toward Sashegy Hill foundered after heavy losses. On the hill itself, the defending force was compelled to surrender, having run out of food and ammunition.

7 February 1945

CENTRAL SECTOR

The 5th Shock Army attacked the 9th Army around Kustrin, crossing the Oder near Furstenberg and Kustrin. Other elements of the 1st Belorussian Front tackled Army Group Vistula in Pomerania. Heavy fighting erupted at Arnswalde (now Choszno) and Deutsch Krone (now Walcz) as the Russians broke through the flimsy defences of Himmler's ragged armies.

Both towns were isolated as the Russians pushed into the German rear. Zhukov was throwing the 3rd Shock, 1st and 2nd Guards Tank, 47th and 61st Armies (some 359,000 men of the 1st Belorussian Front) and the entire 2nd Belorussian (560,000 men) against the depleted, overextended and badly equipped German units. In Silesia a counter-attack by the German 17th Army regained Grottkau.

SOUTHERN SECTOR
After heavy fighting in Buda the southern railway station fell to Soviet forces. In Yugoslavia the Germans began to evacuate Visegrad and Mostar.

8 February 1945

CENTRAL SECTOR
The 1st Ukrainian Front completed a hurried redeployment and attacked from the Oder bridgeheads north and south of Breslau. Heavy artillery fire hit the 17th Army followed by armoured and infantry assaults. However, the thaw made the going difficult for the Soviet assault teams, as did ferocious German resistance. Even so, a breakthrough was achieved near Steinau by the 52nd Army.

9 February 1945

CENTRAL SECTOR
Thorn fell to the 70th Army, barely 3,000 of the 30,000 strong garrison surviving the battle.

10 February 1945

CENTRAL SECTOR
The 19th Army fought its way towards Neustettin as it pushed into Pomerania.

In East Prussia since 13 January the 2nd Belorussian Front had suffered 36,000 killed and 123,000 wounded.[7] The 3rd Belorussian Front began a new assault against the 4th Army around Heilsberg. In Silesia the 3rd Guards Tank Army forced its way forward from the Oppeln bridgehead, threatening the southern flank of the German defences around Breslau.

GERMAN COMMAND
The Germans raised the new 11th SS Panzer Army upon reinforcements sent up to Army Group Vistula. SS General Steiner commanded this weak force, establishing positions between the 2nd and 9th Armies.

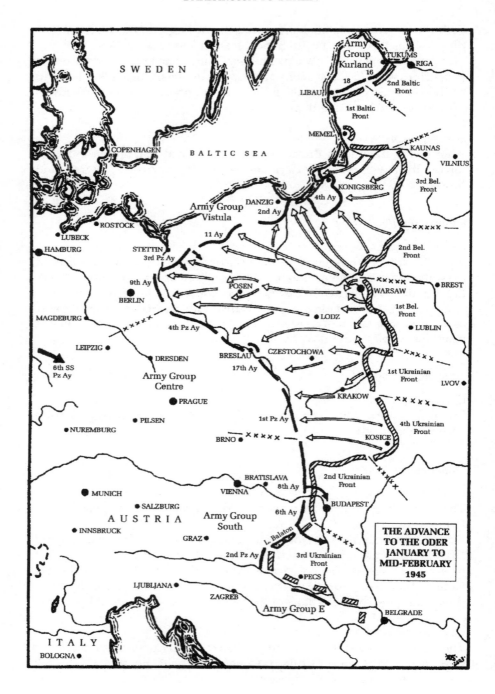

THE ADVANCE
TO THE ODER
JANUARY TO
MID-FEBRUARY
1945

11 February 1945

CENTRAL SECTOR
In East Prussia the German 4th Army abandoned Wormditt to the 48th Army after heavy fighting. In Silesia the 1st Ukrainian Front had comprehensively defeated the 17th Army on the Oder and forced back the 4th Panzer Army to the Niesse river. Glogau had been encircled by the 3rd Guards Army and some 18,000 German soldiers cut off. The 6th Army launched a direct assault upon Breslau but was repulsed. Leignitz was also attacked while Luben (now Lubin), Haynau (Chojnow), Neumarkt (Sroda-Slaska) and Kanth (Katy-Wroklowskie) all fell.

SOUTHERN SECTOR
During the evening the Germans began to assemble in their attack sectors prior to the breakout from Buda. Heavy fighting erupted as the Soviet positions were stormed by some 28,000 men but intense fire inflicted serious losses upon the Germans

12 February 1945

SOUTHERN SECTOR
The Germans resumed their break-out attempt from Buda. A force of nearly 16,000 men reached the hills around Perbal before they were halted by units of the 46th Army. More than 12,000 had been killed or captured inside the city. The remnants of Pfeffer-Wildenbruch's group continued to fight on in the sewers.

13 February 1945

SOUTHERN SECTOR
Organised resistance came to an end in Budapest but fighting continued as isolated pockets of resistance refused to give in. The battle of Budapest had cost the German and Hungarian forces 138,000 captured and 50,000 killed. Of the 16,000 that broke out on 12 February and reached Perbal, barely 700 regained the main combat line. The battle had cost the 2nd Ukrainian Front 35,000 killed and 130,000 wounded and the 3rd Ukrainian Front a further 45,000 killed and 109,000 wounded.[8]

> *The battle for Budapest had cost the Soviets and Germans dear. The entire German–Hungarian garrison was destroyed in a ferocious street battle lasting two months but the added experience the Soviets gained in urban fighting would prove valuable during the battles for Berlin and Vienna. Budapest honed Soviet urban fighting skills to a level of expertise unsurpassed by any other army.*

GERMAN COMMAND

Guderian proposed a counter-attack in Pomerania aimed at nipping off the spearheads of the 1st Belorussian Front. His plan called for a double pincer movement from Frankfurt and Stargard but Hitler amended this to a single pincer striking south from Stargard. Guderian suggested the appointment of General Wenck to lead the assault but at this Hitler exploded, deriding Guderian for the implication that Himmler could not lead the attack. After protracted argument Wenck was appointed, but only subordinately to Himmler. Operation Sonnenwende was conceived. The attack was to be launched by the 11th SS Panzer Army with six under-strength divisions. Hitler believed these divisions to be at full strength and fully equipped.

14 February 1945

CENTRAL SECTOR

Army Group Vistula assembled its force for the counter-attack at Stargard. Arrayed on a thirty-mile front, the attack force was split into three groups. The Central Group comprised Decker's 3rd SS Panzer Korp with the SS Nordland and Nederland, the Führer-Begleit Division and SS Langemarck and aimed to relieve Arnswalde. Western Group deployed Unrein's 29th Panzer Korp (Holstein and 10th SS Panzer Divisions, Polizei and Wallonien SS Divisions). The Eastern Group was to push the left flank towards Landsberg on the Warthe. It had the Führer Grenadier Division, 281st and 163rd Infantry Divisions. The Russians were well aware of the German build up and had moved their 2nd Guards Tank and 61st Armies into defensive positions to counter the attack. The 1st Guards Tank, 47th and 3rd Shock Armies formed a second echelon.[9]

The 5th Guards Army launched a strong attack from Brieg and linked up with the 3rd Guards Army near Breslau, encircling 80,000 civilians and 35,000 soldiers inside the city. Most of the 269th Infantry Division was isolated. The Soviet 6th Army invested Breslau with 150,000 men. A counter-attack by the 19th Panzer Division established a tenuous connection with the garrison, but an immediate Russian counter-attack prevented the escape of any forces or reinforcement of the garrison.

Other elements of the 1st Ukrainian closed up to the Niesse and took Sorau and Grunberg. A 4th Panzer Army counter-attack with the Grossdeutschland and 24th Panzer Korps west of the Bobr failed to halt the Russian drive.

In Pomerania the Soviet attacks succeeded in taking Schneidmuhl and Deutsch Krone. Arnswalde continued to resist. Heavy fighting also raged along the Oder near Berlin, the 9th Army launching fierce counter-attacks around Frankfurt.

15 February 1945

NORTHERN SECTOR
Army Group Kurland was again heavily attacked. The Germans had established strong positions between Tukums and Libau and resisted all 2nd Baltic Front attacks.

CENTRAL SECTOR
The 11th SS Panzer Army attacked from Stargard. Its 3rd SS Panzer Korp made limited progress towards Arnswalde amid fierce resistance.

In East Prussia the 65th and 49th Armies made good progress as they thrust deeply into the positions of the 4th Army, leading elements of the two armies advancing some ten miles during the 15th. Fierce battles also raged at Frauenberg (now Frombork) and Zinten (Ilaweckie) as the Russians pushed along the Baltic coast towards Heiligenbeil. The 4th Army had by this stage of the battle taken over control of those forces of the 3rd Panzer Army left behind in the pocket following the evacuation of its headquarters of the army to Pomerania. The new 3rd Panzer began to take control of the units on the lower reaches of the Oder. General Gonell requested permission to break out from Posen. Himmler refused but Gonell ordered his units west of the Warthe to break out anyway.

West of the Bobr river the Grossdeutschland and 24th Panzer Korps continued to counter-attack but again failed to halt the 1st Ukrainian Front's right wing.

16 February 1945

CENTRAL SECTOR
The 11th SS Panzer Army opened a general offensive around Stargard after the previous days probing attacks. Once again progress was limited, the greatest gains being made by the Western Group, but even their success was slender.

The 1st Ukrainian Front defeated the Hermann Goering Panzer Korp and took Sagan after a brief battle. Some 2,000 men of the Posen garrison succeed in breaking out of the city and attempted to escape to the west.

SOUTHERN SECTOR
The last German forces still resisting in Buda surrendered, General Pfeffer-Wildenbruch being captured in the final battles.

17 February 1945

NORTHERN SECTOR
Army Group North ordered the Samland and Konigsberg groups to

counter-attack and regain contact. General Lasch, commanding the Konigsberg garrison, was to push west with the 5th Panzer, 1st Infantry and 561st Volksgrenadier Divisions.[10]

CENTRAL SECTOR

With its 2nd Army holding an overextended front in Pomerania, Army Group Vistula requested permission to pull the army back west to link up with the 11th SS Panzer Army. Hitler refused. The 11th SS Panzer Army continued its attack at Stargard. Progress slowed as casualties mounted. During one of his trips from Berlin to report direct to Hitler, Wenck was wounded. General Krebs had to take over co-ordination of the attack.

Renewed attacks along the Bobr by the Grossdeutschland and 24th Panzer Korps embroiled the 4th Tank Army in bitter fighting. The 3rd Guards Tank and 52nd Armies moved to support the left and right flanks of the 4th. Against this strengthened force the Germans threw six worn out armoured divisions.

SOUTHERN SECTOR

The 6th SS Panzer Army began to deploy with Army Group South. The 1st SS Panzer Korp deployed against the Hron bridgehead and immediately attacked the 7th Guards Army, taking the Soviet force by surprise and pushing them back towards the river. A Soviet counter-attack failed to halt the German thrust, the 1st SS striving to destroy the bridgehead and restore the strong front along the Hron.

18 February 1945

CENTRAL SECTOR

Marshal Chernakhovsky, commanding the 3rd Belorussian Front, was killed near Mehlsack. Marshal Vasilevsky took over the front for the remainder of the war. Vasilevsky incorporated the 1st Baltic Front into the 3rd Belorussian, renaming it the Samland Group.

The German offensive around Stargard sputtered out after a total lack of success. There was further heavy fighting along the Bobr river. The 8th Guards attacked Posen, heavy fighting following as the remnants of the garrison fought on.

SOUTHERN SECTOR

The fighting in the Hron bridgehead continued as the 1st SS Panzer Korp hit the 7th Guards in the flank, forcing it back across the river. Army Group E evacuated Mostar.

19 February 1945

CENTRAL SECTOR
The battle for the Konigsberg corridor began as Group Samland attacked. Three divisions of the 28th Korp, supported by the fire of the battle cruiser *Admiral Scheer*, struck the 39th Army in Samland. Simultaneously Lasch began his attack and after fierce fighting Metgethen fell. The 2nd Belorussian Front continued to hit the 4th Army in the Heiligenbeil pocket.

The Soviet 6th Army attacked Breslau but failed to break the German line while the 4th Panzer Army abandoned its attack along the Bobr.

20 February 1945

CENTRAL SECTOR
Groups Samland and Lasch linked up to rejoin Konigsberg with the Samland Peninsula. Civilian refugees began flooding the road west to Pillau to escape the city. Russian artillery and air strikes inflicted a heavy price on the fleeing masses.

The 2nd Belorussian Front was exhausted after protracted fighting in East Prussia. After a month of continual battle there were barely 300 operational tanks left and many combat divisions were down to less than a thousand combat infantry.

The 1st Belorussian Front, in a similar state of disrepair as the 2nd, attacked the Germans on a 200-mile line in Pomerania, while its 8th Guards Army was embroiled in heavy fighting at Posen and Kustrin. Some 15,000 Germans continued to resist in Posen.

The defenders of Breslau attempted a counter-attack but were repulsed by the 6th Army and pinned down in the southern park. The in-experienced Volksturm suffered heavy losses under concentrated Russian fire.

SOUTHERN SECTOR
There was heavy fighting in the Hron bridgehead as the 7th Guards Army was squeezed by the 1st SS Panzer Korp. Between Lakes Balaton and Velencei the 6th Army was active once again, attacking the 3rd Ukrainian Front. The German 8th Army though was attacked by the 46th Army near Esztergom.

21 February 1945

CENTRAL SECTOR
After days of heavy fighting the 8th Guards Army made limited gains in the German defences around Posen.

22 February 1945

CENTRAL SECTOR
The 8th Guards hit Posen with tanks and infantry. Fierce fighting raged in the citadel but a demand to surrender was refused. Gonell ordered his force to break out before he committed suicide. All efforts prove fruitless though as repeated attempts were repulsed. By dusk the battle was over as Colonel Mattern surrendered the surviving 12,000 men.

23 February 1945

CENTRAL SECTOR
The last remnants of the Posen garrison surrendered. Arnswalde was also taken.

SOUTHERN SECTOR
The 7th Guards Army abandoned its bridgehead on the Hron river. Dietrich's 6th SS Panzer Army was forming in strength around Vienna as it prepared for the counter-offensive. The attack aimed to break the Soviet forces on the west bank of the Danube and guarantee the safety of the Hungarian oilfields.

GERMAN COMMAND
During the first three weeks of February the Germans had significantly reinforced Army Group Vistula. The army group now deployed thirty-four divisions with 450,000 men, 5,000 artillery pieces and 1,000 panzers or assault guns.[11]

24 February 1945

CENTRAL SECTOR
The 2nd Belorussian Front attacked in eastern Pomerania. It had been reinforced with the 19th Army on its left wing. The German 11th SS Panzer Army was renamed 3rd Panzer Army.

25 February 1945

CENTRAL SECTOR
The 19th Army ripped a thirty-five-mile hole in the right wing of the 2nd Army and advanced thirty miles towards Koslin. Danzig and the entire 2nd Army were threatened with isolation by this new advance.

26 February 1945

CENTRAL SECTOR
The 19th Army pushed its armoured component forward near Neustettin in an effort to reach the Baltic coast. To deflect this blow the 2nd Army attempted to assemble its 7th Panzer Korp around Rummelsburg.

27 February 1945

SOUTHERN SECTOR
Army Group E opened the road to Sarajevo after it had been cut by partisans. This road had to be kept open until the units south of the city had been withdrawn otherwise the southern wing of Army Group E would be annihilated.

28 February 1945

CENTRAL SECTOR
Neustettin (now Szczecinek) fell to elements of the 19th Army after a bitter battle. Prechlau was also captured.

THE OSTHEER
The fighting on the Eastern Front during the first two months of 1945 saw more outstanding achievements by the Red Army and catastrophic defeats for the Ostheer. All Poland had fallen to the Russians, some 400,000 Germans being killed or captured at a cost of over half a million Soviet killed or missing. Across the whole front the Germans deployed twenty-eight panzer, fourteen panzer grenadier and 131 infantry divisions while Hungary deployed eleven divisions.[12] The vast majority of these divisions barely had the strength of a regiment, let alone a division.

GERMAN DEPLOYMENT
On the northern wing Army Group Kurland remained incarcerated with its 250,000 men. The 18th Army deployed the 10th, 1st, 50th and 2nd Korps and the 16th Army the 38th Panzer, 6th SS, 16th and 63rd Korps.[13]
Army Group North in East Prussia had around 400,000 soldiers in the Danzig/Eastern Pomeranian, Heiligenbeil and Konigsberg pockets. The 4th Army was deployed between the Samland–Konigsberg pocket (designated Detachment Samland), and the Heiligenbeil pocket. The Samland Detachment had the 9th Korp and Fortress Konigsberg under command, while the Heiligenbeil group had the 26th, 6th and 20th Korps and 41st Panzer Korp. To the west were the badly battered armies of Army Group Vistula, spread out on a line from the Oder to the eastern tip of Pomerania. This group comprised the 9th Army on the Oder with around

150,000 men among its 5th SS Mountain, 11th SS and 101st Korps and the 56th Panzer Korp. At Stettin and east into Pomerania was the 3rd Panzer Army with around 100,000 men in the 3rd SS Panzer and 10th SS Korps and Group Tettau. The 2nd Army covered eastern Pomerania with the 7th Panzer, 18th Mountain, 66th Panzer, 27th and 23rd Korps and Korp Group Rappart.

Holding the line from the Niesse river to central Slovakia was Army Group Centre. This group had the 4th Panzer Army south-east of Berlin, the 17th Army covering the Czech–Silesian border and the 1st Panzer Army on the southern flank in Slovakia. The 4th Panzer had around 120,000 men and 200 panzers between the 5th, 24th Panzer, Gross-deutschland and 40th Panzer Korps, while the 17th Army comprised the 8th, 17th, 48th Panzer, 57th Panzer and 39th Panzer Korps. The 1st Panzer Army deployed the 39th Mountain, 59th and 11th Korps and Korp Group Schlesein.

Arrayed from Slovakia to the Drava river were the armies of Army Group South. This force deployed the 8th Army in Slovakia (4th Panzer, 72nd and 29th Korps), 3rd Hungarian Army, battered and demoralised, south of the Danube with its 2nd Hungarian and 3rd Panzer Korps, and between Lakes Balaton and Velencei the 6th Army with its 4th SS Panzer and 8th Hungarian Korps. South of Lake Balaton was the 2nd Panzer Army with its 67th and 22nd Korps, completing the line to the Drava. From here on the combat line was fluid as Army Groups E and F struggled to escape from the partisan war in Yugoslavia. However, behind Army Group South the 6th SS Panzer Army (1st and 2nd SS and 3rd Panzer Korps) was beginning to assemble in preparation for Operation Frühlingserwachen.

Impressive though the German dispositions might seem, the bulk of these divisions were vastly under strength and lacked all kinds of essential equipment. Despite having some of the most technologically advanced weapons of the war, the German army was no longer the modern force it used to be, being rendered immobile through lack of fuel. Air support, so vital to the success of many offensives, was a thing of the past, the Luftwaffe having been drawn west to deal with the Allied bomber offensive and the remainder grounded by lack of aviation fuel.

THE RED ARMY

While the Ostheer continued its preparations for the attack in Hungary, the Red Army assembled its forces on the northern flank to strike at the German armies in Pomerania. The 1st Belorussian had swung its main weight north, deploying the 47th, 61st, 2nd Guards Tank, 3rd Shock, 1st Guards Tank and 1st Polish Armies between the Oder and Neustettin, while the 2nd Belorussian Front was already in the process of severing the 2nd Army from the 3rd Panzer Army. The 2nd Belorussian had the 19th,

70th, 49th, 65th and 2nd Shock Armies deployed for the attack that was scheduled to begin on 1 March.

1 March 1945

CENTRAL SECTOR

With the now customary artillery and air support, 1st Belorussian Front launched its offensive into Pomerania. The 1st and 2nd Guards Tank Armies and 3rd Shock Army pushed north from Arnswalde, while the 47th Army attacked west of Pyritz and the 61st Army east of Stargard. The main assault hit the junction of the 3rd and 10th SS Korps.

The 24th Panzer Korp launched a strong counter-attack near Lauban but after initially taking the 3rd Guards Tank Army by surprise, it was brought to a halt and suffered heavy losses. Over the next few days the 4th Tank Army pulled out of the combat line and moved to Oppeln to support 21st Army.

2 March 1945

CENTRAL SECTOR

The 1st Belorussian front had ripped apart the 3rd Panzer Army defences north of Arnswalde and had isolated the 10th SS Korp and Korp Group Tettau around Dramberg. The 3rd Shock Army was thrusting to the north-east towards Belgard and north-west towards the Isle of Wollin, while the 1st and 2nd Guards Tank Armies moved upon Kolberg and Stettin respectively. To the east of Dramberg the 1st Polish Army enveloped the left wing of the 10th SS Korp as it also pushed towards Belgard and Kolberg.

In Silesia the 24th Panzer Korp continued its fruitless attacks near Lauban.

3 March 1945

CENTRAL SECTOR

The right flank of the 3rd Panzer Army began to abandon the Schwedt bridgehead as the 2nd Guards Tank, 61st and 47th Armies converged upon Stettin on the lower Oder. Heavy fighting raged around Lauban in Silesia.

4 March 1945

CENTRAL SECTOR

The 1st Guards Tank Army reached the Baltic coast near Kolberg. Elements of the 1st Polish Army linked up with the tankers to invest the garrison of 3,200 soldiers and 68,000 civilians. Regenswalde also fell as the 10th SS Korp fought for its survival around Dramberg. Stargard fell to the 61st Army.

The 24th Panzer Korp drew closer to Lauban, inflicting heavy losses upon the 3rd Guards Tank Army.

5 March 1945

CENTRAL SECTOR

Lead elements of the 19th Army reached Koslin and took the town after a bitter struggle. The 2nd Belorussian Front now prepared to strike east to pin the Germans against the coast around Danzig. To the west the 47th Army attacked towards Altdamm, inflicting heavy casualties upon the 3rd Panzer Army's right wing. The 10th SS Korp at Dramberg was fiercely attacked by units of the 3rd Shock Army from the south, west and north and by the 1st Polish Army from the east. The korp commander was wounded and captured during heavy fighting as his forces attempted to break out to the west. Korp Group Tettau, fighting south of Belgard, began a difficult march north-west towards the coast in an effort to escape destruction. It had around 15,000 troops but also tried to ensure the safety of 40,000 civilians moving along with the pocket.[14]

The 24th Panzer Korp recaptured Lauban as it pushed the 3rd Guards back.

SOUTHERN SECTOR

Army Group South completed its preparations for Operation Frühlingserwachen. Wohler had been reinforced with Dietrich's 6th SS Panzer Army and had managed to stockpile a reserve of fuel. However, the land around Lake Balaton where the attack was to be made was heavily flooded and would prove difficult to negotiate. For the attack the Germans had assembled the 6th SS Panzer Army (1st and 2nd SS panzer Korps and 3rd Panzer Korp totalling ten armoured and five infantry divisions), 6th Army (4th SS panzer Korp and 8th Hungarian Korp comprising three infantry and five armoured divisions) and 2nd Panzer Army (44th and 67th Korps comprising four infantry divisions), a force of 430,000 troops, 5,600 artillery pieces and 880 panzers or assault guns. The Luftwaffe had 850 aircraft but was short of aviation fuel.[15] North of the Danube bend the 8th Army (nine infantry and two armoured divisions) and 3rd Hungarian Army (one armoured division and two infantry divisions) held off the 2nd Ukrainian Front in Slovakia.

Against the main attack sector Tolbukhin's 3rd Ukrainian Front had the 4th Guards Army near Lake Velencei and 26th Army near Lake Balaton, the junction of the two armies being between the lakes, right at the point where the Germans were going to attack. In reserve behind the junction of the two armies was the 27th Army, while the 57th Army was south of Lake Balaton, between the lake and the Drava river. The 1st Bulgarian and 3rd Yugoslav Armies held the northern bank of the Drava against Army Group E while the 17th Air Army supported the ground forces. In all the 3rd Ukrainian Front fielded 407,000 troops, 7,000 artillery pieces, 400 tanks or Su's and 960 aircraft[16]. In Stavka reserve behind the 3rd Ukrainian was the 9th Guards Army. From the junction with the 3rd Ukrainian south of Biscke was Malinovsky's 2nd Ukrainian Front with the 46th Army around Esztergom and the 6th Guards Tank Army to its south, the 7th Guards Army on the line of the Hron, north of the Danube, the 53rd Army, 4th Rumanian and 40th Armies holding the line running north-east along the general line of the Hungarian–Slovak border. The 5th Air Army provided aerial support.

The German intention was for the 6th SS Panzer Army to break through the junction of the 4th Guards and 26th Armies and reach the Danube at Dunapentele in the north and near Baja in the south. The northern wing would then push directly north along the western bank of the river to recapture Budapest and destroy those elements of the 2nd and 3rd Ukrainain Fronts trapped on the west bank. The southern wing meanwhile would link up with Army Group E which was to cross the Drava and reach the Danube near Mohacs. The 2nd Panzer Army would pin the 57th Army down south of Lake Balaton. The scope of the attack was fairly limited and would in no way alter the otherwise disastrous German position on the Eastern Front.

6 March 1945

CENTRAL SECTOR

Heavy fighting raged around Altdamm as the 47th Army closed upon Greifenhagen on the Oder and the 61st Army pushed in from the east.

Grudziadz fell to the 65th Army of the 2nd Belorussian Front while the 2nd Shock Army marched north to outflank the German Nogat defences. Belgard fell to elements of the 3rd Shock and 1st Polish Armies after hard fighting.

SOUTHERN SECTOR

With limited artillery and air support the Germans launched Operation Frühlingserwachen. Dietrich's 6th SS Panzer Army hit the junction of the 26th and 4th Guards Armies and immediately became embroiled in bitter fighting. Intense action followed as the Germans launched repeated attacks in an effort to break the Russian line. However, rather then breaking through the SS merely shoved the Soviet armies back. The 3rd Panzer Korp repeatedly hit the junction of the two armies while the 1st SS Panzer Korp struck the 26th Army frontally. Unfortunately a heavy snowfall turned the ground into a quagmire, preventing the 2nd SS Panzer Korp from moving up to its attack positions.

7 March 1945

SOUTHERN SECTOR

The fighting north of Lake Balaton intensified as leading elements of the 2nd SS Panzer Korp attacked between the 1st SS to its south and 3rd Panzer to the north. The 26th Army was hit by upwards of 170 panzers and assault guns but fought doggedly in the waterlogged ground, holding up the German spearheads long enough for Tolbukhin to reinforce the battered army with his remaining reserves. To the south the 2nd Panzer Army and Army Group E joined the offensive, the 2nd Panzer managing to penetrate the 57th Army's forward positions after hard fighting. Along the Drava Army Group E also attacked but only managed to establish small bridgeheads on the north bank in the face of determined resistance by the 1st Bulgarian and 3rd Yugoslav Armies near Donji Miholjac and Valpovo.

8 March 1945

CENTRAL SECTOR

Stolp fell to the 19th Army without a fight as the 2nd Belorussian Front poured west towards Danzig and Gotenhafen. The 1st Belorussian handed over its 1st Guards Tank Army to the 2nd for a limited period to aid this attack. Together with 1,500,000 civilians and 100,000 wounded soldiers the Germans had the remnants of the 4th SS Polizei and 4th and 7th Panzer Divisions together with eleven infantry divisions and a Luftwaffe field division.

SOUTHERN SECTOR

The German advance in Hungary was far short of expectations, three days of bitter fighting having pushed the line forward just four miles. In an effort to effect a breakthrough Wohler committed more units to the battle, the 2nd SS Panzer Korp assembling more than 250 panzers and assault guns to smash its way through the 26th Army. Fierce battles raged along both banks of the Sarviz Canal as the 1st SS Panzer Korp made progress on the west bank, but the 2nd stalled yet again on the eastern bank. The 2nd Panzer Army also continued its attack but was also becoming bogged down as the 57th Army piled forces up against the narrow attack sector north of Nagyatad.

Army Group E was involved in bitter fighting around Sarajevo as Tito's rebel army harried the retreating Germans.

9 March 1945

CENTRAL SECTOR

Fighting in Pomerania intensified as elements of the 2nd Belorussian Front closed upon Danzig from the south and west. Marienburg fell to the 2nd Shock Army after a long battle. To the west elements of the 3rd Shock Army (1st Belorussian Front) reached the mouth of the Oder river opposite the Isle of Wollin.

The Germans counter-attacked towards Striegau with two weak divisions. Heavy fighting developed.

SOUTHERN SECTOR

In Hungary the 6th SS Panzer Army committed more forces to the attack. More than 600 tanks were operating against the 4th Guards and 26th Armies but had failed to achieve a decisive breakthrough. Furthermore, the Germans were facing difficulties in the terrible terrain, the clinging mud using up massive amounts of the slender German fuel supplies. With the attack already running out of steam, the Stavka began to move the forces up to block any further progress. The 27th Army inserted into the line between the 26th and 4th Guards Armies while the 6th Guards Tank Army redeployed so as to strike from the area south of Biscke, into the rear of the exposed German salient. The Stavka also allocated the 9th Guards Army to the 3rd Ukrainian Front but refused to allow Tolbukhin to commit it to battle until the Germans had completely exhausted themselves.

There was further heavy fighting along the Drava as the 3rd Yugoslav Army attempted to destroy Army Group E's Valpovo bridgehead. Despite bitter fighting the Germans managed to hold on.

SOVIET COMMAND

The Soviet High Command planned its Hungarian counter-offensive in conjunction with its redeployment of forces. The 3rd Ukrainian Front was to deliver the main blow as it attacked with the 4th and 9th Guards Armies north of Lake Velencei towards Papa and Veszprem. The 26th Army would attack from its positions on the eastern side of Lake Balaton and drive into the right wing of the 6th SS Panzer Army to envelop the 1st and 2nd SS Panzer and 3rd Panzer Korps before Szekesfehervar. The 46th and 6th Guards Tank Armies of the 2nd Ukrainian Front were to attack between the Danube and Biscke to isolate the 3rd Hungarian Army around Tatabanya.

Following these attacks the 2nd and 3rd Ukrainian Fronts would launch a general advance aimed at capturing Vienna.

10 March 1945

CENTRAL SECTOR

The 19th Army captured Lauenburg on the approaches to Gotenhafen. Elements of the 1st Guards Tank Army were now operating in conjunction with the 19th, overwhelming the hastily erected German defences.

The 1st Ukrainian Front pounded the 17th Army and 4th Panzer Army along the Niesse and Oder lines, particularly heavy fighting raging near Oppeln, Grottkau and Lauban. Striegau was isolated by German forces after heavy fighting. The Russians defend fiercely but were gradually forced back. A little farther south the 4th Ukrainian Front also attacked around Morava Ostrava but quickly became stuck in the well established 1st Panzer Army defences.

SOUTHERN SECTOR

The Germans were suffering under intense Soviet air attacks as their attack around Lake Balaton bogged down entirely. Tolbukhin requested permission to commit the 9th Guards Army in order to halt the German attack completely but the Stavka refused.

11 March 1945

CENTRAL SECTOR

Fierce fighting raged around Kustrin as the 5th Shock Army and 8th Guards Army attempted to dislodge the isolated garrison. General Rendulic was appointed to command Army Group Kurland, General Weiss, Army Group North and General Manteuffel the 3rd Panzer Army. Von Saucken took over the remains of the 2nd Army in East Prussia.

12 March 1945

CENTRAL SECTOR

Elements of the 1st Guards Tank Army reached the outer defences around Gotenhafen. Only the remnants of the 7th Panzer Korp opposed them.

SOUTHERN SECTOR

The German offensive in Hungary had virtually ground to a halt, the attacking units having exhausted themselves after a week of bitter fighting. Hitler was furious at the failure to break through to the Danube and ordered the attack to be resumed, raging against both the army and the SS.

13 March 1945

CENTRAL SECTOR
The 3rd Belorussian began a new offensive aimed at destroying the remnants of the 4th Army holed up around Heiligenbeil, Konigsberg and Samland. Marshal Vasilevsky had massed seven armies to defeat the Germans and opened his attack with overwhelming artillery and air strikes. The initial attack hit the Konigsberg corridor and the Heiligenbeil pocket.

In Pomerania heavy fighting broke out at Kolberg as the 1st Polish Army began to reduce the garrison.

14 March 1945

CENTRAL SECTOR
Heavy fighting raged at Kolberg. The Poles demanded the surrender of the town but the garrison commander, General Fullreide, refused. He was aided in his defence by two naval destroyers lying offshore.

Fighting at Altdamm intensified as the 47th Army renewed its attacks. The 3rd Panzer Army had steadily strengthened its positions over the previous few days and withheld the Soviet attack.

SOUTHERN SECTOR
The 6th SS Panzer Army launched a last ditch effort to break through the positions of the 27th Army. Two hundred panzers, with artillery and infantry support, surged forwards but became embroiled in bitter fighting. To the north the 2nd Ukrainian Front captured Zvolen.

15 March 1945

CENTRAL SECTOR
Heavy fighting raged on the approaches to Gotenhafen and Danzig as the 70th, 49th, 65th and 2nd Shock Armies moved closer to the ports. The German defence was aided by naval artillery fire from the cruisers *Schlesein*, *Prinz Eugen* and *Leipzig*. Polish troops broke into Kolberg and fought their way through the town. Many of the civilians had already been evacuated but the bulk of the garrison remained to hold off the enemy.

Hitler began to transfer elements of the 3rd Panzer Army away from Altdamm to support the battle at Kustrin, fundamentally weakening the positions Manteuffel had carefully built up.

Fighting erupted in Silesia once again as the 1st Ukrainian Front attacked from Oppeln with the aim of reaching Neustadt. The 21st and 4th Tank Armies attacked from Grottkau, while the 59th and 60th Armies struck the German line around Ratibor.

SOUTHERN SECTOR

The German offensive in Hungary came to an end, the attacking forces having lost more than 500 panzers and assault guns, 3,000 artillery pieces and over 40,000 infantry in just ten days of bitter fighting. The 6th SS Panzer Army and 6th Army were left in a vulnerable salient following their failed offensive, under threat of a counter-attack against their exposed flanks

To launch just such an attack the 3rd Ukrainian Front had been strengthened by the addition of the 6th Guards Tank Army from the 2nd Ukrainian Front. With more than 400 tanks and Su's the 6th would spearhead the attack.

The failure of the German counter-offensive in Hungary left the initiative in the south firmly in the hands of the Soviet armies. Hitler had squandered his last operational reserve and pinned his strongest armoured units down in the south, hundreds of miles from the Oder where Soviet armies were already entrenched. With Berlin and Konigsberg already under threat, Vienna would be the next of the Reich's major cities to feel the approach of the Soviet forces.

16 March 1945

CENTRAL SECTOR

During a day of intense fighting the remaining civilians were evacuated from Kolberg. To the south elements of the 4th Tank Army crossed the Niesse river.

SOUTHERN SECTOR

Tolbukhin's 3rd Ukrainian Front, with 536,700 men, began the Vienna Offensive Operation.[17] The 4th and 9th Guards pounded the 6th Army between Szekesfehervar and Mor. Already fully committed south of Lake Velencei, Wohler had nothing left with which to meet this attack. Only the desperation of the German defence prevented an immediate breakthrough, a hard day of fighting gaining the Soviet forces just two miles.

17 March 1945

CENTRAL SECTOR

The 1st Polish Army unleashed an overwhelming assault upon Fullreide's dwindling force in Kolberg. The Germans were reduced to a precarious strip of territory against the sea and made their final preparations to evacuate their force now that the civilians had all escaped.

The 4th Ukrainian Front abandoned its attacks around Morava Ostrava after limited progress. For his failure, General Petrov was dismissed from command of the 4th Ukrainian and Eremenko appointed in his place.

SOUTHERN SECTOR
The 100,000 men of the 46th Army joined the counter-offensive in Hungary, striking the 3rd Hungarian Army so hard it began to disintegrate. As this battle raged the 6th Army and 6th SS Panzer Army were both massively attacked, the 6th struggling to hold off the attacks of the two guards armies while the 6th SS was pinned down by aggressive attacks from the 26th and 27th Armies. The continued massive weight of forces hitting the 6th Army threatened to destroy its positions north-west of Lake Velencei and bring about disaster for the whole of the 6th SS Panzer Army to the south. In southern Hungary Army Group E began to fall back across the Drava, abandoning the Valpovo and Donji Miholjac bridgeheads.

18 March 1945

CENTRAL SECTOR
After a week of bad weather and brutal fighting the skies over East Prussia cleared and the Red Air Force began to pound the 4th Army. German resistance seemed to slacken immediately as the air armies pulverised anything that moved. Under heavy attack, the 6th Korp of the 4th Army requested permission to withdraw but was denied, even though it meant the korp would likely be destroyed. The simple fact was there was nowhere to withdraw to. In Pomerania, Kolberg fell to the 1st Polish Army as Group Fullreide escaped to the west.

19 March 1945

CENTRAL SECTOR
At Danzig and Gotenhafen the 2nd Belorussian Front made steady gains despite extremely aggressive German resistance. The Zoppot Heights fell after bitter fighting and Danzig was brought under intense artillery fire. The 7th Panzer Korp was now fighting just one mile outside the city.

The 47th and 2nd Guards Tank Armies reached the Oder south of Altdamm, prompting Manteuffel to order the evacuation of the bridgehead.

In Silesia the 59th Army linked up with the 4th Tank Army, encircling a large part of the Hermann Goering Panzer Korp near Oppeln and ripping open the southern wing of the 17th Army. Elements of the 24th Panzer Korp were moved to plug the hole but were too weak to relieve the pocket.

SOUTHERN SECTOR

The Soviet counter-offensive in Hungary gathered speed as Tolbukhin committed his armour. Leading units of the 6th Guards Tank Army punched their way into the rear of the 6th SS Panzer Army. In immediate danger of isolation, Dietrich began to pull his men out of the salient. Dietrich was unwilling to sacrifice his army despite a direct order from Hitler to stand and fight, and almost certainly to be annihilated.

GERMAN COMMAND

Hitler ordered the implementation of a nationwide scorched earth policy. He aimed to take Germany down in a deluge of destruction and leave nothing to the Allies. Speer and others actively intrigued to prevent the implementation of the policy.

20 March 1945

CENTRAL SECTOR

The 3rd Panzer Army abandoned its bridgehead in Pomerania at Altdamm. The 3rd Belorussian Front made progress as it advanced northeast along the Baltic coast. Braunsberg fell after a bloody battle. Near Danzig the 49th Army attacked Zoppot while Allied bombers launched a massive raid upon German shipping in the bay.

In Silesia the 21st and 4th Tank Armies destroyed those elements of the Herman Goering Para Panzer Korp isolated at Oppeln. The Germans lost 30,000 killed and 15,000 captured in the bitter fighting.

Himmler, reduced to a state of nervous exhaustion after his brief period in command of Army Group Vistula, was relieved and General Heinrici appointed in his place. General Nehring of the 24th Panzer Korp took command of the 1st Panzer Army.

21 March 1945

CENTRAL SECTOR

General Muller requested permission to evacuate the remnants of his 4th Army and its remaining heavy equipment from Heiligenbeil. Hitler predictably refused. Fighting had reached Heiligenbeil itself.

The last units of the 3rd Panzer Army trapped on the eastern bank of the Oder near Altdamm were destroyed. This battle had cost the Germans another 40,000 killed and 12,000 captured.[18]

SOUTHERN SECTOR

In Hungary Tatabanya fell to the 46th Army. A little to the south elements of the 9th Guards Army entered Szekesfehervar after heavy fighting with the 6th Army. The 6th was fighting desperately to gain time for the 6th SS Panzer Army to escape the developing cauldron near Lake Balaton.

22 March 1945

CENTRAL SECTOR
The 49th Army breached the 7th Panzer Korp line at Zoppot and reached the Baltic, isolating the garrison of Danzig from that in Gotenhafen. Vasilevsky prepared to begin the systematic destruction of both pockets. To the east the 4th Army was pounded relentlessly at Heiligenbeil.

The 8th Guards and 5th Shock Armies (1st Belorussian Front) launched fierce attacks against Busse's 9th Army around Kustrin. After heavy fighting the two armies linked up near Golzow, isolating 2,000 men in Kustrin. Heinrici ordered General Busse to relieve the garrison.

SOUTHERN SECTOR
The 4th and 9th Guards and 6th Guards Tank Armies overwhelmed the 6th Army and swept into the rear of the 6th SS Panzer Army. Realising the danger this posed to his force, Dietrich ordered his men to fight their way west, out of the developing pocket. Bloody fighting raged as the Germans struggled to escape, abandoning much of their heavy equipment as they fled.

23 March 1945

CENTRAL SECTOR
Severe fighting erupted in the outer defences around Danzig as the 49th Army pressed in from the north, the 65th from the west and 2nd Shock from the south.

A counter-attack by two divisions of the 9th Army towards Kustrin was repulsed by the 8th Guards Army. A second attack later in the day also failed.

SOUTHERN SECTOR
Komarno and its oilfields fell to the 7th Guards Army as did Esztergom to the 46th Army as the 3rd Hungarian Army was destroyed south of the Danube and the 8th Army thrown back to its north.

The 6th SS Panzer Army narrowly escaped from the Balaton area as the 26th Army to the south linked up with the 4th and 9th Guards pushing in from the north-east. German defences around Veszprem disintegrated as the 6th SS and 6th Armies began a headlong retreat into Austria.

24 March 1945

CENTRAL SECTOR

After days of bitter fighting Soviet forces captured the railway station at Heiligenbeil.

The 4th Ukrainian Front began a new offensive in Slovakia in order to capture the Moravska Ostrava industrial region. The 38th, 1st Guards and 18th Armies were committed to the attack against the 1st Panzer Army. In Silesia the 59th Korp lost at Sorau (now Zary) to elements of the 1st Ukrainian Front.

SOUTHERN SECTOR

In Hungary Mor and Kisber fell to the 4th Guards as the 6th Army fought a last ditch rearguard. Veszprem fell to the 26th Army. Nearer to the Danube the remnants of the 3rd Hungarian Army counter-attacked towards Esztergom but were repulsed with heavy losses. On Army Group South's southern wing the 2nd Panzer Army was attacked by the 57th Army and fought a delaying action as it slowly withdrew. The 3rd Ukrainian Front intended to drive along the western bank of Lake Balaton from the north with the 27th Army and envelop the 2nd Panzer south of the lake as the 27th and 57th Armies linked up.

25 March 1945

CENTRAL SECTOR

The 3rd Belorussian Front captured Heiligenbeil after a long battle. Muller's 4th Army was pressed back into a narrow strip of land against the Baltic coast. The main points of resistance were around the small settlements of Laysuhnen, Rosenberg and Balga.

The 19th Army attacked the outer defences at Gotenhafen while the 2nd Shock Army hit Danzig.

SOUTHERN SECTOR

The German 8th Army was hit by a new attack as the 2nd Ukrainian Front, launching an offensive across the Hron river aimed at Bratislava. Units of the 53rd, 7th Guards and 1st Rumanian Armies crossed the river and established a strong bridgehead, enabling Mobile Group Pliev to break through the main line of German resistance and press into the interior. The 5th Air Army provided overwhelming air support, hitting anything that moved on the German side of the line. On the far right wing the 40th and 4th Rumanian Armies also attacked, their target being the Hron at Banska Bystrica.

In Hungary Papa fell to leading units of the 6th Guards Tank Army. Fighting also developed in Devecser as the 26th Army advanced and at

Pecel as the 27th pushed along Lake Balaton. Tata also fell to the 46th Army. With Army Group South broken and routed, Hitler relieved Wohler of command and appointed General Rendulic in his place. However, Rendulic was in Kurland and would not be able to take up his new post until the middle of April, by which time Army Group South, renamed Army Group Ostmark, would have lost Vienna and eastern Austria to the Red Army.

26 March 1945

CENTRAL SECTOR
The 19th Army began the assault upon Gotenhafen.

SOUTHERN SECTOR
The 26th Army captured Devecser as the 6th SS Panzer Army fell back to try and establish a line of defence on the Raab river. North of the Danube the 40th Army (2nd Ukrainian Front) took Banska Bystrica.

27 March 1945

CENTRAL SECTOR
The remnants of the German 4th Army disintegrated on the shores of the Frisches Haff. The remnants of three divisions isolated at Laysuhnen were wiped out after a bloody last stand while others were destroyed at Rosenberg. Only a small force continued to resist on the Balga Peninsula.

Gotenhafen fell to the 19th Army as the 8,000 survivors of the garrison withdrew north to the Oxhoft Peninsula. Units of the 2nd Shock and 19th Armies broke through to the final German defence line north and south of Danzig. During the night of 27–28 March General von Saucken ordered the evacuation of his remaining forces inside the port.

Busse's 9th Army counter-attacked from Frankfurt with four armoured divisions in an effort to reach Kustrin. Taking the 8th Guards Army by surprise the attack initially made good progress, leading units breaking into Kustrin late in the day. However, strong Soviet counter-attacks pushed the Germans back and Kustrin was once again isolated. After a day of ferocious fighting 8,000 German troops had been lost.[19]

In Silesia the 1st Ukrainian Front captured Strehlen (now Strzelin) and Rybnik after a bitter battle.

SOUTHERN SECTOR
The bulk of the 3rd Hungarian Army, almost 100,000 men, was isolated north of Tatabanya as the 46th Army reached the Danube. Heavy fighting raged along the line of the Raab as the 6th SS Panzer Army tried to stem the Soviet advance towards Austria.

28 March 1945

CENTRAL SECTOR
As fog grounded the Soviet air armies the Germans evacuated the bulk of their remaining forces from Balga in East Prussia. Covering the retreat a single infantry division fought to the very end, making a last stand at Balga. The horrific campaign for control of the Heiligenbeil pocket had cost the 4th Army 93,000 killed and 47,000 wounded plus 605 panzers, 3,600 artillery pieces 1,400 mortars and 130 aircraft destroyed or captured.[20] Essentially, the 4th Army no longer existed.

SOUTHERN SECTOR
Elements of the 46th Army took Gyor and forced the 6th Army back from the Raab. Sarvar also fell as the 26th Army pushed the 6th SS Panzer Army back.

GERMAN COMMAND
Guderian was dismissed from his post as Chief of the Army General Staff and General Krebs, formerly military attache to the Soviet Union before the war, was appointed in his place.

29 March 1945

CENTRAL SECTOR
The fighting on the lower Oder reached a climax as the 8th Guards and 5th Shock Armies finally crushed the German forces in Kustrin. Around 1,000 survivors of the garrison broke out after a day of ferocious fighting and reached the main German line. Hitler immediately had the garrison commander arrested.

SOUTHERN SECTOR
Soviet forces in Hungary continued to advance. Kapuvar fell to the 6th Guards Tank Army, Szombathely to the 26th and Koszeg to the 9th Guards. The 2nd Panzer Army was hit hard by the 57th Army and 1st Bulgarian Army as it fought its way west. However, the 27th Army was deep in the rear of the 2nd Panzer and, together with the 57th Army, isolated the northern wing of the German force just south of Lake Balaton.

30 March 1945

CENTRAL SECTOR
After a bloody battle Danzig fell to the 2nd Shock Army, the German garrison having been entirely destroyed. The Soviets claimed 10,000 prisoners during the battle and captured or destroyed 140 panzers and

assault guns and forty-five U-Boats. Elements of Von Saucken's 2nd Army fought on to the bitter end in the Vistula delta. In the centre the 60th Army and 4th Tank Army of the 1st Ukrainian Front took Ratibor.

SOUTHERN SECTOR
The 9th Guards Army pushed forward from Koszeg and entered Austria. A little to the north the 7th Guards Army (2nd Ukrainian Front) approached Bratislava.

31 March 1945

SOUTHERN SECTOR
The 7th Guards Army crossed the Vah river off the march while supporting forces took Nitra. Galanta also fell to second echelon elements of the 7th Guards. On the Austrian border Kormend and Szentgotthard fell to the 27th Army while Sopron was attacked by the 6th Guards Tank.

THE OSTHEER
German deployment on the eastern front stood at thirty-two panzer, fifteen panzer grenadier and 132 infantry divisions.[21]

1 April 1945

CENTRAL SECTOR
The German 9th Army launched an unsuccessful counter-attack at Kustrin. Farther south, the 13th Army of the 1st Ukrainian Front took Glogau after a long struggle.

SOUTHERN SECTOR
The 2nd Ukrainian Front pressed home its attack across the Vah, the 7th Guards Army beginning to envelop the German forces which were trying the bar the road to Bratislava. Farther south Sopron fell to the 6th Guards Tank Army after a brief battle.

The Stavka issued new orders for the 46th Army to envelop Vienna from the east while the 3rd Ukrainian Front, while the 4th and 9th Guards and 6th Guards Tank Armies approached from the south and west. With Hungary under Soviet control, many surviving Hungarian soldiers began to surrender. There would still be some Hungarians fighting on with Army Group Ostmark until the very end of the war though.

2 April 1945

CENTRAL SECTOR
Marshal Vasilevski had built up his armies around Konigsberg in order to

crush the German garrison. The 11th Guards Army was poised south of the city while the 50th and 43rd Armies were ready to the north and north-west. The 39th Army was to sever the link with the Samland Group. In preparation for the attack, Soviet artillery began softening the German defences.

SOUTHERN SECTOR
Masonmagyarovar fell to the 46th Army in north-west Hungary, while the 6th Guards Army reached the shores of Lake Neuseidler. In western Hungary the Nagykanitsa oilfields, Germany's last source of natural oil, fell to the 57th Army.

3 April 1945

CENTRAL SECTOR
The 4th Ukrainian Front was reinforced with the 60th Army (1st Ukrainian), bringing the strength of the 4th to 265,000 men with 6,000 artillery pieces, 300 tanks and Su's and 435 aircraft.[22] Facing this host the 1st Panzer Army had 300 panzers and 280 planes, the majority of which were inoperable due to the lack of fuel. Many of the German tanks were used as fixed firing positions during the fighting.

SOUTHERN SECTOR
The 7th Guards Army began to attack the outer defences of Bratislava as the German 8th Army crumbled. In Austria the 46th Army reached open ground east of Vienna and advanced rapidly towards the city. The 6th SS Panzer Army was falling back to cover the city defences but was also threatened by the advance of the 6th Guards Tank, 4th and 9th Guards Armies on its right wing. Weiner Neustadt fell to the 9th Guards.

4 April 1945

CENTRAL SECTOR
The 3rd Belorussian Front launched a series of fierce attacks around the Konigsberg perimeter, testing the German defences. The 48th, 50th, 11th Guards and 39th Armies all attacked during the course of the day, inflicting heavy casualties.

With the fighting in Pomerania over, the Soviets assessed the cost. The 1st Belorussian Front had lost 12,000 killed and 40,000 wounded since February and the 2nd Belorussian 40,000 killed and 132,000 wounded.[23]

SOUTHERN SECTOR
The 7th Guards Army captured Bratislava after a brief battle. General Kreysing drew his broken army west, falling back upon Brno.

5 April 1945

SOUTHERN SECTOR
The 46th Army began its attack towards Vienna, crossing the Danube west of Bratislava in order to envelop the city from the north. The 4th Guards Army was already attacking to the south-east. Dietrich's 6th SS planned to make a stand in Vienna and fight for every street.

6 April 1945

CENTRAL SECTOR
The 3rd Belorussian Front launched its offensive against Konigsberg. Some 138,000 men, 5,000 artillery pieces and 538 tanks or Su's were committed against Group Lasch, with just 35,000 men in four infantry divisions and eight Volkssturm brigades. Massive air and artillery fire accompanied the attack as the 1st and 15th Air Armies ravaged the German positions. Bitter fighting erupted as the Soviet forces attacked from the north, east and south, puncturing the German lines at numerous points and penetrating into the city by the end of the first day of fighting. The 11th Guards Army closed upon the railway station while the 43rd Army annihilated a Volksgrenadier division in hard fighting. One by one, the outer forts fell.

SOUTHERN SECTOR
The 2nd and 3rd Ukrainian Fronts opened their offensive upon Vienna, the 4th Guards Army fighting its way into the southern suburbs despite fierce resistance from the 6th SS Panzer Army. Russian casualties were severe as the Germans fought in every street. The 6th Guards Tank Army suffered particularly heavy losses as it entered the city, the deadly Panzerfaust taking its toll. Mattresses tied to the front of the tanks prevented some losses but enough Germans found their mark to whittle away the strength of the tank army. In an effort to slow the Soviet advance the SS destroyed all bridges across the Danube except one, placing units of the 2nd SS Das Reich here to defend it. As the battle for Vienna raged the 2nd Panzer Army withdrew towards Graz.

7 April 1945

CENTRAL SECTOR
The fighting around Konigsberg intensified as the 11th Guards pushed into the city and the 43rd Army widened the hole it had ripped in the German front. The 39th Army had pinned the 5th Panzer Division down in Samland, preventing it from offering any aid to the city.

SOUTHERN SECTOR

The 4th Guards and 6th Guards Tank Armies penetrated deep into Vienna but fierce battles slowed their advance. While the bulk of the 6th SS Panzer Army fought inside Vienna, others units were pushed back to the west by the 9th Guards Army as it closed upon St Polten.

8 April 1945

CENTRAL SECTOR

The situation in Konigsberg had deteriorated greatly, Group Lasch having been isolated from the Samland Group as the 11th Guards Army crossed the Pregel and linked up with the 43rd Army. Muller ordered Lasch to break out and rejoin but Lasch maintained that his forces were too weak.

SOUTHERN SECTOR

Elements of the 6th Guards Tank Army penetrated into Vienna city centre as they strove to link up with the 4th Guards Army. The 6th SS Panzer Army defended every step of the way.

9 April 1945

CENTRAL SECTOR

With his force on the verge of total annihilation, General Lasch surrendered Konigsberg. More than 92,000 German soldiers were captured while 42,000 soldiers and 25,000 civilians had died during the battle. Hitler descended into a furious rage at news of Lasch's surrender and ordered the arrest of his family and relatives. Lasch was sentenced to death in absentia and Muller, commander of the defunct 4th Army, dismissed. The last vestiges of the 4th Army continued to resist in Samland.

10 April 1945

SOUTHERN SECTOR

The 6th SS Panzer Army began to pull out of Vienna city centre while the remnants of the 6th Army and other units of the 6th SS fought on near Wiener Neustadt and Baden.

11 April 1945

CENTRAL SECTOR

General von Saucken was appointed to command the Army of East Prussia following Muller's sacking. Saucken had six divisions and a host of miscellaneous units, totalling 65,000 men, in Samland.

SOUTHERN SECTOR

The 27th Army (3rd Ukrainian Front) threw the 2nd Panzer Army back towards the Mur river as it advanced upon Graz while the 26th closed upon Neuenkirchen. Inside Vienna the Parliament building and City Hall fell to the 4th Guards Army as the Soviets fought their way across the Danube canal.

THE WESTERN FRONT

American forces reached the Elbe at Magdeburg and forced a crossing but halted there instead of pushing towards Berlin. Eisenhower had forbidden the advance east as Berlin was to be left to the Soviets. The advance of the US 9th Army to the Elbe had thrown Wenck's 12th Army back to the Harz Mountains. Wenck was well placed to turn and march towards Berlin should the need arise but his army was nothing more than a band of exhausted, demoralised men, without heavy weapons.

12 April 1945

CENTRAL SECTOR

The 3rd Belorussian Front unleashed a massive attack against Group Samland. Two divisions on the German left wing came under intense pressure but held on.

SOUTHERN SECTOR

Soviet forces in Austria began to advance south of Vienna, the 26th, 27th and 57th Armies pushing forward on a broad front. Inside the city the Germans were fighting around Florisdorf Bridge, the defenders having just six panzers left. Strong Soviet attacks quickly destroyed four tanks but the SS continued to hold.

13 April 1945

CENTRAL SECTOR

Fierce fighting continued in Samland as the remnants of the 26th, 9th and 55th Korps fought on.

SOUTHERN SECTOR

The battle for Vienna drew to a close as the 3rd Ukrainian Front crushed the remnants of the 6th SS Panzer Army still in the city. By dusk the city had fallen but was a gutted ruin. The fighting in the south since 16 March had cost the Germans 134,000 captured and thirty-two divisions destroyed. For Army Group Ostmark the end was in sight. The battle had not only been costly for the Germans though, it had cost the 3rd Ukrainian

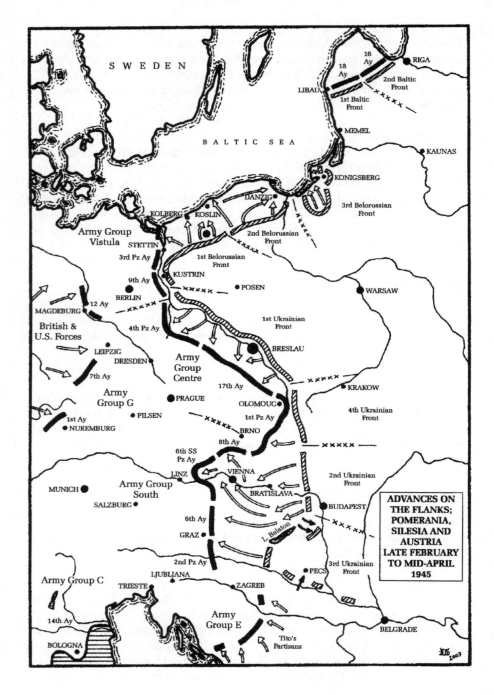

ADVANCES ON
THE FLANKS;
POMERANIA,
SILESIA AND
AUSTRIA
LATE FEBRUARY
TO MID-APRIL
1945

Front 32,000 killed and 106,000 wounded and the 46th Army 5,800 killed and 22,000 wounded.[24]

14 April 1945

CENTRAL SECTOR
The fighting in Samland intensified as the German line of resistance crumbled. The survivors fell back upon Pillau in the hope of evacuation by the Navy.

SOVIET COMMAND
Following correspondence with General Eisenhower at the end of March, Stalin ordered the start date for the Berlin Operation be brought forward but typically, judging everyone by his own devious standards, informed the Western Allies that he did not intend to begin the offensive until May at the earliest. The 1st and 2nd Belorussian and 1st Ukrainian Fronts had spent the first half of April feverishly preparing for the offensive, the 2nd Belorussian being particularly hard pressed to meet the start date as it redeployed across 200 miles of ravaged Pomeranian countryside to the line of the Oder. By mid-April the Soviets had largely completed their redeployment, massing a force of 2,500,000 men, 41,000 artillery pieces, 6,200 tanks and Su's and 7,200 aircraft between the three fronts. The armies were well provided with over 100,000 motor vehicles to keep the infantry moving forward.

The Soviet plan intended for the 1st Belorussian Front, with 908,000 men and 1st Ukrainian Front with 550,900, was to destroy the German 9th and 4th Panzer Armies on the line of the Oder and Niesse rivers and then push rapidly forward to envelop Berlin. To give the attack a competitive edge, Stalin drew the front boundary line short, leaving it a few miles east of Berlin and declaring that the first front to reach the city would have the glory of conquering it. The competition was not as one sided as it may at first appear, as the 1st Belorussian Front, despite being only fifty miles from the city at Kustrin, was faced with lines of formidable German defences. To overcome the German forces Zhukov aimed to use a novel technique. Placing searchlights close to the front line, he ordered his tanks to attack with lights blazing, hoping to reflect the light back off the low clouds over the battlefield and illuminate the German positions. The 1st Belorussian Front deployed for the offensive the 61st Army on its northern wing, 1st Polish Army, 47th and 3rd Shock Armies, 5th Shock Army north of Kustrin, 8th Guards Army south of the town, 69th Army opposite Frankfurt and 33rd Army on the southern wing. Behind the 5th Shock Army was the 2nd Guards Tank and behind the 8th Guards the 1st Guards Tank. The 3rd Army was held in front reserve.

Koniev's 1st Ukrainian Front, despite being deployed to the south along the Niesse, was not faced with the extensive defences that had been erected before Berlin. It aimed to tear the 4th Panzer Army in two and push rapidly north-west. The main obstacle in his line of advance was the Niesse but Koniev planned to cross under the cover of a smoke barrage. On his northern flank, opposite Forst, Koniev had the 3rd Guards Army, followed on a line running south by the 13th, 5th Guards, 2nd Polish and 52nd Armies, the latter deployed north of Gorlitz. Behind the 3rd Guards and 13th Armies were the 3rd and 4th Guards Tank Armies. The 28th Army was held in front reserve.

To the north the 2nd Belorussian Front, with 441,000 men, was to begin its offensive a few days later and pin down the 3rd Panzer Army. The 3rd aimed to reach the Baltic and cut the Allied line of advance into Denmark. The British were already racing for this region, trying to do the reverse to the Russians. For this task Rokossovsky had the 2nd Shock Army on its right wing, 65th and 70th Armies in the centre and south of Stettin and the 49th Army opposite Schwedt.

While the bulk of the 1st Belorussian and 1st Ukrainian Fronts destroyed the Germans in Berlin the outer pincers were to push to the Elbe river and link up with the Western Allies. Each of the Soviet fronts was provided with massive air support, the 2nd Belorussian Front having the 4th Air Army, the 1st Belorussian the 16th and 18th Air Armies and the 1st Ukrainian Front the 2nd Air Army.

Facing this mighty array was Heinrici's Army Group Vistula and the northern wing of Schorner's Army Group Centre. Group Vistula had the 3rd Panzer and 9th Armies, Manteuffel's 3rd Panzer having ten divisions between the 32nd, 51st, 46th Panzer and 10th SS Korps while Busse's 9th Army had the 5th SS Mountain, 11th SS and 101st Korps with fifteen divisions. In army group reserve, situated immediately behind the 9th Army was Weidling's 56th Panzer Korp with three panzer and three panzer grenadier divisions. To the south Graeser's 4th Panzer Army of Army Group Centre deployed fourteen divisions between the 57th Panzer, Grossdeutschland Panzer and 5th Korps and Korp Group Moser. In support the Luftwaffe had 300 aircraft but many were grounded due to the lack of fuel.

The comparative strengths of the German and Soviet combat forces concentrated for the battle of Berlin showed just how much the Red Army had grown and how the Ostheer had wasted away after four years of brutal and costly fighting. The 3rd Panzer and 9th Armies totalled barely 200,000 men with 750 panzers and assault guns and 1,500 artillery pieces, while the 1st and 2nd Belorussian Fronts had 1,400,000 men, 4,100 tanks and Su's and 23,600 artillery pieces. On the Niesse the 4th Panzer had another 100,000 men and 200 panzers but the 1st Ukrainian opposed it with 1,100,000 men and 2,150 tanks and Su's.

By the evening of 15 April 1945, with the ruins of Vienna in Soviet hands, the 1st Belorussian and 1st Ukrainian Fronts were ready to begin the offensive against Hitler's own city. The 2nd Belorussian, still redeploying from Pomerania, would begin its attack on the 20th.

In the middle of the combat line the 2nd and 4th Ukrainian Fronts had been reinforced and prepared to crush the German forces in Slovakia, the two fronts having a combined strength of 750,000 men, 8,300 artillery pieces, 580 tanks and Su's and 1,400 aircraft. Facing this concentration of armies were the weakened 17th and 1st Panzer Armies of Army Group Centre.

The loss of both Konigsberg and Vienna proved beyond doubt that the end of Nazi Germany was in sight. The trapped armies in East Prussia had been wiped out, the Kurland forces contained and prevented from influencing the battles to the west and the Hungarian forces finally swept from the field. With these victories behind him, Stalin had turned his attention to the capture of Berlin, to influence the post-war settlement of European frontiers. Western armies were already on the Elbe at Magdeburg while the Soviets faced the Germans across the Oder to the east of the city. Yet again, overwhelming force would be brought to bear to annihilate the Germans before their capital.

NOTES

1   Duffy, *Red Storm on the Reich*, p103. This is an excellent book on the advance of the Soviet armies through Poland and into Germany in the first quarter of 1945.
2   Ellis, *The World War II Databook*, Table 14, p230
3   Ellis, *The World War II Databook*, Table 20, p233
4   Ellis, *The World War II Databook*, p176
5   Ungvary, *The Battle for Budapest*, p146
6   Kirosheev, *Soviet Casualties and Combat Losses in the Twentieth Century*, Table 75
7   Kirosheev, *Soviet Casualties and Combat Losses in the Twentieth Century*, Table 75
8   Kirosheev, *Soviet Casualties and Combat Losses in the Twentieth Century*, Table 75
9   Duffy, *Red Storm on the Reich*, p183
10   Duffy, *Red Storm on the Reich*, p165
11   Duffy, *Red Storm on the Reich*, p177
12   Ellis, *The World War II Databook*, p176 for German divisional strengths, p178 for Hungarian.
13   Ellis, *The World War II Databook*, pp171–4 for German order of battle across the Eastern Front on 1 March
14   Duffy, *Red Storm on the Reich*, p197
15   Erickson, *The Road to Berlin*, p510
16   Erickson, *The Road to Berlin*, p512
17   Kirosheev, *Soviet Casualties and Combat Losses in the Twentieth Century*, Table 67

18 Duffy, *Red Storm on the Reich*, p238
19 Duffy, *Red Storm on the Reich*, pp245–6
20 Duffy, *Red Storm on the Reich*, p206
21 Ellis, *The World War II Databook*, p177
22 Kirosheev, *Soviet Casualties and Combat Losses in the Twentieth Century*, Table 67
23 Kirosheev, *Soviet Casualties and Combat Losses in the Twentieth Century*, Table 75
24 Kirosheev, *Soviet Casualties and Combat Losses in the Twentieth Century*, Table 75

CHAPTER IX

Annihilation

Hitler's Thousand Year Reich lay in ruins. East Prussia had fallen to Soviet armies, Hungary was conquered and Austrian invaded. Vienna was no longer German, the might of the Waffen SS lying broken in its streets. In a final cycle of violence the Stavka inflicted the coup de grâce upon the mortally wounded German armies, first aiming to destroy those around Berlin, before annihilating the remnants of the once mighty Ostheer in a final battle of encirclement in Bohemia.

16 April 1945

CENTRAL SECTOR

As Group Samland disintegrated the survivors massed at Pillau. Amid chaotic scenes Russian troops broke into Fischhausen, close to Pillau. A rearguard action by the 5th Panzer Division saw the unit annihilated.

Before dawn the battle for Berlin was launched, Zhukov's 1st Belorussian Front unleashing an overwhelming artillery barrage upon the German defences on the Seelow Heights. However, General Heinrici had identified the preparations for the attack and skilfully withdrew his first line back to the main line of resistance just before the artillery strike began. This spared the 9th Army many casualties during the bombardment. Following closely behind the artillery fire the 5th Shock and 8th Guards Armies advanced. The 8th Guards Army quickly became embroiled in bitter fighting with the defending Germans and ground to a halt, Zhukov's searchlight tactic backfiring as the clouds of dust and smoke blown up by the artillery fire obliterated the German positions but lit up his own units, leaving them vulnerable to German counter-fire. Despite repeated attacks the Russians failed to break the German line. In a towering rage Zhukov vented his anger on Chuikov. Furious at the delay Zhukov made a cardinal error and ordered the commitment of the armour before the main line of enemy resistance had been broken. This move predictably also failed as the 1st Guards Tank Army became ensnared in the mother of all traffic jams behind the 8th Guards Army. The 2nd

Guards Tank Army was also committed, spreading havoc behind the 5th Shock Army. Despite these difficulties the 8th Guards managed to fight its way into Seelow, but bloody battles along the main street, the Germans firing 88s at point blank range against the Russian tanks, prevented the advance from reaching any farther. Casualties mounted as German anti-tank teams, armed with the deadly Panzerfaust, picked off stranded tanks while concentrated fire from the high ground pinned down the Soviet infantry.

To the south the 1st Ukrainian Front also began its attack preceded by light artillery bombardment. Smoke bombs were dropped across the river to obscure the movement of the 3rd Guards, 13th and 5th Guards Armies to the left bank. Within hours Koniev had secured a bridgehead and hastily constructed pontoons strong enough to hold his tanks. As the first-wave armies smashed through the 4th Panzer Army's forward positions, the 3rd and 4th Guards Tank Armies had begun to cross the Niesse in force.

SOUTHERN SECTOR

The 3rd Ukrainian Front continued to press Army Group Ostmark back in Austria, St Polten and Furstenfeld falling after heavy fighting. The 2nd Ukrainian Front pushed closer to Brno.

17 April 1945

CENTRAL SECTOR

The offensive towards Berlin continued as Zhukov piled more and more units up against the 9th Army on the Seelow Heights. Artillery fire and air attacks hit the Germans, striking the deeply committed front-line units. German casualties were heavy, but when the 8th Guards, 5th Shock and 1st and 2nd Guards Tank Armies resumed their attacks they were again held up. Busse was using the entire strength of the 9th Army at Seelow in an effort to prevent the Soviets from achieving a breakthrough. By late afternoon Seelow fell to the 8th Guards Army but the Germans merely retired to their next defensive position.

Koniev's 1st Ukrainian Front fared far better, the 13th, 3rd Guards and 5th Guards Armies punching a hole through the centre of the 4th Panzer Army. With their line of advance clear, he committed the 4th Tank and 3rd Guards Tank Armies across the Niesse and towards the Spree river. Koniev requested that he be allowed to direct his attack northward to envelop the German forces at Berlin from the south. Stalin agreed, directing that the 3rd Guards Tank and 4th Tank Armies move towards Zossen and Potsdam.

There was heavy fighting in East Prussia as the 3rd Belorussian Front attacked Samland Group around Pillau (now Baltaisk). Fischhausen fell after very heavy fighting.

SOUTHERN SECTOR

In Austria Wilhelmsdorf and Zisterdorf fell as the 46th Army pushed the 6th SS Panzer Army back north of Vienna.

18 April 1945

CENTRAL SECTOR

The 1st Belorussian Front launched another massive artillery bombardment upon the German Seelow defences. This final barrage finally broke German resistance as the 9th Army began to crumble. Repeated attacks by the 5th Shock, 8th Guards and 1st and 2nd Guards Tank Armies began to break down the German positions. With the main line of resistance collapsing Busse committed the 56th Panzer Korp in an effort to hold back the Russians. Furious fighting raged, but despite the panzer troops' best efforts, the 8th Guards Army and 1st Guards Tank Army managed to break through towards Berlin. To the north the 47th Army, 3rd and 5th Shock Armies also moved forward.

The 1st Ukrainian Front split the 4th Panzer Army in two as it pushed north-west from the Niesse. Spremberg was encircled by the 5th Guards Army and Cottbus by the 3rd Guards as the 3rd Guards Tank moved quickly towards Zossen and the 4th Guards Tank strove to reach Potsdam.

19 April 1945

CENTRAL SECTOR

After a long and bloody battle the 1st Belorussian Front began its general advance upon Berlin. The struggle for the Seelow Heights had cost Zhukov 30,000 killed and enabled the 1st Ukrainian Front to gain valuable time in the advance upon the city from the south. The race to Berlin was now on. Munchberg fell to the 8th Guards while the 3rd Shock and 47th Armies, now supported by the 2nd Guards Tank Army, started to advance to outflank Berlin from the north. Busse was no longer able to bar the road to the city as he had lost the bulk of his army in the fierce battle for the heights.

The 1st Ukrainian Front also advanced rapidly, the 5th Guards Army pushing towards Torgau on the Elbe, the 13th Army towards Wittenberg also on the Elbe, while the 3rd Guards with the 3rd and 4th Guards Tank Armies pushed north-west towards Berlin. Elements of the 2nd Polish Army, on the southern wing, took Rothenberg.

20 April 1945

CENTRAL SECTOR

The Western Allies launched their last air raid upon Berlin. No sooner had the bombs stopped falling on the city than the artillery of Zhukov's 1st Belorussian Front began to pound the eastern suburbs. Despite stiff resistance Bernau fell to the 47th Army as it advanced north of Berlin while the 3rd Shock Army began to press straight towards Berlin from the north-east. Hitler ordered the 9th Army to continue to resist on the Oder despite the threat of encirclement. The 33rd Army joined the offensive as it struck the southern wing of the army, pushing it back towards the isolated northern wing of the 4th Panzer Army west of Frankfurt and Guben.

The 1st Ukrainian Front pushed forward, the 3rd Guards Tank Army taking Barut, just twenty miles south of Zossen and the OKH headquarters. The 28th Army moved up from the reserve to support the 3rd Guards Tank. Late in the day Juterbog, main armaments depot for the German forces around Berlin, fell to the 4th Guards Tank. Behind the main advance the 5th Guards Army attacked elements of the 4th Panzer Army near Cottbus, inflicting heavy casualties.

On the right wing of the Soviet offensive the 2nd Belorussian Front began to hit the 3rd Panzer Army. Heavy artillery fire and strong air support suppressed the Germans while the 65th, 70th and 49th Armies attempted a crossing of the Oder between Schwedt and Stettin. Initial German resistance was intense and brought the attacks of the 70th and 49th Armies to a halt. Only the 65th Army managed to penetrate the German positions just south of Stettin.

21 April 1945

CENTRAL SECTOR

Rokossovsky reinforced the 65th Army to place the main weight of his attack here. Fierce fighting continued as the 3rd Panzer Army tried to prevent the Soviet forces breaking into Mecklenberg. Once again the 70th and 49th Armies were held up but the 65th made steady gains.

The 1st Belorussian increased its artillery bombardment of Berlin. Elements of the 3rd Shock Army entered the north-east suburbs while the 5th Shock broke in from the east. The 8th Guards Army and 1st Guards Tank Army remained heavily committed in bloody fighting around Furstenwalde as the 9th Army launched repeated counter-attacks. Inside Berlin, factories still producing weapons fell silent as electricity and gas supplies were cut. North of the city the 1st Polish and 61st Armies were involved in heavy fighting near Eberswalde, while the 47th and 2nd Guards Tank Armies crossed the main Autobahn north of Berlin. The 47th Army was pushing east towards Potsdam and Ketzin while the 2nd Guards Tank Army attempted to push straight into the city from the north.

South of Berlin, the 3rd Guards Tank Army took Zossen, isolating the southern wing of the 9th Army and half of the 4th Panzer Army between Frankfurt and Guben, a force of 200,000 men with 2,000 artillery pieces and 200 panzers. The group was under heavy attack by the 33rd and 69th Armies from the east and north and by the 28th Army to the south and west.

22 April 1945

CENTRAL SECTOR
The 2nd Belorussian Front continued its bitter battle to smash the 3rd Panzer Army along the Oder. Farther south the 1st Belorussian Front struck into Berlin in force. Units of the 3rd Shock Army were embroiled in the north-east suburbs, while the 5th Shock and 1st Guards Tank and 8th Guards Armies moved up to provide support in the eastern suburbs. The 47th Army meanwhile had crossed the Havel near Oranienberg as it outflanked the Germans to the north. Elements of the 2nd Tank Army had wheeled south to enter the Hennigsdorf suburb in north-west Berlin. Furstenberg, Strausberg and Bernau all fell to the 1st Belorussian Front in a day of hard fighting.

South of the city the 3rd Guards Tank and 28th Armies (1st Ukrainian Front) entered the southern suburbs, lead units reaching the Teltow Canal. The 4th Guards Tank Army was also pushing up from the south and neared Potsdam. On the opposite wing of Koniev's front the 2nd Polish Army neared Dresden.

Hitler announced that he would stay in Berlin, assuming control of the city defences. He maintained he would fight and die in the city if the Russians were not repulsed. The failure of an attack he had ordered a few days before north of the city by SS General Steiner's mixed force threw him into one of his towering rages. After an abusive tirade at the uselessness of the army, the SS and the German people, he finally accepted that the war was lost.

In Moravia the 60th Army (4th Ukrainian Front) broke into Opava after a bloody battle with the 1st Panzer Army. After a furious battle the town fell.

23 April 1945

CENTRAL SECTOR
Kietel attempted to organise a counter-attack to throw the Russians back from Berlin. He ordered Wenck's 12th Army to march east from the Elbe to drive the Soviets back but this force was an army in name only.

In Berlin itself were nearly 300,000 German soldiers, all of whom were ordered to fight to the last bullet. Heavy fighting raged as the 8th Guards and 3rd Guards Tank Armies linked up, the 1st Belorussian and 1st

Ukrainian Fronts having joined hands in the south-east suburbs. Around the city the Germans lost Oranienberg, Pulsnitz, Beelitz, Trebbin, Tetlow and Dahlewitz to the Soviet forces.

Frankfurt and Cottbus fell to the 69th and 3rd Guards Armies respectively. The 4th Panzer Army launched a counter-attack with 100 panzers from Bautzen. The 2nd Polish and 52nd Armies were surprised by the German attack and the junction of the two forces was severed. Bitter fighting raged throughout the day as the Soviets launched immediate counter-attacks.

SOUTHERN SECTOR
The 2nd Ukrainian Front began a new attack upon Brno with the 53rd and 6th Guards Tank Armies. The 8th Army was overwhelmed by the attack and began to disintegrate.

GERMAN POLITICS
Goering offered to assume control of the Reich, stating that he would seek peace terms with the west. This came as a blow to Hitler, Goering having been a loyal servant throughout the twelve years of Nazi power. Betrayed, Hitler ordered Goering's arrest and stripped him of his offices.

24 April 1945

CENTRAL SECTOR
The Soviet armies inside Berlin launched intense attacks towards the city centre, the 3rd Guards Tank and 28th Armies pushing in from the south to link up in force with the 8th Guards, 3rd and 69th Armies. The 3rd and 5th Shock and 1st Guards Tank attacked from the east. To the north the 2nd Guards Tank also pressed through the German defences. At the western end of the city, heavy fighting raged near Potsdam as the 4th Guards Tank Army moved to link up with the 47th Army.

South of Berlin, the counter-attack by the 4th Panzer Army around Bautzen was halted as 52nd and 2nd Polish Armies and 2nd Air Army pounded the German forces. Casualties mounted alarmingly, compelling the 4th Panzer to abandon its attack and fall back. West of Berlin, the 12th Army began its relief attack, hitting units of the 13th Army and 4th Guards Tank Army as it pushed towards Treuerbreitzen. The Soviets were again surprised by the counter-attack and the 13th began to fall back.

In Moravia the 6th Guards Tank Army of the 2nd Ukrainian Front reached Brno but were halted as the 8th Army counter-attacked. The Soviets suffered heavy losses and in bitter fighting were prevented from taking the town.

25 April 1945

CENTRAL SECTOR

The 47th Army of the 1st Belorussian Front and 4th Guards Tank Army of the 1st Ukrainian Front linked up at Ketzin near Potsdam, isolating the Berlin garrison. Germany itself was also split in two as the 5th Guards Army reached the Elbe at Torgau and linked up with the men of the 5th Corp, US 1st Army.

Around Berlin, Gatow airfield was brought under intense heavy artillery fire and was put out of action. Fighting in the northern, eastern and southern suburbs also intensified. The 12th Army renewed its attack but was halted by the 13th Army. Fierce fighting raged at Beelitz, where the remnants of the Frankfurt–Guben Group were trying to break through to the west. Counter-attacks by the 13th threw the 12th Army back with heavy casualties.

In East Prussia the 3rd Belorussian Front took Pillau after a bitter six-day battle. The remnants of Group Samland still would not give up, falling back to the narrow strip of land south of the town. Fighting in East Prussia since January had cost the 3rd Belorussian Front 89,400 killed and 332,000 wounded.[1]

SOUTHERN SECTOR

The 60th Army launched new attacks upon Moravska Ostrava while the 6th Guards Tank Army continued its battle for Brno.

26 April 1945

CENTRAL SECTOR

The Soviets began the final phase of their offensive aimed at crushing the Berlin garrison. Some 460,000 soldiers, supported by 12,000 artillery pieces and 1,500 tanks and Su's and the aircraft of the 16th and 18th Air Armies, hit the 300,000 German troops in the city. The Moabitt and Neukolin districts fell after hard fighting, while Potsdam was heavily attacked and Templehof airfield captured.

To the north the 3rd Belorussian Front broke through the Oder line, Stettin falling to the 65th Army. South of Berlin, the Frankfurt–Guben group was fighting its last battle against the 3rd, 69th, 33rd, 3rd Guards and 28th Armies. The Germans launched fierce attacks west, hitting the junction of the 3rd Guards and 28th Armies near Halbe. Farther west, the 12th Army attacked towards Berlin once again but the 13th Army inflicted crippling casualties.

The remnants of the Samland Group began to surrender but elements continued to fight on at the tip of the Pillau Peninsula. More than 30,000 had surrendered during the fighting but nearly as many continued to fight on.

SOUTHERN SECTOR

The 2nd and 4th Ukrainian Fronts routed the 8th Army around Brno, the town falling as the Germans fell back. During the battle the Soviets lost 38,000 killed and 140,000 wounded.[2]

27 April 1945

CENTRAL SECTOR

The 3rd Panzer Army disintegrated, enabling Rokossovksy to plunge into Mecklenberg. Prenzlau fell to the 70th Army and Angermunde to the 49th as the 3rd Panzer fled west.

Spandau and Grunewalde were attacked and Potsdam fell as the Russians surged through Berlin. The Soviet armies were keeping up the pace of the attack by rotating their combat troops to ensure fresh troops were in action around the clock.

The break-out attempt by the Frankfurt–Guben Group around Halbe came to an end as the Soviets massacred the ranks of desperate German soldiers. Cohesion collapsed as the 9th and 4th Panzer Armies broke up.

28 April 1945

CENTRAL SECTOR

The 3rd Shock Army took the Alt Moabitt district of Berlin and pushed on to the Spree at the Moltke Bridge. Moabitt prison was also taken and furious fighting raged in the Tiergarten as the 8th Guards Army pushed forwards. Russian spearheads were just a mile from Hitler's headquarters in the Chancellery bunker, but the Russian attacks were directed towards the Reichstag, which was believed to be the seat of Nazi power. After heavy fighting elements of the 1st Ukrainian Front cleared the Pots-dammerstrasse, reducing the pocket to ten by three miles. Other units of the 1st Ukrainian were fighting on the Unter-den-Linden. German resistance was fanatical, many of the defending units being foreign SS troops with no hope of escape even if they survived the battle. By dusk the Soviets completed the capture of the Potsdammer Bridge and the Ministry of Internal Affairs was the scene of furious room-by-room fighting.

With the 3rd Panzer Army broken, Heinrici reported to the OKH that he was no longer able to hold on to the Oder line and informed them of his decision to pull back west to avoid encirclement. Hitler expressly forbade this move but Heinrici responded that he would continue to withdraw, refusing to sacrifice an army in a pointless battle. Hitler immediately sacked Heinrici and appointed General Student, commanding the German armies in Holland, to take over the vacant post. However, Student would be unable to join the armies in the east before the end so Tippelskirch deputised as army group commander.

THE ITALIAN FRONT

Mussolini was captured by Communist partisans near Lake Como and, with his mistress, Clara Petacci, was executed. His body was strung up by the feet from a lamp post in the streets of Milan, as jeering crowds mutilated and beat the defunct dictator. When his end was reported to Berlin, it confirmed Hitler's decision to take his own life rather than fall into the hands of the Russians. He also left explicit instructions to his followers to thoroughly burn his body so that no trace could be found.

29 April 1945

CENTRAL SECTOR

The German forces in Berlin suffered massive losses during the ferocious fighting. Potsdam station fell and Wilmersdorf was attacked. The Moltke Bridge fell to the 3rd Shock Army. Bitter fighting raged in the Interior Ministry Building and the City Hall while the Flak Towers resisted all attempts at capture. Inside these massive structures hundreds of civilians lay alongside wounded soldiers while all around shells burst. Bloody battles were being fought along the Potsdammerstrasse, in Belle Allianz Platz and around the Chancellery, underneath which Hitler directed the movement of his imaginary armies. General Weidling, commanding the 56th Panzer Korp near the Reichstag, reported that his men were almost out of ammunition and that food and water had run out. Hitler ordered Weidling to fight on to the last man.

With Soviet forces just yards away, Hitler wrote his last will and testament. He blamed the German defeat upon the Jews and appointed Admiral Karl Doenitz his successor. Even from the grave he meddled in the pointless politics of a ruined and defeated Germany, naming the ministers of the new government. As a final act he married Eva Braun.

The Frankfurt–Guben Group launched another desperate counterattack, this time near Beelitz while the 12th Army attacked at Belzig. The 12th was able to inflict heavy casualties upon the 4th Guards Tank Army and advanced east, leading elements entering Potsdam late in the day. The attacks of the Frankfurt–Guben Group had been partially successful as minor elements linked up with the 12th near Beelitz. Over the next two days more than 30,000 men made a dash for the west.

The 2nd Shock Army of the 2nd Belorussian Front captured Anklam. The 49th, 70th and 65th Armies were pursuing the retreating 3rd Panzer Army and taking huge chunks of Mecklenburg as they surged forward. The battle was developing into a race to outrun the Soviets in order to surrender to the advancing British.

In Moravia the 38th Army was involved in fierce fighting at Moravska Ostrava, units breaking into the town. The 1st Guards Army moved down from the north to support the attack. As it did so the German defences began to collapse.

30 April 1945

CENTRAL SECTOR

Russian forces in Berlin broke through the German defences in the city centre and crossed the Königsplatz to enter the Reichstag. Furious battles erupted as SS troops held up the 3rd Shock Army, inflicting heavy losses. Sheer firepower swung the balance of the battle, Soviet troops breaking into the ground floor and battling their way into the heavily defended rooms. The Germans refused to give any quarter and fought for each room, bitter battles raging across corridors and through broken walls.

Hitler bade farewell to his staff and Party colleagues in the bunker and retired to his private quarters. There, at approximately 1530 hours, he and Eva Braun committed suicide, Hitler shooting himself in the head with a pistol and Eva Braun taking poison. Their bodies were carried up the stairs into the cratered Chancellery garden and were incinerated. Fritz Linge, Hitler's personal bodyguard, burned the corpses and buried the ashes and bones in a crater to prevent their capture by the Russians. His efforts would prove to be in vain as Soviet secret operations personnel located them after the battle. After twelve years in power, the man who had dragged Europe into its most bloody war and sent millions to their deaths in the concentration camps and gas chambers, was dead.

In Mecklenberg the 2nd Belorussian Front advanced rapidly, the 2nd Shock Army closing upon Stralsund, the 70th on Waren and the 49th upon Wittenberge. To the south, in Bohemia, Moravska Ostrava fell to the 38th Army and 1st Guards Army.

PRODUCTION

With the Reich in ruins or occupied, German industrial capability collapsed. During the first four months of 1945 it had produced 3,935 panzers and assault guns, 9,318 motor vehicles and 7,544 aircraft.[3]

1 May 1945

CENTRAL SECTOR

In Berlin the Tiergarten fell to 8th Guards Army. The Reichstag fell to the 3rd Shock Army after a bloody battle. Half of the 5,000 defenders were killed during the fighting.

With Hitler gone the Germans in Berlin began to seek terms for surrender. After much deliberation with Bormann and Goebbels, General Krebs, the Chief of the General Staff, crossed the Soviet lines under a flag of truce to discuss the options for surrender. He was taken to General

Chuikov of 8th Guards Army who relayed his request by telephone to Zhukov and he in turn to Stalin. Krebs tried to seek a settlement whereby the fighting ceased and then terms were discussed, but the Russians demanded the complete and unconditional surrender of all German armies. Krebs was unable to agree to this and returned to the Bunker, informing Bormann and Goebbels of the Russian demands. Goebbels refused to surrender.

Around the Chancellery the Germans came under massive attack. Many of the German units had run out of ammunition and began to surrender of their own accord. Weidling recognised this fact and decided to surrender his surviving forces the following day.

The 12th Army and remnants of the 9th Army struggled to beat off the attacks of the Soviet forces south of Berlin while in Bohemia Prague rose in revolt.

SOUTHERN SECTOR
On the Adriatic coast, Tito's partisans linked up with the 2nd New Zealand Division of the British 8th Army advancing from Italy. The meeting of the two forces at Montefalcone sealed the fate of the 150,000 men of Army Group E in Croatia and Slovenia.

2 May 1945

CENTRAL SECTOR
Weidling surrendered the remnants of the Berlin garrison, bringing the fighting to an end. The battle cost the Germans around half a million killed and captured and 1,500 tanks, 4,500 aircraft and 8,600 artillery pieces lost. However, the cost had also been high for the Soviet forces, the 2nd Belorussian losing 13,000 killed and 46,000 wounded, the 1st Belorussian 37,000 killed and 141,000 wounded and the 1st Ukrainian 27,000 killed and 86,000 wounded. Equipment losses amount to 2,156 tanks and Su's, 1,220 artillery pieces and 527 aircraft.[4]

By 1500 hours the guns had fallen silent and an eerie quiet settled over the city. Josef Goebbels poisoned his six children and then he and his wife Magda committed suicide. Like Hitler and Eva Braun, the adults' bodies were burned but not so thoroughly. The corpses were later identified by the Russians. General Krebs also committed suicide but Bormann attempted to escape from Berlin with a small band of followers. Unconfirmed reports list Bormann as killed when the tank he was taking cover behind was destroyed.

The remnants of the Frankfurt–Guben Group continued their battle but by nightfall the bulk of the force was destroyed and the 12th Army thrown back to the west. Nearly 120,000 German soldiers surrendered while 60,000 had been killed in the fighting.

On the Baltic coast the 2nd Shock Army reached Stralsund and Rostock fell to the 70th Army.

3 May 1945

NORTHERN SECTOR

The German High Command gave its consent to the evacuation of forces from Kurland. Over the next few days 26,000 soldiers were be evacuated. Over 190,000 would be left behind.

CENTRAL SECTOR

The advance of the 2nd Belorussian Front along the Baltic coast was brought to an abrupt halt as the 70th Army contacted the leading elements of the British 2nd Army near Wismar, the British winning the race to secure the approaches to Denmark. On the line of the Elbe the American 1st and 9th Armies joined hands in force with the 1st Belorussian and 1st Ukrainian Fronts. The 61st Army reached the river south of Wittenberge, the 1st Polish Army near Sandau, the 47th just to its south, the 3rd south of Stendal and the 69th and 33rd Armies north and south of Magdeburg. The remnants of the 12th Army began to fall back to the west to surrender to the US 1st Army.

With the battle for Berlin over, the 1st Ukrainian Front began to redeploy its forces to the line between the Elbe and Niesse to strike the German forces in Bohemia.

SOUTHERN SECTOR

Croatia declared independence and raised a defence force of 12,000 men. Tito directed fourteen divisions against them.

4 May 1945

CENTRAL SECTOR

Schwerin fell to the 70th Army as the rearguards of the 3rd Panzer Army were destroyed. The revolt in Prague broke out in force. The Germans were attacked by Czech partisans and civilians.

5 May 1945

CENTRAL SECTOR

The 2nd Shock Army destroyed isolated elements of the 3rd Panzer Army at Swinemunde and Peenemunde. German forces in East Prussia and Breslau came under fierce attack while Army Group Centre was pressed around Olomouc and south-east of Moravska Ostrava. A limited counter-

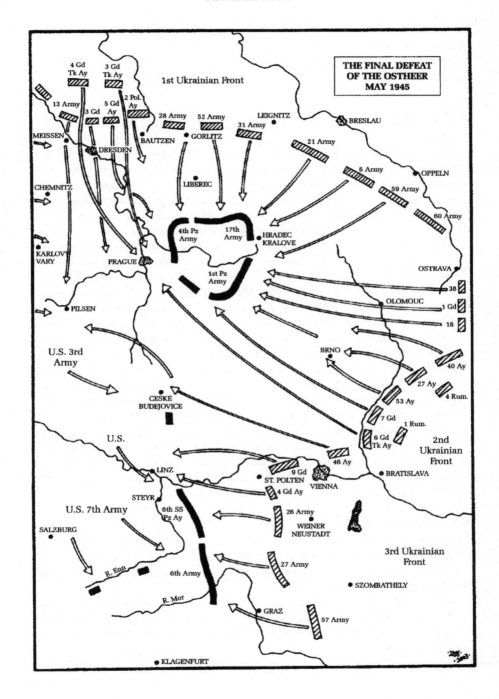

THE FINAL DEFEAT
OF THE OSTHEER
MAY 1945

4 Gd
Tk Ay

3 Gd
Tk Ay

1st Ukrainian Front

13 Army

3 Gd

5 Gd
Ay

2 Pol.
Ay

28 Army

52 Army

LEIGNITZ

31 Army

BRESLAU

MEISSEN

21 Army

DRESDEN

BAUTZEN

GORLITZ

6 Army

OPPELN

CHEMNITZ

LIBEREC

59 Army

60 Army

KARLOVY
VARY

PRAGUE

4th Pz
Army

17th
Army

HRADEC
KRALOVE

OSTRAVA

38

PILSEN

1st Pz
Army

OLOMOUC

1 Gd

18

U.S. 3rd
Army

BRNO

40 Ay

27 Ay

4 Rum.

CESKE
BUDEJOVICE

53 Ay

7 Gd

1 Rum.

U.S.

6 Gd
Tk Ay

46 Ay

2nd
Ukrainian
Front

LINZ

9 Gd
ST. POLTEN

VIENNA

BRATISLAVA

STEYR

U.S. 7th Army

6th SS
Pz Ay

4 Gd Ay

26 Army

3rd Ukrainian
Front

SALZBURG

WEINER
NEUSTADT

27 Army

SZOMBATHELY

R. Enn

6th Army

R. Mor

GRAZ

57 Army

KLAGENFURT

attack by the 17th Army around Wansen was easily repulsed by the 1st Ukrainian Front.

In Prague the revolt gathered pace, Vlassov's Cossack army defecting to the rebels.

6 May 1945

CENTRAL SECTOR

After a long struggle Breslau surrendered to the Soviet 6th Army. Of the 40,000-strong garrison some 30,000 had been killed but 6th Army had suffered 60,000 casualties. The treatment of the German garrison once it had surrendered was brutal, Soviet soldiers exacting terrible revenge.

On the main combat line the 1st, 2nd, 4th and 3rd Ukrainian Fronts began a massive offensive aimed at enveloping Army Group Centre. The 1st Ukrainian Front pushed down from the north and north-east with the 4th Guards Tank, 13th, 3rd Guards Tank, 3rd and 5th Guards, 2nd Polish, 28th, 52nd, 31st, 21st, 6th and 59th Armies, the 4th Ukrainian from the east with the 60th, 38th, 1st Guards and 18th Armies, the 2nd Ukrainian from the south-east with the 40th, 4th Rumanian, 27th, 53rd, 1st Rumanian, 7th Guards and 6th Guards Tank Armies and the 3rd Ukrainian Front from Austria with the 4th and 9th Guards and 46th Armies. The Stavka had massed 806,000 men with the 1st Ukrainian, 351,000 with the 4th Ukrainian and 613,000 with the 2nd Ukrainian Fronts, 30,000 artillery pieces, 2,000 tanks and Su's and 3,000 aircraft to defeat the Germans.[5] Army Group Centre was short of ammunition, equipment and fuel.

The German front broke under the massive weight of the attack, the 1st Ukrainian slicing through the 4th Panzer and 17th Armies to push into the rear of the 7th Army near Chemnitz. The 4th Ukrainian Front punched a hole through the 1st Panzer Army and the 2nd Ukrainian through the 8th Army. On the northern wing Meissen fell to the 3rd Guards Army while the 8th Army defences around Brno collapsed.

SOUTHERN SECTOR

There were fierce battles in Croatia as Army Group E launched a desperate effort to break through to the west. The 97th Korp, fighting on the western flank, became separated and, after a bloody battle against the 4th Yugoslav Army, surrendered.

The independent Slovene defence force surrendered to Tito's forces. Over the next few days Tito's men murdered 110,000 Croats near Bleiburg, another 30,000 at Kocevje and then a further 200,000 over the coming months.

7 May 1945

CENTRAL SECTOR
Army Group Centre was rapidly crushed as the Ukrainian fronts advanced. In East Prussia fierce fighting raged at Vogelsang.

8 May 1945

NORTHERN SECTOR
Army Group Kurland began to surrender. Over 189,000 German soldiers marched into Soviet captivity as the 16th and 18th Armies laid down their arms.

CENTRAL SECTOR
Fighting continued in East Prussia and Bohemia as the Soviets pounded the remnants of the Ostheer. Dresden fell to the 5th Guards Army and the 4th Ukrainian Front was involved in fierce fighting around Olomouc. The town fell late in the day. German forces began to surrender in large numbers.

SOUTHERN SECTOR
In Croatia Yugoslav partisans took Zagreb, confining Army Group E to a narrow strip of land along the Austro–Slovene border.

THE WESTERN ALLIES
The 8 May was declared VE Day as the surrender of the German Army was ratified on the Luneburg Heath by Field Marshal Montgomery. However, for the Soviets the German surrender was not complete until the 9th, this being declared VE Day in the Soviet Union. Even so, despite the official surrender, the fighting in East Prussia, Bohemia and Austria continued.

9 May 1945

NORTHERN SECTOR
The surrender of Army Group Kurland continued, just a few bands continuing to resist.

CENTRAL SECTOR
In the Vistula delta and the Baltic Spit the Germans began to surrender. The 2nd Baltic Front landed men on Bornholm Island and took 12,000 prisoners as the Germans gave up.

Tanks of the 3rd and 4th Guards Tank Armies entered Prague, isolating the bulk of the 17th Army and 1st Panzer Army to the east. Elements of the

2nd Ukrainian Front approached from the south, having virtually destroyed the 8th Army. On the northern wing Gorlitz was attacked by the 52nd Army.

SOUTHERN SECTOR
Army Group South was isolated in Austria following the destruction of the 8th Army while Army Group E struggled on in Slovenia. The large-scale surrender of the German forces in the south began.

10 May 1945

CENTRAL SECTOR
German forces in the Prague pocket began to surrender.

SOVIET COMMAND
The Soviet High Command ordered the Ukrainian fronts to push west and link up with the Allies.

11 May 1945

CENTRAL SECTOR
Army Group Centre was breaking up as its forces surrendered by the thousand. The remnants of German forces in East Prussia also surrendered in large numbers.

The final campaign around Prague cost the 1st Ukrainian Front 6,000 killed and 17,000 wounded, the 2nd 2,500 killed and 11,800 wounded and the 4th Ukraine 2,300 killed and 9,200 wounded.[6]

SOUTHERN SECTOR
Army Group Ostmark began to lay down its arms. Army Group E fought on but was also breaking up.

13 May 1945

CENTRAL SECTOR
The majority of German forces, cut off in East Prussia, in the Vistula Delta and along the Baltic coast, had surrendered.

14 May 1945

CENTRAL SECTOR
More than 150,000 German soldiers had surrendered in East Prussia.

15 May 1945

SOUTHERN SECTOR

The 150,000 men of Army Group E laid down their arms around Slovenigradesk.

19 May 1945

CENTRAL SECTOR

The Soviet Army destroyed the last pocket of organised German resistance in Bohemia.

The Cost of the Russo–German War

Four years of brutal fighting had finally come to an end. During the various campaigns Germany, one of Europe's foremost military powers, had been absolutely destroyed and the Soviet Union, a fledgling military state in 1941, had risen to be a world super-power.

It can reasonably be argued that the campaign in Russia was the most decisive campaign of the Second World War. In losses alone the scale of the conflict is overwhelming. Germany lost 1,001,000 killed, 1,287,000 missing and 3,968,000 wounded while 1,500,000 surrendered to the Red Army at the end. Some ninety-eight German divisions were wiped out during the fighting, fifty-six surrendered between 1941 and 1944 and ninety-three at the close of hostilities. Germany's allies suffered equally severe casualties, the Hungarian military losing 136,000 killed and 250,000 wounded, while 300,000 civilians also lost their lives. Rumania lost 71,000 killed, 310,000 missing and 243,000 wounded fighting alongside the Ostheer and another 170,000 killed, wounded and missing fighting for the Soviets. More than 340,000 Rumanian civilians lost their lives. Bulgaria suffered 32,000 military and 50,000 civilians casualities.

The Soviet Union suffered by far the greatest loss of any combatant, 13,500,000 military personnel being killed or captured. Of 6,000,000 captured a fraction survived. Even after liberation their ordeal was not over, many being imprisoned by Stalin for surrendering to the Germans. Another 18,000,000 were wounded while the civil population lost more than 10,000,000. The successful Soviet campaigns during the late stages of the war still cost the Red Army dear. More than a million men were killed or wounded, 140,000 losing their lives in Hungary, 70,000 in Rumania, 140,000 in Czechoslovakia, 26,000 in Austria, 102,000 in Berlin and 10,000 in Yugoslavia. The Polish 1st and 2nd Armies lost 40,000 men fighting alongside the Russians.

Any number of theories on the causes of the German defeat, the manner in which the conflict was fought and the other aspects of the war have been promoted. This book does not seek to deliver any conclusions, but to record the sacrifices and the daily military history of the war, to give the reader the knowledge of the battles so that with that knowledge, history will not be repeated.

NOTES

1   Kirosheev, *Soviet Casualties and Combat Losses in the Twentieth Century*, Table 75
2   Kirosheev, *Soviet Casualties and Combat Losses in the Twentieth Century*, Table 75
3   Ellis, *The World War II Databook*, Table 87 (tanks), Table 91 (trucks) and Table 92 (aircraft)
4   Kirosheev, *Soviet Casualties and Combat Losses in the Twentieth Century*, Table 75
5   Kirosheev, *Soviet Casualties and Combat Losses in the Twentieth Century*, Table 67
6   Kirosheev, *Soviet Casualties and Combat Losses in the Twentieth Century*, Table 75

Bibliography

Adair, Paul, *Hitler's Greatest Defeat*, Arms & Armour Press, 1994
Ailsby, Christopher, *SS Hell on the Eastern Front*, Spellmount, 1998
Barr, Niall and Hart, Russell (eds), *Panzer*, Aurum Press, 1999
Bor-Komorovski, T, *The Secret Army*, London, 1950
Buchner, Alex, *Ostfront 1944*, Schiffer Military, 1991
_____ *The German Infantry Handbook*, Schiffer Military, 1991
Carell, P, *Hitler's War on Russia, vol 1*, Corgi, 1967
_____ *Scorched Earth. Hitler's War on Russia vol 2*, Harrap, 1970
Carruthers, Bob and Erickson, John, *The Russian Front 1941–1945*, Cassell, 1999
Cross, Robin, *Citadel*, BCA, 1993
Chuikov, VI, *The Beginning of the Road*, MacGibbon & Kee, 1963
_____ *The End of the Third Reich*, MacGibbon & Kee, 1967
Clark, Alan, *Barbarossa*, Cassell, 2000
Duffy, Christopher, *Red Storm on the Reich*, Routledge, 2001
Ellis, John, *Brute Force*, Andre Deutsch, 1990
_____ *The World War II Databook*, Aurum Press, 1993
Erickson, John, *The Road to Stalingrad*, Weidenfeld & Nicolson, 1993
_____ *The Road to Berlin*, Weidenfeld & Nicolson, 1983
Glantz, David M, *Barbarossa 1941*, Tempus, 2001
_____ *Zhukov's Greatest Defeat*, Kansas, 1999
_____ *From the Don to the Dnepr*, Cass, 1991
Glantz, David M, & House, Jonathan, *When Titans Clashed*, Birlinn, 2000
Gorbatov, A, *Years of my Life*, Constable, 1964
Gilbert, Martin, *Second World War*, Fontana, 1990
Guderian, Heinz, *Panzer Leader*, Arrow Books, 1990
Halder, F, *Hitler as Warlord*, Putnam, 1950
Healy, Mark, *Kursk 1943* (Osprey Campaign Series), Osprey, 1992
Hughes, Matthew & Mann, Chris, *The T-34 Tank*, Spellmount, 1999
Lederrey, E, *Germany's Defeat in the East*, War Office, 1959
Liddell-Hart, BH, *The Other Side of the Hill*, Cassell, 1948
Lucas, James, *German Army Handbook 1939-1945*, Sutton, 1998
_____ *Last Days of the Reich*, BCA, 1986

_____ *Storming Eagles*, Guild, 1988

_____ *The Last Year of the German Army*, BCA, 1994

_____ *War on the Eastern Front*, Greenhill, 1991

Macksey, Kenneth, *Tank versus Tank*, Guild, 1988

Manstein, Erich von, *Lost Victories*, Greenhill, 1987

Mellenthin, F W von, *Panzer Battles*, Oklahoma Press, 1989

Minasyan, M M, *Great Patriotic War of the Soviet Union* (official work) Moscow, 1974

Mitcham, S W, *Hitler's Legions: the German Army Order of Battle, World War II*, Leo Cooper/Secker & Warburg, 1985

Perrett, Bryan, *Knights of the Black Cross*, London, 1986

Quarrie, Bruce, *Hitler's Samurai*, BCA, 1985

_____ *Hitler's Teutonic Knights*, Patrick Stephens, 1987

_____ *Weapons of the Waffen SS*, Patrick Stephens, 1988

Rauss, Erhard & Natzmer, Oldwig von, *The Anvil of War*, Greenhill, 1994

Salisbury, Harrison E, *The 900 Days*, Pan Books, 2000

Seaton, Albert, *The Russo German War 1941–45*, Presidio, 1990

Shirer, William L, *The Rise and Fall of the Third Reich*, Secker & Warburg, 1984

Speer, Albert, *Inside the Third Reich*, Phoenix, 1995

Tarrant, V E, *Stalingrad*, Leo Cooper, 1992

Trevor-Roper, H R, (ed), *Hitler's War Directives 1939–45*, Pan, 1973

Werth, A, *Russia at War 1941-45*, Corgi, 1965

Young, Peter, *The Almanac of World War II*, London, 1981

Zaloga, Steven J, & Grandsen, James, *Soviet Tanks and Combat Vehicles of World War II*, Arms & Armour Press, 1984

Ziemke, E F, *Stalingrad to Berlin: the German Defeat in the East*, GPO Washington, 1968

Zhukov, Georgi K, *Marshal Zhukov's Greatest Battles*, London, 1969

Index of Places

Index of People